T0178314

Lecture Notes in Computer Science

Lecture Notes in Artificial Intelligence 13859

Founding Editor

Jörg Siekmann

Series Editors

Randy Goebel, *University of Alberta, Edmonton, Canada*
Wolfgang Wahlster, *DFKI, Berlin, Germany*
Zhi-Hua Zhou, *Nanjing University, Nanjing, China*

The series Lecture Notes in Artificial Intelligence (LNAI) was established in 1988 as a topical subseries of LNCS devoted to artificial intelligence.

The series publishes state-of-the-art research results at a high level. As with the LNCS mother series, the mission of the series is to serve the international R & D community by providing an invaluable service, mainly focused on the publication of conference and workshop proceedings and postproceedings.

Yasufumi Takama · Katsutoshi Yada ·
Ken Satoh · Sachiyo Arai
Editors

New Frontiers
in Artificial Intelligence

JSAI-isAI 2022 Workshop, JURISIN 2022, and JSAI 2022
International Session, Kyoto, Japan, June 12–17, 2022
Revised Selected Papers

Editors
Yasufumi Takama ⓘ
Tokyo Metropolitan University
Tokyo, Japan

Katsutoshi Yada ⓘ
Kansai University
Osaka, Japan

Ken Satoh ⓘ
National Institute of Informatics
Tokyo, Japan

Sachiyo Arai ⓘ
Chiba University
Chiba, Japan

ISSN 0302-9743   ISSN 1611-3349 (electronic)
Lecture Notes in Artificial Intelligence
ISBN 978-3-031-29167-8   ISBN 978-3-031-29168-5 (eBook)
https://doi.org/10.1007/978-3-031-29168-5

LNCS Sublibrary: SL7 – Artificial Intelligence

This Springer imprint is published by the registered company Springer Nature Switzerland AG
The registered company address is: Gewerbestrasse 11, 6330 Cham, Switzerland

Preface

The JSAI annual conference (JSAI 2022) and the fourteenth JSAI International Symposia on Artificial Intelligence (JSAI-isAI 2022) were held together on June 12 through 17,2022 at Kyoto International Conference Center, Kyoto, Japan. JSAI annual conferences are held every year since 1987 by the Japanese Society for Artificial Intelligence (JSAI) as main events for the society. The international sessions held at these conferences play a key role for the society in its efforts to share Japan's research on artificial intelligence with other countries.

JSAI-isAI has hosted a number of international workshops every year since 2009, supported by JSAI. It has provided a unique and intimate forum where AI researchers gather and share their knowledge in a focused discipline. While the JSAI annual conference and JSAI-isAI have been conducted separately in different places and schedules, we have decided to hold JSAI-isAI 2022 in conjunction with JSAI 2022 to exploit the synergetic effect of both events.

JSAI 2022 had 736 papers, which include 41 papers presented at the international sessions, for 3,033 participants. JSAI-isAI 2022 hosted 2 workshops (JURISIN 2022 and SCIDOCA 2022) and had 3 invited talks and 32 oral presentations for 91 participants from 13 countries. The sixteenth International Workshop on Juris-Informatics (JURISIN 2022) was organized to discuss both the fundamental and practical issues in Juris-informatics among people from various backgrounds such as law, social science, information and intelligent technology, logic, and philosophy, including the conventional "AI and law" area. The sixth International Workshop on SCIentific DOCument Analysis (SCIDOCA 2022) gathered researchers and experts who are aiming at scientific document analysis from various perspectives.

This volume is the post-proceedings of JSAI-isAI 2022 and JSAI 2022. From the 67 papers submitted to JURISIN 2022 and the international sessions of JSAI 2022, 18 papers were selected on the basis of a single-blind review by at least two reviewers and the quality of the extended versions of the papers was carefully checked by the program committee members. The acceptance rate was about 27%, which ensures the quality of the post-proceedings.

Although JSAI-isAI 2022 and JSAI 2022 were held in a hybrid format, overseas participants could not attend the events onsite because of the entry restrictions to Japan due to COVID-19. We hope this book will introduce readers to the state-of-the-art research outcomes of JSAI-isAI 2022 and JSAI 2022, and motivate them to organize and/or participate in JSAI events in the future.

February 2023

Yasufumi Takama
Katsutoshi Yada
Ken Satoh
Sachiyo Arai

Organization

Program Committee Chairs

Yasufumi Takama	Tokyo Metropolitan University, Japan
Katsutoshi Yada	Kansai University, Japan
Ken Satoh	National Institute of Informatics and Sokendai, Japan
Sachiyo Arai	Chiba University, Japan

JURISIN 2022

Workshop Chairs

Makoto Nakamura	Niigata Institute of Technology, Japan
Satoshi Tojo	Japan Advanced Institute of Science and Technology, Japan

Steering Committee

Yoshinobu Kano	Shizuoka University, Japan
Takehiko Kasahara	Toin University of Yokohama, Japan
Le-Minh Nguyen	Japan Advanced Institute of Science and Technology, Japan
Makoto Nakamura	Niigata Institute of Technology, Japan
Yoshiaki Nishigai	Chiba University, Japan
Katsumi Nitta	Tokyo Institute of Technology, Japan
Yasuhiro Ogawa	Nagoya University, Japan
Seiichiro Sakurai	Meiji Gakuin University, Japan
Ken Satoh	National Institute of Informatics and Sokendai, Japan
Satoshi Tojo	Japan Advanced Institute of Science and Technology, Japan
Katsuhiko Toyama	Nagoya University, Japan
Masaharu Yoshioka	Hokkaido University, Japan

Advisory Committee

Trevor Bench-Capon	The University of Liverpool, UK
Tomas Gordon	Frauenhofer FOKUS, Germany
Henry Prakken	Utrecht University & University of Groningen, The Netherlands
John Zeleznikow	Victoria University, Australia
Robert Kowalski	Imperial College London, UK
Kevin Ashley	University of Pittsburgh, USA

Program Committee

Thomas Ågotnes	University of Bergen, Norway
Michał Araszkiewicz	Jagiellonian University, Poland
Ryuta Arisaka	National Institute of Informatics, Japan
Marina De Vos	University of Bath, UK
Juergen Dix	Clausthal University of Technology, Germany
Kripabandhu Ghosh	Indian Institute of Technology Kanpur, India
Saptarshi Ghosh	Indian Institute of Technology Kharagpur, India
Randy Goebel	University of Alberta, Canada
Guido Governatori	NICTA, Australia
Tokuyasu Kakuta	Chuo University, Japan
Yoshinobu Kano	Shizuoka University, Japan
Takehiko Kasahara	Toin University of Yokohama, Japan
Mi-Young Kim	University of Alberta, Canada
Le-Minh Nguyen	Japan Advanced Institute of Science and Technology, Japan
Makoto Nakamura	Niigata Institute of Technology, Japan
María Navas-Loro	Universidad Politécnica de Madrid, Spain
Yoshiaki Nishigai	Chiba University, Japan
Tomoumi Nishimura	Osaka University, Japan
Katsumi Nitta	Tokyo Institute of Technology, Japan
Yasuhiro Ogawa	Nagoya University, Japan
Monica Palmirani	CIRSFID, Italy
Ginevra Peruginelli	IGSG-CNR, Italy
Juliano Rabelo	University of Alberta, Canada
Julien Rossi	Amsterdam Business School, Netherlands
Seiichiro Sakurai	Meiji Gakuin University, Japan
Ken Satoh	National Institute of Informatics and Sokendai, Japan
Jaromir Savelka	Carnegie Mellon University, USA

Yunqiu Shao	Tsinghua University, China
Akira Shimazu	Japan Advanced Institute of Science and Technology, Japan
Kazuko Takahashi	Kwansei Gakuin University, Japan
Yoichi Takenaka	Kansai University, Japan
Satoshi Tojo	JAIST, Japan
Katsuhiko Toyama	Nagoya University, Japan
Vu Tran	The Institute of Statistical Mathematics, Japan
Josef Valvoda	University of Cambridge, UK
Sabine Wehnert	Otto-von-Guericke-Universität Magdeburg, Germany
Yueh-Hsuan Weng	Tohoku University, Japan
Hannes Westermann	University of Montreal, Canada
Hiroaki Yamada	Tokyo Institute of Technology, Japan
Takahiro Yamakoshi	Nagoya University, Japan
Masaharu Yoshioka	Hokkaido University, Japan

JSAI 2022 International Session

Conference Chair

Chie Morita	Toshiba Corporation, Japan

Executive Committee Chairs

Hiroyuki Toda	NTT Corporation, Japan
Toshiyuki Nomura (Vice)	NEC Corporation, Japan

Program Committee Chairs

Naohiro Matsumura	Osaka University, Japan
Sachiyo Arai (Vice)	Chiba University, Japan
Tadanobu Furukawa (Sub)	Fujitsu Ltd., Japan

Program Committee

Akinori Abe	Chiba University, Japan
Yu-Sheng Chen	ASYS Corporation, Taiwan

Shunichi Hattori	Central Research Institute of Electric Power Industry, Japan
Toshihiro Hiraoka	University of Tokyo, Japan
Yoshihisa Ijiri	LINE Corporation, Japan
Felix Jimenez	Aichi Prefectural University, Japan
Hisashi Kashima	Kyoto University, Japan
Daisuke Katagami	Tokyo Polytechnic University, Japan
Kazuki Kobayashi	Shinshu University, Japan
Makoto Koshino	National Institute of Technology, Ishikawa College, Japan
Naoki Masuyama	Osaka Metropolitan University, Japan
Tomoki Miyamoto	The University of Electro-Communications, Japan
Yuya Moroto	Hokkaido University, Japan
Jun Ernesto Okumura	Eureka Inc., Japan
Takuma Otsuka	NTT Corporation, Japan
Rafał Rzepka	Hokkaido University, Japan
Hiroki Shibata	Tokyo Metropolitan University, Japan
Yasufumi Takama	Tokyo Metropolitan University, Japan
Takahiro Uchiya	Nagoya Institute of Technology, Japan
Bartosz Wojcik	Jagiellonian University, Poland
Katsutoshi Yada	Kansai University, Japan

Sponsored By

The Japan Society for Artificial Intelligence (JSAI)

Contents

JSAI 2022 International Session

JURISIN 2022

Juris-Informatics (JURISIN) 2022

Makoto Nakamura[1] and Satoshi Tojo[2]

[1] Niigata Institute of Technology, Japan
[2] Japan Advanced Institute of Science and Technology, Japan

The Sixteenth International Workshop on Juris-Informatics (JURISIN 2022) was held with a support of the Japanese Society for Artificial Intelligence (JSAI) in association with JSAI International Symposia on AI (JSAI-isAI 2022). JURISIN was organized to discuss legal issues from the perspective of information science. Compared with the conventional AI and law, JURISIN covers a wide range of topics, including any theories and technologies which is not directly related with juris-informatics but has a potential to contribute to this domain.[1]

Thus, the members of Program Committee (PC) are leading researchers in various fields, including computer scientists, lawyers and philosophers, to contribute to the advancement of juris-informatics and it is also expected to open novel research areas.

This year, JURISIN have a session on the Competition on Legal Information Extraction/Entailment (COLIEE 2022) which consists of twelve papers, together with a comprehensive overview report. Despite the short announcement period, twenty-six papers were submitted for general and COLIEE sessions. Each paper was reviewed by three members of PC. The collection of papers covers various topics such as data mining, machine translation, text classification, legal reasoning, argumentation theory, application of AI and informatics to law and so on.

The workshop consisted of a COLIEE session on the first day and a general session on the second day. The workshop was held both in face-to-face and online. The face-to-face workshop was held for the first time in three years after the Covid-19 pandemic.

As invited speakers, we have Professor Enrico Francesconi from IGSG-CNR, Italy and Professor Randy Goebel from Alberta University, Canada. Both invited speakers participated online.

After the workshop, fourteen papers were submitted for the post proceedings. They were reviewed by PC members again and eleven papers were finally selected, as follows.

- Takahiro Yamakoshi, Yasuhiro Ogawa and Katsuhiko Toyama proposed a Transformer-based differential translation architecture that targets statutory sentences partially modified by amendments.
- Wachara Fungwacharakorn, Kanae Tsushima and Ken Satoh tackled defeasible logic for representing legal theories.
- Hiroki Cho, Ryuya Koseki, Aki Shima and Makoto Nakamura proposed a system that automatically maps similar provisions between Japanese and foreign laws for comparative legal research.

---

[1] PC members are found at https://www.niit.ac.jp/jurisin2022/#PCmember.

- Mi-Young Kim, Juliano Rabelo, Randy Goebel, Masaharu Yoshioka, Yoshinobu Kano and Ken Satoh presented a summary of the ninth Competition on Legal Information Extraction and Entailment (COLIEE 2022).
- Quan Minh Bui, Chau Nguyen, Dinh-Trung Do, Nguyen-Khang Le, Dieu-Hien Nguyen, Thi-Thu-Trang Nguyen, Minh-Phuong Nguyen and Minh Le Nguyen participated in the competition for Tasks 1, 2, 3 and 4 with deep learning approaches for tackling long and ambiguous legal documents.
- Juliano Rabelo, Mi-Young Kim and Randy Goebel proposed a method for Task 1, which was ranked first among all participants in the competition.
- Shubham Kumar Nigam, Navansh Goel and Arnab Bhattacharya proposed neural models using Sentence-BERT and Sent2Vec for Tasks 1 and 2.
- Masaharu Yoshioka, Youta Suzuki and Yasuhiro Aoki prpposed a method for Tasks 3 and 4 that utilizes three different IR systems.
- Sabine Wehnert, Libin Kuttyu and Ernesto William De Luca combines the scores of a TF-IDF model with a sentence-embedding based similarity score to produce answer rankings.
- Masaki Fujita, Takaaki Onaga, Ayaka Ueyama and Yoshinobu Kano employed an ensemble of their rule-based method for Task 4, using predicate-argument structures which extends their previous work, and added BERT-based methods.
- Minae Lin, Sieh-chuen Huang and Hsuan-lei Shao participated in Tasks 3 and 4, restructuring given data to a dataset of the disjunctive union strings from training queries and articles.

Finally, we wish to express our gratitude to all those who submitted papers, PC members, discussant and attentive audience.

Differential-Aware Transformer for Partially Amended Sentence Translation

Takahiro Yamakoshi[1,3][✉], Yasuhiro Ogawa[1,2], and Katsuhiko Toyama[1,2]

[1] Graduate School of Informatics, Nagoya University,
Furo-cho, Chikusa-ku, Nagoya 464-8601, Japan
[2] Information Technology Center, Nagoya University,
Furo-cho, Chikusa-ku, Nagoya 464-8601, Japan
[3] Legal AI Inc., JP Tower Nagoya 23F, Meieki 1-1-1,
Nakamura-ku, Nagoya 450-6323, Japan
yamakoshi@legalai.jp

Abstract. We propose a Transformer-based differential translation architecture that targets statutory sentences partially modified by amendments. In translating post-amendment statutory sentences, translation *focality*—modifying only the amended expressions in the translation and retaining the others—is important to avoid misunderstanding the amendment's contents. To sharpen the translation's focality, we introduce a neural network architecture called a *Copiable Translation Transformer* that can copy expressions in the pre-amendment translated sentence as needed and generate expressions from the post-amendment original sentence. In experiments, we showed that our method outperformed the naive Transformer with a training corpus of partially amended sentences.

Keywords: Differential Translation · Amendment · Transformer · Copying Mechanism

1 Introduction

In the world's globalized society, governments must quickly publicize their statutes to facilitate international trade, financial investments, legislation support, and so on. In April 2009, the Japanese government addressed this issue by launching the Japanese Law Translation Database System (JLT) [11], where it publicizes English translations of its statutes. After amending a statute, its translation must be promptly updated to avoid confusion among international readers about whether it remains in effect. Unfortunately, the pace of translation work lags behind statutory amendments. According to Yamakoshi et al. [16], as of January 2020, only 23.4% (163/697) of the translated statutes in JLT correspond to their latest versions. On the other hand, translating post-amendment

Y. Takama et al. (Eds.): JSAI-isAI 2022 Workshop, LNAI 13859, pp. 5–22, 2023.
https://doi.org/10.1007/978-3-031-29168-5_1

statutory sentences is crucial because most enacted statutes in Japan's legislative bodies are amendment laws. For example, 78% (73/94) of the acts enacted in 2019 are amendment laws.

Updating the translations of statutory sentences according to an amendment resembles a differential translation, where we must consider the *focality* of translations [15]. Focal translations modify the expressions related to the amendment and keep those unrelated to it. For example, consider the following sentence: "申立ては、事故の事実を示して、書面でこれをしなければならない。" (The request shall be made in a document stating the facts of the accident.) Its amendment changed "事故" (*jiko*; accident) to "海難" (*kainan*; marine accident). The following revision satisfies the focality requirement: "The request shall be made in a document stating the facts of the <u>marine accident</u>" because it contains minimum modifications. On the other hand, although "The <u>petition</u> shall be made in a document <u>describing</u> the facts of the marine accident" is a fluent and adequate translation, it is an unsuitable revision from the focality perspective because "申立て" (*moshitate*; request) and "示して" (*shimeshite*; stating), which are irrelevant to the amendment, were changed.

Some studies on machine translation methods retain the focality of post-amendment statutory sentences. Kozakai et al. [7] proposed a method for post-amendment Japanese statutory sentences based on a statistical machine translation (SMT) method from Koehn et al. [6]. These methods are *template-aware*: they can reuse expressions in a given target-language sentence (translation template). Yamakoshi et al. [15] proposed a machine translation method that generates translation candidates by Transformer [12], a neural machine translation (NMT) architecture, and selects the best one by comparing the candidates with the output of a template-aware SMT model (e.g., Koehn et al. [6] and Kozakai et al. [7]). The combination of an NMT model and a template-aware SMT model complements their respective weaknesses. An NMT model can output more fluent sentences than an SMT model; a template-aware SMT model can keep expressions that are common in the amendment, which a naive Transformer cannot do. However, the latter advantage is weak in the method because it just chooses a candidate from a naive Transformer and does not postedit it. That is, when the Transformer model does not output an expression that should be retained in any candidate, the expression cannot be salvaged even if the template-aware SMT model successfully translated it.

In this paper, we propose new NMT architecture for partially amended Japanese statutory sentences and address the issue in Yamakoshi et al.'s method. We call our architecture *Copiable Translation Transformer*. Our NMT architecture is based on the naive Transformer in terms of using an attention mechanism. The differences are (1) that it receives a pre-amendment translated sentence with a post-amendment original sentence and (2) it can either copy a word in the pre-amendment translated sentence or generate a word for each word output. This mechanism resembles a *copying mechanism* for text summarization (e.g., Gu et al. [1] and Xu et al. [14]). However, their mechanisms, which are for monolingual sentence generation, take a single sentence and copy words from that sentence.

On the other hand, our mechanism is for bilingual text generation and takes two sentences of different languages—a post-amendment original sentence and a pre-amendment translated sentence—and copies the words from the latter.

This paper contributes to post-amendment statutory sentence translation tasks by proposing a Transformer-based machine translation architecture and describing its performance. Although we apply our Copiable Translation Transformer to Japanese-English translation in this paper, it can be used with any language pairs.

This paper is organized as follows. In Sect. 2, we position our task by introducing the amendment procedure in Japanese legislation. In Sect. 3, we explain related work and describe our neural architecture in Sect. 4. Sections 5 and 6 present our evaluation experiments and discussions. Finally, we summarize and conclude in Sect. 7.

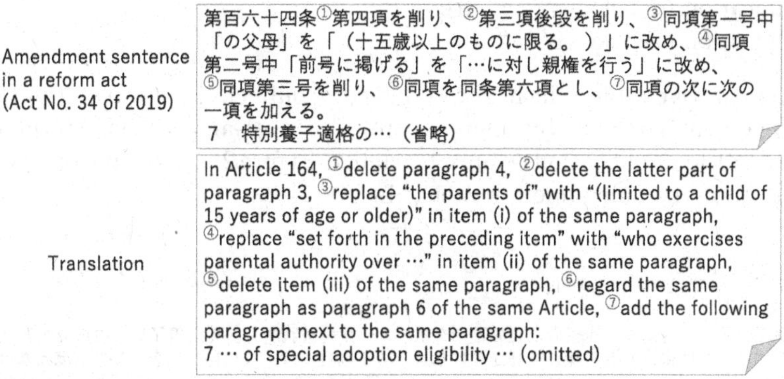

Amendment sentence in a reform act (Act No. 34 of 2019)

第百六十四条①第四項を削り、②第三項後段を削り、③同項第一号中「の父母」を「（十五歳以上のものに限る。）」に改め、④同項第二号中「前号に掲げる」を「…に対し親権を行う」に改め、⑤同項第三号を削り、⑥同項を同条第六項とし、⑦同項の次に次の一項を加える。
7　特別養子適格の…（省略）

Translation

In Article 164, ①delete paragraph 4, ②delete the latter part of paragraph 3, ③replace "the parents of" with "(limited to a child of 15 years of age or older)" in item (i) of the same paragraph, ④replace "set forth in the preceding item" with "who exercises parental authority over …" in item (ii) of the same paragraph, ⑤delete item (iii) of the same paragraph, ⑥regard the same paragraph as paragraph 6 of the same Article, ⑦add the following paragraph next to the same paragraph:
7 … of special adoption eligibility … (omitted)

Fig. 1. Amendment sentence

2 Task Definition

In this section, we clarify the background and the objective of our task. First, we introduce the amendment process in Japanese legislation from the viewpoint of document modification and identify it as a differential translation task.

2.1 Partial Amendments in Japanese Legislation

In Japanese legislation, partial amendments are done by "patching" modifications to the target statute, prescribed as amendment sentences in a reform statute. Such modifications can be categorized as follows [9]:

1. Modification of part of a sentence: (a) replacement, (b) addition, and (c) deletion.
2. Modification of such statute structure elements as sections, articles, items, etc.: (a) replacement, (b) addition, and (c) deletion.

3. Modification of element numbers: (a) renumbering, (b) attachment, and (c) shift.
4. Combined modification of an element's renumbering and replacing its title string.

In modifying part of a sentence, the Japanese legislation rules [3] indicate that the expressions to be modified must be uniquely specified by chunks of meaning.

Figure 1 shows an example of an actual amendment sentence prescribed by a reform act. Any of its seven modifications can be assigned to one of the above categories:

- Modifications ① and ⑤ belong to 2. (c) of a paragraph and an item, respectively;
- Modification ② belongs to 1. (c);
- Modifications ③ and ④ belong to 1. (a);
- Modification ⑥ belongs to 3. (a);
- Modification ⑦ belongs to 2. (b).

A comparative table, which corresponds to a publicized reform statute, shows the amendment contents by aligning pre- and post-amendment statutes and underlining the modifications chunk by chunk. Figure 2 is a sample of a comparative table for the amendment sentence in Fig. 1.

Post-amendment statute	Pre-amendment statute
（省略） 6　家庭裁判所は、特別養子縁組の成立の審判をする場合には、次に掲げる者の陳述を聴かなければならない。② ⑥ ③ 一　養子となる者（十五歳以上のものに限る。） 二　養子となるべき者に対し親権を行う者（養子となるべき者の父母及び養子となるべき者の親権者に対し親権を行う者を除く。）及び養子となるべき者の未成年後見人　④ （削除）⑤ （削除）① 7　特別養子適格の…　⑦ （省略）	（省略） 3　家庭裁判所は、特別養子縁組の成立の審判をする場合には、次に掲げる者の陳述を聴かなければならない。この場合において、第一号に掲げる者の同意がないにもかかわらずその審判をするときは、その者の陳述の聴取は、審問の期日においてしなければならない。 一　養子となる者の父母 二　養子となるべき者に対し親権を行う者（前号に掲げる者を除く。）及び養子となるべき者の未成年後見人 三　養子となるべき者の父母に対し親権を行う者及び養子となるべき者の父母の後見人 4　家庭裁判所は、… （省略）

Fig. 2. Comparative table: red circled numbers correspond to modifications described in Fig. 1 (Color figure online)

2.2 Differential Translation for Partial Amendments

We focus on the sentence-level differential translation task proposed by Yamakoshi et al. [15]. It targets category 1 (i.e., replacement, addition, and deletion of part of a sentence), described in the previous section. In the case of

Fig. 1, our targets are modifications ③ and ④. It also targets those that insert an additional sentence (e.g., a proviso) to an existing element or delete a sentence from the element, since additions or deletions obviously affect the main sentence. For example, modification ② in Fig. 1, which removed the latter part, is such a case.

Figure 3 illustrates this task. It involves four sentences from bilingual documents paired by two amendment versions. It takes a triplet of sentences (*a pre-amendment original sentence, a post-amendment original sentence*, and *a pre-amendment translated sentence*) as input and generates a translation for the post-amendment by the original sentence called *a post-amendment translated sentence*.

In generating post-amendment translated sentences, from the viewpoint of precise publicization, it is better to only modify expressions that are changed by the amendment without modifying the others for two reasons. First, such sentences clearly represent the amendment contents and clarify them for international readers. Second, since the expressions in pre-amendment translated sentences are reliable, reusing them ensures translation quality. In the case of Fig. 3, we should replace "the facts of the marine accident" with "the facts of ... of the examinee" and retain the other expressions that correspond to the following instruction: "Replace 「海難の事実」 (*kainan no jijitsu*) with 「海難の事実及び...過失の内容」 (*kainan no jijitsu oyobi ... kashitsu no naiyo*)". We call this requirement *focality*, which is the third requirement along with fluency and adequacy that are the primary metrics of general machine translation.

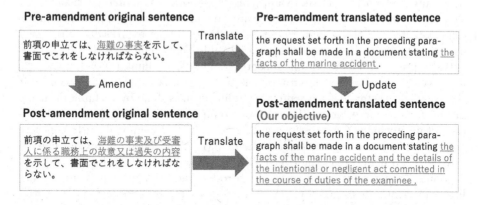

Fig. 3. Differential translation in an amended statutory sentence

We summarize our task as follows:

Input:
    Pre-amendment original sentence S_{PrO};
    Post-amendment original sentence S_{PoO};
    Pre-amendment translated sentence S_{PrT}.

Output: Generated post-amendment translated sentence $\hat{S}_{\text{PoT}}$.

Requirements:

focality: $\hat{S}_{\text{PoT}}$ must be generated based on the expressions of S_{PrT}, and $\hat{S}_{\text{PoT}}$ must exactly reflect the amendment from S_{PrO} to S_{PoO};

fluency: $\hat{S}_{\text{PoT}}$ must have natural phrasing and syntax;

adequacy: $\hat{S}_{\text{PoT}}$ must contain the contents in S_{PoO} without excesses or inadequacies.

3   Related Work

In this section, we review related work and respectively introduce methods, evaluation criteria, and corpora suitable for difference translations in Sects. 3.1, 3.2, and 3.3.

3.1   Translation Methods

Koehn et al. [6] proposed a statistical machine translation (SMT) based method that can be applied to differential translation. It can reuse expressions in a sentence chosen from translation memory (TM). It determines common expressions between the input sentence and the TM original sentence using an edit distance algorithm. Such common expressions are retained in the output sentence, and only other expressions are generatively translated by an SMT system, such as Moses [5]. Kozakai et al. [7] adapted this method to a post-amendment statutory sentence translation task by applying the following two modifications. First, they used a pre-amendment original sentence and its translation instead of a relevant pair from TM. Second, to determine the common expressions, they used underlined information in a comparative table that highlights the differences between pre- and post-amendment sentences chunk by chunk instead of the edit distance. The underlined information is more reasonable as a translation unit than the edit distance since sentence modification is done by a chunk of meaning in Japanese legislation. These above template-aware SMT-based methods can retain unchanged expressions well, although they cannot fluently generate translations because of the limitations of SMT. The fluency problem can be solved with a neural machine translation (NMT), such as Transformer [12].

Some Transformer-based methods introduce additional components to utilize expressions in target-language sentences that are suitable for differential translation. Xia et al. [13] proposed a method that incorporates the Transformer network with TM by embedding TM-reference sentences using a graph network. However, since the method lacks a mechanism to output the input as it is, it may make unnecessary modifications to unchanged expressions. Yamakoshi et al. [15]'s method combined a template-aware SMT with Transformer. It generates translate candidates by Transformer and chooses the best candidate by comparing them with the output of a template-aware SMT method. It tries to keep as many unchanged expressions in the pre-amendment translated sentence as possible. However, it cannot salvage such expressions if the Transformer model did not output them in any candidate.

The copying mechanism for neural networks offers the choice of directly outputting input words. Gu et al. [1] proposed this mechanism with the usage in the sequence-to-sequence NMT. Xu et al. [14] utilized it in the Transformer architecture. However, since these methods are designed for text summarization, they assume that input and output sentences share a language. Therefore, we cannot directly use the copying mechanism for translations like our task.

3.2 Evaluation Criteria

As discussed in Sect. 2.2, fluency, adequacy, and focality are the three requirements of differential translation quality. For fluency and adequacy, we can use the standard criteria for machine translation, including BLEU [10] and RIBES [2]. However, they are insensible to focality. To evaluate focality, Yamakoshi [15] proposed a focality score that uses n-gram recall between a pre-amendment translation and the system output. Yamakoshi [16] proposed an integrated criterion for differential translation named the Inclusive Score for DIfferential Translation (ISDIT). ISDIT consists of two factors: (1) the n-gram recall of expressions unaffected by the amendment and (2) the n-gram precision of the output compared to the reference.

3.3 Corpora

Kozakai et al. [7] used JLT bilingual resources to compile corpora for their experiment. For training data, they gathered 158,928 Japanese-English sentence pairs from 407 statutes provided in JLT. For test data, they selected 17 amendments available in JLT[1] from which they compiled 158 examples of sentence amendments, each of which consists of quartets (S_{PrO}, S_{PrT}, S_{PoO}, S_{PoT}). However, some of these examples are not focal because they contain modifications irrelevant to the amendment.

Yamakoshi et al. [16] compiled a corpus of focal quartets by the following procedure. First, they listed versions of statutes in JLT and e-LAWS[2]. Then they chose statutes whose JLT version lags behind its e-LAWS version and collected sentence-level amendments for such statutes. Finally, they manually translated the post-amendment sentences so that they retained their focality. Their corpus consists of 1,483 differential translation examples from 62 amendment cases.

---

[1] JLT has a function for browsing statutes and the translations of different amendment versions.

[2] https://elaws.e-gov.go.jp/ The e-Legislative Activity and Work Support System (e-LAWS) provides an open governmental database of the most recent, original national statutes (i.e., written in Japanese).

4   Proposed Architecture

In this section, we describe our proposed architecture, *Copiable Translation Transformer*, which expands the Transformer network so that it can copy expressions in pre-amendment translated sentences. Copiable Translation Transformer has a copying mechanism that takes two sentences of different languages: post-amendment original sentence S_{PoO} and pre-amendment translated sentence S_{PrT}. That is, it requires a dataset with triplets $(S_{\mathrm{PrT}}, S_{\mathrm{PoO}}, S_{\mathrm{PoT}})$ for training, where S_{PrT} and S_{PoO} are the input to the system, and S_{PoT}, the post-amendment translated sentence, is the answer. The Copiable Translation Transformer does not use pre-amendment original sentences S_{PrO}, following the insights of Xia et al. [13]. The source-side TM-reference sentence (S_{PrO} in our task) is less informative because most words in it also appear in the input sentence (S_{PoO} in our task); ignoring the former sentence reduces memory and time consumption.

Figure 4 shows the network connection of the Copiable Translation Transformer. It generates i-th word output's representation R^i_{PoT} by decoding the words of the post-amendment translated sentence that already output $\hat{S}^{<i}_{\mathrm{PoT}}$ using encoded representation of post-amendment original sentence S_{PoO}:

$$R^i_{\mathrm{PoT}} = \mathrm{decoder}(\mathrm{encoder}_{\mathrm{PoO}}(S_{\mathrm{PoO}}), \hat{S}^{<i}_{\mathrm{PoT}}),\tag{1}$$

where R^i_{PoT} is a vector with dimension d. From R^i_{PoT}, it generates the word likelihood over vocabulary V that we call *word generation likelihood* l^i_{gen}:

$$l^i_{\mathrm{gen}} = \mathrm{ff}(R^i_{\mathrm{PoT}}),\tag{2}$$

where l^i_{gen} is a vector with a dimension of vocabulary size $|V|$ and ff is a feedforward module. These steps are identical to those of the naive Transformer.

The Copiable Translation Transformer additionally encodes pre-amendment translated sentence S_{PrT} to earn its word representations R_{PrT}:

$$R_{\mathrm{PrT}} = \mathrm{encoder}_{\mathrm{PrT}}(S_{\mathrm{PrT}}),\tag{3}$$

where R_{PrT} is a matrix with dimension $d \times |S_{\mathrm{PrT}}|$. It then calculates the word likelihood over S_{PrT} that we call the *word copy likelihood* l_{copy} by multiplying R^i_{PoT} and R_{PrT}:

$$l^i_{\mathrm{copy}} = R^i_{\mathrm{PoT}}R_{\mathrm{PrT}},\tag{4}$$

where l^i_{copy} is a vector with dimension $|S_{\mathrm{PrT}}|$. Finally, it chooses next word $\hat{S}^i_{\mathrm{PoT}}$ with the maximum likelihood among l^i_{gen} and l^i_{copy}:

$$x = \mathrm{argmax}[l^i_{\mathrm{gen}}; l^i_{\mathrm{copy}}],\tag{5}$$

$$\hat{S}^i_{\mathrm{PoT}} = \begin{cases} x\text{-th word in } V & (\text{if } x \leq |V|) \\ (x - |V|)\text{-th word in } S_{\mathrm{PrT}} & (\text{otherwise}) \end{cases},\tag{6}$$

where x is the index of the maximum value in concatenated vector $[l^i_{\mathrm{gen}}; l^i_{\mathrm{copy}}]$. If a word from the vocabulary is selected, then it *generates* it; otherwise, it *copies* it.

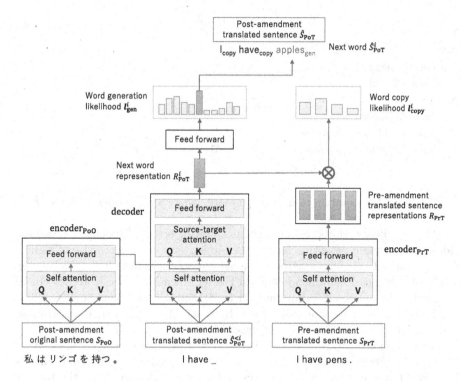

Fig. 4. Network connection of Copiable Translation Transformer

5   Experiment

Next we experimentally evaluated the effectiveness of our method.

5.1   Outline

We built training and test datasets from a focal differential translation corpus [16] with 1,483 differential translation examples from 62 amendment cases. The corpus contains many quartets $(S_{\text{PrO}}, S_{\text{PrT}}, S_{\text{PoO}}, S_{\text{PoT}})$, where we used S_{PrT}, S_{PoO}, and S_{PoT} for the Copiable Translation Transformer and S_{PoO} and S_{PoT} for the naive Transformer. We divided the corpus into 1,150 examples (46 amendment cases) for the training dataset and 201 examples (eight amendment cases) for the test dataset[3]. To evaluate the effect of augmenting the training dataset, we newly compiled a focal differential translation corpus with 1,670 examples (34 amendment cases) with the same protocol as Yamakoshi et al. [16] and used these examples as an additional training dataset.

We compared the performance of our Copiable Translation Transformer and the naive Transformer [12] with/without the additional training dataset and

---

[3] We kept the remaining 132 examples (eight amendment cases) for a development dataset for future use.

Table 1. Experimental options

Name	Transformer	Use template-aware SMT?	Use additional dataset?
Naive-SMT-noadd	Naive	Yes	No
Naive-noSMT-add	Naive	No	Yes
Naive-SMT-add	Naive	Yes	Yes
Copiable-SMT-noadd	Copiable	Yes	No
Copiable-noSMT-add	Copiable	No	Yes
Copiable-SMT-add	Copiable	Yes	Yes

with/without the combination of a template-aware SMT model. Table 1 shows the options.

We used these architectures under the following settings: six encoder/decoder hidden layers, eight attention heads, 512 hidden vectors, a batch size of eight, a dropout rate of 0.1. The maximum input sequence length is 256, which covers 92.3% of sentence-level amendments in the 96 amendment cases above. For all the models, we set the iteration number to 20,000. We used SentencePiece [8] as a tokenizer and set the vocabulary size to 8,192. We implemented the training and prediction codes based on the TensorFlow official model[4].

For a template-aware SMT model, we use Kozakai et al.'s template-aware SMT model (hereinafter "Kozakai model") as proposed by Yamakoshi et al. [15]. Each NMT model outputs 4-best candidates from which we chose the top one by calculating the BLEU scores between a candidate and the output from the template-aware SMT model. For simplification, we do not apply the Monte Carlo dropout, which is a candidate augmentation trick, unlike their proposed method.

We evaluated the fluency and adequacy with BLEU and RIBES. For the focality evaluation, we utilized ISDIT [16]. We set maximum n-gram length N to 4 for calculating ISDIT and BLEU.

5.2   Results

Table 2 shows the experimental results. The Copiable Translation Transformer-based methods achieved better performance in all of the evaluation criteria. With the template-aware SMT's assistance and the additional dataset, the Copiable Translation Transformer one (Copiable-SMT-add) outperformed the naive Transformer one (Naive-SMT-add) by 31.80 BLEU, 33.20 RIBES, and 37.74 ISDIT points.

The additional dataset also raised its performance. For example, the Copiable Translation Transformer with the addition dataset (Copiable-SMT-add) achieved better performance than the same architecture one without it (Copiable-SMT-noadd) by 6.49 BLEU, 4.41 RIBES, and 12.79 ISDIT points.

The combination of NMT and template-aware SMT raised the performance regardless of the NMT type. Among the models, the Copiable Translation

---

[4] https://github.com/tensorflow/models/.

Table 2. Experimental results

Model	BLEU	RIBES	ISDIT
Naive-SMT-noadd	18.40	50.75	8.37
Naive-noSMT-add	21.19	52.56	9.68
Naive-SMT-add	22.32	53.89	10.52
Copiable-SMT-noadd	47.63	82.68	35.47
Copiable-noSMT-add	36.00	77.05	40.05
Copiable-SMT-add	**54.12**	**87.09**	**48.26**

Table 3. Successful case

Model	Output
(Sentence S_{PrO})	第百四十四条の三<u>第五項</u>において準用する第百二十四条の規定による手続が終了した日
(Sentence S_{PrT})	the day that the process under article 124 as applied mutatis mutandis pursuant to article 144-3, <u>paragraph (5)</u> is complete;
(Sentence S_{PoO})	第百四十四条の三<u>第六項</u>において準用する第百二十四条の規定による手続が終了した日
(Sentence S_{PoT})	the day that the process under article 124 as applied mutatis mutandis pursuant to article 144-3, <u>paragraph (6)</u> is complete;
Naive-SMT-add	the day on which the procedure under the provisions of article 13-3, paragraph (6) of the companies act as applied mutatis mutandis pursuant to article 156
Copiable-SMT-add	the day that the process under 124 as applied mutatis mutandis pursuant to article 144-3, <u>paragraph (6)</u> is complete

Transformer-based one raised its performance more drastically (Copiable-SMT-add vs. Copiable-noSMT-add; 18.12 BLEU, 10.04 RIBES, and 8.21 ISDIT) than that with the naive Transformer (Naive-SMT-add vs. Naive-noSMT-add; 1.13 BLEU, 1.33 RIBES, and 0.84 ISDIT).

Table 3 shows a successful case. This example contains a modification of an element number: "paragraph (5)" to "paragraph (6)". The Copiable Translation Transformer one copied most of the unchanged expressions and modified the paragraph number. The naive Transformer one output such irrelevant expressions as "the companies act".

Table 4 shows a failure case for both Transformers. It contains a deletion of the expression "or the petitioner for an objection." The Copiable Translation Transformer one output meaningless words at the beginning of the sentence and the expression to be deleted. The naive Transformer one output lacked such unchanged expressions as "must specify" and "notify the requestor".

Table 4. Failure case

Model	Output
(Sentence S_{PrO})	経済産業大臣は、前条の意見の聴取の期日及び場所を定め、審査請求人又は異議申立人に通知しなければならない。
(Sentence S_{PrT})	the minister of economy, trade and industry must specify the date and place of the hearing of opinions prescribed in the preceding article, and notify the requestor for review or the petitioner for objection.
(Sentence S_{PoO})	経済産業大臣は、前条の意見の聴取の期日及び場所を定め、審査請求人に通知しなければならない。
(Sentence S_{PoT})	the minister of economy, trade and industry must specify the date and place of the hearing of opinions prescribed in the preceding article, and notify the requestor for review.
Naive-SMT-add	the minister of economy, trade and industry shall, in accordance with the procedures provided for in the preceding item, and the day on which the label set forth in the preceding article.
Copiable-SMT-add	in of ofy, and notify the foreign national must specify the date and place of the hearing of opinions prescribed in the preceding article, and notify the requestor for review or the petitioner for review.

6 Discussion

We further examine our proposed architecture in this section.

6.1 Using Pre-amendment Sentences in Naive Transformer

The focal differential translation corpus [16] contains quartets (S_{PrO}, S_{PrT}, S_{PoO}, S_{PoT}). That is, we can arrange two translation pairs, (S_{PrO}, S_{PrT}) and (S_{PoO}, S_{PoT}), from the corpus, which doubles the training dataset. To assess the effect of doubling, we trained the naive Transformer with the doubled dataset.

Table 5. Effect of doubled dataset

Model	BLEU	RIBES	ISDIT
Naive-SMT-add	22.32	53.89	10.52
Naive-SMT-doubled	24.02	56.10	12.55
Copiable-SMT-add	**54.12**	**87.09**	**48.26**

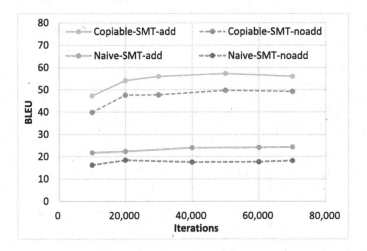

Fig. 5. BLEU scores in different iterations

Table 5 shows the result. We trained each model and combined it with the Kozakai model as the hyperparameters specified in Sect. 5.1. The naive Transformer with the doubled dataset (Naive-SMT-doubled in Table 5) slightly outperformed the conventional dataset by around 2 points of BLEU, RIBES, and ISDIT. However, the Copiable Translation Transformer achieved a far better performance than the two other models.

6.2 Training Iterations

We investigated the transition of the performance on different training iterations to exclude the results from chance. Figures 5 and 6 show BLEU and ISDIT with different iterations. The tendency of the translation performance discussed above was kept in all the iterations. In all the models and criteria, the performance did not drastically improve as the iteration number grew.

6.3 Using a Large-Scaled Bilingual Corpus

We can acquire bilingual corpora with hundreds of thousands of Japanese-English statutory sentence pairs [7,15,16]. In this section, we trained a naive Transformer with a large-scaled corpus containing 391,758 sentence pairs [16]. We set the iteration number to 2,000,000 for training the model and identical values as Sect. 5.1 for the other hyperparameters. We combined the naive Transformer model with the Kozakai model, as explained in Sect. 5.1.

Table 6 shows the experimental result. "Naive-SMT-large" in the table indicates the model trained with the large-scaled corpus. The large-scaled corpus drastically raised the naive Transformer's performance, which supersedes the best performance from our Copiable Translation Transformer. However, researching our method remains valuable since it achieved a better performance than naive Transformer with the same amount of training data.

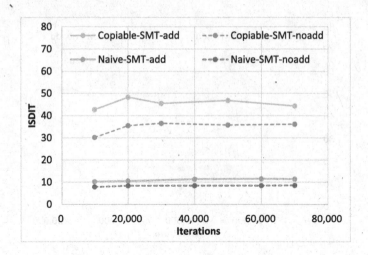

Fig. 6. ISDIT scores in different iterations

Table 6. Performance of naive Transformer with a large-scaled corpus

Model	BLEU	RIBES	ISDIT
Naive-SMT-add	22.32	53.89	10.52
Naive-SMT-large	**83.00**	**94.16**	**74.14**
Copiable-SMT-add	54.12	87.09	48.26

Table 7 shows the system outputs of the example in Table 4. The naive Transformer model with a large-scaled corpus output a very accurate translation. However, it was not completely focal because of an unnecessary modification from "requestor" (審査請求人 ; *shinsaseikyunin*) to "applicant of the request." The Copiable Translation Transformer model retained that word.

6.4   Investigation into *n*-Best Candidates

To assess how stably NMT models generate translations, we calculate the following statistical parameters of the 4-best candidate sentences output by the models:

- Average word count;
- Standard deviation of word count;
- Average BLEU score;
- Standard deviation of BLEU scores.

We compared the following models' parameters: a naive Transformer with the additional dataset (Naive-add), a naive Transformer with a large-scaled dataset (Naive-large), and a Copiable Translation Transformer with an additional dataset (Copiable-add).

Table 7. Output of naive Transformer trained with a large-scaled corpus

Model	Output
(Sentence S_{PrO})	経済産業大臣は、前条の意見の聴取の期日及び場所を定め、審査請求人又は異議申立人に通知しなければならない。
(Sentence S_{PrT})	the minister of economy, trade and industry must specify the date and place of the hearing of opinions prescribed in the preceding article, and notify the requestor for review or the petitioner for objection.
(Sentence S_{PoO})	経済産業大臣は、前条の意見の聴取の期日及び場所を定め、審査請求人に通知しなければならない。
(Sentence S_{PoT})	the minister of economy, trade and industry must specify the date and place of the hearing of opinions prescribed in the preceding article, and notify the requestor for review.
Naive-SMT-add	the minister of economy, trade and industry shall, in accordance with the procedures provided for in the preceding item, and the day on which the label set forth in the preceding article.
Naive-SMT-large	the minister of economy, trade and industry must specify the date and place of the hearing of opinions prescribed in the preceding article, and notify the applicant of the request for review.
Copiable-SMT-add	in of ofy, and notify the foreign national must specify the date and place of the hearing of opinions prescribed in the preceding article, and notify the requestor for review or the petitioner for review.

Table 8. Statistical parameters of n-best candidates

Parameter	Naive-add	Naive-large	Copiable-add
Average word count	74.60	67.93	52.14
Standard deviation of word count	9.42	1.24	9.58
Average BLEU score	19.42	75.40	47.89
Standard deviation of BLEU scores	2.18	4.54	8.13

Table 8 shows the result. We averaged the parameters over all 201 examples in the test data. Naive-large has the smallest standard deviation of word count, which indicates the stability of its sentence generation. Naive-add and Copiable-add have similar standard deviations of word count. Copiable-add has the smallest word count, perhaps because of the cases that only generated a few words (i.e., just outputting "the").

As for the BLEU score's standard deviation, Copiable-add has the largest value, followed by Naive-large and Naive-add, which indicates that Copiable-add is the most unstable. Perhaps insufficiency of the training data caused this result because the Copiable Translation Transformer has approximately 1.5 times more neural units than the naive Transformer. This result identifies an insight into the performance of the Copiable Translation Transformer without a template-aware SMT model in Sect. 5.2. Since the output of the Copiable Translation Transformer was more unstable, the assistance of the template-aware SMT was more effective.

Next we discuss the actual 4-best candidates output by each model, shown in Table 9. Naive-large's candidates are close to the reference and have only minor differences from each other. Although Naive-add apparently generated candidates more stably than copiable-add, they contain more irrelevant words (e.g., "fee-charging employment placement") that may degrade the evaluation criteria scores.

Table 9. 4-best candidates generated by each model

Source	Sentence
Reference	the term "commodity" as used in this act means:
Naive-add #1	the term "employment placement service provider" as used in this act means a fee-charging employment placement business;
Naive-add #2	the term "employment placement service provider" as used in this act means a fee-charging employment placement service provider of another person who does not work provided for in this act.
Naive-add #3	the term "employment placement service provider" as used in this act means a fee-charging employment placement service provider of another person who do not work provided for in this act.
Naive-add #4	the term "employment placement service provider" as used in this act means a fee-charging employment placement service provider of another person who holds a license provided for in this act.
Copiable-add #1	the term "financial instruments business" as used in this act means the following goods:
Copiable-add #2	the term ")" as used in this act means the following goods:
Copiable-add #3	the term "business" as used in this act means the following goods:
Copiable-add #4	the term "financial instruments business operator" as used in this act means the following goods: .
Naive-large #1	the term "commodities" as used in this act means the following:
Naive-large #2	the term "commodity" as used in this act means the following:
Naive-large #3	the term "commodity" as used in this act means any of the following:
Naive-large #4	the term "commodity" as used in this act shall mean the following:

7   Summary

We proposed architecture for Transformer that aims for differential translations for amended statutory sentences. Our architecture, Copiable Translation Transformer, has a copying mechanism tuned for translation tasks. In the prediction of the next word, it can either generate a word from the vocabulary or copy one from a pre-amendment statutory sentence. The copying mechanism raises the focality of the system output more than the naive Transformer. With a dataset of a few thousand examples, our Copiable Translation Transformer outperformed the naive Transformer in both ISDIT and BLEU and RIBES. However, it failed to reach the performance of the naive Transformer trained by a large-scaled bilingual corpus with hundreds of thousands of examples.

Toward practical use of our architecture, our future work will address the following tasks. First, we will search for a method to artificially augment the amount of training data for the Copiable Translation Transformer because manually translating post-amendment statutory sentences is very expensive. Second, we will search for a method to utilize the knowledge of a large-scaled corpus in training a Copiable Translation Transformer model. Third, we will investigate other methods that have a copying mechanism with dual-language inputs. An example is Huang et al. [4]'s method for automatic post-editing.

Acknowledgments. This work was partly supported by JSPS KAKENHI Grant Number 21H03772.

References

1. Gu, J., Lu, Z., Li, H., Li, V.O.: Incorporating copying mechanism in sequence-to-sequence learning. In: Proceedings of the 54th Annual Meeting of the Association for Computational Linguistics, pp. 1631–1640 (2016)
2. Hirao, T., Isozaki, H., Sudoh, K., Duh, K., Tsukada, H., Nagata, M.: Evaluating translation quality with word order correlations. J. Nat. Lang. Process. **21**(3), 421–444 (2014). (In Japanese)
3. Hoseishitsumu-Kenkyukai: Workbook Hoseishitsumu (newly revised second edition). Gyosei (2018). (In Japanese)
4. Huang, X., Liu, Y., Luan, H., Xu, J., Sun, M.: Learning to copy for automatic post-editing. In: Proceedings of the 2019 Conference on Empirical Methods in Natural Language Processing and the 9th International Joint Conference on Natural Language Processing (EMNLP-IJCNLP), pp. 6122–6132 (2019)
5. Koehn, P., et al.: Moses: open source toolkit for statistical machine translation. In: Proceedings of the ACL 2007 Demo and Poster Sessions, pp. 177–180 (2007)
6. Koehn, P., Senellart, J.: Convergence of translation memory and statistical machine translation. In: AMTA Workshop on MT Research and the Translation Industry, pp. 21–31 (2010)
7. Kozakai, T., Ogawa, Y., Ohno, T., Nakamura, M., Toyama, K.: Shinkyutaishohyo no riyo niyoru horei no eiyaku shusei. In: Proceedings of NLP2017, 4 p. (2017) (In Japanese)
8. Kudo, T., Richardson, J.: Sentencepiece: a simple and language independent subword tokenizer and detokenizer for neural text processing. In: Proceedings of the 2018 Conference on Empirical Methods in Natural Language Processing (System Demonstrations), pp. 66–71 (2018)
9. Ogawa, Y., Inagaki, S., Toyama, K.: Automatic consolidation of Japanese statutes based on formalization of amendment sentences. In: Satoh, K., Inokuchi, A., Nagao, K., Kawamura, T. (eds.) JSAI 2007. LNCS (LNAI), vol. 4914, pp. 363–376. Springer, Heidelberg (2008). https://doi.org/10.1007/978-3-540-78197-4_34

10. Papineni, K., Roukos, S., Ward, T., Jing Zhu, W.: BLEU: a method for automatic evaluation of machine translation. In: Proceedings of the 40th Annual Meeting of the Association for Computational Linguistics, pp. 311–318 (2002)
11. Toyama, K., et al.: Design and development of Japanese law translation system. In: Law via the Internet 2011, 12 p. (2011)
12. Vaswani, A., et al.: Attention is all you need. In: Proceedings of Advances in Neural Information Processing Systems, vol. 30, pp. 6000–6010 (2017)
13. Xia, M., Huang, G., Liu, L., Shi, S.: Graph based translation memory for neural machine translation. In: Proceedings of the Thirty-Third AAAI Conference on Artificial Intelligence, pp. 7297–7304 (2019)
14. Xu, S., Li, H., Yuan, P., Wu, Y., He, X., Zhou, B.: Self-attention guided copy mechanism for abstractive summarization. In: Proceedings of the 58th Annual Meeting of the Association for Computational Linguistics, pp. 1355–1362 (2020)
15. Yamakoshi, T., Komamizu, T., Ogawa, Y., Toyama, K.: Differential translation for Japanese partially amended statutory sentences. In: Okazaki, N., Yada, K., Satoh, K., Mineshima, K. (eds.) JSAI-isAI 2020. LNCS (LNAI), vol. 12758, pp. 162–178. Springer, Cham (2021). https://doi.org/10.1007/978-3-030-79942-7_11
16. Yamakoshi, T., Komamizu, T., Ogawa, Y., Toyama, K.: Evaluation scheme of focal translation for Japanese partially amended statutes. In: Proceedings of the 8th Workshop on Asian Translation (WAT2021), pp. 124–132 (2021)

On Complexity and Generality
of Contrary Prioritized Defeasible Theory

Wachara Fungwacharakorn[✉], Kanae Tsushima, and Ken Satoh

National Institute of Informatics, Sokendai University, Tokyo, Japan
{wacharaf,k_tsushima,ksatoh}@nii.ac.jp

Abstract. This paper studies defeasible logic for representing legal theories. In defeasible logic, a literal can be ambiguous since a theory can support both the literal and its contrary. There have been several policies in handling ambiguities but choosing a policy is under judges' discretion, which is unpredictable and possibly contradicts the legislators' intentions. To prevent such a problem, this paper studies *contrary prioritization*, which restricts a defeasible theory to prioritize all pairs of rules in which heads are contrary to each other. This paper analyzes the complexity of contrary prioritization and the generality of contrary prioritized defeasible theories in the translations between such defeasible theories and stratified logic programs. This paper presents that contrary prioritization requires an effort of finding a correct assignment of the priorities between contrary pairs, and the effort makes the problem of contrary prioritization *NP-complete*. Furthermore, every contrary prioritized defeasible theory can be translated to a stratified logic program and vice versa. Hence, a contrary prioritized defeasible theory is as general as a stratified logic program.

Keywords: Legal reasoning · Legal representation · Priority

1 Introduction

For a long time, researchers have been interested in using logic programs to represent legal theories. There are two types of logic programs that are commonly used to represent legal theories. The first type is a normal logic program, in which each rule is an extended Horn clause with negation as failure. This includes many programming languages for representing statutes such as PROLOG [31,33,34], PROLEG [29], and CATALA [22]. The second type is a defeasible logic program, in which each rule is a defeasible rule that does not use negation as a failure, but instead uses priorities between rules. This includes several frameworks for legal reasoning such as legal reasoning in Defeasible Logic [24] and legal reasoning in ASPIC+ [26].

One distinct feature of a defeasible logic program is that a literal in a defeasible logic program can be *ambiguous* [6] when there are at least two chains of monotonic reasoning such that one supports the literal but another supports

Y. Takama et al. (Eds.): JSAI-isAI 2022 Workshop, LNAI 13859, pp. 23–35, 2023.
https://doi.org/10.1007/978-3-031-29168-5_2

its contrary, and a priority cannot resolve this conflict. In some legal contexts, ambiguous legal conclusions lead to uncertainties. For example, ambiguous normative conclusions lead to normative conflicts of who has a right or a power to do [5]. For such legal contexts, legislators should prevent ambiguities in legislation. This paper aims to assist legislators in checking whether there is a possible prototypical case that makes the conclusion ambiguous, and if a legislator specifies an anticipated derivation for the conclusion of that prototypical case, what should a priority be to meet the legislator's intention.

In this paper, we explore *contrary prioritization* – a policy which prioritizes all pairs of rules in which heads are contrary to each other, hence ambiguous literals can be resolved if a dependency graph of a program is acyclic and a priority is transitive. We prove that the problem of contrary prioritization is *NP-complete* since it requires finding a correct assignment of unknown priorities between pairs of rules of which heads are contrary to each other. Since it is common to prevent ambiguities in legal theories by representing them as stratified normal logic programs [21], we show that every contrary prioritized defeasible theory can be translated to a stratified logic program and vice versa. This implies that a contrary prioritized defeasible theory is as general as a stratified logic program.

This paper is structured as follows. Section 2 provides basic definitions of normal logic programs, defeasible logic programs, and common policies handling ambiguity. Section 3 describes contrary prioritization and analyzes the complexity of contrary prioritization and the generality of a contrary prioritized defeasible theory. Section 4 compares contrary prioritization with other policies handling ambiguity. Finally, Sect. 5 provides a conclusion of this paper.

2   Backgrounds

In this paper, we restrict attention to propositional logic programs for representing laws in civil law systems, where statutes are the primary source of a decision. In civil law systems, judges usually develop legal theories from statutes in order to make consistent interpretations across courts. For example, judges in the Japanese Legal Training Institute developed a legal theory known as the Japanese Presupposed Ultimate Facts Theory or *Yoken-jijitsu-ron* [17]. Since there are similarities between legal theories and computational logic programs, researchers have become interested in codifying legal theories into logic programs [21,31].

2.1   Normal Logic Program

There are two types of logic programs that are commonly used to codify a legal theory. One common type is a normal logic program or a PROLOG program. PROLOG is one of the most popular logic programming languages and it was the first logic programming language for representing laws [33]. Although recent programming languages for laws, such as PROLEG [29] and CATALA [22], typically separate exception parts from requisite parts, it has been demonstrated that such separation has the same expressive power as original PROLOG [30].

Definition 1 (Normal Logic Program). *A normal logic program is a set of rules of the form*

$$h \leftarrow b_1, \ldots, b_m, not\ b_{m+1}, \ldots, not\ b_n. \tag{1}$$

where $h, b_1, \ldots, b_n$ are propositions. Let R be a rule of the form (1), we have

- *h as a head of a rule or a conclusion of a rule denoted by $head(R)$,*
- *$\{b_1, \ldots, b_m\}$ as a positive body of a rule denoted by $pos(R) \cdot$ (each element of a positive body is called a requisite),*
- *$\{b_{m+1}, \ldots, b_n\}$ as a negative body of a rule denoted by $neg(R)$ (each element of a negative body is called an exception),*

A rule is called a fact *if the body of the rule is empty.*

not in a rule is a negation as failure, namely *not p* is derived if p cannot be derived. Negation as failure can be used for representing default assumptions, which the opposite can attack by proving their negations [31, 32]. Typically, legal rules would express this behavior with the terms "except" or "unless", etc.

In civil litigation, a judge takes factual situations in a case as inputs. Then, the judge concludes a legal decision based on related statutes. To reflect this civil litigation, we divide propositions into *fact propositions*, which must not occur in the head of a rule (except the rule with empty body i.e. a fact), and *rule propositions* for otherwise. Let F be a set of fact propositions and R_n be a set of rules. $\langle F, R_n \rangle$ is a normal logic program built by appending facts (rules with empty bodies) constructed from all fact propositions in F into R_n. A set of propositions which can be concluded $\langle F, R_n \rangle$ is called an *answer set*. In other words, an answer set indicates a legal decision in the case (represented by F) based on the statute (represented by R_n).

To reflect the constraint that judges require a distinct and unambiguous interpretation of statutes, judges usually describe a legal theory as a stratified logic program since it would produce only one answer set [9].

Definition 2 (A stratified program [4, 18]). *A normal logic program T is stratified if there is a partition $T = T_0 \cup T_1 \cup \ldots \cup T_n$ (T_i and T_j disjoint for all $i \neq j$) such that*

- *if a proposition p is in a positive body of rule in T_i then a rule with p in the head is only contained within $T_0 \cup T_1 \cup \ldots T_j (j \leqslant i)$*
- *if a proposition p is in a negative body of rule in T_i then a rule with p in the head is only contained within $T_0 \cup T_1 \cup \ldots T_j (j < i)$*

2.2 Defeasible Logic Program

A defeasible logic program [23] is another common logic program for codifying a legal theory. In a defeasible logic program, there are three kinds of rules: *strict* rules, *defeasible* rules, and *defeaters*. For the sake of simplicity, in this paper, we focus on a defeasible logic program that only contains defeasible rules.

Definition 3 (Defeasible Logic Program). *A defeasible logic program is a set of defeasible rules of the form*

$$l_1, \ldots, l_n \Rightarrow l_0 \tag{2}$$

where $l_0, \ldots, l_n$ are literals, which are propositions or classical negations of propositions. Let l be a literal, we say $\bar{l}$ is contrary to l, namely $\bar{p} = \neg p$ and $\overline{\neg p} = p$ where p is a proposition. Let R be a rule of the form (2), we have

- l_0 *as a head of a rule or a conclusion of a rule denoted by head(R),*
- $\{l_1, \ldots, l_n\}$ *as a body of a rule denoted by body(R).*

Rules in defeasible logic programs interact via priorities. Hence, knowledge in defeasible logic is structured as a defeasible theory defined as follows.

Definition 4 (Defeasible Theory). *A defeasible theory is a triple $(F, R_d, >)$ where*

- *F is a consistent set of literals constructed from fact propositions (that is p and $\neg p$ cannot occur in the same F)*
- *R_d is a set of defeasible rules*
- *$>$ is a priority - an ordering relation on $R_d{}^1$ such that for all $r_i, r_j, r_k \in R_d$, $r_i \not> r_i$ (irreflexive) and if $r_i > r_j$ and $r_j > r_k$ then $r_i > r_k$ (transitive). If $r_i > r_j$, we say r_i has a higher priority than r_j or r_i overrides r_j.*

Defeasible logic has its own proof theory [23]. Generally speaking, a conclusion is derived when it is supported by some rules and there are no counterattacks or all counterattacks are from lower prioritized rules. There are several types of derivation in defeasible logic but we focus only on defeasible derivations. Following [6], general defeasible derivations are denoted by a proof tag d_f i.e. $(F, R_d, >) \vdash +d_f l$ if a literal l is defeasibly provable and $(F, R_d, >) \vdash -d_f l$ if a literal l is defeasibly refuted. In this paper, we restrict only a *decisive* defeasible theory, of which a dependency graph is acyclic. In such a theory, a literal can be either defeasibly provable or defeasibly refuted [12].

In legal reasoning, there are many legal principles introducing priorities among rules [14]. Example 1 shows one example from the Brazilian Penal Code.

Example 1 (The Brazilian Penal Code). Consider these two articles in the Brazilian Penal Code regulating about abortion [20].

Article 124 ... *abortion is forbidden* ...
Article 128 ... *It is permitted to abort upon consent if the woman's life is endangered or if pregnancy is the result of sexual abuse* ...

---

[1] Generally, $>$ in defeasible logic is not required to be transitive. However, in this paper, we assume the transitivity to ensure that a closure of the priority is acyclic.

The articles can be represented by the following defeasible logic program[2].

r_1 : abort $\Rightarrow$ guilty-due-to-abortion.

r_2 : abort, upon-consent, woman-life-endangered $\Rightarrow$ ¬guilty-due-to-abortion

r_3 : abort, upon-consent, sexual-abuse $\Rightarrow$ ¬guilty-due-to-abortion

For this example, legal scholars often interpret that Article 128 overrides Article 124 as it covers more specific cases than Article 124. This corresponds to a legal principle *lex specialis* – a specific act can override a general act. Given a case $F = \{abort, upon\text{-}consent, woman\text{-}life\text{-}endangered\}$ and a priority $\{r_2 > r_1, r_3 > r_1\}$ expressing the interpretation by legal scholars, we have that $(F, R_d, >) \vdash +d_f$¬*guilty-due-to-abortion* and $(F, R_d, >) \vdash -d_f$*guilty- due-to-abortion* since r_2 overrides r_1.

2.3   Ambiguity Blocking and Ambiguity Propagation

A literal l is said to be ambiguous if there is a monotonic chain of reasoning that supports l, another that supports the contrary $\bar{l}$, and the priority does not resolve this conflict [6]. There are two common policies to deal with ambiguity in defeasible logic. One is an *ambiguity blocking* (commonly denoted by a proof tag ∂), which intuitively means both derivations of ambiguous l and $\bar{l}$ are determined as failure. Another is an *ambiguity propagation* (commonly denoted by a proof tag δ), which intuitively means both derivations of ambiguous l and $\bar{l}$ are determined as success.

Example 2. Consider a defeasible theory [11] with the following defeasible rules and the empty priority.

$$r_1 : evidenceA \Rightarrow responsible$$
$$r_2 : evidenceB \Rightarrow \neg responsible$$
$$r_3 : responsible \Rightarrow guilty$$
$$r_4 :\Rightarrow \neg guilty$$

Without a priority to determine which rule overrides which, when both *evidenceA* and *evidenceB* are given, the literal *responsible* becomes ambiguous. With ambiguity blocking, the ambiguity is blocked at *responsible* (neither $+\partial responsible$ nor $+\partial\neg responsible$ is derived), and thus *guilty* is not ambiguous (only $+\partial\neg guilty$ is derived). With ambiguity propagation, *guilty* is ambiguous (both $+\delta guilty$ and $+\delta\neg guilty$ are derived), since the ambiguity propagates from *responsible* to them (both $+\delta responsible$ and $+\delta\neg responsible$ are derived).

Although ambiguity blocking and ambiguity propagation share of the same goal of making a conclusion without adding new priorities in civil litigation,

---

[2] This is a simplified representation for ease of exposition. A proper representation requires considering deontic modalities and strengths of permission cf. [13].

they reflect different proof standards [10,16,25,32] (for further discussion, see [6,11,35]). From the example, ambiguity blocking reflects the concept that a person is considered innocent until proven guilty beyond reasonable doubt, and the reasonable doubt is reflected by ambiguity. On the other hand, ambiguity propagation reflects the concept that the conclusion needs to be consider from the weight of the evidence proportionally. Hence, the decision may vary and differ from what the legislators anticipated.

3   Contrary Prioritization

For some legal conclusions, legislators have to prevent ambiguities in drafting or revising legislation, especially when they consider normative conclusions of whether or not a particular person has a right or has a power. One simple policy to prevent ambiguities is *contrary prioritization*, which prioritizes all pairs of rules in which heads are contrary to each other. Below defines contrary prioritization in both absolute and relative ways.

Definition 5 (Contrary Prioritized Defeasible Theory). *Let* $D = (F, R_d, >)$ *be a decisive defeasible theory of which a dependency graph is acyclic.*

- *We say* D *is* absolutely contrary prioritized *if and only if for all* $r_i, r_j \in R_d$ *such that* $head(r_i) = \overline{head(r_j)}$, $r_i > r_j$ *or* $r_j > r_i$.
- *We say* D *is* relatively contrary prioritized *if and only if for every absolutely contrary prioritized* $D^* = (F, R_d, >^*)$ *such that* $r_i > r_j$ *implies* $r_i >^* r_j$, $D^* \vdash \pm d_f p$ *if and only if* $D \vdash \pm d_f p$ *for every proposition* p.

We define relative contrary prioritization in supporting a concept of *team defeat* [19] where absolute contrary prioritization is not required for preventing ambiguity because a set of rules would be packed as a team to defeat other rules. In other words, the program produces the same derivations regardless of how to complete the priority. For instance, the following defeasible theory $D = (\{a, b, c, d\}, R_d, >)$ is relatively contrary prioritized because either $r_2 > r_3$ or $r_3 > r_2$ is introduced, they both produce the same derivations.

$$r_1 : a \Rightarrow p \qquad r_3 : c \Rightarrow p.$$
$$r_2 : b \Rightarrow \neg p \qquad r_4 : d \Rightarrow \neg p.$$
$$r_2 > r_1, \ r_4 > r_3$$

Since every relatively contrary prioritized defeasible theory can be translated into an absolutely contrary prioritized defeasible theory, a contrary prioritized defeasible theory in the rest of paper refers to an absolute one.

Example 3 demonstrates a problem of a defeasible theory without contrary prioritization in a fictional example from the Brazilian Penal Code.

Example 3. Continuing from Example 1, suppose there was a case that a woman had a pregnancy as a result of sexual abuse and went to a non-authorized abortion clinic for having an abortion upon her consent. The court may consider that going to a non-authorized abortion clinic shows an intention of abortion hence it should be guilty. Then, legislators may consider this case and introduce a rule r_4 overriding r_3 ($r_4 > r_3$) to reflect the court decision. However, since we do not know a priority between r_2 and r_4, it leads to ambiguity in legal interpretation when there is a case in which a woman's life is endangered but she goes to a non-authorized clinic.

r_1 : abort $\Rightarrow$ guilty-due-to-abortion.

r_2 : abort, upon-consent, woman-life-endangered. $\Rightarrow$ ¬guilty-due-to-abortion

r_3 : abort, upon-consent, sexual-abuse $\Rightarrow$ ¬guilty-due-to-abortion.

r_4 : non-authorized-abort $\Rightarrow$ guilty-due-to-abortion.

$(r_2 > r_1), (r_3 > r_1), (r_4 > r_3)$

3.1   Complexity

Contrary prioritization can be divided into two steps. This first step is to check whether there is a possible prototypical case that makes the conclusion ambiguous. If there is such a case, then we show it to the user (i.e. a legislator) and ask for an anticipated derivation for the conclusion of the case. The second step is to find a correct priority that meets the anticipation.

In the first step, contrary prioritization needs to find all pairs of rules of which the heads are contrary to each other and the priorities are unknown. The first step requires finding the transitive closure of priorities so Warshall's Algorithm may be used. The complexity of the algorithm is known to be $O(n^3)$ where n is the number of nodes in the closure, which is the number of rules in this context. In the second step, contrary prioritization finds a correct assignment of such unknown priorities to see which one leads to the anticipated derivation. This problem can be considered as a kind of problem in defeasible preference revision [12,14,15].' As the direct consequence of their results, the problem of finding a correct assignment of unknown priorities between contrary pairs is reducible to the 3-SAT problem, and thus the problem is *NP-complete*.

Theorem 1. *The problem of finding a correct assignment of unknown priorities between contrary pairs is reducible to the 3-SAT problem.*

Proof. Given a 3-SAT formula $\Gamma = \bigwedge_{i=1,\ldots,n}(l_{i1} \vee l_{i2} \vee l_{i3})$. Let f and s be new propositions that never occurred in Γ. Consider a defeasible theory $(\{f\}, R_d, \varnothing)$ where R_d contains only two types of rules as follows.

1. $\overline{l_{i1}}, \overline{l_{i2}}, \overline{l_{i3}} \Rightarrow s$ for every $i = 1 \ldots n$
2. $f \Rightarrow p$ and $f \Rightarrow \neg p$ for every proposition p in Γ

If we can find priorities between contrary pairs, which occur only within rules type 2, so that s is derived, then Γ is not satisfiable according to De Morgan's Law. Hence, the problem of finding a correct assignment of unknown priorities between contrary pairs is reducible to the 3-SAT problem.   □

From Example 3, there are three possible priorities between r_2 and r_4 as in Fig. 1. The legislators have to consider the anticipated derivation of *guilty-due-to-abortion* in a case in which both r_2 and r_4 are applicable. Then, contrary prioritization needs to try all possible priorities between r_2 and r_4 to see which one leads to the anticipated derivation.

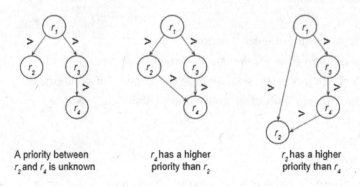

A priority between r_2 and r_4 is unknown r_4 has a higher priority than r_2 r_2 has a higher priority than r_4

Fig. 1. Possible priorities between r_2 and r_4

3.2 Generality in Translation to and from Stratified Logic Program

The next question is how general a contrary prioritized defeasible theory is. Since stratified normal logic programs are ambiguity-free, we compare a contrary prioritized defeasible theory to a stratified normal logic program. Relations between defeasible logic programs and normal logic programs have been long studied [1,2,7]. In this paper, we focus on the relation between a contrary prioritized defeasible theory and a stratified normal logic program. We have that a contrary prioritized defeasible theory is translatable to a stratified logic program back and forth.

Theorem 2. *Every contrary prioritized defeasible theory is translatable to a stratified logic program.*

Proof. For each pair of prioritized rules in which heads are contrary to each other

$$r_1 : l_{11}, \ldots, l_{1m} \Rightarrow l_0.$$
$$r_2 : l_{21}, \ldots, l_{2n} \Rightarrow \overline{l_0}.$$

where l_0, l_{ij} are literals, and $r_2 > r_1$, we can translate them into a normal logic program by introducing *not e* where e is a new proposition for each pair of such rules [4,27] while left classical negative literals are treated as a new proposition.

$$r_1' : l_0 \leftarrow l_{11}, \ldots, l_{1m}, not\ e.$$
$$r_2' : e \leftarrow l_{21}, \ldots, l_{2n}.$$

Since the dependency graph and the priority of contrary prioritized defeasible theory are acyclic, the dependency graph of the translated program has no cycles containing a negative edge. Therefore the translated program is stratified [4]. □

Theorem 3. *Every stratified logic program is translatable to a contrary prioritized defeasible theory.*

Proof. Following the translation from a defeasible theory to a logic program [3], we can simulate a negation as failure *not b* as $r_1 :\Rightarrow b'$. $r_2 : b \Rightarrow \neg b'$. where $r_2 > r_1$ and b' is a new proposition corresponding to *not b*. This translated theory is contrary prioritized since those contraries occurring in the heads of rules are all new propositions. □

Example 4 demonstrates a translation of a defeasible logic program from Example 1 to a normal logic program. The result can be interpreted as *abortion is forbidden except the woman's life is endangered or the pregnancy is the result of sexual abuse*. This interpretation corresponds to the legal principle *exceptio firmat regulam* – general rules can apply unless exceptional situations occur.

Example 4. We can translate the defeasible logic program in Example 1 into a normal logic program as follows.

> guilty-due-to-abortion ← abort, *not* exception1, *not* exception2.
>> exception1 ← abort, upon-consent, woman-life-endangered.
>> exception2 ← abort, upon-consent, sexual-abuse.

The following two revisions demonstrate all of the possible priorities introduced by the new rule in the same manner as all of the possible priorities between r_2 and r_4 in Example 3.

Revision 1 (equivalent to $r_2 > r_4$)

> guilty-due-to-abortion ← abort, *not* exception1, *not* exception2.
>> exception1 ← abort, upon-consent, woman-life-endangered.
>> exception2 ← abort, upon-consent, sexual-abuse,
>>> **not exception3**.
>> exception3 ← non-authorized-abort.

Revision 2 (equivalent to $r_4 > r_2$)

> guilty-due-to-abortion ← abort, *not* exception1, *not* exception2.
>> exception1 ← abort, upon-consent, woman-life-endangered,
>>> **not exception3**.
>> exception2 ← abort, upon-consent, sexual-abuse,
>>> **not exception3**.
>> exception3 ← non-authorized-abort.

4   Discussion

In this paper, we investigate a defeasible logic program when there are two monotonic reasoning chains, one supports an anticipated conclusion but another supports its contrary, and a priority cannot resolve this conflict. This phenomenon is usually referred to as *ambiguity*. This paper mainly investigates a contrary prioritized policy, preventing ambiguity by having a priority for every pair of rules in which heads are contrary to each other. This policy ensures that, with a transitive priority, we can always resolve such a conflict in a defeasible logic program with an acyclic dependency graph.

In this section, we compare the contrary prioritized policy to other policies dealing with ambiguity, especially *ambiguity blocking* and *ambiguity propagation* (see Sect. 2.3) which are two most common policies in defeasible logic. Although ambiguity blocking and ambiguity propagation reflect different proof standards, they share the same goal of making a conclusion without adding new priorities. The effort of minimizing new priorities or exceptions is usually found in civil litigation as judges tend to limit themselves from legislative issues. This effort is usually referred to as *minimal revision* i.e. revising the theory as few as possible, only to justify the decision for the new case [8, 12, 28].

Contrary prioritization, on the other hand, would be more appropriate for legislators than judges since the policy respects coherentist revision (usually from legislators' perspective) rather than minimal revision (usually from judges' perspective). From Example 3, contrary prioritization considers a case in which a woman's life is endangered but she goes to a non-authorized clinic, where both r_2 and r_4 are applicable. This case is prototypical because it was not the case that went to the court. Hence, the revision in Example 3 is obviously not minimal. However, from the coherentist perspective, a defeasible theory with ambiguous literals leads to varied and possibly unanticipated decisions. To prevent unanticipated decisions, the coherentist tends to avoid ambiguous or inconsistent conclusions (see [20]), and contrary prioritization may serve as heuristics for revising the theory.

5   Conclusion

To resolve ambiguities in defeasible theories, this paper explores *contrary prioritized* defeasible theories, which restricts prioritizing every pair of rules whose heads are contrary to each other. To make a contrary prioritized defeasible theory, we find pairs of rules of which the priorities are unknown and find a correct assignment of such unknown priorities that gives an anticipated result. Since the problem of finding a correct assignment of unknown priorities between contrary pairs is reducible to the 3-SAT problem, the problem of contrary prioritization is *NP-complete*. We show that every contrary prioritized defeasible theory is translatable to a stratified logic program and vice versa. This demonstrates that contrary prioritization can indeed resolve ambiguity.

Acknowledgements. The authors would like to thank all anonymous reviewers for insightful suggestions and comments. This work was supported by JSPS KAKENHI Grant Numbers, JP17H06103 and JP19H05470 and JST, AIP Trilateral AI Research, Grant Number JPMJCR20G4.

References

1. Antoniou, G.: Relating defeasible logic to extended logic programs. In: Vlahavas, I.P., Spyropoulos, C.D. (eds.) SETN 2002. LNCS (LNAI), vol. 2308, pp. 54–64. Springer, Heidelberg (2002). https://doi.org/10.1007/3-540-46014-4_6
2. Antoniou, G., Billington, D., Governatori, G., Maher, M.J.: Embedding defeasible logic into logic programming. Theory Pract. Logic Program. **6**(6), 703–735 (2006)
3. Antoniou, G., Maher, M.J., Billington, D.: Defeasible logic versus logic programming without negation as failure. J. Log. Program. **42**(1), 47–57 (2000)
4. Apt, K.R., Blair, H.A., Walker, A.: Towards a theory of declarative knowledge. In: Foundations of Deductive Databases and Logic Programming, pp. 89–148. Morgan Kaufmann, Burlington (1988)
5. Araszkiewicz, M., Płeszka, K.: The concept of normative consequence and legislative discourse. In: Araszkiewicz, M., Płeszka, K. (eds.) Logic in the Theory and Practice of Lawmaking. Legisprudence Library, pp. 253–297. Springer, Cham (2015). https://doi.org/10.1007/978-3-319-19575-9_10
6. Billington, D., Antoniou, G., Governatori, G., Maher, M.: An inclusion theorem for defeasible logics. ACM Trans. Comput. Log. (TOCL) **12**(1), 1–27 (2010)
7. Brewka, G.: On the relationship between defeasible logic and well-founded semantics. In: Eiter, T., Faber, W., Truszczyński, M. (eds.) LPNMR 2001. LNCS (LNAI), vol. 2173, pp. 121–132. Springer, Heidelberg (2001). https://doi.org/10.1007/3-540-45402-0_9
8. Fungwacharakorn, W., Tsushima, K., Satoh, K.: On semantics-based minimal revision for legal reasoning. In: Proceedings of the 18th International Conference on Artificial Intelligence and Law - ICAIL 2021. ACM, New York (2021)
9. Gelfond, M., Lifschitz, V.: The stable model semantics for logic programming. In: Kowalski, R., Bowen, Kenneth (eds.) Proceedings of International Logic Programming Conference and Symposium, vol. 88, pp. 1070–1080. MIT Press, Cambridge (1988)
10. Governatori, G., Maher, M.J.: Annotated defeasible logic. Theory Pract. Logic Program. **17**(5–6), 819–836 (2017)
11. Governatori, G., Maher, M.J., Antoniou, G., Billington, D.: Argumentation semantics for defeasible logic. J. Log. Comput. **14**(5), 675–702 (2004)
12. Governatori, G., Olivieri, F., Cristani, M., Scannapieco, S.: Revision of defeasible preferences. Int. J. Approximate Reasoning **104**, 205–230 (2019)
13. Governatori, G., Olivieri, F., Rotolo, A., Scannapieco, S.: Computing strong and weak permissions in defeasible logic. J. Philos. Log. **42**(6), 799–829 (2013)
14. Governatori, G., Olivieri, F., Scannapieco, S., Cristani, M.: Superiority based revision of defeasible theories. In: Dean, M., Hall, J., Rotolo, A., Tabet, S. (eds.) RuleML 2010. LNCS, vol. 6403, pp. 104–118. Springer, Heidelberg (2010). https://doi.org/10.1007/978-3-642-16289-3_10
15. Governatori, G., Olivieri, F., Scannapieco, S., Cristani, M.: The hardness of revising defeasible preferences. In: Bikakis, A., Fodor, P., Roman, D. (eds.) RuleML 2014. LNCS, vol. 8620, pp. 168–177. Springer, Cham (2014). https://doi.org/10.1007/978-3-319-09870-8_12

16. Governatori, G., Sartor, G.: Burdens of proof in monological argumentation. In: Legal Knowledge and Information Systems, pp. 57–66. IOS Press (2010)
17. Ito, S.: Basis of Ultimate Facts. Yuhikaku (2001)
18. Kunen, K.: Signed data dependencies in logic programs. Technical report, University of Wisconsin-Madison Department of Computer Sciences (1987)
19. Maher, M.J.: Propositional defeasible logic has linear complexity. Theory Pract. Logic Program. 1(6), 691–711 (2001)
20. Maranhão, J.S.A.: Conservative coherentist closure of legal systems. In: Araszkiewicz, M., Płeszka, K. (eds.) Logic in the Theory and Practice of Lawmaking. LL, vol. 2, pp. 115–136. Springer, Cham (2015). https://doi.org/10.1007/978-3-319-19575-9_4
21. McCarty, L.T.: Some arguments about legal arguments. In: Proceedings of the 6th International Conference on Artificial Intelligence and Law, pp. 215–224 (1997)
22. Merigoux, D., Chataing, N., Protzenko, J.: Catala: a programming language for the law. In: International Conference on Functional Programming. Proceedings of the ACM on Programming Languages, pp. 1–29. ACM, Virtual, South Korea (2021)
23. Nute, D.: Defeasible logic. In: Bartenstein, O., Geske, U., Hannebauer, M., Yoshie, O. (eds.) INAP 2001. LNCS (LNAI), vol. 2543, pp. 151–169. Springer, Heidelberg (2003). https://doi.org/10.1007/3-540-36524-9_13
24. Prakken, H.: Logical Tools for Modelling Legal Argument: A Study of Defeasible Reasoning in Law. Kluwer Academic Publishers (1997)
25. Prakken, H., Sartor, G.: Formalising arguments about the burden of persuasion. In: Proceedings of the 11th International Conference on Artificial Intelligence and Law, pp. 97–106 (2007)
26. Prakken, H., Wyner, A., Bench-Capon, T., Atkinson, K.: A formalization of argumentation schemes for legal case-based reasoning in ASPIC+. J. Log. Comput. 25(5), 1141–1166 (2015)
27. Przymusinska, H., Przymusinski, T.: Semantic issues in deductive databases and logic programs. In: Formal Techniques in Artificial Intelligence. Citeseer (1990)
28. Rotolo, A., Roversi, C.: Constitutive rules and coherence in legal argumentation: the case of extensive and restrictive interpretation. In: Dahlman, C., Feteris, E. (eds.) Legal Argumentation Theory: Cross-Disciplinary Perspectives. Law and Philosophy Library, vol. 102, pp. 163–188. Springer, Dordrecht (2013). https://doi.org/10.1007/978-94-007-4670-1_11
29. Satoh, K., et al.: PROLEG: an implementation of the presupposed ultimate fact theory of Japanese civil code by PROLOG technology. In: Onada, T., Bekki, D., McCready, E. (eds.) JSAI-isAI 2010. LNCS (LNAI), vol. 6797, pp. 153–164. Springer, Heidelberg (2011). https://doi.org/10.1007/978-3-642-25655-4_14
30. Satoh, K., Kogawa, T., Okada, N., Omori, K., Omura, S., Tsuchiya, K.: On generality of PROLEG knowledge representation. In: Proceedings of the 6th International Workshop on Juris-Informatics (JURISIN 2012), Miyazaki, Japan, pp. 115–128 (2012)
31. Satoh, K., Kubota, M., Nishigai, Y., Takano, C.: Translating the Japanese presupposed ultimate fact theory into logic programming. In: Proceedings of the 2009 Conference on Legal Knowledge and Information Systems: JURIX 2009: The Twenty-Second Annual Conference, pp. 162–171. IOS Press, Amsterdam (2009)
32. Satoh, K., Tojo, S., Suzuki, Y.: Formalizing a switch of burden of proof by logic programming. In: Proceedings of the First International Workshop on Juris-Informatics (JURISIN 2007), pp. 76–85 (2007)

33. Sergot, M.J., Sadri, F., Kowalski, R.A., Kriwaczek, F., Hammond, P., Cory, H.T.: The British nationality act as a logic program. Commun. ACM **29**(5), 370–386 (1986)
34. Sherman, D.M.: A prolog model of the income tax act of Canada. In: Proceedings of the 1st International Conference on Artificial Intelligence and Law, pp. 127–136. Association for Computing Machinery, New York (1987)
35. Stein, L.A.: Resolving ambiguity in nonmonotonic inheritance hierarchies. Artif. Intell. **55**(2–3), 259–310 (1992)

Mapping Similar Provisions Between Japanese and Foreign Laws

Hiroki Cho[1], Ryuya Koseki[1], Aki Shima[2], and Makoto Nakamura[1(✉)]

[1] Faculty of Engineering, Niigata Institute of Technology, Niigata, Japan
mnakamur@niit.ac.jp
[2] The Institute of Education and Student Affairs, Niigata University, Niigata, Japan
shimaaki@me.com

Abstract. A system that automatically maps similar provisions between Japanese and foreign laws is useful in comparative legal research. The purpose of this study is to develop a system for automatically mapping similar provisions. It uses the similarity of document vectors generated by the BERT model to find related provisions. We experimentally found that (1) the BERT model effectively maps similar provisions, (2) the BERT model, which was pre-trained in daily English, falls short in performance for Japanese law translated into English, and (3) LEGAL-BERT, a BERT model specific to the legal domain, may not be effective for English translations of Japanese laws. In addition, we performed mapping between Japanese and foreign laws in English and showed that the performance exceeded simple word-based mapping.

Keywords: comparative law · similar provisions · BERT

1 Introduction

When conducting business with foreign individuals/companies or actually going abroad on business, a good grasp of the laws of that other country is required. Focusing on the similarities with the laws of one's own country simplifies understanding what is common and what is different. Here we consider comparisons with foreign laws from an academic perspective. Comparative law is the study of laws that belong to different legal systems for identifying their similarities and differences. This study compares the laws of one's own country with those of a foreign country on a provision-by-provision basis and considers the correspondence of similar provisions (Fig. 1). Experts endure severe challenges when mapping similar provisions and struggle to identify correspondences between similar provisions in multiple laws for the following reasons:

1. Different languages are used,
2. the sheer number of potential combinations to be compared makes it difficult to manually check each one, and
3. both the text and its social context must be read.

© The Author(s), under exclusive license to Springer Nature Switzerland AG 2023
Y. Takama et al. (Eds.): JSAI-isAI 2022 Workshop, LNAI 13859, pp. 36–50, 2023.
https://doi.org/10.1007/978-3-031-29168-5_3

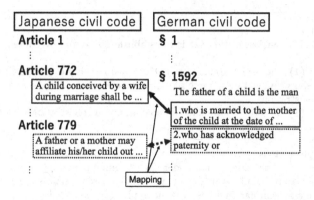

Fig. 1. Example of mapping between Japanese and foreign laws

Non-experts generally solve the problem in the following order. Item 1 can be addressed by using government-provided English translation data or machine translation. In this case, we previously confirmed that the correspondence accuracy depends on the translation accuracy [4]. Checking all the correspondences in item 2 is onerous [8]. If it can be solved, the correspondence cost can be reduced. Therefore, this study's purpose is to develop a tool that automates the correspondence of similar provisions in comparative law research. Automating items 1 and 2 will simplify addressing item 3.

To map similar provisions, we must first resolve the correspondence on a law-by-law basis. However, for large bodies of laws, such as civil code, for example, mapping similar provisions resembles a similar document search where the provisions are a single document. One method of similar document retrieval is ranking with the Jaccard coefficient [8], which is a typical method that focuses on the number of word matches. BM25 [14, 15] is another well-known method in information retrieval.

Although methods for counting word matches are simple and fast, they ignore the meaning or the context of words. Two documents that use different words are judged to be completely dissimilar even if they have similar content. To solve this problem, we proposed a method that uses word vectors obtained from language models. This study employs the latest language model: BERT [6].

In this study, experiments were conducted with the goal of mapping Japanese law to foreign law. First, we performed mapping between Japanese laws and evaluated how well BERT mapped similar provisions. Next, English translations of Japanese laws were mapped to verify the performance of a law-specific model. Finally, we did a mapping between Japanese and German laws and evaluated the results.

We explain similar document retrieval in Sect. 2 and describe our proposed method in Sect. 3. Section 4 shows our experimental settings and how to make correct data, and the experimental results are shown in Sect. 5. Finally, we conclude in Sect. 6.

(Purpose)
Article 1 The purpose of this Act is to establish fair control over foreign ...
(Definition)
Article 2 (1) The term "foreign national" as used in this Act means a person ...
(2) A person who has two or more nationalities other than Japanese ...
(Initial Registration)
Article 3 (1) All foreign nationals in Japan apply for registration with the ...
(i) one application form for alien registration;
(ii) passport;
(iii) two phtographs.
(2) In the case of the application under the preceding paragraph, a person ...
(3) If the head of a municipality finds unavoidable circumstances exist in the ...
(4) Where a foreign national has filed the application provided for in ...

Fig. 2. Basic Structure of Japanese Law (Alien Registration Act (Act No. 125, 1952))

2   Similar Document Search

We approach this study's purpose, i.e., mapping similar provisions, as a similar document search by considering each article as a single document. There are two methods of similar document retrieval: treating a document as a set of words and calculating the similarity, and calculating the similarity from a distributed representation of documents obtained using a neural network.

2.1   Document Unit

For mapping similar provisions, we must consider whether to use an *article* or a *paragraph* as the basic unit. As shown in Fig. 2, an article consists of a set of paragraphs. An article that does not contain a paragraph, such as Article 1, can be regarded as an article that actually consists of a single paragraph. We believe that considering a paragraph as a document is more effective.

In this paper, however, based on the results of preliminary experiments, we chose to use an article as the basic unit for the following reasons:

- Extremely short paragraphs reduce the mapping performance during the vectorization process (described in Sect. 2.3).
- The larger the number of documents is, the more difficult is the task of creating a correct dataset because it is represented by a bipartite graph with a computational complexity of $O(n^2)$, which is difficult by hand. Since an article consists of one or more paragraphs, it follows that |articles| ≤ |paragraphs|.
- Laws between two countries do not necessarily deal with identical subject matter. Many cannot be mapped to each other in terms of provisions. Since the nature of the problem requires that as many relevant provisions as possible be shown, using a paragraph as the basic unit is overly detailed.

– Even if a paragraph is used as the basic unit, it does not solve the problem of documents that frequently exceed BERT's 512-token limit. In fact, although using an article as the unit of measurement is preferred, unfortunately, such a choice fails to solve the implementation problem since many documents exceed 512 tokens, even in a single paragraph.

2.2 Similarity of Bag of Words

In this section, we introduce two evaluation methods for similarity using bag of words.

The Jaccard Coefficient. The Jaccard coefficient in Eq. (1) is a method of expressing the similarity between two sets:

$$\text{Jaccard}(A, B) = \frac{|A \cap B|}{|A \cup B|}. \tag{1}$$

In similar document retrieval, the Jaccard coefficient can be calculated by considering each document as a set of words. Although the Jaccard coefficient is simple to compute, one disadvantage is that it does not account for the importance of words; even synonyms are treated as completely different words.

BM25. Okapi BM25 [14, 15] is a weighting method that is generally more accurate than *TF-IDF* in the field of information retrieval. Consider document vector $\bar{d} = (d_1, \ldots, d_V)$ that belongs to collection C, where d_j denotes the *term frequency* of the j-th term in $\bar{d}$ (term j) and V is the total number of terms in the vocabulary. Term weighting function $w_j(\bar{d}, C)$, which exploits the term frequency as well as such factors as the document's length and the collection statistics, can be formalized by Eq. (2):

$$w_j(\bar{d}, C) = \frac{(k_1 + 1)d_j}{k_1((1 - b) + b\frac{dl}{avdl}) + d_j} \log \frac{N - df_j + 0.5}{df_j + 0.5}, \tag{2}$$

where N is the number of documents, df_j is the document frequency of term j, dl is the document length, $avdl$ is the average document length across the collection, and k_1 and b are free parameters that are set to 1.2 and 0.75.

The document score is obtained by adding the document term weights of terms that match query q:

$$W(\bar{d}, q, C) = \sum_j w_j(\bar{d}, C) \cdot q_j, \tag{3}$$

where $q_j = 1$ if the term $j \in q$, and otherwise, $q_j = 0$.

2.3 Similarity of Vectors

Based on the distribution hypothesis [7], which argues that the meaning of a word is formed by its surrounding words, a neural network (NN) can represent the meaning of a word as a vector by learning with a large amount of text data. As an example, a vector close to "queen" can be obtained by performing the following vector operation: "king − man + woman".

BERT is a language model proposed by Devlin et al. [6] that has shown high performance on many NLP tasks. Currently, several pre-trained models are publicly available that can perform highly accurate classification simply by performing fine tuning. The final layer's output can be extracted to obtain a word vector for each token of the input document.

However, the basic BERT model, which is based on a corpus of such general documents as Wikipedia, has performed poorly in certain domains, including medicine [9]. In the legal domain, the LEGAL-BERT model [3] has been published as an English model.

3 Proposed Method

In this study, we used an article as the smallest unit of provisions. The following mapping flow to foreign laws is shown in Fig. 3:

1. Unify the language in English if the two laws to be mapped are in different languages.
2. Input each article as a document into BERT.
3. Make the output averages into a document vector.
4. Calculate the cosine similarity between the document vectors of the home and foreign laws.
5. Map the articles based on cosine similarity.

First, a translation into the unified language is needed. It is sufficient to select a language based on the translation availability in the target country or on machine translation accuracy. In this study, we used English translated laws provided by governments. In item 5, the system calculates the similarity of each of the two sets of documents to all the documents in the other set and assigns a mapping to the document pair with the largest similarity in both directions (bottom in Fig. 3).

4 Experiments

This section explains our experiment that confirmed the proposed method in the previous section. Section 4.1 describes its purpose, and Sect. 4.2 shows the procedure to achieve it. Sections 4.3 explains how to create a dataset of correct answers used in this experiment for comparisons between Japanese laws, and Sect. 4.4 explains the comparisons between Japanese and foreign laws. Finally, Sect. 4.5 evaluates our experiment.

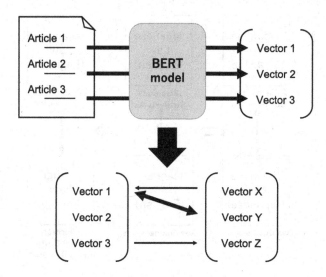

Fig. 3. Vector

4.1   Purpose

In this section, we mapped similar provisions between the Japanese Civil Code (Family Law) and the German Civil Code to verify whether the proposed method effectively maps Japanese law to foreign law.

We conducted a three-step experiment (Fig. 4):

1. Mapping articles between Japanese laws in Japanese;
2. Mapping articles between Japanese laws in English;
3. Mapping articles between Japanese and foreign laws in English.

Since it is difficult to make correct data when mapping to a foreign law, this experiment tests the mapping of Japanese laws to each other. We used the Electricity Business Act (Act No. 170 of 1964) and the Gas Business Act (Act No. 51 of 1954), which have similar legal contents. Although the similarity of document vectors is used to map similar articles, vectorization by BERT is not always effective for legal documents or general documents. Therefore, we verified BERT's performance when mapping similar articles through the first experiment by comparing BERT's mapping performance with Jaccard coefficients and BM25.

Second, since we must use English translations of documents when mapping to a foreign law, we performed mapping using English translations of Japanese laws and examined whether it was performed identically as in the Japanese case. Since the LEGAL-BERT model, which is specific to the legal domain, is publicly available for the English BERT model, we compared its performance with the commonly used BERT-BASE.

Finally, following the above steps, we made a correspondence between the family law of the Japanese and German Civil Codes. Although we created correct

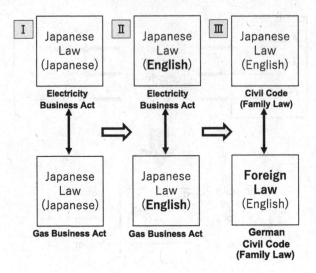

Fig. 4. Plan of experiments

data using the method described below, not every correspondence is necessarily listed, and so the evaluation cannot be guaranteed.

4.2 Procedure of Experiments

Documents from the experimental data were input into a pre-trained BERT model in Japanese, and the output, excluding [CLS] and [PAD] in the final layer, was averaged into a document vector. The pre-trained model was cl-tohoku/bert-base-japanese-whole-word-masking. Since the maximum number of input tokens for BERT is set to 512, we ignored those exceeding that number. The cosine similarity between the document vectors of different laws was calculated for all the combinations. Every document refers to the document with the highest cosine similarity. If the referenced document has the highest similarity to the source document, the two documents are mapped. The mapping results between the Electricity and Gas Business Acts were then evaluated using correct data.

Next, to compare the results with those using Jaccard coefficients, the same set of documents was divided into words by a morphological analyzer called MeCab, and the Jaccard coefficients between two documents were used for the similarity to map the documents. Neologd was used for MeCab's dictionary. The same process was performed using BM25.

Finally, we conducted a mapping experiment with BERT on the English translation of the laws using bert-base-uncased and legal-bert-base-uncased as the English pre-trained models of BERT and compared their performance.

For Experiment 3, each law was entered into the BERT model (BERT-BASE) on an article-by-article basis and vectorized and mapped using the same method as in Experiment 2. We found that one-to-one mapping using Experiment 2's

Table 1. Number of articles and paragraphs (as of February 24, 2022)

	Language	#Articles	#Paragraphs
Electricity Business Act	Japanese	315	705
	English	304	675
Gas Business Act	Japanese	207	505
	English	221	539

method produced almost no correct answers. Therefore, we changed the method to mapping one article of Japanese law to the top five similar articles of German law. The results were evaluated based on the data of correct answers. For comparison, the methods using the Jaccard coefficient and BM25 were also evaluated using the same procedure.

4.3   Creating a Correct Dataset: Japanese Laws

For the correspondence between Japanese laws, we used the Electricity Business Act (Act No. 170 of 1964) and the Gas Business Act (Act No. 51 of 1954). They are both infrastructure-related laws, and their definitions and structures resemble each other.

The laws used in these experiments are listed in Table 1. As of April 2022, there are 315 and 207 articles in the Electricity Business Act and the Gas Business Act. Note that the last article, Article 123 in the former and Article 207 in the latter, does not give the correct number because of deletions and additions by branch number in both laws.

The Japanese law data and the English translation data of Japanese laws were obtained from the e-Gov[1] and the Japanese Law Translation Database System[2] in XML format. The text under the article tag was extracted from each file, and each was treated as one document.

The differences in the number of articles between the Japanese and English versions (e.g., the Electricity Business Act has 315 articles in the Japanese version versus 304 articles in the English version) reflect that both the Electricity and Gas Business Acts were amended after their translations. The English versions are translations of the laws as of 2017, whereas the Japanese versions use the laws as amended in 2020. Therefore, the correct data created for the Japanese version do not necessarily match the English version. As a result, experiments with the English mapping version are predicted to have a lower evaluation value.

We asked two legal experts to create a correspondence table showing these two laws. One graduated from the Faculty of Law, Nagoya University and is currently a team leader in a company that is undertaking the national project e-LAWS. The other is the third author of this paper, a researcher specializing

---

[1] https://www.e-gov.go.jp.
[2] http://www.japaneselawtranslation.go.jp.

Table 2. Laws Compared in the Experiment

	Articles
Japanese Civil Code	725–886
German Civil Code	1297–1921

in criminal law. They used different methods to create correct data. The former expert calculated the inter-document similarity for each article for the two laws based on surface strings, which were then manually checked to produce correct data. The correspondence was made on a one-to-one basis for each article. The latter expert completely read through both laws and made comparisons by replacing the mutatis mutandis reading of the applicable provisions. For each article of the Electricity Business Act, some articles had more than one corresponding article in the Gas Business Act.

Since the Electricity Business Act has more articles than the Gas Business Act, we looked at the former article-by-article, and if we found an article with similar content in the latter, we mapped both articles. Correspondence with articles in multiple locations was allowed.

The results showed that the two experts made identical correspondence for 109 of the 315 articles. For 134 articles both determined that no correspondence existed. Thus, the agreement between their results was 0.79.

4.4   Creating a Correct Dataset: Foreign Laws

In this paper, we focus on family law. Table 2 shows the laws and their scope used in the experiment. We used the English translations provided by the governments[3].

We used legal commentaries to create correct data. Thus far, the following three editions of legal commentaries have been published by a leading Japanese publisher:

1. Annotated Civil Code: The original series began publication in 1964. It does not correspond to the subsequent legal changes.
2. New edition of the Annotated Civil Code: Although this sequel series of the Annotated Civil Code was published in 1988 to respond to changes in the law, more than 30 years have passed since then.
3. New Annotated Civil Code: The content of this series, which began publication in 2016, is different from the above two series because it was planned as an independent book.

A diagram of the relationship between the three-book series is shown in Fig. 5.

We attempted to create correct data using the latest New Annotated Civil Code (3) [11], even though only its first half has been published. Its latter part

---

[3] https://www.gesetze-im-internet.de/Teilliste_translations.html.

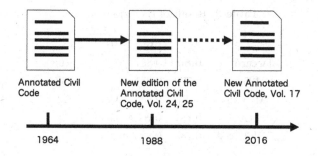

Fig. 5. Relationship among three-book series of legal commentaries

(Sharing of Living Expenses)
Article 760 A husband and wife shall share the expenses that arise from the marriage taking into account their property, income, and all other circumstances.
[Contrast] German Civil Code 1360-1361, Swiss Civil Code 163-165, French Civil Code 214
[Amendment] 798

Fig. 6. Example of an entry in the New Annotated Civil Code [11]

was extracted from the new edition of the Annotated Civil Code (2) [10,12]. Therefore, perhaps some of the entries will not correspond to the current law or maybe the policies for comparative laws are inconsistent.

Figure 6 shows how the New Annotated Civil Codes are displayed at the beginning of each article. We extract this [Contrast]section from the books and made a list by articles. As a result, 108 articles of the scope shown in Table 2 correspond to one or more articles of the German Civil Code.

Note, however, that this list of comparative laws extracted from the legal commentaries is not entirely accurate. For example, Article 766 (Determination of Matters regarding Custody of Child after Divorce, etc.), which was amended in 2011, should be mentioned. Because of the detailed description of the trends in foreign laws on approximately two pages, no list of comparative laws is provided that starts with '[Contrast]'. Since our part-time worker mechanically created the correct data from the [Contrast] section, processing this description was outside the scope of our current study. Therefore, no list of comparative laws extracted from detailed descriptions is included in the correct data of this experiment.

4.5   Evaluation Method

The mapping results of the Electricity to Gas Business Acts were compared with the correct data.

The number of mappings included in both the results and the correct data was defined as TP, the number of mappings included in the results but not in the correct data as FP, the number of mappings included in neither the results

Table 3. Result of the experiment 1

	Acc	Pre	Rec	F1
Jaccard	**0.803**	0.827	**0.717**	**0.768**
BM25	0.778	0.831	0.662	0.737
BM25+SW	0.773	0.832	0.642	0.724
BERT	0.787	**0.859**	0.649	0.736
BERT+SW	0.785	0.835	0.651	0.731

nor the correct data as TN, and the number of mappings not included in the results but in the correct data as FN.

In addition, since the correct data were created by our two experts, semi-correct answers were introduced for the mappings in which they did not agree. TP, TN, FP, and FN were defined as the number of cases in which they both agreed, SP as the number of cases in which the mapping was identical as that of just one of them, and SN as the number of cases without such mapping from either expert. We calculated the Accuracy, Recall, Precision, and F-measure:

$$\text{Accuracy} = \frac{2TP + SP + 2TN + SN}{2TP + 2SP + 2FP + 2TN + 2SN + 2FN} \tag{4}$$

$$\text{Precision} = \frac{2TP + SP}{2TP + 2SP + 2FP} \tag{5}$$

$$\text{Recall} = \frac{2TP + SP}{2TP + SP + 2FN + SN} \tag{6}$$

$$\text{F-measure} = \frac{2\text{Recall} \cdot \text{Precision}}{\text{Recall} + \text{Precision}} \tag{7}$$

5 Experimental Results

5.1 Experiment 1: Japanese Laws in Japanese

Table 3 shows the evaluation results of the mapping between the Electricity and Gas Business Acts in Japanese.

The score is highest when the Jaccard coefficient is used; the scores of both BM25 and BERT are about the same. This result was probably caused by the word-for-word similarity of the provisions of the Electricity and Gas Business Acts. There were negligible differences in accuracy with and without stop-words.

In Experiment 1, the Jaccard coefficient had the highest overall value. However, when Jaccard coefficients were used in the preliminary experiment to map Japanese law to German law in terms of provisions, satisfactory results were not obtained. This may be due to the fact that the words used are different even if their contents are similar. Therefore, in subsequent experiments we expect that the similarity of the document vectors obtained using NN can be used to map provisions with similar meanings.

Table 4. Result of the experiment 2

	Acc	Pre	Rec	F1
Jaccard	0.763	0.774	0.686	0.727
BM25	**0.783**	**0.809**	**0.701**	**0.751**
BERT-BASE	0.747	0.783	0.628	0.697
LEGAL-BERT	0.742	0.771	0.639	0.699

5.2 Experiment 2: Japanese Laws in English

Table 4 shows the evaluation results of the mapping between the Electricity Business Act and the Gas Business Act in English translation.

The purpose of this experiment is twofold. One is to see how the evaluation results change when the two target laws are translated into English, and the other is to compare the evaluations of BERT-BASE and LEGAL-BERT.

The main reason for the overall lower evaluation value (compared to Experiment 1) can be explained by the discrepancy in the correct answer data, as described in Sect. 4.3. The correct answer data created for the Japanese version do not necessarily match the English version. As a result, experiments with an English mapping version resulted in a lower evaluation value.

The BM25 evaluation showed the highest value, suggesting that even minor differences in the Japanese laws may more often appear as surface differences than in the Japanese text when it is translated into English. In this case, giving a higher score to the characteristic words that appear in the provisions will improve the evaluation more than with the Jaccard coefficient.

A comparison of BERT-BASE and LEGAL-BERT identified no significant differences. Therefore, our expectation that using the latter will dramatically improve performance was not met. Although LEGAL-BERT is a model specialized for the legal domain, only such English legal documents as EU law, UK law, and US contract documents were used for training; no Japanese legal data were included in it. This might explain why LEGAL-BERT is not superior.

Therefore, the following experiment only used BERT-BASE.

5.3 Experiment 3: Japanese Civil Code and German Civil Code in English

The results of the mapping evaluation are shown in Table 5. Note that in this experiment, we used English translations of both Japanese and German laws provided by the respective governments. The correct data consist of 108 mappings. In this experiment, we labeled a mapping as correct if at least one correct answer was included in the articles up to the fifth place of prediction.

BERT was evaluated higher than the Jaccard coefficient. Since different countries' laws use various words, the contextual analysis is more useful. However, BM25 represents the highest evaluation value, perhaps because few common

Table 5. Result of Experiment 3

	Correct answers (%)
Jaccard	21/108 = 19.4 (%)
BM25	36/108 = 33.3 (%)
BERT	33/108 = 30.6 (%)

Japan: Civil Code (Act No. 89 of 1896)   **Article 792** A person who has attained the age of majority may adopt another as his/her child.
Germany: Civil Code   **Section 1742** An adopted child may, as long as the adoption relationship exists, in the lifetime of an adoptive parent only be adopted by that parent's spouse.

Fig. 7. Example of mapping by BERT

characteristic words are well matched to the provisions. On the other hand, maybe the pre-training using daily English is unable to satisfactorily vectorize the English translations of the Japanese and German laws.

Figure 7 shows the correspondence that wasn't found by the method using the Jaccard coefficients, but that was found by BERT.

6 Conclusion

We used BERT to map similar provisions between Japanese and foreign laws. In our experiment, we performed mapping between Japanese laws in Japanese and Japanese laws in English as well as between Japanese and German laws in English. The results show that similar provisions can be mapped using the BERT-based method. Our results also found no difference in performance between BERT-BASE and LEGAL-BERT when mapping Japanese laws.

Our proposed method enabled a commercial laptop computer to automatically map similar provisions in a mapping process that was completed in a few minutes. This possibility is expected to significantly reduce such process cost compared to the manual process. If the correspondence accuracy can be further improved, a system can be constructed for practical use.

On the other hand, we found that BM25 earned the highest evaluation, except for the mapping of Japanese laws to each other in Japanese. In other words, at present, mapping by BERT is insufficient, and feature word matching is more highly evaluated than context vectorization.

It is clear that the BERT model was greatly affected by the 512-token limit. Since only 512 tokens from the beginning of each article were targeted, long articles were not handled well. Implementation options that might solve this problem include Doc2Vec [2], DocBERT [1], SentenceBERT [13], etc. This is an issue for future work.

We used the Electricity Business Act and the Gas Business Act to compare Japanese laws because they are both infrastructure-related laws, and their definitions and structures resemble each other. However, actual mapping revealed that they are less similar than expected. Two non-experts for the preliminary experiments and two experts for this paper created correct data, although this task was very burdensome. We chose document units as articles to reduce the burden of creating correct answer data. In future experiments, we must start from the selection of similar laws. It is also possible to change the unit to a paragraph by limiting the range of the law instead of the entire law.

We could also discuss the unit setting in relation to BERT's input length constraints by presenting detailed experimental results when the document unit is a paragraph. This might lead to a discussion over which type of units should be compared for each type of law when the structure of legal documents differs, such as between Japanese law and U.S. code.

For Experiment 3, we used English translations of both Japanese and German laws, since government-provided English translations of both laws were available. If we were to more aggressively confront language barriers, we could use a pretrained *multilingual* language model, such as XLM-RoBERTa [5] and evaluate how it performs in a cross-language matching task.

Acknowledgements. This research was partly supported by JSPS KAKENHI Grant Number JP19H04427.

References

1. Adhikari, A., Ram, A., Tang, R., Lin, J.: DocBERT: BERT for document classification (2019). https://doi.org/10.48550/ARXIV.1904.08398, https://arxiv.org/abs/1904.08398
2. Bhattacharya, P., Ghosh, K., Pal, A., Ghosh, S.: Legal case document similarity: you need both network and text. CoRR abs/2209.12474 (2022). https://doi.org/10.48550/arXiv.2209.12474
3. Chalkidis, I., Fergadiotis, M., Malakasiotis, P., Aletras, N., Androutsopoulos, I.: LEGAL-BERT: the muppets straight out of law school. In: Findings of the Association for Computational Linguistics: EMNLP 2020, pp. 2898–2904. Association for Computational Linguistics (2020). https://doi.org/10.18653/v1/2020.findings-emnlp.261
4. Cho, H., Nakamura, M.: The relationship between translation accuracy and mapping of similar provisions to foreign laws in Comparative Law Study (in Japanese). In: Proceedings of IEICE Shin-Etsu Section Conference, p. 8B-2 (2021)
5. Conneau, A., et al.: Unsupervised cross-lingual representation learning at scale. CoRR abs/1911.02116 (2019). http://arxiv.org/abs/1911.02116
6. Devlin, J., Chang, M.W., Lee, K., Toutanova, K.: BERT: pre-training of deep bidirectional transformers for language understanding. In: Burstein, J., Doran, C., Solorio, T. (eds.) NAACL-HLT (1), pp. 4171–4186. Association for Computational Linguistics (2019)
7. Harris, Z.: Distributional structure. Word **10**(2–3), 146–162 (1954). https://doi.org/10.1007/978-94-009-8467-7_1

8. Koyama, K., Sano, T., Takenaka, Y.: The legislative study on Meiji civil code by machine learning. In: Proceedings of the 15th International Workshop on Juris-Informatics (JURISIN2021), pp. 41–53 (2021)

9. Lee, J., et al.: BioBERT: a pre-trained biomedical language representation model for biomedical text mining. Bioinformatics **36**(4), 1234–1240 (2020). https://doi.org/10.1093/bioinformatics/btz682. Funding Information: This research was supported by the National Research Foundation of Korea (NRF) funded by the Korea government (NRF-2017R1A2A1A17069645, NRF-2017M3C4A7065887, NRF-2014M3C9A3063541). Publisher Copyright: 2020 Oxford University Press. All rights reserved

10. Nakagawa, Z., Yamahata, M.: New Annotated Edition-The Civil Code 24, Family 4 (in Japanese). Yuhikaku Publishing Inc., Japan (1994)

11. Ninomiya, S.: New Annotated Civil Code 17, Family 1 (in Japanese). Yuhikaku Publishing Inc., Japan (2017)

12. Oho, F., Nakagawa, J.: New Annotated Edition-The Civil Code 25, Family 5 (in Japanese). Yuhikaku Publishing Inc., Japan (2004)

13. Reimers, N., Gurevych, I.: Sentence-BERT: sentence embeddings using siamese BERT-networks (2019). https://doi.org/10.48550/ARXIV.1908.10084, https://arxiv.org/abs/1908.10084

14. Robertson, S., Walker, S., Jones, S., Hancock-Beaulieu, M., Gatford, M.: Okapi at TREC-3. In: TREC, pp. 109–126 (1994)

15. Robertson, S., Zaragoza, H., Taylor, M.: Simple BM25 extension to multiple weighted fields. In: Proceedings of the Thirteenth ACM International Conference on Information and Knowledge Management, CIKM 2004, pp. 42–49. ACM, New York (2004)

COLIEE 2022 Summary: Methods for Legal Document Retrieval and Entailment

Mi-Young Kim[3]([✉]), Juliano Rabelo[1,2], Randy Goebel[1,2], Masaharu Yoshioka[4], Yoshinobu Kano[5], and Ken Satoh[6]

[1] Alberta Machine Intelligence Institute, Edmonton, AB, Canada
[2] Department of Computing Science, University of Alberta, Edmonton, AB, Canada
{rabelo,rgoebel}@ualberta.ca
[3] Department of Science, Augustana Faculty, Camrose, AB, Canada
miyoung2@ualberta.ca
[4] Faculty of Information Science and Technology, Hokkaido University, Kita-ku, Sapporo-shi, Hokkaido, Japan
yoshioka@ist.hokudai.ac.jp
[5] Faculty of Informatics, Shizuoka University, Naka-ku, Hamamatsu-shi, Shizuoka, Japan
kano@inf.shizuoka.ac.jp
[6] National Institute of Informatics, Hitotsubashi, Chiyoda-ku, Tokyo, Japan
ksatoh@nii.ac.jp

Abstract. We present a summary of the 9th Competition on Legal Information Extraction and Entailment (COLIEE 2022). The competition consists of four tasks on case law and statute law. The case law component includes an information retrieval task (Task 1), and the confirmation of an entailment relation between an existing case and an unseen case (Task 2). The statute law component includes an information retrieval task (Task 3) and an entailment/question answering task (Task 4). Participation was open to any group, using any approach. Ten different teams participated in the case law competition tasks, most of them in more than one task. We received competition submissions from 9 teams for Task 1 (26 runs) and 5 teams for Task 2 (14 runs). On the statute law task, there were 11 different teams participating, most in more than one task. Five teams submitted a total of 15 runs for Task 3, and 6 teams submitted a total of 18 runs for Task 4. We summarize the technical details of all approaches, describe our official evaluation, and provide an overall analysis on our data and submission results.

Keywords: Legal Documents Processing · Textual Entailment · Information Retrieval · Classification · Question Answering

1 Introduction

The Competition on Legal Information Extraction/Entailment (COLIEE) was created to build a community to develop the state of the art for information

Y. Takama et al. (Eds.): JSAI-isAI 2022 Workshop, LNAI 13859, pp. 51–67, 2023.
https://doi.org/10.1007/978-3-031-29168-5_4

retrieval and entailment using legal texts. It is usually co-located with JURISIN, the Juris-Informatics workshop series, which was created to promote community discussion on both fundamental and practical issues on legal information processing. The intention is to embrace a variety of disciplines, including law, social sciences, information processing, logic and philosophy, including the existing conventional "AI and law" area. In alternate years, COLIEE is organized as a workshop with the International Conference on AI and Law (ICAIL), which was the case in 2017, 2019, and 2021. Until 2018, COLIEE consisted of two tasks: information retrieval (IR) and entailment using Japanese Statute Law (civil law). Since COLIEE 2018, IR and entailment tasks using Canadian case law were introduced.

Task 1 is a legal case retrieval task that involves, given a query case, extracting supporting cases from the provided case law corpus, which are hypothesized to support the decision for the query case. Task 2 is a legal case entailment task, which requires the identification of a paragraph or paragraphs from existing cases, which entail a given fragment of a new case. Task 3 and 4 is the statute law retrieval and entailment task using Japanese Civil law. Recently, the performance of the submitted results has been improved by using deep learning techniques. However, largely due to the small size of labelled training and test data, the performance based on deep learning techniques has been inconsistent. This is especially true for Task 4. In that ask, since the system returns a yes/no answer for each question, it is necessary to consider the effect of correct answer selection by chance. Therefore, for Task 4 in this year, we asked all participants to submit results using previous COLIEE parameters, to evaluate the system using a larger corpus of labelled test data; this allows direct comparison with previous COLIEE results.

The rest of our paper is organized as follows: Sects. 2, 3, 4, 5 describe each task, presenting their definitions, datasets, list of approaches submitted by the participants, and results attained. Section 6 presents final some final remarks.

2   Task 1 - Case Law Information Retrieval

2.1   Task Definition

This task consists in finding which cases, amongst a set of provided candidate cases, should be "noticed" with respect to a given query case[1]. More formally, given a query case q and a set of candidate cases $C = \{c_1, c_2, ..., c_n\}$, the task is to find the supporting cases $S = \{s_1, s_2, ..., s_n \mid s_i \in C \land noticed(s_i, q)\}$ where $noticed(s_i, q)$ denotes a relationship which is true when $s_i \in S$ is a noticed case with respect to q.

2.2   Dataset

The dataset is comprised of a total of 5,978 case law files. Also given is a labelled training set of 4,415, of which 900 are query cases. On average, the training data

---

[1] "Notice" is a legal technical term that denotes a legal case description that is considered to be relevant to a query case.

includes approximately 4.9 noticed cases per query case, which are to be identified among the 4,415 cases. To prevent competitors from merely using existing embedded conventional citations in historical cases to identify cited cases, citations are suppressed from all candidate cases and replaced by a "FRAGMENT_SUPPRESSED" tag indicating that a fragment was removed from the case contents. A test set consists of a total of 1,563 cases, with 300 query cases and a total of 1,263 true noticed cases. The test dataset contains on average 4.21 noticed cases per query case. Initially, the golden labels for that test set are not provided to competitors.

2.3 Approaches

We received 26 submissions from 9 different teams for Task 1. In this section, we present an overview of the approaches taken by the 7 teams which submitted papers describing their methods. Please refer to the corresponding papers for further details.

- **TUWBR (2 runs)** [5] start from two assumptions: first, that there is a topical overlap between query and notice cases, but that not all parts of a query case are equally important. Secondly, they assume that traditional IR methods, such as BM25, provide competitive results in Task 1. They perform document level and passage level retrieval, and also augment the system by adding external domain knowledge by extracting statute fragments and explicitly adding those fragments to the documents.
- **JNLP (3 runs)** [3] applies an approach that first splits the documents into paragraphs, then calculates the similarities between cases by combining term-level matching and semantic relationships on the paragraph level. An attention model is applied to encode the whole query in the context of candidate paragraphs, and then infer the relationship between cases.
- **DoSSIER (3 runs)** [1] combined traditional and neural based techniques in Task 1. The authors investigate lexical and dense first stage retrieval methods aiming for a high recall in the initial retrieval and then compare shallow neural re-ranking with the MTFT-BERT model to the BERT-PLI model. They then investigate which part of the text of a legal case should be taken into account for re-ranking. Their results show that BM25 shows a consistently high effectiveness across different test collections in comparison to the neural network re-ranking models.
- **LeiBi (3 runs)** [2] applied an approach which consists of the following steps: first, given a legal case as a query, they augment it by heuristically identifying several "meaningful" sentences or n-grams. The authors then use the pre-processed query case to retrieve an initial set of possible relevant legal cases, which are further re-ranked. Finally, the team aggregates the relevance scores obtained by the first stage and the re-ranking models to further improve retrieval effectiveness. The query cases are reformulated to be shorter, using three different statistical methods (KLI, PLM, IDF-r), in addition to using models that leverage embeddings (e.g., KeyBERT). Moreover, the authors investigate if automatic summarization using Longformer-Encoder-Decoder

(LED) can produce an effective query representation for this retrieval task. Furthermore, the team proposes a re-ranking cluster-driven approach, which leverages Sentence-BERT models to generate embeddings for sentences from both the query and candidate documents. Finally, the authors employ a linear aggregation method to combine the relevance scores obtained by traditional IR models and neural-based models.

- **UA (3 runs)** [9] use a transformer-based model to generate paragraph embeddings, and then calculate the similarity between paragraphs of a query case and positive and negative cases. These calculated similarities are used to generate feature vectors (10-bin histograms of all pair-wise comparisons between 2 cases). They then use a Gradient Boosting classifier to determine if those cases should be noticed or not. The UA team also applies pre- and post-processing heuristics to generate their final results, which were ranked first in Task 1 of the current COLIEE edition;

- **nigam (3 runs)** [8] developed an approach which combines transformer-based and traditional IR techniques; more specifically, they used Sentence-BERT and Sent2Vec for semantic understanding, combined with BM25. The nigam team first selects the top-K candidates according to the BM25 rankings, and then use pre-trained Sentence-BERT and Sent2Vec models to generate representation features of each sentence. The authors also used cosine similarity with a max-pooling strategy to get the final document score for ranking the relationshp between the query and noticed cases.

- **siat (3 runs)** [15] show how longformer-based contrastive learning is able to process sequences of thousands of tokens (which are usually restricted to between 512 and 1024 tokens). In addition to this longformer-based approach, the siat team also explores traditional retrieval models. They achieved second place overall in Task 1 of COLIEE 2022.

2.4   Results

Table 1 shows the results of all submissions received for Task 1 for COLIEE 2022. A total of 26 submissions from 9 different teams were evaluated. Similar to what happened in COLIEE 2021 [11], the f1-scores are generally low, which reflects the fact that the task is now more challenging than its previous formulation[2]. However, in the current edition, we still see a relevant improvement in those scores, with the top teams achieving scores above 0.35 (up from 0.19 as the best score in the COLIEE 2021 edition).

Most of the participating teams applied some form of traditional IR techniques such as BM25, transformer based methods such as BERT, or a combination of both. The best performing team was UA, with an f1-score of 0.3715, who used an approach that relied on creating an embedding representation for the cases, and then calculated the similarity between each query case and positives and negatives samples from the training dataset. The resulting distances are then

---

[2] for a description of the previous Task 1 formulation, please see the COLIEE 2020 summary [10].

bucketed into 10-bin histograms, which are used to train a Gradient Boosting classifier. Also worth mentioning is the siat team, whose approach made use of a novel longformer-based model and achieved second place overall.

Table 1. Task 1 results

Team	File	F1 Score	Precision	Recall
UA	pp_0.65_10_3.csv	0.3715	0.4111	0.3389
UA	pp_0.7_9_2.csv	0.3710	0.4967	0.2961
siat	siatrun1.txt	0.3691	0.3005	0.4782
siat	siatrun3.txt	0.3680	0.3026	0.4695
UA	pp_0.65_6.csv	0.3559	0.3630	0.3492
siat	siatrun2.txt	0.2964	0.2522	0.3595
LeiBi	run_bm25.txt	0.2923	0.3000	0.2850
LeiBi	run_weighting.txt	0.2917	0.2687	0.3191
JNLP	run3.txt	0.2813	0.3211	0.2502
nigam	bm25P3M3.txt	0.2809	0.2587	0.3072
JNLP	run2.txt	0.2781	0.3144	0.2494
DSSR	DSSR_01.txt	0.2657	0.2447	0.2906
JNLP	run1.txt	0.2639	0.2446	0.2866
DSSR	DSSR_03.txt	0.2461	0.2267	0.2692
TUWBR	TUWBR_LM_law	0.2367	0.1895	0.3151
LeiBi	run_clustering.txt	0.2306	0.2367	0.2249
TUWBR	TUWBR_LM	0.2206	0.1683	0.3199
nigam	sbertP3M3RS.txt	0.1542	0.1420	0.1686
nigam	s2vecP3M3RS.txt	0.1484	0.1367	0.1623
DSSR	DSSR_02.txt	0.1317	0.1213	0.1441
LLNTU	2022.task1.LLNTUtfidCos	0.0000	0.0000	0.0000
LLNTU	2022.task1.LLNTUtanadaT	0.0000	0.0000	0.0000
LLNTU	2022.task1.LLNTU3q4clii	0.0000	0.0000	0.0000
Uottawa	Task1Run3_UottawaLegalBert.txt	0.0000	0.0000	0.0000
Uottawa	Task1Run1_UottawaMB25.txt	0.0000	0.0000	0.0000
Uottawa	Task1Run2_UottawaSentTrans.txt	0.0000	0.0000	0.0000

To better understand the details of the Task 1 challenge, we have performed a deeper error analysis, focusing on which characteristics of the query and candidate cases may influence the difficulty of this task. We considered only high level contents features because performing actual legal analysis would require manual inspection of the whole dataset, which is a very laborious task given the dataset size, and would require deep legal domain expertise.

Our more shallow analysis first calculates how many false positives and false negatives correlate with statistics such as the query case length (in bytes) and

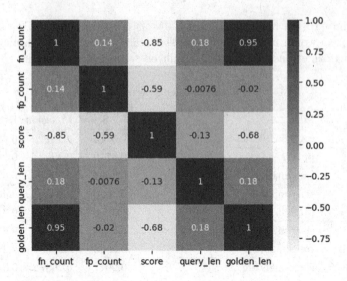

Fig. 1. Correlation matrix of metrics collected from all teams' results in the test dataset + the query file size and the number of true noticed cases.

to the number of expected noticed cases. Figure 1 shows the correlation matrix. Here, fn_count is the total number of false negatives per query case across all teams[3], fp_count is the total number of false positives, query_len is the size of the query case in bytes, golden_len is the number of noticed cases for each query case, and score is given by a simple formula:

$$score_i = TP_i - FP_i - FN_i$$

In this error analysis, we used this score metric instead of f1 because f1 would be zero when either precision or recall are zero, and would not capture relevant errors[4].

From the correlation matrix, we can see there is very little correlation between the FP counts and query_len and golden_len, a somewhat relevant positive correlation of 0.18 between fn_count and query_len, and a strong correlation of 0.95 between fn_count and golden_len. This means that all methods submitted, in general, fail to find noticed cases when the expected number of noticed cases is high (the average number of noticed cases in the test dataset is 4.21). That is expected for methods such as [9] in which the authors limit the number of cases found as noticed based on a priori probabilities, but other methods may have that property as an intrinsic part of their architecture. From those results, we can see that all methods could be improved if they do not limit their outputs to

---

[3] Results from the LLNTU and UOttawa teams were not considered because they had an f1-score of 0, which may indicate some problem in their submission.

[4] For example, when recall is zero it means all FN errors where captured, but there might be FP errors which would not be captured.

a "safe" number of cases. Of course, that is easier said than done: limiting the outputs based on a priori probabilities is an effective way of decreasing FP, and implementing a method that is able to decrease FN while not increasing FP is a big challenge in Task 1.

For future editions of COLIEE, we intend to make the distributions of the training and test datasets more similar with respect to average and standard deviation of number of noticed cases. There are still some issues we need to adjust in the dataset, such as two different files with the exact same contents (i.e., the same case represented as two separate files). This is a problem with the original dataset from where the competition's data is drawn, and knowing that dataset presents those issues we will improve our collection methods to correct them. Fortunately, those issues were rare and did not have a relevant impact on the final results.

3 Task 2 - Case Law Entailment

3.1 Task Definition

Given a base case and a specific text fragment from it, together with a second case relevant to the base case, this task consists in determining which paragraphs of the second case entail that fragment of the base case. More formally, given a base case b and its entailed fragment f, and another case r represented by its paragraphs $P = \{p_1, p_2, ..., p_n\}$ such that $noticed(b, r)$ as defined in Sect. 2 is true. The task consists in finding the set $E = \{p_1, p_2, ..., p_m \mid p_i \in P\}$ where $entails(p_i, f)$ denotes a relationship which is true when $p_i \in P$ entails the fragment f.

3.2 Dataset

In Task 2, 525 query cases were provided for training against 18,740 paragraphs. There were 100 query cases against 3278 candidate paragraphs as part of the testing dataset. On average, there are 35.627 candidate paragraphs for each query case in the training dataset and 32.455 candidate paragraphs for each query case in the testing dataset. The average number of relevant paragraphs for Task 2 was 1.14 paragraphs for training and 1.18 paragraphs for testing.

3.3 Approaches

Five teams submitted a total of 14 runs to this task. They used LegalBERT, BM25, zero shot models, and some other heuristic approaches. More details on the approaches are described below. Here, we introduce three teams' approaches that described their methods in more detail in their respective papers.

- **JNLP (3 runs)** [3] applied LegalBERT and BM25. In their first run, they combined the two scores from LegalBERT and BM25, and then ranked the outputs. In the second run, they used a knowledge representation technique called "Abstract Meaning Representation" (AMR) to capture the most important words in the query and corresponding candidate paragraph. In the third run, instead of combining the two scores from LegalBERT and BM25, they identified relevant paragraphs through the interaction between the top N candidates in LegalBERT and top M candidates in AMR + BM25.

- **nigam (2 runs)** [8] submitted two official runs both of which are based on the BM25 model. Run-1 uses only entailed fragment text as a query, and run-2 uses the filtered base case which combines a search entailed fragment text into the base case, and is then provided as input to the model as searched results (along with previous and following sentences to capture the other relevant information). Every query case predicts one case law paragraph because the average number of relevant paragraphs is approximately 1.14 in the training dataset.
- **NM (3 runs)** [13] used monoT5, which is an adaptation of the T5 model. During inference, monoT5 generates a score that measures the relevance of a document to a query by applying a softmax function to the logits of the tokens "true" and "false." NM also extend a zero-shot approach, and they fine-tune the T5-base and T5-3B models for 10k steps, which corresponds to almost one epoch or approximately 530,000 query-passage pairs from the MS MARCO training set. They refer to the resulting models as monoT5-base-zero-shot and monoT5-3b-zero-shot. In the third run, they combine the answers from the two models. They apply their own answer selection method to determine the final set of answers from the two models. Their ensemble model was ranked first in the COLIEE 2022 Task 2 competition.

3.4 Results

The F1-measure is used to assess performance in this task. The actual results of the submitted runs by all participants are shown on Table 2, from which it can be seen that the NM team attained the best results. Among the three submissions from NM, two submissions were ranked first and second.

Table 2. Results attained by all teams on the test dataset of task 2.

Team	Submission File	F1-score	Precision	Recall
NM	**monot5-ensemble.txt**	**0.6783**	0.6964	0.6610
NM	monot5-3b.txt	0.6757	0.7212	0.6356
JNLP	run2_bert_amr_remove_reduntdant_filter.txt	0.6694	0.6532	0.6864
JNLP	run3_bert_BM25.txt	0.6612	0.6452	0.6780
jljy	run2_task2.txt	0.6514	0.7100	0.6017
jljy	run3_task2.txt	0.6514	0.7100	0.6017
JNLP	run1_bert_amr_remove_reduntdant.txt	0.6452	0.6154	0.6780
jljy	run1_task2.txt	0.6330	0.6900	0.5847
NM	monot5-base.txt	0.6325	0.6379	0.6271
UA	res_score-0.95_max-1.txt	0.5446	0.6105	0.4915
UA	res_score-0.5_max-1.txt	0.5363	0.7869	0.4068
UA	res_score-0.95_max-5.txt	0.4121	0.3049	0.6356
nigam	bm25EF.txt	0.3204	0.1980	0.8390
UA	bm25BC.txt	0.2104	0.1300	0.5508

4   Task 3 - Statute Law Retrieval

4.1   Task Definition

Task 3 is essentially a pre-processing step for the legal textual entailment (Task 4), whose goal is to extract a subset of Japanese Civil Code Articles $S_1, S_2,...,S_n$ from the entire Civil Code articles considered appropriate for answering the legal bar exam question Q such that

$$Entails(S_1, S_2, ..., S_n, Q) \text{ or } Entails(S_1, S_2, ..., S_n, notQ).$$

4.2   Dataset

For Task 3, questions related to Japanese civil code articles were selected from a history of questions from the Japanese bar exam. However, since that corpus was updated in 2020, we use civil law articles that have official English translation (768 articles in total) as the target civil code. The number of questions classified by the number of relevant articles is listed in Table 3.

Table 3. Number of questions classified by number of relevant articles

number of relevant article(s)	1	2	3	4	5	total
number of questions	94	11	2	1	1	109

4.3   Approaches

The following 5 teams submitted their results (15 runs in total). All teams had experience in submitting results in previous competitions and extended their previous approaches. Ordinal IR models such as BM25 [12] and term-frequency inverse document frequency (TF-IDF) are still appropriate for producing good performance. Deep learning (DL) based approaches (e.g., using BERT [4] and other variants) are also effective components for the task. There are several runs that combine these different approaches.

- **HUKB (3 runs)** [16] uses a BM25 IR model with adjusted document article databases (original article, rewritten articles using reference, and the judicial decision part of the articles). Since use of the judicial decision portion database is helpful to retrieve different relevant articles which can not be retrieved using ordinal keyword-based IR, a simple merging technique is used to retrieve relevant articles with different characteristics.
- **JNLP (3 runs)** [3] uses a deep learning (DL) based approach that begins with identification of the question type. There are two types of questions: one is an ordinal question to check whether the examinee knows the article is appropriate or not. The other is the use-case questions used to understand the mapping of use-case objects to concepts in the relevant articles. Because of the different characteristics of these two types, they propose to use two different models.

- **LLNTU (3 runs)** previously used a BERT-based method, but there paper has no clear explanation about adjustments for this year's task.
- **OvGU (3 runs)** [14] combines the scores of a TF-IDF model with a sentence-embedding based similarity score to produce answer rankings. To find the relevant article for the use-case question, domain knowledge that explains how to apply the articles for the particular case is useful. They proposed a method to extract such knowledge from related legal documents such as journal articles, textbooks and web resources for calculating sentence-embedding.
- **UA (3 runs)** uses the TF-IDF model and BM25 model as an IR module, but there paper has no clear explanation about any adjustments from previous competition approaches.

4.4   Results

Table 4 shows the evaluation results of submitted runs. The official evaluation measures were macro average (average of evaluation measure values for each query over all queries) of F2 measure[5], precision, and recall.

$$precision = \frac{number\ of\ retrieved\ relevant\ articles}{number\ of\ returned\ articles} \tag{1}$$

$$recall = \frac{number\ of\ retrieved\ relevant\ articles}{number\ of\ relevant\ articles} \tag{2}$$

$$f2 = \frac{5 \times precision \times recall}{4 \times precision + recall} \tag{3}$$

We also calculate the mean average precision (MAP) and recall at k (R_k: recall calculated by using the top k ranked documents as returned documents) by using the long ranking list (100 articles).

Table 4 shows the results of the evaluation of submitted results. Due to the limitation of the size of paper, the best performance run in terms of F2 are selected from each team runs.

Table 4. Evaluation results of submitted runs (Task 3) and the corresponding organizers' run

sid	return	retrieved	F2	Precision	Recall	MAP
HUKB2	136	101	0.820	0.818	0.841	0.843
OVGU_run3	161	96	0.779	0.778	0.805	0.836
JNLP.longformer	178	101	0.770	0.687	0.838	0.793
UA_TFIDF2	115	90	0.764	0.807	0.764	0.829
LLNTU0066cc	114	74	0.642	0.674	0.639	0.700

---

[5] Since Task 3 is a pre-processing step for the legal textual entailment (task 4), it is important to have all relevant articles in the retrieved results. So we emphasize recall in this evaluation.

Figure 2, 3, 4 shows the average of evaluation measures for all submission runs. The number of questions whose relevant article is 1 and F2 (average of all submission) is higher than 0.8 is 65.9% (62/94). This is better than the COLIEE 2021 29.2% (19/65). This may reflect the different characteristics of the COLIEE 2022 dataset and participation of well-experienced teams; at the very least, this result shows that we have almost succeeded to develop a method for identifying easy questions. From Fig. 2, we confirmed that there are many easy questions for which almost all system can retrieve the relevant article. The easiest question is R03-2-A "The obligee may not exercise the right of the obligor, if the right is immune from attachment" whose relevant article contains sentences with same vocabulary. However, there are also many queries for which none of the systems can retrieve the relevant articles. R03-07-E is an example of this question: "After A sold land X owned by A to B, B resold land X to C, and each of them was registered as such. Later, the sales contract between A and B was voided on the grounds that A was an adult ward. If C did not know without negligence that A was an adult ward, A may not claim that the ownership of land X belongs to A," and relevant article is Article 121 "An act that has been rescinded is deemed void ab initio." This article uses specific legal terminology such as "rescinded" and "void ab initio." This is almost impossible to handle with an ordinal keyword-based IR system. It is also difficult for the DL-based approach, because one can not exploit a simple semantic association matching. For the question with multiple relevant articles, it is difficult to determine a significant difference from the viewpoint of overall evaluation. We still have the challenge of determining the whole set of relevant articles compared with single relevant article cases.

A new approach proposed in this year's competition is as follows:

1. Using different document database (e.g., article text database and texts for judicial decision part database) for calculating the score to merge [16].
2. Using external knowledge (text related to the articles) to enrich the sentence-embedding information of the article. [14]
3. Classification of the query types; use-case queries or others. [3]

This new method proposed by [16] suggests there are possibly broader criteria to determine the relevance between the question and articles. Therefore, we suppose simple inclusion of the articles whose rank are second or third is not good enough to distinguish multiple relevant articles required for some questions.

Similarly, methods proposed by [14] and [3] suggest that there are questions that ordinal keyword based search is insufficient to find the appropriate relevant articles. Since those questions are mostly use-case ones, [3] suggests that it is better to use different settings and [14] proposed to use additional external knowledge for solving the problem caused by keyword mismatch.

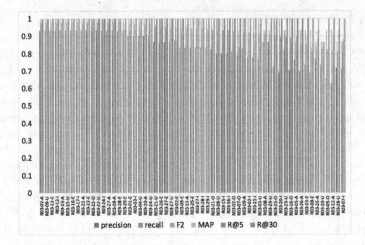

Fig. 2. Averages of precision, recall, F2, MAP, R_5, and R_30 for easy questions with a single relevant article

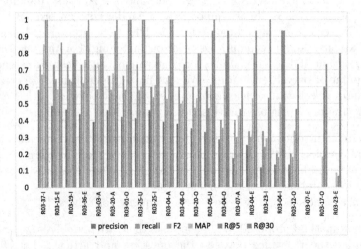

Fig. 3. Averages of precision, recall, F2, MAP, R_5, and R_30 for noneasy questions with a single relevant article

Those approaches are confirmed to be effective in this year's test data, and we expect that the combination of those approaches may improve the retrieval performance compared with this year's system.

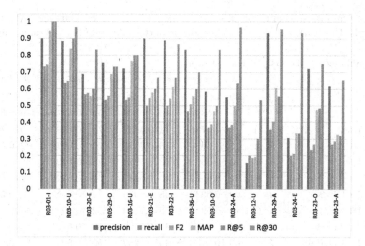

Fig. 4. Averages of precision, recall, F2, MAP, R_5, R_10, and R_30 for noneasy questions with a single relevant article

5   Task 4 - Statute Law Entailment

5.1   Task Definition

Task 4 is for determining whether an entailment relationship holds between a given problem sentence and article sentences. Competitor systems should answer "yes" or "no" for the given problem sentences and article sentences. Participants can use any external data, but it is assumed that they do not use the test dataset and/or something which could directly contain the correct answers of the test dataset, because this task is intended to be a pure textual entailment task. To encourage deeper analysis, we asked participants to submit their output answers to the part of the training dataset (H30-R02), in addition to the formal runs.

5.2   Dataset

Our datasets are the same as for Task 3. Questions related to Japanese civil law were selected from the Japanese bar exam. The organizers provided a data set used in previous years as training data (887 questions) and new questions selected from the 2022 Japanese bar exam as test data (109 questions).

5.3   Approaches

We describe approaches for each team as follows, shown as a header format of **Team Name (number of submitted runs)**.

– **HUKB (3 runs)** [16] proposed a method to select relevant portions from the articles (**HUKB-2**) supplemented with a new data augmentation method

Table 5. Evaluation results of submitted runs (Task 4). L: Dataset Language (J: Japanese, E: English), *: submission ID unique letters, #: number of correct answers

Team	Submission ID	L	*	Formal Run		R02		R01		H30	
				#	Accuracy	#	Accuracy	#	Accuracy	#	Accuracy
N/A	Total	–	–	109	1.0000	81	1.0000	111	1.0000	70	1.0000
N/A	BaseLine	–	–	58	0.5320	43	0.5309	59	0.5315	36	0.5143
KIS	KIS2	J	H	74	0.6789	44	0.5432	71	0.6396	49	0.7000
HUKB	HUKB-1	J	A	73	0.6697	50	0.6173	73	0.6577	42	0.6000
KIS	KIS1	J	G	72	0.6606	48	0.5926	68	0.6126	46	0.6571
KIS	KIS3	J	I	72	0.6606	49	0.6049	68	0.6126	47	0.6714
HUKB	HUKB-2	J	B	69	0.6330	48	0.5926	74	0.6667	41	0.5857
HUKB	HUKB-3	J	C	69	0.6330	58	0.7160	72	0.6486	44	0.6286
LLNTU	LLNTUdeNgram	J	J	66	0.6055	47	0.5802	60	0.5405	33	0.4714
LLNTU	LLNTUdiffSim	J	K	63	0.5780	49	0.6049	56	0.5045	36	0.5143
OVGU	OVGU3	?	–	63	0.5780	–	–	–	–	–	–
UA	UA_e	?	L	59	0.5413	44	0.5432	69	0.6216	32	0.4571
UA	UA_r	?	M	59	0.5413	44	0.5432	69	0.6216	32	0.4571
UA	UA_structure	?	N	59	0.5413	44	0.5432	69	0.6216	32	0.4571
JNLP	JNLP1	J	D	58	0.5321	50	0.6173	59	0.5315	40	0.5714
JNLP	JNLP2	J	E	58	0.5321	49	0.6049	58	0.5225	40	0.5714
OVGU	OVGU2	?	–	58	0.5321	–	–	–	–	–	–
JNLP	JNLP3	J	F	56	0.5138	48	0.5926	65	0.5856	42	0.6000
	OVGU1	?	–	52	0.4771	–	–	–	–	–	–

(**HUKB-1**). This was in addition to their system from COLIEE 2021 (**HUKB-3**) which used an ensemble of BERT with data augmentation, extraction of judicial decision sentences, thus creating positive/negative data from articles.

- **JNLP (3 runs)** [3] compared ELECTRA, RoBERTa, and LegalBERT, which is pre-trained using large legal English texts. They also compared impacts of negation data augmentation, and paragraph-level entailments.
- **KIS (3 runs)** [6] employed an ensemble of their rule-based method, using predicate-argument structures which extends their previous work, and added BERT-based methods. Their BERT-based methods use data augmentation (**KIS2**), with data selection (**KIS1**), and with person name inference (**KIS3**). They also employed an ensemble of different trials of fine-tunings.
- **LLNTU (2 runs)** [7] restructured given data to a dataset of the disjunctive union strings from training queries and articles, and established a longest uncommon sub-sequence similarity comparison model, without stopwords (**LLNTUdiffSim**), and with stopwords (**LLNTUdeNgram**). One of their runs was retracted because they used their dataset via web crawling that could potentially include the correct answers of the test dataset.

Table 6. Statistics of linguistic categories of the past problems, and correct answers of submitted runs for each category in percentages. # shows number of problems, alphabetical letters correspond to submission ID unique letters in Table 5.

Category	#	A	B	C	D	E	F	G	H	I	J	K	L	M	N
Person role	126	.58	.54	**.65**	.52	.5	.55	.6	.6	.59	.52	.52	.52	.52	.52
Person relationship	136	.6	.57	**.65**	.51	.49	.54	.6	.59	.59	.53	.49	.51	.51	.51
Anaphora	75	.61	.65	**.68**	.56	.55	.55	.65	.61	.63	.56	.47	.53	.53	.53
Case role	32	**.63**	.59	.53	.53	.53	.5	.53	.56	.59	.53	.47	.47	.47	.47
Predicate argument	114	.64	.64	**.65**	.57	.57	.62	.57	.6	.58	.54	.54	.6	.6	.6
Negation	128	.54	.59	.6	.63	.63	**.65**	.57	.59	.58	.48	.53	.55	.55	.55
Abstract role	48	.48	.44	**.69**	.5	.48	.48	.56	.48	.56	.5	.6	.42	.42	.42
Dependency	62	.65	.65	**.68**	.55	.55	.56	.58	.61	.56	.53	.6	.47	.47	.47
Paraphrases	13	.62	.62	**.69**	.31	.31	.23	.62	**.69**	.46	.54	.31	.46	.46	.46
Entailment	14	**.93**	.79	.79	.5	.5	.57	.71	.57	.71	.71	.43	.43	.43	.43

- **OvGU (3 runs)** [14] employed an ensemble of graph neural networks (GNNs) as their previous work (**OvGU1**), concatenated with referring textbook nodes (**OvGU2** and averaged sentence embeddings (**OvGU3**). There was no submission for the past training datasets.
- **UA (3 runs)** [9] provides no detailed description for Task 4.

5.4 Results

Table 5 shows evaluation results of Task 4, including the formal run results and training dataset. The evaluation results of the training dataset consider either of R02, R01, or H30 as a test dataset, using corresponding former years' dataset (-R01, -H30, -H29) as training datasets; these configurations correspond to the formal runs of COLIEE 2021, 2020, and 2019, respectively. Table 6 shows statistics of manually classified linguistic categories, which are required to solve the problems. This statistic suggests that the solvers might sometimes answer correctly without analyzing entire linguistic structures, because the correct answer ratios are sometimes too high considering the difficulty of the linguistic issues.

6 Conclusion

We have summarized the systems and their performance as submitted to the COLIEE 2022 competition. For Task 1, UA submitted by the University of Alberta team was the best performing team with an F1 score of 0.3715. In Task 2, the winning team was NM, and combined T5-base and T5-3B models to achieve an F1 score of 0.6783. For Task 3, the top ranked team is HUKB and achieved an F2 score of 0.8204. KIS was the Task 4 winner, with an Accuracy of 0.6789.

We intend to further continue to improve dataset quality in future editions of COLIEE so the tasks more accurately represent real-world problems.

Acknowledgements. This competition would not be possible without the significant support of Colin Lachance from vLex, Compass Law and Jurisage, and the guidance of Jimoh Ovbiagele of Ross Intelligence and Young-Yik Rhim of Intellicon. Our work to create and run the COLIEE competition is also supported by our institutions: the National Institute of Informatics (NII), Shizuoka University and Hokkaido University in Japan, and the University of Alberta and the Alberta Machine Intelligence Institute in Canada. We also acknowledge the support of the Natural Sciences and Engineering Research Council of Canada (NSERC), [including DGECR-2022-00369, RGPIN-2022-0346]. This work was also supported by JSPS KAKENHI Grant Numbers, JP17H06103 and JP19H05470 and JST, AIP Trilateral AI Research, Grant Number JPMJCR20G4.

References

1. Abolghasemi, A., Althammer, S., Hanbury, A., Verberne, S.: Dossier@coliee2022: dense retrieval and neural re-ranking for legal case retrieval. In: Sixteenth International Workshop on Juris-informatics (JURISIN) (2022)
2. Askari, A., Peikos, G., Pasi, G., Verberne, S.: Leibi@coliee 2022: aggregating tuned lexical models with a cluster-driven bert-based model for case law retrieval. In: Sixteenth International Workshop on Juris-informatics (JURISIN) (2022)
3. Bui, M.Q., Nguyen, C., Do, D.T., Le, N.K., Nguyen, D.H., Nguyen, T.T.T.: Using deep learning approaches for tackling legal's challenges (COLIEE 2022). In: Sixteenth International Workshop on Juris-informatics (JURISIN) (2022)
4. Devlin, J., Chang, M., Lee, K., Toutanova, K.: BERT: pre-training of deep bidirectional transformers for language understanding. CoRR abs/1810.04805 (2018)
5. Fink, T., Recski, G., Kusa, W., Hanbury, A.: Statute-enhanced lexical retrieval of court cases for COLIEE 2022. In: Sixteenth International Workshop on Juris-informatics (JURISIN) (2022)
6. Fujita, M., Onaga, T., Ueyama, A., Kano, Y.: Legal textual entailment using ensemble of rule-based and bert-based method with data augmentations including generation without excess or deficiency. In: Sixteenth International Workshop on Juris-informatics (JURISIN) (2022)
7. Lin, M., Huang, S.C., Shao, H.L.: Rethinking attention: an attempting on revaluing attention weight with disjunctive union of longest uncommon subsequence for legal queries answering. In: Sixteenth International Workshop on Juris-informatics (JURISIN) (2022)
8. Nigam, S.K., Goel, N.: Legal case retrieval and entailment using cascading of lexical and semantic-based models. In: Sixteenth International Workshop on Juris-informatics (JURISIN) (2022)
9. Rabelo, J., Kim, M.Y., Goebel, R.: Semantic-based classification of relevant case law. In: Sixteenth International Workshop on Juris-informatics (JURISIN) (2022)
10. Rabelo, J., Kim, M.Y., Goebel, R., Yoshioka, M., Kano, Y., Satoh, K.: COLIEE 2020: methods for legal document retrieval and entailment, pp. 196–210, June 2021. https://doi.org/10.1007/978-3-030-79942-7_13
11. Rabelo, J., Kim, M.Y., Goebel, R., Yoshioka, M., Kano, Y., Satoh, K.: Overview and discussion of the competition on legal information extraction/entailment (COLIEE) 2021. Rev. Socionetwork Strateg. **16**, 111–133 (2022.) https://doi.org/10.1007/s12626-022-00105-z

12. Robertson, S.E., Walker, S.: Okapi/Keenbow at TREC-8. In: Proceedings of the TREC-8, pp. 151–162 (2000)
13. Rosa, G.M., Bonifacio, L.H., Jeronymo, V., de Alencar Lotufo, R., Nogueira, R.: 3b parameters are worth more than in-domain training data: a case study in the legal case entailment task. In: Sixteenth International Workshop on Juris-informatics (JURISIN) (2022)
14. Wehnert, S., Kutty, L., Luca, E.W.D.: Using textbook knowledge for statute retrieval and entailment classification. In: Sixteenth International Workshop on Juris-informatics (JURISIN) (2022)
15. Wen, J., Zhong, Z., Bai, Y., Zhao, X., Yang, M.: Siat@coliee-2022: legal case retrieval with longformer-based contrastive learning. In: Sixteenth International Workshop on Juris-informatics (JURISIN) (2022)
16. Yoshioka, M., Suzuki, Y., Aoki, Y.: HUKB at the COLIEE 2022 statute law task. In: Sixteenth International Workshop on Juris-informatics (JURISIN) (2022)

JNLP Team: Deep Learning Approaches for Tackling Long and Ambiguous Legal Documents in COLIEE 2022

Quan Minh Bui[✉], Chau Nguyen, Dinh-Truong Do, Nguyen-Khang Le,
Dieu-Hien Nguyen, Thi-Thu-Trang Nguyen, Minh-Phuong Nguyen,
and Minh Le Nguyen

Japan Advanced Institute of Science and Technology (JAIST), Nomi, Japan
{quanbui,chau.nguyen,truongdo,lnkhang,ndhien,trangttn,
phuongnm,nguyenml}@jaist.ac.jp

Abstract. Competition on Legal Information Extraction/Entailment (COLIEE) is an annual competition associated with the International Workshop in Juris-Informatics. The challenge for this competition is required not only the skills in processing long documents but also the ability to resolve ambiguity in the legal domain. For lengthy documents, we proposed a document-level attention mechanism (Task 1) and passage mining (Task 3, 4). Regarding ambiguity in the legal domain, we propose 2 methods that use abstract meaning representation to remove noise in given query and candidate documents (Task 2), and the second approach is *use-case* identification (Task 3). By categorizing the given query, we have different approaches to solving questions. The results reflect the difficulty level and competitiveness in this competition.

Keywords: Deep Learning · Legal Text Processing · JNLP Team · Information Retrieval

1 Introduction

The competition is built around the goal of developing machine learning and other methods for the law domain. The applications based on this method will effectively support lawyers in reducing the time and effort of searching for necessary information for a certain trial. There are two types of data in COLIEE competition:

1. Case law: a database of predominantly Federal Court of Canada case laws, provided by Compass Law.
2. Statue law: answering yes/no questions from Japanese legal bar examinations.

Supported by JSPS Kakenhi Grant Number 20H04295, 20K20406, and 20K20625.

And 4 tasks:

1. Task 1 (The Legal Case Retrieval Task): For a given case law and corpus, the machine learning approaches need to identify which cases relate to or support the given case law in the corpus, which contains a massive number of documents.
2. Task 2 (The Legal Case Entailment task): For the given decision and a set of candidate paragraphs, the same as task 1 competitor needs to find a method to identify the relevant paragraph correctly.
3. Task 3 (The Statute Law Retrieval Task): In this task, the competitor's systems are required to retrieve an appropriate subset $(S_1, S_2, ..., S_n)$ of Japanese Civil Code Articles from the Civil Code texts dataset, used for answering a Japanese legal bar exam question Q.
4. Task 4 (The Legal Textual Entailment Data Corpus): The competitor's systems are required to determine textual entailment relationships between a given problem sentence and relevant article sentences. The systems must answer "yes" or "no" regarding the given problem sentences and given article sentences.

In previous years, the commonly used method was lexical matching which calculates the word overlapping between query and candidate. However, this approach performs poorly on complex structure documents such as legal cases and statute law. The possibility of overlapping between documents is very high with extremely long documents. To tackle this issue, we suggest using a pre-trained model such as BERT [6], one of the recent state-of-the-art pre-trained language models trained on massive training data. Leveraging this approach, the fine-tuned model can learn the latent information between query-candidate pairs in the training sample of a specific task.

We have proposed some methods using deep learning approaches based on our analysis. Our proposals can be applied to practical applications or research to resolve legal problems.

2   Related Work

2.1   Case Law

In previous years, we can see that lexical matching is the selection the teams always want to use. For examples:

– UBIRLED team extracted keywords using Python Keyphrase Extraction Toolkit[1] and then applied the combined K-NN algorithm with TF-IDF for ranking candidates for task2 COLIEE 2018.
– iiest team used the BM25 algorithm with a configured score function to enhance the ability to capture lexical information between candidate paragraphs and the base judgments in task 2 COLIEE 2020.

---

[1] https://github.com/boudinfl/pke.

– UB team used learning to rank approach based on BM25 and TF-IDF algorithm in task 1 COLIEE 2020.

Because of the complexity of the legal domain, using only lexical matching can not achieve state-of-the-art results, especially in competitive competitions such as COLIEE. For the exact purpose of demonstrating this statement, we can take a look at task the winner's method such as:

– JNLP teams used not only lexical features but also latent features obtained by a summary from several encoders. This approach significantly improves the performance and helps them achieve state-of-the-art research with nearly 16%(F score) away from the 2nd team in task 1 2018.
– Cyber team [12] used a universal sentence encoder and SVM model on the output representation of query and candidate in TF-IDF space. This delicate combination makes them win the first prize in task 1 2020.
– Also in 2020, by using training data from the organizer, JNLP generated silver data automatically. This approach increased the amount of data to hundreds of thousands. Its effectiveness is demonstrated by JNLP winning first place in task2 2020.

2.2   Statue Law

For the statute law information retrieval task (Task 3), in previous years, all the participants used pre-trained language models in their submissions. Team HUKB [20] built a BERT-based retrieval system along with Indri [17] with two different ways of forming the content of an article. JNLP [11] also built a BERT-based retrieval system. They further employed a sliding window and a self-labeled technique to deal with the challenge of long articles. OvGU [19] utilized both a BERT-based retrieval system (specifically, using sentence-BERT) and TF-IDF with metadata-enriched articles and external data from the web. TR [15] employed Word Mover's Distance [9] and BERT based on the spaCy large language model. UA [8] utilized not only BERT but also BM25 and TF-IDF for different submissions.

Pre-trained language models are also popular for the statute law textual entailment task (Task 4). HUKB [20] augmented the positive/negative samples with rules, fine-tuned 10 variants of BERT models, and ensemble them differently. JNLP [11] ensembled various BERT-based classification models for article-statement pairs. KIS [7] extended their previous works of a classic NLP approach with the analysis of predicate-argument structure; they also designed an ensemble method. OvGU [19] ensembled a graph neural network approach and a LEGAL-BERT-based [3] system. TR [15] made use of T5 [13] and GPT-3 [2], Electra [5], and distilled RoBERTa [10] in their approached. UA [8] employed BERT with semantic information.

In summary of the approaches for Task 3 and Task 4, language model-based systems are popular, along with ensemble approaches.

3 Approaches

3.1 Case Law

For task 1 and task 2, we have the same approach for ranking candidates of a given query. As shown in Fig. 1, we use LEGAL-BERT to capture the semantic information and the BM25 algorithm to capture the lexical information of the given query and corresponding candidates. However, each task has its own difficulty, and we have some appropriate adjustments for the related task.

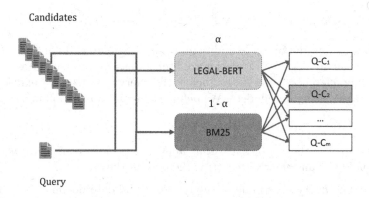

Fig. 1. A High-level look of Task 1 and 2 Approaches

Task 1. In COLIEE 2022 Task 1, we observe that both the query and candidate cases are complex long texts. For example, the average number of words in each case is 4010. It is challenging to represent the whole case law well in a limited semantic space. Thus, we split the documents into paragraphs inspired by the success of BERT-PLI [16] and our previous work [11]. Then, in Runs 1 and 2, we calculate the similarities between cases by combining term-level matching and semantic relationships on the paragraph level. In Run 3, we propose an attention model to encode the whole query in the context of candidate paragraphs, then infer the relationship between cases.

Run 1 and Run 2: Combine Lexical and Semantic Relationships. Our previous work [11] has competitive performance in COLIEE 2021 Task 1. Thus, Runs 1 and 2 mainly use the lexical and semantic relationships between paragraphs. Given the query $q = \{q_1, q_2, ..., q_N\}$ and the candidate case $k = \{k_1, k_2, ..., k_M\}$, where N and M denote the number of paragraphs in q and k, respectively, we use the BM25 model [14] to calculate the lexical mapping score for each paragraph in q and k. To extract the semantic relationship between the query paragraph and the candidate paragraph, we leverage one of the largest pre-trained models for the legal domain called LEGAL-BERT [4]. The particular reason for us to use this model is the massive data used for training. The training data contains over 300,000 documents collected from different sources, and the training architecture is based on BERT [6], one of the state-of-the-art deep learning architectures.

We use the following formula to calculate the combined score:

$$combined\_score = score_{BM25} + \alpha * score_{LEGAL-BERT} \qquad (1)$$

where α is a scaling factor and the purpose is to combine the lexical and semantic information. For each paragraph of the query, we get the most relevant candidate paragraph and then calculate a similarity score between q and the candidate k as follows:

$$similarity\_score_{qk} = \frac{\sum_{i=1}^{N} \max_j(combined\_score_{q_i k_j})}{N} \qquad (2)$$

After that, we obtain the top 5 candidates from the whole candidate pool. In Run 2, we additionally design a regulation to filter unreasonable candidates. Because a query only references cases judged before the query case itself, we extract dates from law cases using datefinder[2]. We define the regulation as follows:

$$Rank_1 = \{c|c \in Rank_0 \wedge max(dates(c)) \leq max(dates(q))\} \qquad (3)$$

where $dates(c)$ is the set of dates that appeared in document c, $Rank_0$ is the top-5 candidates and $max(dates(c))$ is the date of the case c.

Run 3: The query q and one of the top 200 candidate documents k are represented by paragraphs, denoted as $q = \{q_1, q_2, ..., q_N\}$ and $k = \{k_1, k_2, ..., k_M\}$, where N and M denote the number of paragraphs in q and k, respectively. As Fig. 2, we use the pre-trained model for the legal domain LEGAL-BERT [3] to encode each paragraph. For each query paragraph q_i, we employ the attention mechanism to infer the importance of each candidate paragraph k_j to q_i. The attention weight of each candidate paragraph is measured by:

$$\alpha_{q_i k_j} = \frac{exp(\mathbf{e}_{k_j} \cdot \mathbf{e}_{q_i})}{\sum_{j'} exp(\mathbf{e}_{k_{j'}} \cdot \mathbf{e}_{q_i})} \qquad (4)$$

where $\mathbf{e}_{q_i}$ and $\mathbf{e}_{k_j}$ are the encoding of the query paragraph q_i and candidate paragraph k_j, respectively.

We then get the representation of the query paragraph in the context of candidate paragraphs via attentive aggregation:

$$\mathbf{h}_{qik} = \sum_j \alpha_{q_i k_j} \mathbf{e}_{k_j} \qquad (5)$$

The attention mechanism is also employed to infer the importance of each paragraph position to the whole query case. The attention weight of each paragraph position is measured by:

$$\alpha_{qik} = \frac{exp(\mathbf{h}_{qik} \cdot \overline{\mathbf{e}_k})}{\sum_{i'} exp(\mathbf{h}_{qik'} \cdot \overline{\mathbf{e}_k})} \qquad (6)$$

---

[2] https://pypi.org/project/datefinder/.

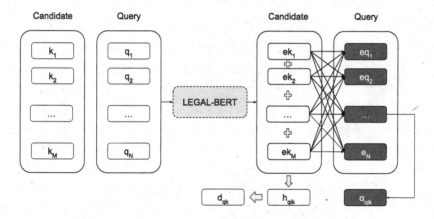

Fig. 2. Attention Mechanism for Document Level

We can then get the case-level representation via attention aggregation:

$$\mathbf{d}_{qk} = \sum_i \alpha_{qik} \mathbf{h}_{qik} \tag{7}$$

Finally, the representation d_{qk} is passed through a linear layer followed by a softmax function to predict as follows:

$$\mathbf{y}_{qk} = softmax(\mathbf{W}_p \cdot \mathbf{d}_{qk} + \mathbf{b}_p) \tag{8}$$

where R denotes the set of relevance labels, e.g., $R = \{0, 1\}$.

During the training procedure, we optimize the following cross-entropy loss:

$$L_{qk}(\hat{\mathbf{y}_{qk}}, \mathbf{y}_{qk}) = -\sum_{r=1}^{|R|} y_{qkr} log(\hat{y_{qk}}) \tag{9}$$

As for testing, we return top-5 candidates that are predicted as relevant cases corresponding to a given query case by our proposed model. We also apply the date filter similar to Run 2 and combine the semantic score to the lexical score as the two above runs.

3.2 Task2

As we mentioned above, case-law often has a complex structure and the likelihood that lexical information can be resolved is very low. As we can see in Fig. 3, the candidate and the given query also contain a long matched span text *"United Nations Convention Relating to the Status of Refugees"*, but this candidate is not a relevant paragraph of the given query.

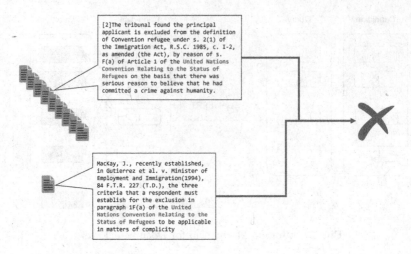

[2]The tribunal found the principal
applicant is excluded from the definition
of Convention refugee under s. 2(1) of
the Immigration Act, R.S.C. 1985, c. I-2,
as amended (the Act), by reason of s.
F(a) of Article 1 of the United Nations
Convention Relating to the Status of
Refugees on the basis that there was
serious reason to believe that he had
committed a crime against humanity.

MacKay, J., recently established,
in Gutierrez et al. v. Minister of
Employment and Immigration(1994),
84 F.T.R. 227 (T.D.), the three
criteria that a respondent must
establish for the exclusion in
paragraph 1F(a) of the United
Nations Convention Relating to the
Status of Refugees to be applicable
in matters of complicity

Fig. 3. Ambiguity of lexical matching

To help the system distinguish the differences in this example, we used transformer [18], the state-of-the-art deep learning model. In previous research, domain adaptation is essential to enhance the performance of deep learning models for specific domains. For maximizing the performance of our method, we chose LEGAL-BERT [4], one of the most significant pre-trained models for the legal domain, and task 2 COLIEE dataset for fine-tuning training data

Although the performance of the transformer model is impressive, it still has the weakness of not working well with too long sentences (>512 tokens). During prediction phases, for a given query Q and a corresponding candidate C, if the total length of Q and C is more than 512 tokens, we will use spacy[3] to apply sentence segmentation on C and obtain a set of sentences $S_c = \{c_1, c_2, c_3, ..., c_N\}$.

After the fine-tuning process, we perform the combination between lexical matching and semantic matching as follows:

LEGAL-BERT Combine with BM25: If the total tokens are more than 512, we will apply sentence segmentation (as above) to obtain the total semantic matching score (TSMS) for the given query and candidate paragraph as:

$$TSMS = \frac{\sum_{i=1}^{N} O_i}{N} \qquad (10)$$

where N is the total number of sentences after applying sentence segmentation, O_i is the semantic score of the candidate sentence c_i, and the corresponding query sentence is provided by LEGAL-BERT. According to Fig. 4, cross-encoder using LEGAL-BERT does not use to generate sentence embedding but the similarity of the input query and the corresponding candidate. Then we used equation (1) to obtain the combination score of LEGAL-BERT [3] and the BM25 algorithm. After having all the candidate scores for the given query, the highest score

---
[3] https://github.com/explosion/spaCy.

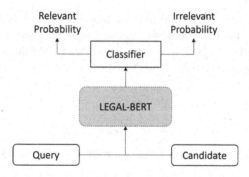

Fig. 4. Cross-encoder for Semantic Relationships

was assigned as the relevant paragraph. Furthermore, we identify other relevant paragraphs by setting a threshold. The candidate will be assigned as a relevant paragraph if a candidate's score exceeds the threshold.

LEGAL-BERT Combine with BM25 (AMR + spacy POS tagging): In our observation, sentences always have a lot of meaningless words, such as stop words, pronouns, etc. These words have no value in searching or measuring similarity. In this run, we use Abstract Meaning Representation (AMR) to capture the most important words in the query and corresponding candidate paragraph. For example, in Fig. 5, an AMR parser can transform the sentence *he stole the bike and ran away* into a semantic graph, and this graph contains the abstract meaning of the given sentence. We expect AMR representation to remove noises such as functional words in the query and candidates, and then the BM25 algorithm can perform better. After that, we performed the BM25 algorithm on these semantic words. At last, we combined the lexical and semantic scores as the first run to get the set of relevant paragraphs.

he stole the bike and ran away

Fig. 5. Example of AMR Representation

Union Result: In this run, we didn't combine the lexical and semantic scores. We used LEGAL-BERT [3] and set up a threshold to get top N candidates, and AMR combined with BM25 as the second run to obtain M candidates. The relevant paragraphs are identified by $N \cap M$.

3.3   Task 3

Table 1. Some examples of training data for Task 3. 1: Normal case, 2: *use-case*

Example	Statement	Relevant Articles	Decision
1	Juristic act subject to a condition subsequent which is impossible is impossible shall be void.	**Article 133** (1) A juridical act subject to an impossible condition precedent is void. (2) A juridical act subject to an impossible condition subsequent is an unconditional juridical act	No
2	The family court appointed B as the administrator of the property of absentee A, as A went missing without appointing the one. In cases where A owns land X, B needs to obtain the permission of a family court in order to sell Land X as an agent of A.	**Article 28** If an administrator needs to perform an act exceeding the authority provided for in Article 103, the administrator may perform that act after obtaining the permission of the family court. [...] **Article 103** An agent who has no specifically defined authority has the authority to perform the following acts only: (i) acts of preservation; [...]	Yes

As mentioned in our previous work [11], there are two main challenges for Task 3.

1. The system has to deal with ambiguity and lengthy documents.
2. Use-case detection (see example 2 in Table 1): The use-case statements are challenging because they replace the meaningful nouns in normal statements with concrete entities like A or B, making it difficult for retrieval models based on lexical similarity (TF-IDF, BM25) or semantic similarity (BERT variants) to identify the relevant articles.

Figure 6 shows the flow of our system. Briefly, we:

1. Firstly, employ fine-tuning with many BERT variants on the full data.
2. Second, filter use-case statements and fine-tune a BERT model on them.
3. Finally, selectively ensemble those models' predictions to construct the final prediction.

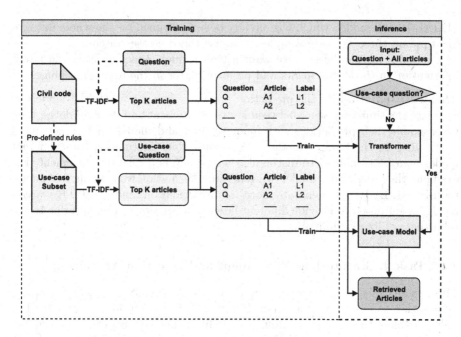

Fig. 6. Overview of the system for Task 3

Fine-tuning with BERT Variants. We fine-tune the pre-trained models of many BERT variants (e.g., Longformer [1], LEGAL-BERT [4], ELECTRA [5], RoBERTa [10]) on the provided training dataset as sentence pair classification task. Specifically, for a given statement, we get a positive sample by pairing it with one of its relevant articles; for negative examples, we pair a given statement with its non-relevant articles, selected based on their top k TF-IDF score. Based on the results in Table 2, the performance of the TF-IDF algorithm is better than BM25 on task 3 of COLIEE 2020, which is why TF-IDF was selected to generate negative and positive samples.

Table 2. Lexical Algorithm Comparison on task 3 COLIEE 2020 Dataset

Algorithm	Precision
BM25	0.4875
TF-IDF	**0.5054**

Addressing Use-Case Statements. First, we build the training data by filtering the use-case statements. As mentioned above, most use-case statements are written with characters indicating a person or a legal person. Firstly, We design a regular expression to filter out the use-case statements, then we use a

LEGAL-BERT model, which has already been fine-tuned on the whole data, to fine-tune on these use-case samples. Because the use-case statements are complex samples in this dataset, we want a transformer model to learn the latent information in these statements and perform better in the prediction phase.

Model Ensembling. In the prediction phase, we use the fine-tuned models to calculate the similarity score between a given statement and its candidates, then we ensemble their predictions with many settings and choose the best setting of ensembling for the final prediction. We assume that information from different models can be combined to distinguish which one is a relevant statement. For example, the Longformer model can generate information from a long document, the LEGAL-BERT can generate more *legal* information, and ELECTRA architecture is supposed to provide different latent information of the data due to the robustness of its discriminator.

3.4   Task 4. Statute Law Entailment and Question Answering

Through analysis, we find out that there is always a passage containing important information to answer the question. Based on this assumption, we employ TF-IDF to explore the most important passage from the given article. Furthermore, we use the same approach as Task 3 to create the use-case model. Similar to Task 3, we experimented with many BERT variants and ensemble their predictions for the final prediction because different BERT variants can learn different aspects of the data. Figure 7 shows the overall of our framework for Task 4.

Paragraph Level Entailment. The paragraphs in an article is denoted by prefix number such as (1), (2), etc. (as can be seen in the first example of Table 1). Based on this hint, we split each article into paragraphs since each paragraph describes a separate subject and does not contain information from other paragraphs.

Negation. In previous competitions, data augmentation using negation proves to provide a better result. Therefore, we employ negation at the paragraph level to generate more training data.

Fine-Tuning with BERT Variants. We fine-tune the pre-trained models of many BERT variants (e.g., Longformer [1], LEGAL-BERT [4], ELECTRA [5], RoBERTa [10]) on the provided training dataset with the task of sentence pair classification. The training data for fine-tuning the transformer models using paragraph level and negation are as follows:

1. Apply article segmentation on all the candidate articles.
2. For the given query, we measure the similarity with all the paragraphs by TF-IDF.
3. The paragraph with the highest TF-IDF score is assigned as a positive sample. The rest will be negative samples.

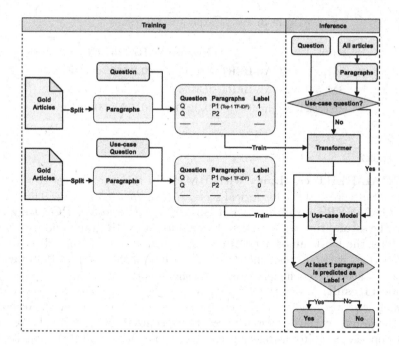

Fig. 7. Overview of the system for Task 4

Use-Case Statements and Model Ensemble. Similar to Task 3, we also address use-case statements and model ensemble. The approach to use-case statements is the same as in Task 3. For each pair of query-candidate, we use several variants of the transformer model to measure the semantic similarity. The final score is the sum of all similarity scores from different transformer models.

4   Experiments and Results

4.1   Task 1

Based on a comparison between the performances with different α values, we set the hyperparameter α to be 0.8 for Run 1 and α to be 0.3 for Run 2. Another key hyperparameter that needs to determine is K, the number of retrieved cases per query. According to the evaluation results on the training set, the optimized value for K is 5.

Table 3 shows the performance on the test set. The result shows that the date filter in Runs 2 and 3 significantly improves the retrieval model's performance. Employing the attention model to encode the whole query in the context of the candidate paragraphs and infer the candidate relevance (Run 3) achieves competitive performance, which shows that our proposed model is effective in legal case retrieval.

Table 3. Task 1 experimental results

Run	Precision	Recall	F1
BM25 + LEGAL-BERT	0.2446	**0.2866**	0.2639
BM25 + LEGAL-BERT	0.3144	0.2494	0.2781
Attention Mechanism	**0.3211**	0.2502	**0.2813**

4.2   Task2

1. **LEGAL-BERT combines with BM25:** In this run, we set $\alpha = 0.9$ for semantic score and 0.1 for lexical score, $threshold = top1_{score} - 0.003$
2. **LEGAL-BERT combines with BM25(AMR + spacy POS tagging):** For the second run, we parsed sentences into an AMR graph and used spacy to filter the most important POS tagging such as verb, noun, adjective, etc. After that, we performed the BM25 algorithm on these sets of POS tagging. We also keep the coefficient α and threshold as the first run.
3. **Union Result:** As described in Sect. 3, we only set up $alpha$ and threshold for semantic scores to get top N semantic-based relevant paragraphs. According to the results on the development set, the optimized value for N is 1. We chose the top M candidates as relevant paragraphs for the lexical-based candidates, and the optimized value for M is 2. Finally, we performed a union between semantic and lexical relevant paragraphs to obtain the final set of candidate paragraphs.

All the results of our methods are shown in Table 4.

Table 4. Task 2 experimental results

Run	Precision	Recall	F1
BM25 + LEGAL-BERT	0.6612	0.6452	0.6780
BM25(AMR) + LEGAL-BERT	0.6452	0.6154	0.6780
Union	**0.6694**	**0.6532**	**0.6864**

4.3   Task 3

Metadata. Metadata of the article includes the information about Parts, Chapters, Sections, Subsections, Division, and Annotations of the articles. These experiments try to assess whether this metadata enhances the model's performance. The result shows that the metadata significantly improves the model prediction.

From our observation from experiments, we decide to employ the TF-IDF filter to 100 candidates, the ratio of positive-negative is 1:100, and include metadata. We conduct experiments with these settings on various Transformer models. Table 5 shows the performance of these models on the development set.

Table 5. Task 3 result of chosen Transformer models

Method	Macro F2	Precision	Recall	Return	Retrieved
LEGAL-BERT$_{Base}$	70.93	0.68	**0.74**	104	**65**
ELECTRA$_{Base}$	**71.87**	**0.73**	0.73	93	64
RoBERTa$_{Base}$	69.42	0.70	0.71	94	63
Longformer$_{Base}$	69.09	**0.73**	0.69	86	62
ALBERT	68.72	0.70	0.69	86	60
DeBERTa	67.22	0.72	0.67	82	59

We also conduct experiments on the use-case question subset to verify the efficiency of the use-case model and report the result in Table 6.

Table 6. Task 3 result on Use-case question subset

Method	Macro F2	Precision	Recall	Return	Retrieved
LEGAL-BERT$_{Base}$	58.06	0.61	0.58	33	20
LEGAL-BERT$_{Base}$ Use-Case	**58.42**	0.58	0.60	36	20

Finally, we ensemble models, including Use-case models, and present the result in Table 7. The result indicates that the ensemble models have better results than single models, and Use-case models can further enhance recall and F2 score. We selected 3 methods from the result to submit our 3 runs.

Table 7. Task 3 Result of ensemble models including Use-case models. (*) Indicates that the models are used in the 3 submission runs with positive-negative ratio = 1:100

Method	Macro F2	Precision	Recall	Return	Retrieved
ELECTRA + Longformer + RoBERTa + Use-case (*)	77.27	0.63	**0.86**	155	**80**
ELECTRA + Longformer + RoBERTa	76.58	0.65	0.83	139	77
RoBERTa + Longformer + Use-case (*)	**77.84**	0.67	0.85	139	78
RoBERTa + Longformer	75.52	**0.69**	0.80	119	73
ELECTRA + LEGAL-BERT + Longformer + RoBERTa (*)	76.21	0.63	0.85	154	78

4.4 Task 4

According to our experiments, we conclude that data argumentation and important passage mining affect the performance of an information retrieval system.

Finally, we ensemble models after applying negative data argumentation and important passage mining. The results are in Table 8. We choose the 3 most robust methods for the blind test.

Table 8. Task 4 Result of ensemble models. (*) Indicates that the models are used in the 3 submission runs with positive-negative ratio = 1:100

Method	Accuracy
ELECTRA$_{Base}$ (*)	64.19
ELECTRA$_{Base}$ + LEGAL-BERT (*)	64.19
ELECTRA$_{Base}$ + LEGAL-BERT + Use-case (*)	61.72
ELECTRA$_{Base}$ + Longformer	62.96
ELECTRA$_{Base}$ + RoBERTa	55.55

5   Conclusion

In this paper, we have addressed several issues of processing legal documents in COLIEE 2022. Firstly, the lengthy document is handled by using an attention mechanism on the document level (Task 1) or sentence segmentation and the TF-IDF algorithm for mining the most critical passages in the given documents. Second, we have proposed 2 new approaches (1) Using AMR representation to remove document noise (Task 2), and (2) By addressing the *use-case*, we can have different methods to solve different types of questions in the legal domain.

References

1. Beltagy, I., Peters, M.E., Cohan, A.: Longformer: the long-document transformer (2020). arXiv:2004.05150
2. Brown, T., et al.: Language models are few-shot learners. Adv. Neural Inf. Process. Syst. **33**, 1877–1901 (2020)
3. Chalkidis, I., Fergadiotis, M., Malakasiotis, P., Aletras, N., Androutsopoulos, I.: LEGAL-BERT: the muppets straight out of law school (2020). arXiv preprint arXiv:2010.02559
4. Chalkidis, I., Fergadiotis, M., Malakasiotis, P., Aletras, N., Androutsopoulos, I.: LEGAL-BERT: the muppets straight out of law school. In: Findings of the Association for Computational Linguistics: EMNLP 2020, pp. 2898–2904, Online, November 2020. Association for Computational Linguistics (2020)
5. Clark, K., Luong, M.T., Le, Q.V., Manning, C.D.: ELECTRA: pre-training text encoders as discriminators rather than generators. In: ICLR (2020)
6. Devlin, J., Chang, M.W., Lee, K., Toutanova, K.: Bert: pre-training of deep bidirectional transformers for language understanding (2018). arXiv preprint arXiv:1810.04805
7. Fujita, M., Kiyota, N., Kano, Y.: Predicate's argument resolver and entity abstraction for legal question answering: kis teams at COLIEE 2021 shared task. In: Proceedings of the Eighteenth International Conference on Artificial Intelligence and Law (2021)
8. Kim, M.Y., Rabelo, J., Goebel, R.: Bm25 and transformer- based legal information extraction and entailment. In: Proceedings of the Eighteenth International Conference on Artificial Intelligence and Law (2021)

9. Kusner, M., Sun, Y., Kolkin, N., Weinberger, K.: From word embeddings to document distances. In: International Conference on Machine Learning, pp. 957–966. PMLR (2015)

10. Liu, Y., et al.: Roberta: a robustly optimized BERT pretraining approach (2019). CoRR, abs/1907.11692

11. Nguyen, H.-T., et al.: JNLP team: deep learning approaches for legal processing tasks in COLIEE 2021 (2021). arXiv preprint arXiv:2106.13405

12. Rabelo, J., Kim, M.-Y., Goebel, R., Yoshioka, M., Kano, Y., Satoh, K.: COLIEE 2020: methods for legal document retrieval and entailment. In: Okazaki, N., Yada, K., Satoh, K., Mineshima, K. (eds.) JSAI-isAI 2020. LNCS (LNAI), vol. 12758, pp. 196–210. Springer, Cham (2021). https://doi.org/10.1007/978-3-030-79942-7_13

13. Raffel, C., et al.: Exploring the limits of transfer learning with a unified text-to-text transformer (2019). arXiv preprint arXiv:1910.10683

14. Robertson, S.E., et al.: Okapi at TREC-3. Nist Special Publication Sp, 109, p. 109 (1995)

15. Schilder, F., et al.: A pentapus grapples with legal reasoning. In: Proceedings of the Eighteenth International Conference on Artificial Intelligence and Law (2021)

16. Shao, Y., et al.: BERT-PLI: modeling paragraph-level interactions for legal case retrieval. In: IJCAI, pp. 3501–3507 (2020)

17. Strohman, T., Metzler, D., Turtle, H., Croft, W.B.: Indri: A language model-based search engine for complex queries. In: Proceedings of the International Conference on Intelligent Analysis, vol. 2, pp. 2–6. Citeseer (2005)

18. Vaswani, A., et al.: Attention is all you need. Adv. Neural Inf. Process. Syst. **30** (2017)

19. Wehnert, S., Sudhi, V., Dureja, S., Kutty, L., Shahania, S., De Luca, E.W.: Legal norm retrieval with variations of the Bert model combined with TF-IDF vectorization. In: Proceedings of the Eighteenth International Conference on Artificial Intelligence and Law, pp. 285–294 (2021)

20. Yoshioka, M., Aoki, Y., Suzuki, Y.: BERT-based ensemble methods with data augmentation for legal textual entailment in COLIEE statute law task. In: Proceedings of the Eighteenth International Conference on Artificial Intelligence and Law, pp. 278–284 (2021)

Semantic-Based Classification of Relevant Case Law

Juliano Rabelo[1,3](✉) ⓘ, Mi-Young Kim[1,2], and Randy Goebel[1,3]

[1] Alberta Machine Intelligence Institute, University of Alberta, Edmonton, Canada
{rabelo,miyoung2,rgoebel}@ualberta.ca
[2] Department of Science, Augustana Faculty, University of Alberta,
Edmonton, Canada
[3] Department of Computing Science, University of Alberta, Edmonton, Canada

Abstract. The challenge of information overload in the legal domain increases every day. The COLIEE competition has created four challenges which are intended to encourage the development of systems and methods to alleviate some of that pressure: a case law retrieval (Task 1) and entailment (Task 2), and a statute law retrieval (Task 3) and entailment (Task 4). In this paper, we describe our method for Task 1, which was ranked first among all participants in the COLIEE 2022 competition. Our approach relies on measuring the similarity between paragraphs of legal cases by generating feature vectors based on those similarities, and then using a classifier to determine if those cases should be noticed or not. We also apply simple pre- and post-processing heuristics to generate the final results.

Keywords: Legal textual retrieval · Semantic text representation · Document similarity · Binary classification · Imbalanced datasets

1 Introduction

Every day, large volumes of legal data are produced by law firms, law courts, independent attorneys, legislators, and many others. Within that context, management of legal information becomes manually intractable, and requires the development of tools which automatically or semi-automatically aid legal professionals to handle the information overload. The COLIEE competition[1] [9], addresses four facets of that challenge: case law retrieval, case law entailment, statute law retrieval and statute law entailment. Here we summarize the details of our approach to the first task, evaluate the results achieved and comment on future work to further improve our models.

Task 1 is the case law retrieval task and, according to [9] "consists in finding which cases, amongst a set of provided candidate cases, should be "noticed" with respect to a given query case. More formally, given a query case q and a set of candidate cases $C = \{c_1, c_2, ..., c_n\}$, the task is to find the supporting cases $S = \{s_1,$

---

[1] https://sites.ualberta.ca/~rabelo/COLIEE2022/.

Y. Takama et al. (Eds.): JSAI-isAI 2022 Workshop, LNAI 13859, pp. 84–95, 2023.
https://doi.org/10.1007/978-3-031-29168-5_6

$s_2, ..., s_n \mid s_i \in C \land noticed(s_i, q)\}$ where $noticed(s_i, q)$ denotes a relationship which is true when $s_i \in S$ is a noticed case with respect to q" (see [9] for more details).

Our approach for Task 1 relies on a transformers-based model to create a multidimensional numeric representation of each case paragraph; we then calculate the cosine distances between each paragraph from a query case and a candidate case. Next, we create a histogram from the resulting distances and train a binary classifier with those inputs. In addition, we do some simple pre-processing (e.g., removal of French fragments) and post-processing (e.g., removal of candidates which have dates more recent than the query case, thus establishing a maximum number of noticed cases per query case based on priors drawn from the training dataset, and applying a minimum confidence score for the classifier outputs) to generate the final results. This approach achieved an f1-score of 0.3715 in the official test dataset, which was the best among all competitors in Task 1 of the COLIEE 2022 competition.

Our paper is organized as follows: Sect. 2 presents a brief state-of-the-art analysis; Sect. 3 describes our method in more detail; Sect. 4 analyzes the results; and Sect. 5 provides some final remarks and proposes some future work.

2   Literature Review

Most current methods for legal information retrieval rely on traditional information retrieval (IR) methods, and more recently, on transformers-based techniques. In COLIEE 2021, the main approaches revolved around those two main topics:

Li et al. [11] proposed a pipeline method based on statistical features and semantic understanding models, which enhances the basic retrieval method with both improved recall and use of semantic ranking.

Schilder et al. [16] applied a two-phase approach for Task 1: first, they generate a candidate set which is optimized for recall. They attempt to include all true noticed cases while removing some of the false candidates. The second step trains a binary classifier[2] which receives as input the pair (*query case, candidate case*) and predicts whether they represent a true noticed relationship.

Rosa et al. [15] presented a generic application of BM25 to the case law retrieval problem. They first index all base and candidate cases present in the given dataset. Before indexing, each document is split into segments of texts using a context window of 10 sentences with overlapping strides of 5 sentences (the 'candidate case segments'). BM25 is then used to retrieve candidate case segments for each base case segment. The relevance score for a (*base case, candidate case*)

---

[2] The authors experimented with logistic regression, naive Bayes, and tree-based classifiers in this step.

pair is the maximum score among all their base case segment and candidate case segment pairs. The candidates are then ranked according to threshold-based heuristics.

Ma et al. [12] applied two methods for the case law retrieval task: the first is a traditional language model for IR, which consists of an application of Likelihood Maximization Inverse Regression (LMIR) on a pre-processed version of the dataset. The TLIR team did not use the full case contents, but rather use the tags inserted in the text to indicate a fragment has been suppressed to identify the most relevant pieces. This specific approach ranked first place among all Task 1 competitors for COLIEE 2021, thus confirming traditional IR methods achieve good results in the case law retrieval task. The second approach used by the TLIR team was a transformer based method, which splits a document into paragraphs and computes interactions between paragraphs using BERT. They have called this model BERT-PLI, because it models the *paragraph-level interactions* of case documents via BERT, then aggregates these interactions to infer the document relevance via a sequential modeling mechanism. Compared with other neural network constructed models, BERT-PLI can take long text representations as an input without truncating them at some threshold.

Althammer et al. [2] combined retrieval methods with neural re-ranking methods using contextualized language models like BERT. Since the cases are typically long documents exceeding BERT's maximum input length, the authors adopt a two phase approach. The first phase combined lexical and dense retrieval methods on the paragraph-level of the cases. Then, they re-rank the candidates by summarizing the cases and applying a fine-tuned BERT re-ranker on said summaries.

Here, we also describe other teams' approaches in the COLIEE 2022 Task 1.

TUWBR (2 runs) [5] start from two assumptions: first, that there is a topical overlap between query and notice cases, but that not all parts of a query case are equally important. Secondly, they assume that traditional IR methods, such as BM25, provide competitive results in Task 1. They perform document level and passage level retrieval, and also augment the system by adding external domain knowledge by extracting statute fragments and explicitly adding those fragments to the documents.

JNLP (3 runs) [4] applies an approach that first splits the documents into paragraphs, then calculates the similarities between cases by combining term-level matching and semantic relationships on the paragraph level. An attention model is applied to encode the whole query in the context of candidate paragraphs, and then infer the relationship between cases.

DoSSIER (3 runs) [1] combined traditional and neural based techniques in Task 1. The authors investigate lexical and dense first stage retrieval methods aiming for a high recall in the initial retrieval and then compare shallow neural re-ranking with the MTFT-BERT model to the BERT-PLI model. They then investigate which part of the text of a legal case should be taken into account for re-ranking. Their results show that BM25 shows a consistently high effectiveness across different test collections in comparison to the neural network re-ranking models.

LeiBi (3 runs) [3] applied an approach which consists of the following steps: first, given a legal case as a query, they augment it by heuristically identifying various meaningful sentences or n-grams. The authors then use the pre-processed query case to retrieve an initial set of possible relevant legal cases, which are further re-ranked. Finally, the team aggregates the relevance scores obtained by the first stage together with the re-ranking models to further improve retrieval effectiveness. The query cases are reformulated to be shorter, using three different statistical methods (KLI, PLM, IDF-r), in addition to models that leverage embeddings (e.g., KeyBERT). Moreover, the authors investigate if automatic summarization using Longformer-Encoder-Decoder (LED) can produce an effective query representation for this retrieval task. Furthermore, the team proposes a re-ranking cluster-driven approach, which leverages Sentence-BERT models to generate embeddings for sentences from both the query and candidate documents. Finally, the authors employ a linear aggregation method to combine the relevance scores obtained by traditional IR models and neural-based models.

nigam (3 runs) [14] developed an approach which was a combination of transformer-based and traditional IR techniques; more specifically, they used Sentence-BERT and Sent2Vec for semantic understanding, combined with BM25. First, the nigam team selects top-K candidates according to the BM25 rankings, and then use pre-trained Sentence-BERT and Sent2Vec models to generate representation features of each sentence. The authors also used cosine similarity with the max-pooling strategy to get the final document score between the query and noticed cases.

siat (3 runs) [17] show how long former-based contrastive learning is able to process sequences of thousands of tokens, (which are usually restricted to between 512 and 1024 tokens). In addition to that longformer-based approach, the siat team also explores traditional retrieval models. They achieved second place overall in Task 1 of COLIEE 2022.

Task 1 has been recently changed in COLIEE. The new configuration made the task harder and usual Information Retrieval methods, even augmented with transformers-based approaches, did not show great results in the 2021 edition [9]. Given most of the current approaches work at the document level, we intended to experiment with the documents at the sentence level to try and capture more localized information. More details of the approach are presented in Sect. 3.

3   Our Method

3.1   Dataset Analysis

The training dataset consists of 4,415 files, with 900 of those identified as query cases. There are a total of 4,206 noticed cases, an average of 4.67 noticed cases per query case. One case may potentially be marked as noticed by more than one query case, but we found that to be rare: there are 3,126 cases that are noticed only once. Among cases that are noticed more than once, 293 are noticed twice, 66 three times, 20 are noticed four times, and 29 are noticed five or more times. In the provided test dataset there were 300 query cases and a total of 1,563 files.

3.2   Details of the Approach

Our approach to the case law retrieval task relied on the use of a sentence-transformer model (see more details below) to generate a multidimensional numeric representation of text. This model is applied to each paragraph from both the query case and every candidate case. We then use a cosine measure to determine the distances between the 768-dimension vectors from the query paragraphs and the candidate paragraphs. A 10-bin histogram of those distances is generated and a Gradient Boosting [6] binary classification model is trained on those inputs.

Given the formulation of the problem, we had to make some choices to produce a reasonable training dataset: since the test set contains a total of approximately 1,500 of which 300 are query cases; we assumed we should generate a training dataset with around 1,000 negative samples per query case. So we needed to down-sample the negative samples in the training dataset to 1,000. At the same time, the positive class is far underrepresented (less than 5 samples per query case in average), so we over-sampled those examples by simple replication.

We also implemented some simple pre-processing steps:

Removal of French contents through a language identification model based on a naive Bayesian filter [13];

Splitting of input text into paragraphs based on simple pattern matching relying on the common format used in cases. The method relies on finding a sequence of numbered paragraphs with digits between brackets as the first characters in the line starting at [1] and looking for the next natural number;

Extraction of dates mentioned in the cases through the application of a named entity recognition model [7]. These dates are used later to remove candidate cases which mention dates more recent than the most recent date mentioned in a query case, under the assumption those candidates cannot be a true noticed case because they are more recent than the query case. So, we basically extract all Date entities in both the query and the candidate case and if the query case contains a date which is more recent than the most recent date in the candidate case, that candidate case will be removed from the list.

At inference time we used the following steps:

Date filtering: we apply the same date pre-processing steps mentioned above;

Histograms: we generate histograms for every pair of query document and each candidate which does not contain dates more recent than the query document dates;

Apply model: we use those histograms as inputs to our trained model.

Based on an analysis of the training dataset, we also apply some simple post-processing steps:

Number of noticed cases per query case: the average number of noticed cases per query case in the training dataset is 4.67, so we establish a range of 3 to 10 maximum noticed cases per query case;

Confidence score: we establish a minimum confidence score for the classifier, disregarding outputs which are below a given threshold;

Repeating noticed cases: if the same case is noticed across many different query cases, we also remove that noticed case from our final answer as it is observed in the training dataset that this is an uncommon situation.

We experimented with a range of parameters for each one of those post-processing criteria and selected the 3 combinations which produced the best output in a validation set containing 50 query cases[3].

We also explored two other approaches which we could not use in the final submissions due to limited access to hardware resources: usage of the FAISS library [8] for semantic similarity searches, and another one based on fine-tuning an ALBERT model [10] which showed promising results in preliminary evaluations. We intend to further explore these approaches in future editions of the COLIEE competition.

Sentence-Transformer Model. The model used to produce 768-dimensional representations for the case paragraphs was the HuggingFace sentence-transformers/all-mpnet-base-v2 model[4]. That model was trained on very large sentence level datasets using a self-supervised contrastive learning objective using the pretrained Microsoft/mpnet-base model[5] as the base model and fine-tuning it on a 1B sentence pairs dataset. The authors use a contrastive learning objective: given a sentence from the pair, the model should predict which of a set of randomly sampled other sentences was actually paired with it in the dataset.

---

[3] The validation set was randomly drawn from the provided dataset and has no overlap with the cases used for training.

[4] https://huggingface.co/sentence-transformers/all-mpnet-base-v2.

[5] https://huggingface.co/microsoft/mpnet-base?text=The+goal+of+life+is+%3Cmask%3E.

Binary Classification Model. The model used for training was a Gradient Boosting model [6] which was trained on the calculated similarity histograms as described before. Since the training dataset is severely unbalanced, we oversample the positive class by simple duplication, and undersample the negative class by establishing a target maximum number (which was chosen as 1,000 samples). The only hyper-parameter we varied in the classifier itself was the number of estimators, which was set to 1,000, 3,000 and 5,000.

Hyper-parameter Setting. We performed a grid search for 3 hyper-parameters:

- Maximum number of noticed cases per query case: based on the dataset analysis performed, given the average number of noticed cases per query case in the training set is around 5, we experimented with establishing a limit which varied from 3 to 10 (step 1) in an attempt to reduce the false positives;
- Minimum confidence score: we trained a binary classifier to determine if a given case should be noticed with respect to a given query case. With this hyper-parameter we can filter out candidate cases for which the classifier confidence score is below a given threshold. We experimented with values from 0.55 to 0.80 (step 0.05);
- Maximum duplicate noticed cases: we noticed in our validation results that the same case was classified as noticed with respect to more than one query case, which is not common in the training dataset, so we establish the maximum number of times the same case can be present in the output. This parameter was varied from 1 to 5 (step 1).

The 3 best performing combinations where used in our submission. You can see that the best one (max noticed cases = 10, min score = 0.65, max dups = 3) had a good precision but not so good recall. The second best combination (9, 0.7, 2) had an f1-score very close the first one but with a much higher precision. We attribute this to the effect of the minimum confidence score with was higher in this case whereas the other parameters where pretty much the same. Even though the difference in the final f1-score wasn't material, having the ability to tweak parameters and influence precision and recall would be a good feature of the method in real-world applications as users could adopt parameters according to their requirements with respect to precision and recall.

4   Results

The results on the official COLIEE evaluation set are shown in Table 1:

Table 1. Official results for the Case Law Retrieval task.

Team	File	F1 Score	Precision	Recall
UA	**pp_0.65_10_3.csv**	**0.3715**	**0.4111**	**0.3389**
UA	**pp_0.7_9_2.csv**	**0.3710**	**0.4967**	**0.2961**
siat	siatrun1.txt	0.3691	0.3005	0.4782
siat	siatrun3.txt	0.3680	0.3026	0.4695
UA	**pp_0.65_6.csv**	**0.3559**	**0.3630**	**0.3492**
siat	siatrun2.txt	0.2964	0.2522	0.3595
LeiBi	run_bm25.txt	0.2923	0.3000	0.2850
LeiBi	run_weighting.txt	0.2917	0.2687	0.3191
JNLP	run3.txt	0.2813	0.3211	0.2502
nigam	bm25P3M3.txt	0.2809	0.2587	0.3072
JNLP	run2.txt	0.2781	0.3144	0.2494
DSSR	DSSR_01.txt	0.2657	0.2447	0.2906
JNLP	run1.txt	0.2639	0.2446	0.2866
DSSR	DSSR_03.txt	0.2461	0.2267	0.2692
TUWBR	TUWBR_LM_law	0.2367	0.1895	0.3151
LeiBi	run_clustering.txt	0.2306	0.2367	0.2249
TUWBR	TUWBR_LM	0.2206	0.1683	0.3199
nigam	sbertP3M3RS.txt	0.1542	0.1420	0.1686
nigam	s2vecP3M3RS.txt	0.1484	0.1367	0.1623
DSSR	DSSR_02.txt	0.1317	0.1213	0.1441
LLNTU	2022.task1.LLNTUtfidCos	0.0000	0.0000	0.0000
LLNTU	2022.task1.LLNTUtanadaT	0.0000	0.0000	0.0000
LLNTU	2022.task1.LLNTU3q4clii	0.0000	0.0000	0.0000
Uottawa	Task1Run3_UottawaLegalBert.txt	0.0000	0.0000	0.0000
Uottawa	Task1Run1_UottawaMB25.txt	0.0000	0.0000	0.0000
Uottawa	Task1Run2_UottawaSentTrans.txt	0.0000	0.0000	0.0000

Our best result was achieved with the following post-processing parameters: minimum confidence score = 0.65, maximum noticed cases = 10, maximum number of repeated noticed cases = 3^6. Our second best score had similar parameters (0.7, 9 and 2 respectively). In the third submission we only used the minimum score and maximum number of noticed cases (0.65 and 6, respectively). This provided a more balanced trade-off between precision and recall, as opposed to the first two which had a higher precision but a lower recall. This is an interesting characteristic for real world applications, as one could make an informed decision on how to tweak parameters depending on which metric is more important for their particular scenario.

---

[6] We simply remove noticed cases which appear in more than the maximum allowed query cases. An obvious improvement is to keep just the highest scoring noticed cases.

4.1   Error Analysis

A thorough error analysis for this kind of task is very challenging as we would need to read, understand and compare thousands of legal documents. Due to a lack of resources, we performed a more high-level analysis which helped us to postulate a hypothesis on where our method could be improved, which will guide future work.

Through a sample analysis, we observed that our method seemed to be less effective with longer files. To confirm, we began with an idea to calculate the f1-score for individual cases and identify some common characteristics on those cases with a low f1-score. That idea was later put aside because the f1-score for individual cases would not be able to capture how much our method was wrong when either recall or precision was zero. For that reason, we calculated an error score for each case, which is given by the formula below:

$$Err_i = FP_i + FN_i - TP_i$$

where FP_i, FN_i and TP_i are the number of false positives, false negatives and true positives for case i, respectively.

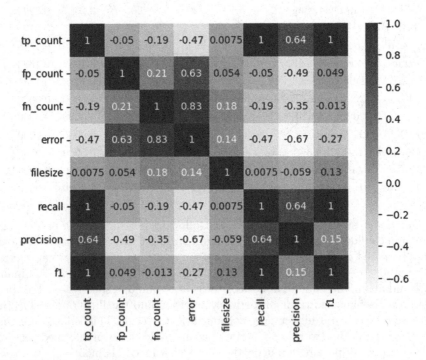

Fig. 1. Correlation matrix of metrics achieved in the test dataset + the query file size considering the whole dataset.

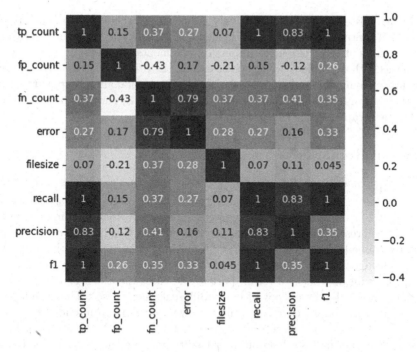

Fig. 2. Correlation matrix of metrics achieved in the test dataset + the query file size. Cases were sorted in descending order according to the error score defined above and only the top 25% cases were considered.

We then calculated a correlation matrix between our results in the official COLIEE test dataset and the size of each query file in that dataset ("filesize" in Fig. 1).

That correlation matrix shows a small but still relevant correlation between the query file size and the error score. We then ordered the dataset by the error score in descending order, and split it into four subgroups, and observed that the correlation increased when we considered only the cases with more errors. Figure 2 shows the correlation matrix for the 25% cases where we had more errors, where the correlation between the file size and the error score is 0.28, twice as much the value considering the whole dataset:

That correlation was 0.097, –0.24 and –0.26 for the other 3 quadrants (the next 3 groups of 25% cases ordered by the error score - respectively, the cases from 25% to 50%, from 50% to 75%, and from 75% to the end of the dataset. We notice that correlation is the highest for the first group (where the errors are more frequent), and then decreases to a very low correlation on the second quadrant, and keeps decreasing to be negative values for the third and fourth quadrants. Those scores confirm our hypothesis that errors are more common when the query files are larger[7]. That is likely because past cases are usually

---

[7] We intend to run similar experiments considering now the candidate file sizes.

cited when a fragment of that cited case is relevant in the context of the present case which contains the citation, and when the files are longer our method is less effective in identifying the more important fragments/contexts.

To tackle that problem, we intend to extend the proposed method by focusing specifically on highly-similar fragments. Since our method already splits the cases into their paragraphs, it should be easy to extend it to consider only the most similar paragraphs in the comparison, for example.

5   Final Remarks

We have presented our approach for the Case Law Retrieval task in COLIEE 2022. Our team was ranked first among all competitors in that task (9 teams, which sent 26 submissions altogether) with an approach that combined semantic similarity representation at the sentence level with a Gradient Boosting binary classifier trained on 10-bin histograms containing similarity scores between sentences of the query and candidate cases. As future work, we intend to refine our post-processing approach to retain part of the cases identified as noticed when they are present in the output of many different query cases. That would be a simple extension of our current method. However, the main intended extension to this work is a more disruptive approach fully based on transformer-based models, which we had to abandon in this edition of the competition due to lack of hardware resources. We also intend to focus on specific paragraphs, as cases tend to cite other cases in a context that usually is constrained to a small number of paragraphs (usually only one).

Acknowledgments. This research was supported by the Alberta Machine Intelligence Institute (AMII), the University of Alberta, and the Natural Sciences and Engineering Research Council of Canada (NSERC), [funding reference numbers DGECR-2022-00369 and RGPIN-2022-0346].

References

1. Abolghasemi, A., Althammer, S., Hanbury, A., Verberne, S.: Dossier@coliee2022: dense retrieval and neural re-ranking for legal case retrieval. In: Sixteenth International Workshop on Juris-informatics (JURISIN) (2022)
2. Althammer, S., Askari, A., Verberne, S., Hanbury, A.: Dossier@coliee 2021: leveraging dense retrieval and summarization-based re-ranking for case law retrieval. In: Proceedings of the COLIEE Workshop in ICAIL (2021)
3. Askari, A., Peikos, G., Pasi, G., Verberne, S.: Leibi@coliee 2022: aggregating tuned lexical models with a cluster-driven bert-based model for case law retrieval. In: Sixteenth International Workshop on Juris-informatics (JURISIN) (2022)
4. Bui, M.Q., Nguyen, C., Do, D.T., Le, N.K., Nguyen, D.H., Nguyen, T.T.T.: Using deep learning approaches for tackling legal's challenges (COLIEE 2022). In: Sixteenth International Workshop on Juris-informatics (JURISIN) (2022)
5. Fink, T., Recski, G., Kusa, W., Hanbury, A.: Statute-enhanced lexical retrieval of court cases for COLIEE 2022. In: Sixteenth International Workshop on Juris-informatics (JURISIN) (2022)

6. Friedman, J.H.: Greedy function approximation: a gradient boosting machine. Ann. Stat. 1189–1232 (2001)
7. Honnibal, M., Johnson, M.: An improved non-monotonic transition system for dependency parsing. In: Proceedings of the 2015 Conference on Empirical Methods in Natural Language Processing, pp. 1373–1378. Association for Computational Linguistics, Lisbon, Portugal, September 2015
8. Johnson, J., Douze, M., Jégou, H.: Billion-scale similarity search with GPUs. IEEE Trans. Big Data **7**(3), 535–547 (2019)
9. Rabelo, J., Goebel, R., Kim, M.Y., Kano, Y., Yoshioka, M., Satoh, K.: Overview and discussion of the competition on legal information extraction/entailment (COLIEE) 2021. J. Rev. Socionetwork Strateg. **16**(1) (2022)
10. Lan, Z., Chen, M., Goodman, S., Gimpel, K., Sharma, P., Soricut, R.: ALBERT: a lite BERT for self-supervised learning of language representations. CoRR abs/1909.11942 (2019). http://arxiv.org/abs/1909.11942
11. Li, J., Zhao, X., Liu, J., Wen, J., Yang, M.: Siat@coliee-2021: combining statistics recall and semantic ranking for legal case retrieval and entailment. In: Proceedings of the COLIEE Workshop in ICAIL (2021)
12. Ma, Y., Shao, Y., Liu, B., Liu, Y., Zhang, M., Ma, S.: Retrieving legal cases from a large-scale candidate corpus. In: Proceedings of the 18th International conference on Artificial Intelligence and Law (ICAIL) (2021)
13. Nakatani, S.: Language detection library for java (2010). https://github.com/shuyo/language-detection
14. Nigam, S.K., Goel, N.: Legal case retrieval and entailment using cascading of lexical and semantic-based models. In: Sixteenth International Workshop on Juris-informatics (JURISIN) (2022)
15. Rosa, G.M., Rodrigues, R.C., Lotufo, R., Nogueira, R.: Yes, bm25 is a strong baseline for legal case retrieval. In: Proceedings of the 18th International conference on Artificial Intelligence and Law (ICAIL) (2021)
16. Schilder, F., et al.: A pentapus grapples with legal reasoning. In: Proceedings of the COLIEE Workshop in ICAIL (2021)
17. Wen, J., Zhong, Z., Bai, Y., Zhao, X., Yang, M.: Siat@coliee-2022: legal case retrieval with longformer-based contrastive learning. In: Sixteenth International Workshop on Juris-informatics (JURISIN) (2022)

nigam@COLIEE-22: Legal Case Retrieval and Entailment Using Cascading of Lexical and Semantic-Based Models

Shubham Kumar Nigam[1](✉), Navansh Goel[2], and Arnab Bhattacharya[1]

[1] Indian Institute of Technology, Kanpur, Kanpur, India
{sknigam,arnabb}@cse.iitk.ac.in
[2] Vellore Institute of Technology, Chennai, India

Abstract. This paper describes our submission to the Competition on Legal Information Extraction/Entailment 2022 (COLIEE-2022) workshop on case law competition for tasks 1 and 2. Task 1 is a legal case retrieval task, which involves reading a new case and extracting supporting cases from the provided case law corpus to support the decision. Task 2 is a legal case entailment task, involving the identification of a paragraph from existing cases that entails the decision in a relevant case. We employed the neural models Sentence-BERT and Sent2Vec for semantic understanding and the traditional information retrieval model BM25 for exact matching in both tasks. As a result, our team (named "nigam") ranked 5th among all the teams in Tasks 1 and 2. Experimental results indicate that the traditional information retrieval model BM25 still outperforms neural network-based models.

Keywords: BM25 · Sentence-BERT · Sent2vec · Reduced-Space

1 Introduction

Many countries, such as India, the United States, Canada, Australia, and Africa, follow the case law system. These case law systems are legal systems that give great weight to judicial precedent, and the volume of information produced in the legal sector nowadays is overwhelming. Due to this, it takes significant efforts of legal practitioners to search for relevant cases from the database and extract the entailment parts manually with the rapid growth of digitalized legal documents. Therefore, an efficient legal assistant system to alleviate the heavy document work is necessary for Legal-AI.

The Competition on Legal Information Extraction and Entailment (COLIEE) workshop has been organized for several years to assist the legal research community. They provide the legal texts and specific problems in the legal domain such as question-answering, case law retrieval, case law entailment,

---

S. K. Nigam and N. Goel—These authors contributed equally to this work.

Y. Takama et al. (Eds.): JSAI-isAI 2022 Workshop, LNAI 13859, pp. 96–108, 2023.
https://doi.org/10.1007/978-3-031-29168-5_7

statute law retrieval, and statute law entailment to help the research community develop Legal-AI techniques.

This paper introduces our approaches to completing two case law tasks, Task 1 (*case retrieval* task) and Task 2 (*case entailment* task). We employed both traditional information retrieval models such as BM25 [6] for exact matching and semantic understanding, and neural models such as Sentence-BERT [5], Sent2Vec [4] for both the tasks. We also used a combination for Task 1, where we first select top-K candidates according to the BM25 rankings and afterward get the representation features of each sentence for the document by using pre-trained Sentence-BERT and Sent2Vec via comparing paragraph-level interaction. Furthermore, for each paragraph of the query, we capture the most vital matching signals with the candidate document using the cosine similarity with the max-pooling strategy. Since case law references can be as small as one or two paragraphs, the max-pooling strategy gives the best possible score for a query-candidate case pair over alternative strategies like average-pooling. As a result, our team ranked 5th among all the participants in both tasks. Experimental results suggest that the exact matching using the traditional information retrieval model BM25 still outperforms representation features generated by neural network-based models. We released the codes for all subtasks via GitHub[1].

2   The Task

2.1   Task 1: Legal Case Retrieval

The main objective of legal case law retrieval is to obtain relevant supporting documents for a given query case Q_i. The task involves retrieving noticed cases from the set $N = \{N_1, N_2, ..., N_m\}$, such that $N \subseteq C$ belonging to a given case law corpus of all possible supporting/candidate cases $C = \{C_1, C_2, C_3, ..., C_n\}$. The variables m and n represent the respective sizes of the noticed case set and the supporting case corpus, satisfying the condition $m \leq n$.

The query case documents contain suppressed reference markers instead of actual references to precedent case laws, thereby compelling the participants to design models that can understand the text around the references and return valid noticed cases. A supporting/candidate case $C_k \in C$ is a noticed case for query $Q_i \in Q$ *if and only if* Q_i contains a reference to C_k.

2.2   Task 2: Legal Case Entailment

Task 2 comprises identifying a specific paragraph from a given supporting case that entails the decision for the query case. Thus, given a query case Q_i, a supporting/candidate case C_j and a set of paragraphs $P = \{P_1, P_2, P_3, ..., P_n\}$ such that $P \subseteq C$, the task requires correctly identifying $P_k \in P$ such that it entails the decision for query case Q_i.

---

[1] https://github.com/ShubhamKumarNigam/COLIEE-22.

Table 1. Statistics of the training and test data for Task1 and Task2

	Task 1		Task 2	
	Train	Test	Train	Test
No. of queries	898	300	525	100
No. of candidate cases/paragraphs	3531	1263	18740	3278
avg no. of candidate paragraphs per query	–	–	35.63	32.46
avg no. of relevant candidates/paragraphs	4.68	4.21	1.14	1.18
avg query length (words)	28866.73	32461.27	24966.55	22326.95
avg candidate length (words)	30113.09	29756.87	636.08	643.69

3   Data Corpus

The data corpus for both Task 1 and Task 2 belongs to a database of case law documents from the Federal Court of Canada provided by Compass Law. Table 1 presents the dataset statistics for both the tasks. For Task 1, 898 query cases were given against 3531 candidate cases as a part of the training data corpus. The test dataset had 300 query cases against 1263 candidate cases. For Task 2, 525 query cases were provided for training against 18740 paragraphs. There were 100 query cases against 3278 candidate paragraphs as part of the testing dataset. The organizers provided the candidate paragraphs for a given query case separately. On average, there are 35.63 candidate paragraphs for each query case in the training dataset and 32.46 candidate paragraphs for each query case in the testing dataset.

On further analysis, we found that the average number of relevant candidate cases for Task 1 was 4.68 cases for the training dataset and 4.21 relevant cases for the test dataset. As a part of our methodology, we predict the top-5 possible candidate cases for each query case based on these numbers. The average number of relevant paragraphs for Task 2 was a little over 1 paragraph – 1.14 paragraphs for training and 1.18 paragraphs for testing. These numbers show that most documents for Task 2 had their decisions entailed inside a single paragraph. The table also shows the average length of each document. The average number of words is higher in the testing query dataset than in the training query dataset for Task 1.

On the contrary, the average number of words per candidate document decreases from the training data to the testing data. The opposite trend is observed for Task 2, where the average number of words per query document decreases from training data to testing data. In contrast, the average number of words per candidate paragraph increases from training to testing.

3.1   Preprocessing

Since the given documents are very long, representing an entire document as a single entity is inefficient. Also, it is often noted that case judgments cite multiple cases and write multiple sentences about them. The documents are segmented into meaningful sentences using the Spacy library[2]. The organizers of the competition redacted the citations from query case documents to evaluate the extent of information captured from the text around a given citation. A citation marker "FRAGMENT_SUPPRESSED" was introduced in place of relevant citations or can be considered a mask of citation in query cases. Thus by locating the sentence that contains the citation marker "FRAGMENT_SUPPRESSED", relevant information is further extracted from the text around this sentence. For example, upon assigning the index i to a sentence that contains the citation marker, a window of k sentences around the sentence results in a paragraph ranging from $(i-k)^{th}$ to $(i+k)^{th}$ sentence index. So, the one query case is segmented into paragraphs that contain the citation marker as $Q = (Q_{p1}, Q_{p2}, ..., Q_{pN})$. The subscript pi denotes the index of a paragraph in a query document, such that $1 \leq i \leq N$ and $i \in \mathbb{N}$, where N is the number of paragraphs in the query document containing a valid citation. These paragraphs include all the relevant information regarding the citation, and we call as the context around the citation. These context-around sentences will be input to the models instead of a whole document and serve as a corpus. For example, in the case of syntactic-based models like BM25, this new corpus will be taken for vectorization, and in the case of semantic-based models like Sentence-BERT and Sent2Vec, generate distributed representations of these sentences. Similarly, the citation corpus is segmented into logical paragraphs represented by $C = (C_{p1}, C_{p2}, ..., C_{pM})$. The subscript pj denotes the index of a paragraph in a citation document, such that $1 \leq j \leq M$ and $j \in \mathbb{N}$, where M is the total number of paragraphs in the citation document.

3.2 Evaluation Metrics

The evaluation metrics of Tasks 1 and 2 are precision, recall, and F-measure. All the metrics are micro-average, which means the evaluation measure is calculated using the results of all queries. Definition of these measures are as follows:

$$\text{Precision} = \frac{\text{No. of correctly retrieved cases (paragraphs) for all queries}}{\text{No. of retrieved cases (paragraphs) for all queries}} \quad (1)$$

$$\text{Recall} = \frac{\text{No. of correctly retrieved cases (paragraphs) for all queries}}{\text{No. of relevant cases (paragraphs) for all queries}} \quad (2)$$

$$\text{F-measure} = \frac{2 \times \text{Precision} \times \text{Recall}}{\text{Precision} + \text{Recall}} \quad (3)$$

4 Our Methods

4.1 BM25

In previous COILEE submissions, many participants such as Kim et al. [2], Ma et al. [3], Rosa et al. [7], Shao et al. [8] and Shao et al. [9] in IJCAI-20 concluded

---

[2] https://spacy.io/usage/linguistic-features#sbd.

that traditional bag-of-words IR models have competitive performances in legal case retrieval tasks. So our first preference is to try the exact matching-based BM25 model [6], which is a probabilistic relevance model based on a bag-of-words approach. The score of a document D given a query Q which contains the words $q_1, ..., q_n$ is given by:

$$\text{score}(D, Q) = \sum_{i=1}^{n} \text{IDF}(q_i) \cdot \frac{f(q_i, D) \cdot (k_1 + 1)}{f(q_i, D) + k_1 \cdot (1 - b + b \cdot \frac{|D|}{\text{avgdl}})} \tag{4}$$

where $f(q_i, D)$ is q_i's term frequency in the document D, $|D|$ is the length of the document D in words, $avgdl$ is the average document length in the text collection from which documents are drawn, and k_1 and b are free parameters.

$$\text{IDF}(q_i) = ln\left(\frac{N - n(q_i) + 0.5}{n(q_i) + 0.5} + 1\right) \tag{5}$$

where N is the total number of documents in the collection, and $n(q_i)$ is the number of documents containing q_i[3].

We tried BM25 using Rank-BM25 library[4], where the algorithms are taken from the paper Trotman et al. [10]. Although we are not getting good results, we tried to implement Okapi BM25 with sklearn's TfidfVectorizer[5] which converts a collection of raw documents to a matrix of TF-IDF features. TfidfVectorizer has valuable features; some important feature descriptions are:

- **stop_words:** Either we can pass string 'english' or a list containing stop words, all of which will be removed from the resulting tokens.
- **ngram_range:** The lower and upper boundary of the range of n-values for different n-grams to be extracted. For example, an ngram_range of (1, 1) means only unigrams, and (1, 2) means unigrams and bigrams.
- **max_df:** While building the vocabulary, ignore terms with a document frequency strictly higher than the given threshold (corpus-specific stop words). The range is [0.0, 1.0].
- **min_df:** While building the vocabulary, ignore terms with a document frequency strictly lower than the given threshold. This value is also called a cut-off in the literature. The range is [0.0, 1.0].
- **norm:** Each output row will have a unit norm, either:
  - 'l2': The sum of squares of vector elements is 1. The cosine similarity between two vectors is their dot product when the l2 norm has been applied.
  - 'l1': Sum of absolute values of vector elements is 1.

These features are beneficial for BM25 to extract better features, and even we can restrain these features. Our results depict that after employing TfidfVectorizer, BM25 performed much better.

---

[3] https://en.wikipedia.org/wiki/Okapi_BM25.
[4] https://github.com/dorianbrown/rank_bm25.
[5] https://scikit-learn.org/stable/modules/generated/sklearn.feature_extraction.text.TfidfVectorizer.html.

4.2 Sent2Vec

Sent2Vec is an Unsupervised Learning of Sentence Embedding or distributed representations of sentences using Compositional N-Gram Features. It can be considered an extension of word2vec (CBOW) to sentences. Sentence embedding is the average of the source word embeddings of its constituent words. We generate features from the pre-trained model "sent2vec_wiki_bigrams" from Sent2vec[6] library, and paper Pagliardini et al. [4], which is trained on the English Wikipedia dataset, and embedding dimensions are 700.

We used hierarchical matching to find the document in the candidate dataset that was the most relevant to the query cases. First, we try to find the most relevant paragraph in the candidate document's paragraph, then find the most relevant candidate document. Each relevant paragraph (context-around sentences) of the query case Q and candidate document C is denoted as Q_{pi} and C_{pj} such that $Q = (Q_{p1}, Q_{p2}, ..., Q_{pN})$ and $C = (C_{p1}, C_{p2}, ..., C_{pM})$. Here N and M denote the total number of relevant paragraphs in Q and the total number of paragraphs in C, respectively. For each paragraph in Q and C, a paragraph pair (Q_{pi}, C_{pj}) is constructed, where $1 \leq i \leq N$, $1 \leq j \leq M$, $i, j \in \mathbb{N}$ and given as the input to the model to get the dense representations of the paragraphs.

That way, we can get an interactive table of paragraphs that maintains the semantic relationship between the query paragraph Q_{pi} and the candidate paragraph C_{pj}. For each paragraph of the query, we capture the most vital matching score with the candidate document using cosine-similarity[7] with max-pool strategy. Hence we get a sequence of vectors, denoted as $S_{Q_iC_j} = (S_{QpiCp1}, S_{QpiCp2}, ..., S_{QpiCpN})$. As shown in Eq. 6, each component S_{Q_iC} corresponds to the aggregate of the interactions of all of the paragraphs in the candidate document corresponding to the ith query paragraph.

$$S_{Q_iC} = MaxPool((Q_{pi}, C_{p1}), (Q_{pi}, C_{p2}), ...(Q_{pi}, C_{pM})), S_{Q_iC} \in \mathbb{R} \qquad (6)$$

Finally, we used the max-pooling strategy again between query and candidate cases to get the most similar document.

$$S_{QC} = MaxPool((Q_1, C_1), (Q_2, C_2), ...(Q_N, C_M)), S_{QC} \in \mathbb{R} \qquad (7)$$

Since case law references can be as small as one or two paragraphs, the max-pooling strategy gives the best possible score for a query-candidate case pair over alternative strategies like average-pooling.

4.3 Sentence-BERT

Since we need sentence/paragraph representations, instead of using any transformer and generating sentence embedding using a pooling strategy, it will be more suitable to directly use a model to derive semantically meaningful

---

[6] https://github.com/epfml/sent2vec.
[7] https://scikit-learn.org/stable/modules/generated/sklearn.metrics.pairwise.cosine_similarity.html.

representations for sentences. We use the Sentence-BERT[8] framework based on the paper [5], which provides an easy method to compute dense vector representations for sentences and paragraphs. This model is based on transformer networks like BERT/RoBERTa, but this modification of the pre-trained BERT network uses siamese and triplet network structures to derive semantically meaningful sentence embeddings. We generate dense vectors from the pre-trained model "all-mpnet-base-v2" from Sentence-BERT[9] library, which is trained on a large and diverse dataset of over 1 billion training pairs, max sequence length 384, mean-pooling, and generates 768 dimensions. The max-pooling strategy used in Sect. 4.2 is also followed for this approach. To find the most similar paragraphs between query and candidate cases in a dataset, we compared using cosine-similarity using the max-pool strategy. Finally, we used the max-pooling strategy between query and candidate cases to get the most similar document.

4.4   Reduced-Space

We use a two-step matching approach to find the document in the candidate dataset that is most relevant to the query cases. In Stage 1, we select the top 100 candidates from the initial candidate corpus with respect to the query case Q according to BM25 scores. In Stage 2, we compare the paragraphs of query and output of top-100 candidate cases by BM25 as mentioned in Sect. 4.2, and then get the most relevant candidate document.

As illustrated in Fig. 1, the query corpus comprises of paragraphs; depicted by $Q = (Q_{p1}, Q_{p2}, ..., Q_{pN})$; by extracting sentences containing the "FRAGMENT_SUPPRESSED" marker. The subscript pi denotes the index of a paragraph in a query document, such that $1 \leq i \leq N$ where N is the number of paragraphs in the query document containing a valid citation. Upon assigning the index i to a sentence which contains the citation marker, a window of k sentences around the sentence results in a paragraph ranging from $(i - k)^{th}$ to $(i + k)^{th}$ sentence index. Similarly, the citation corpus consists of segmented logical paragraphs represented by $C = (C_{p1}, C_{p2}, ..., C_{pM})$. The subscript pj denotes the index of a paragraph in a citation document, such that $1 \leq j \leq M$ where M is the total number of paragraphs in the citation document. In total, we obtain $N \cdot M$ pairs of paragraphs.

Further, we used a lexical model to calculate the similarity between a given query and the entire case law corpus on paragraph-wise segmented documents. We limit the search space from 3531 to 100 candidate cases by picking the top 100 cases with the highest BM25 scores for a given query. After reducing the search space to 100 documents, we want to extract the semantic relationship between the query and candidate paragraphs pairs, e.g., $(Q_{pi}; C_{pj})$. To obtain this relationship score, we use the pre-trained model Sentence-BERT and Sent2vec. To find the most similar paragraphs between query and candidate cases in a dataset, we compared using cosine-similarity using the max-pool strategy. Finally, we

---

[8] https://www.sbert.net/.
[9] https://www.sbert.net/docs/pretrained_models.html.

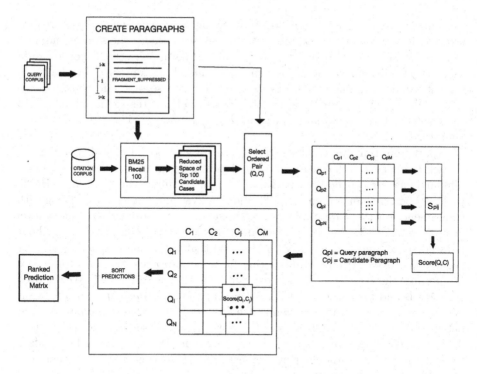

Fig. 1. An illustration of Reduced-Space Architecture.

used the max-pooling strategy between query and candidate cases to get the most similar document. Again, the max-pooling strategy is identical to the approach used in Sect. 4.2.

4.5 Reasons for Max-Pooling

The relevant candidate documents carry essential information related to the query case, but the amount of information is often disputable. There are many candidate cases wherein only one or two paragraphs' worth of relevant information is present in the context of the query case. For such documents, taking alternative pooling strategies such as average pooling can result in a decreased similarity score. With a decrease in the score, the model can find it difficult to identify relevant candidate cases from cases containing general information related to case laws. We consider a 2D max-pooling strategy that allows the model to extract the most similar documents for a given query case to solve this issue.

5 Results and Analysis

5.1 Task-1

We submitted three official runs in Table 2, run-1 is BM25, in a cascaded manner reduced space after using BM25 Recall@100, run-2 is pre-trained Sentence-BERT, and run-3 is pre-trained Sent2vec. All these official runs have done experiments on the paragraph level comparison, and every query case predicts a top-5 citation for both training and test dataset because the average number of relevant cases is approximately 5 in training data. We get the top score in using the traditional model BM25 for exact matching; on the other hand, in semantic understanding models, Sentence-BERT gets second, and Sent2vec gets third. Our team ("nigam") ranked 5th among all the teams in Tasks 1, and the results indicate that the traditional retrieval model BM25 still outperforms neural network-based models.

Apart from that, we tried several experiments without reduced space means the search space was the entire citation corpus in Sent2vec and Sentence-BERT. Similar behavior can be seen in Table 3 for the training dataset, where BM25 performs better than Sentence-BERT and Sent2vec in reduced space. Along with experiments on the paragraph level comparison, we also tried document level comparison, but they did not give good results. We even included results without reduced space, and it can easily be observed that the reduced space results are slightly improved. Training and testing for every query case predict top-5 case law because the average number of relevant cases is approximately 5. We removed stop-words and experimented with a range of values in max_df, min_df, b, $k1$, and $ngram\_range$ parameters while keeping other hyperparameters with their default values. We achieved the best F1 Score under this setting, i.e., $\{max\_df = 0.90, min\_df = 1, b = 0.99, k1 = 1.6, ngram\_range = (2, 6)\}$. The default values worked the best for other hyperparameters, and experimenting with them did not add value to the result.

5.2   Task-2

We submitted two official runs in Table 4; both runs are based on the BM25 model. Run-1 uses only entailed fragment text as a query, and run-2 uses the filtered base case such that search entailed fragment text into the base case then input to the model as searched results along with previous and following sentences to capture the other relevant information. Every query case predicts one case law paragraph because the average number of relevant paragraphs is approximately 1.14 in the training dataset. Our team ("nigam") ranked 5th among all the teams in Tasks 2, and the results indicate that using only fragment text as the query will give better scores. Although, we got the highest Recall score among all participants.

Similar behaviour can be seen in Table 5 for the training dataset, where BM25 performs better when only fragment text as the query and outputs only a single paragraph. Apart from that, we also tried two paragraphs prediction for every query; indeed, that gives a better recall value, but on the other hand, precision values drop significantly. We also tried experiments where along with fragment text, we retrieved preceding and succeeding sentences from the base case after matching fragment text to capture the other relevant information. For example, $[-i, +j]$ means previous i and following j sentences from the matched fragment sentences. However, the results show that results drop as we include the other information. We kept stop-words and experimented with a range of values in

Table 2. Results on the test set of Task 1

Team	F1 Score	Precision	Recall
UA	0.3715	0.4111	0.3389
UA	0.371	0.4967	0.2961
siat	0.3691	0.3005	0.4782
siat	0.368	0.3026	0.4695
UA	0.3559	0.363	0.3492
siat	0.2964	0.2522	0.3595
LeiBi	0.2923	0.3	0.285
LeiBi	0.2917	0.2687	0.3191
JNLP	0.2813	0.3211	0.2502
nigam	**0.2809**	**0.2587**	**0.3072**
JNLP	0.2781	0.3144	0.2494
DSSR	0.2657	0.2447	0.2906
JNLP	0.2639	0.2446	0.2866
DSSR	0.2461	0.2267	0.2692
TUWBR	0.2367	0.1895	0.3151
LeiBi	0.2306	0.2367	0.2249
TUWBR	0.2206	0.1683	0.3199
nigam	**0.1542**	**0.142**	**0.1686**
nigam	**0.1484**	**0.1367**	**0.1623**
DSSR	0.1317	0.1213	0.1441

max_df, min_df, b, $k1$, and $ngram\_range$ parameters while keeping other hyper-parameters with their default values. We achieved the best F1 Score under this setting, i.e. $\{max\_df = 0.65, min\_df = 1, b = 0.7, k1 = 1.6, ngram\_range = (1, 1)\}$. The default values worked the best for other hyperparameters, and experimenting with them did not add value to the result. One thing that can be noticed here is that uni-gram works better because, in Task-2, the length of entailed fragment text is small compared to the query case in Task-1.

Table 3. Task 1 results in the training set. Every query case predicts top-5 case law because the average number of relevant cases is approximately 5. We remove stopwords, max_df = 0.90, min_df = 1, b = 0.99, k1 = 1.6, ngram_range = (2, 6) in BM25. Moreover, other parameters are set to default for all experiments.

Model	F1 Score	Precision	Recall
BM25	**0.1957**	**0.1895**	**0.2023**
Sent2vec	0.0812	0.0786	0.0839
SBERT	0.0844	0.0817	0.0873
BM25 + Sent2vec (Reduced Space)	0.1080	0.0961	0.1234
BM25 + SBERT (Reduced Space)	0.1017	0.0984	0.1051

Table 4. Results on the test set of Task 2

Team	F1 Score	Precision	Recall
NM	0.6783	0.6964	0.661
NM	0.6757	0.7212	0.6356
JNLP	0.6694	0.6532	0.6864
JNLP	0.6612	0.6452	0.678
jljy	0.6514	0.71	0.6017
jljy	0.6514	0.71	0.6017
JNLP	0.6452	0.6154	0.678
jljy	0.633	0.69	0.5847
NM	0.6325	0.6379	0.6271
UA	0.5446	0.6105	0.4915
UA	0.5363	0.7869	0.4068
UA	0.4121	0.3049	0.6356
nigam	**0.3204**	**0.198**	**0.839**
nigam	**0.2104**	**0.13**	**0.5508**

Table 5. Task 2 results in the training set. Every query case predicts either 1 or 2 case law paragraphs because the average number of relevant paragraphs is approximately 1.14. We kept stop-words, max_df = 0.65, min_df = 1, b = 0.7, k1 = 1.6, ngram_range = (1,1). Moreover, other parameters are set to default for all experiments in BM25. Query cases are input such that either only entailed fragment text or search that text into the base case with previous and following sentences.

Query case Input	# Prediction per query	F1 Score	Precision	Recall
consider only Entailed Fragment text	1	**0.6228**	**0.6667**	**0.5843**
	2	0.5106	0.4010	0.7028
using base case [−1, +1]	1	0.4359	0.4667	0.4090
	2	0.4172	0.3276	0.5743
using base case [−1, +2]	1	0.4110	0.4400	0.3856
	2	0.3857	0.3029	0.5309
using base case [−1,+3]	1	0.3790	0.4057	0.3556
	2	0.3663	0.2876	0.5042
using base case [−2, +3]	1	0.3594	0.3848	0.3372
	2	0.3469	0.2724	0.4775
using base case [−3, +3]	1	0.3488	0.3733	0.3272
	2	0.3457	0.2714	0.4758

6   Conclusions

We participated at COLIEE 2022 in Task 1 and Task 2, which allowed exploring information retrieval challenges in the legal case law retrieval and legal entailment. Our main objective was to combine traditional lexical retrieval models BM25 with dense passage retrieval models Sentence-BERT and Sent2vec for re-ranking the results. We show that the paragraph-level retrieval in the first stage outperforms the document-level retrieval. Also, overall ranking after combining lexical and semantic models improves the ranking of dense passage retrieval models alone for task-1. Although usually, neural network-based models perform best in the NLP tasks, especially transformers. Nevertheless, our results and previous COLIEE participants [7] show that many pre-trained models can perform unsatisfactorily in a specialized domain like legal information extraction; traditional lexical retrieval models often outperform. In order to achieve improvements in performance, neural network-based models need appropriate training and fine-tuning on domain-specific data.

Furthermore, in task-2, using only fragment text as the query will give better scores, whereas accommodating other information from the base case only impairs the accuracy. Since we got the highest Recall score among all participants, we should also try the reduced space approach. In the future, we plan to investigate dense retrieval models domain-specific contextualized language models like LegalBERT [1] and graph neural networks [11].

References

1. Chalkidis, I., Fergadiotis, M., Malakasiotis, P., Aletras, N., Androutsopoulos, I.: LEGAL-BERT: the muppets straight out of law school. In: Findings of the Association for Computational Linguistics: EMNLP 2020, pp. 2898–2904. Association for Computational Linguistics (2020). https://doi.org/10.18653/v1/2020.findings-emnlp.261, https://aclanthology.org/2020.findings-emnlp.261
2. Kim, M.Y., Rabelo, J., Okeke, K., Goebel, R.: Legal information retrieval and entailment based on BM25, transformer and semantic thesaurus methods. Rev. Socionetwork Strat. **16**, 157–174 (2022). https://doi.org/10.1007/s12626-022-00103-1
3. Ma, Y., Shao, Y., Liu, B., Liu, Y., Zhang, M., Ma, S.: Retrieving legal cases from a large-scale candidate corpus (2021)
4. Pagliardini, M., Gupta, P., Jaggi, M.: Unsupervised learning of sentence embeddings using compositional n-gram features. In: Proceedings of the 2018 Conference of the North American Chapter of the Association for Computational Linguistics: Human Language Technologies, Volume 1 (Long Papers), pp. 528–540. Association for Computational Linguistics, New Orleans (2018). https://doi.org/10.18653/v1/N18-1049, https://aclanthology.org/N18-1049
5. Reimers, N., Gurevych, I.: Sentence-BERT: sentence embeddings using Siamese BERT-networks. In: Proceedings of the 2019 Conference on Empirical Methods in Natural Language Processing and the 9th International Joint Conference on Natural Language Processing (EMNLP-IJCNLP), pp. 3982–3992. Association for Computational Linguistics, Hong Kong (2019). https://doi.org/10.18653/v1/D19-1410, https://aclanthology.org/D19-1410

6. Robertson, S.E., Walker, S., Jones, S., Hancock-Beaulieu, M.M., Gatford, M., et al.: Okapi at trec-3. NIST SPECIAL PUBLICATION SP, vol. 109, p. 109 (1995)
7. Rosa, G.M., Rodrigues, R.C., Lotufo, R., Nogueira, R.: Yes, BM25 is a strong baseline for legal case retrieval. arXiv preprint arXiv:2105.05686 (2021)
8. Shao, Y., Liu, B., Mao, J., Liu, Y., Zhang, M., Ma, S.: Thuir@ coliee-2020: leveraging semantic understanding and exact matching for legal case retrieval and entailment. arXiv preprint arXiv:2012.13102 (2020)
9. Shao, Y., et al.: BERT-PLI: modeling paragraph-level interactions for legal case retrieval. In: IJCAI, pp. 3501–3507 (2020)
10. Trotman, A., Puurula, A., Burgess, B.: Improvements to BM25 and language models examined. In: Proceedings of the 2014 Australasian Document Computing Symposium, pp. 58–65 (2014)
11. Yang, J., Ma, W., Zhang, M., Zhou, X., Liu, Y., Ma, S.: LegalGNN: legal information enhanced graph neural network for recommendation. ACM Trans. Inf. Syst. (TOIS) 40(2), 1–29 (2021)

HUKB at the COLIEE 2022 Statute Law Task

Masaharu Yoshioka[1,2]([envelope]), Youta Suzuki[2], and Yasuhiro Aoki[2]

[1] Faculty of Information Science and Technology, Hokkaido University,
N14 W9, Kita-ku, Sapporo-shi, Hokkaido, Japan
`yoshioka@ist.hokudai.ac.jp`

[2] Graduate School of Information Science and Technology, Hokkaido University, N14
W9, Kita-ku, Sapporo-shi, Hokkaido, Japan
`suzuki@eis.hokudai.ac.jp, aoki.yasuhiro.k4@elms.hokudai.ac.jp`

Abstract. HUKB group is participating in the Statute Law task (Tasks
3 and 4) in COLIEE 2022. For Task 3, we propose a method that utilizes three different IR systems. Our new proposed IR system utilizes the
similarity of descriptions of judicial decisions between questions and articles. In addition to this new IR system, we also use an ordinal keyword-
based IR system (BM25) and the BERT-based IR system proposed in
COLIEE 2020. Because of the different characteristics of these systems,
ensembled results have better recall without losing too much precision.
Our system, which ensembles the results of our new proposed IR and
keyword-based IR system, achieves the best performance for Task 3. For
Task 4, we extend our previous BERT-based entailment system (the best
performance system of COLIEE 2021) by using a new data augmentation method and a method to select relevant parts from the articles. We
discuss the characteristics of the system using the submitted results.

Keywords: Legal Information Retrieval · Query Analysis · Deep
Neural Network · Keyword-based IR

1 Introduction

The competition on Legal Information Extraction/Entailment (COLIEE) [2,3,
5,7,8,11] serves as a forum to discuss issues related to legal information retrieval
(IR) and entailment. There are two types of tasks in COLIEE 2022. One is case
law tasks (Tasks 1 and 2), and the other is statute law tasks (Tasks 3 and 4).
This year, we participate in the latter two tasks: the statute law retrieval task
(Task 3) and the legal textual entailment task (Task 4).

For Task 3, we proposed a new statute law retrieval system that considers the
similarity of judicial decisions described in the questions and articles. Because
this task is a preprocess for Task 4 to judge whether the question statement is
true or not, the existence of the judicial decision discussed in the question is an
important factor to find out relevant articles. For Task 4, we have extended our

Y. Takama et al. (Eds.): JSAI-isAI 2022 Workshop, LNAI 13859, pp. 109–124, 2023.
https://doi.org/10.1007/978-3-031-29168-5_8

previous system for the COLIEE 2021 [6] (the best performance system for the COLIEE 2021) by introducing a new data augmentation method and a method to select relevant parts of articles from all articles.

In this paper, we introduce our methods for Tasks 3 and 4 in detail and discuss the characteristics of the system using the evaluation results of the submitted runs.

2   Tools and Settings

In this section, we introduce tools and settings used for Tasks 3 and 4. For Task 3, we use an ordinal keyword-based IR system and a BERT-based IR system. For Task 4, we use a BERT-based system that classifies whether the given relevant article pair entails a question or not. In this year, we use almost the same setting for BERT as that used in Tasks 3 and 4.

2.1   Keyword-Based IR System

Because queries about the statute law retrieval task (Task 3) are extracted from the Japanese Bar exam, the queries contain technical terms in the law domain. As a result, the keyword-based system that utilizes such technical terms works well for the questions. However, there are the following two problems in the keyword-based IR system.

(1) Missing judicial decision description
   The most important point for discussing the entailment is describing judicial decisions. However, previous keyword-based systems did not pay any attention to this part, and there are cases where the system returns articles that share many keywords but not judicial decisions.
(2) Difficulty in handling a reference to other articles
   Many articles refer to other articles in civil law. The most significant ones are "*mutatis mutandis*". It is difficult to find the pairs of such articles by using a simple keyword-based IR system.

To tackle this problem, we propose a method to reconstruct the civil law articles database by considering judicial decisions and references.

For the item (1), we select judicial decision parts from the articles and use this text to determine the similarity between the judicial decision parts of the questions. For the articles that have multiple judicial decisions, we also make the subarticle database split the articles to represent each judicial decision.

The general methods to make such texts are as follows.

(A) Split the articles by using items. In most cases, when there are two or more sentences in the article, we split the text into subarticles by considering the item, sentence, and existence of judicial decisions. For the case shown in Fig. 1, underlined text in the sentences refers to judicial decision parts. There are three sentences for the judicial decision, and we split this article into three subarticles.

(B) To make the article database, we used judicial decisions for all items as one for the article. For the article database, all text for the article was used for the text part of the article, and all judicial parts were used for the judicial decision part of the article. For the Fig. 1 case, text shown in the upper part of the figure except for the number of articles was used as the text part, and judicial parts (underlined text) were used for the judicial decision part.

(C) We also made a subarticle database. For the data, one subarticle text has one corresponding judicial decision part (e.g., subarticle 299-(2)A used the judicial decision part of 299-(2)A in Fig. 1). However, for the text part, a concatenation of previous text (including a heading title of the article) was used for the text part because important keywords were only used for the former part of the text.

For item (2), we made new text by combining the information of the original article with that of a refereed article(s).

Figure 2 shows an example of the rewriting process for *"mutatis mutandis"*. In this case, referred article 299 was one for the 留置権 ("right of retention"), and article 350 explains *"mutatis mutandis"* for 質件 ("right of pledges"). Therefore, combined articles use 質 ("pledges") instead of 留置 ("retention").

We used Elasticsearch[1] with basic BM25 [9] settings with kuro-moji_tokenizer[2] as an IR engine. Elasticsearch can use structured queries and multiple indexes for calculating similarity. We used this function for using two indexes; one was for all text, and the other was for the judicial decision part.

For the article and subarticle database, we added the title of the article (e.g., for article 299 we use (留置権者による費用の償還請求) "(Demands for Reimbursement of Expenses by Holders of Rights of Retention)" and for 350+299, we used the title of article 350 (留置権及び先取特権の規定の準用) "(Mutatis Mutandis Application of Provisions on Rights of Retention and Statutory Liens)") for the text of the articles. We also added the judicial decision part text for the index of judicial decisions.

When making a query, we automatically extracted a judicial decision part (details of the method are explained in the following paragraphs) from the question and calculated a similarity score using two indexes. One score was calculated based on the similarity between the whole question text and the article text. The other score was calculated based on the judicial decision part of the article and one of the questions extracted automatically. Those two scores were added for the final similarity score between the question and the article. We extracted judicial decision parts based on the method proposed in [12]. This method analyzes the dependency structure of the question using CaboCha [4] and removes condition parts using clue keywords such as "〜すれば" (if ...), "〜としても" (in case of), "〜場合," (case), "〜限る、" (limited to). However, the previous method makes the judicial decision part text longer, and it may not work well for the preliminary experiment. We selected phrases from the root verb (or root adjective) by

---

[1] https://www.elastic.co/.

[2] https://www.elastic.co/guide/en/elasticsearch/plugins/current/analysis-kuromoji-tokenizer.html.

Japanese:	English:
（留置権者による費用の償還請求） 第二百九十九条　1 <u>留置権者は、</u>留置物について必要費を支出したときは、<u>所有者にその償</u><u>還をさせることができる。</u> 2 留置権者は、留置物について有益費を支出したときは、これによる価格の増加が現存する場合に限り、所有者の選択に従い、<u>その支出した金額</u><u>又は増価額を償還させること</u><u>ができる。</u>ただし、<u>裁判所は、</u>所有者の請求により、<u>その償</u><u>還について相当の期限を許与</u><u>することができる。</u>	(Demands for Reimbursement of Expenses by Holders of Rights of Retention) Article 299 (1) If the holder of a right of retention incurs necessary expenses with respect to the thing retained, that <u>holder</u><u>may have the owner reimburse the same.</u> (2) If the <u>holder of a right of retention</u><u>incurs beneficial expenses</u> with respect to the thing retained, <u>to the extent that</u><u>there is currently an increase in value as</u><u>a result of the same,</u> that holder may have the expenses incurred or the increase in value reimbursed at the owner's choice; provided, however, that <u>the court may,</u> at the request of the owner, <u>grant a</u><u>reasonable period of time for the</u><u>reimbursement of the same</u>.
Japanese: （留置権者による費用の償還請求） • **299-(1)** <u>留置権者は、留</u>置物について必要費を支出したときは、<u>所有者にその</u><u>償還をさせることができる。</u> • **299-(2)A** <u>留置権者は、</u>留置物について有益費を支出したときは、これによる価格の増加が現存する場合に限り、所有者の選択に従い、<u>その支出した金額又は</u><u>増価額を償還させることが</u><u>できる。</u> • **299-(2)B** ただし、<u>裁判</u><u>所は、所有者の請求により、</u><u>その償還について相当の期</u><u>限を許与することができる。</u>	English: (Demands for Reimbursement of Expenses by Holders of Rights of Retention) • 299-(1) If the holder of a right of retention incurs necessary expenses with respect to the thing retained, that <u>holder may have the owner reimburse</u><u>the same.</u> • 299-(2)A If the <u>holder of a right of</u><u>retention incurs beneficial expenses</u> with respect to the thing retained, <u>to the</u><u>extent that there is currently an</u><u>increase in value as a result of the same,</u> that holder may have the expenses incurred or the increase in value reimbursed at the owner's choice; • 299-2(B)provided, however, that <u>the court</u><u>may</u>, at the request of the owner, <u>grant a</u><u>reasonable period of time for the</u><u>reimbursement of the same.</u>

Fig. 1. (Sub)articles database comprising judicial decisions

considering stop words such as "できる", "する", "ある" for verbs and "もの", "こと" "ため" for nouns. For each dependency branch of the root, two connected chunks were used for the judicial decision. If there is no dependency branch of the root (mostly caused by the stop word and/or removing condition parts), two connected chunks just before the root were used for the judicial decision parts.

```
Japanese:
（留置権及び先取特権の規定の
準用）
第三百五十条 第二百九十六条か
ら第三百条まで及び第三百四条
の規定は、質権について準用す
る。
（留置権者による費用の償還請
求）
第二百九十九条 留置権者は、留
置物について必要費を支出した
ときは、所有者にその償還をさ
せることができる。
             ↓
（留置権及び先取特権の規定の
準用）（留置権者による費用の
償還請求）
350+299-(1) 質権者は、質物
について必要費を支出したとき
は、所有者にその償還をさせる
ことができる。
```

```
English:
(Mutatis Mutandis Application of Provisions
on Rights of Retention and Statutory Liens)
Article 350 The provisions of Articles 296
through 300 and those of Article 304 apply
mutatis mutandis to pledges.
(Demands for Reimbursement of Expenses by
Holders of Rights of Retention)
Article 299 (1) If the holder of a right of
retention incurs necessary expenses with
respect to the thing retained, that holder
may have the owner reimburse the same.
             ↓
(Mutatis Mutandis Application of Provisions
on Rights of Retention and Statutory Liens)
(Demands for Reimbursement of Expenses by
Holders of Rights of Retention)
350+299-(1) If the holder of a right of
pledges incurs necessary expenses with
respect to the pledges, that holder may
have the owner reimburse the same.
```

Fig. 2. Making combined articles using reference information

Figure 3 shows an example of this extraction process.

By using this method, the importance of the similarity between judicial decision parts is emphasized.

The final score of the article ($MergeScore_{article}$) is just the simple summation of two IR system scores where $DocumentScore_{article}$ is a score of the article calculated based on the similarity between the whole article and whole query, and $DecisionScore_{article}$ is a score of the article calculated based on the similarity between the decision part of the article and one of the queries.

$$MergeScore_{article} = DocumentScore_{article} + DecisionScore_{article} \quad (1)$$

However, based on the results of preliminary experiments, we found that there are several cases where the system fails to extract appropriate judicial decision parts. In such cases, articles that use similar keywords of the wrongly extracted judicial decision may have larger score, even though the article is not relevant. In addition, there are cases requiring multiple articles with different characteristics; one is for judicial decisions, and another is for analyzing the condition part. For such questions, emphasis on the judicial decision fails to find an article for the condition part. Therefore, we also made a database without judicial decisions. For the database, we used original article text for the text part of the article. We can use our new text for the text part, but preliminary experiments show that IR results with an original text database can find more complementary answers (relevant answers that cannot be found by our proposed IR system with judicial decision information). This may be caused by the side effect of rewriting the article text.

Question:
強迫による意思表示の取消しは、善意でかつ過失がない第三者に対抗することがで
きない。
If the manifestation of intention of a person is held void on
the ground that it does not reflect that person's true
intention, such nullity may be duly asserted against a third
party in good faith acting with negligence.

↓
Dependency Analysis
強迫に–D
よる意思表示の–––D
取消しは、–D
善意でかつ過失がない第三者に対抗する–D
ことができない。

↓
Extraction of judicial decision part
よる意思表示の–––D
取消しは、–D
善意でかつ過失がない第三者に対抗する

↓
Final text ↓
よる意思表示の取消しは、善意でかつ過失がない第三者に対抗する
the manifestation of intention of a person is held void
against a third party in good faith acting with negligence.

Fig. 3. Extraction of judicial decision parts from the question

In addition to finding other types of complementary answers, we also used a BERT-based IR system introduced in the previous COLIEE [13]. Details of the system are discussed in the next section.

To generate final retrieved results, it is necessary to decompose combined articles into original articles. For the postprocess, we replaced the result of combined articles with original ones. However, such results may contain redundant results. For such redundant cases, we selected the highest ranked one for the rank of the article. This is also true for the subarticle retrieved results.

2.2 BERT-Based IR and Entailment System

Bidirectional Encoder Representations from Transformers(BERT) [1] is a deep neural network-based natural language processing (NLP) tool that can be applied to a variety of NLP tasks including IR and entailment. One of the characteristics of the BERT is the usage of a pretrained model trained by the general semantic understanding task. By using this model trained by a large volume of texts, we can make a task-specific model by using a relatively small amount of data for training (fine-tuning) to achieve better performance. Recently, the BERT-based system was used for COLIEE and achieved the best results for

COLIEE 2021 Task 4 [6]. For Task 3, ordinal IR models such as BM25 and BERT-based models have similar performance with different characteristics.

We introduce a BERT-based IR system and entailment system for COLIEE 2022.

BERT-Based IR System. For the IR task, the BERT model was fine-tuned as a binary classification task that classifies whether the pair of query and article are relevant or not [10]. Based on the trained model, the system can calculate a score for all documents for a given question. This score was used to rank the documents.

This year's system uses BERT-Japanese[3] for the BERT-based model instead of the BERT model provided by Kyoto University[4].

To make the training data, we randomly selected 50 negative examples from the article dataset for each query, and we also used (oversampled) relevant documents five times to balance the positive and negative examples.

For the target document database, we used both the article dataset and the subarticle database. All articles and subarticles are sorted by the similarity score and redundant articles are removed by using the same method for the keyword-based IR results.

We made three fine-tuning models and returned all top-ranked documents using the given query.

BERT-based Entailment System. For the entailment task, the BERT model was fine-tuned as a binary classification task that classifies the pair of questions and articles to check whether the articles entail the question. We used almost the same settings for the previous COLIEE [6].

One of the characteristics of [6] is data augmentation using article texts and ensembling results of BERT systems trained with different training sets.

The previous augmentation method decomposes all articles into smaller sentences for judicial decision. For example, "第七百八条 不法な原因のために給付をした者は、その給付したものの返還を請求することができない。ただし、不法な原因が受益者についてのみ存したときは、この限りでない。" ("Article 708 A person that has paid money or delivered thing for an obligation for an illegal cause may not demand the return of the money paid or thing delivered; provided, however, that this does not apply if the illegal cause existed solely in relation to the Beneficiary.") has two sentences. Because it is difficult to understand the meaning of the second sentence by itself, we rewrote the text as "不法な原因のために給付をした者は、その給付したものの返還を請求することができる。" ("If the illegal cause existed solely in relation to the Beneficiary, A person that has

---

[3] https://github.com/cl-tohoku/bert-japanesewithmodel   https://huggingface.co/cl-tohoku/bert-base-japanese-whole-word-masking.

[4] https://nlp.ist.i.kyoto-u.ac.jp/index.php?ku_bert_japanese   日本語   Pretrained モデル (http://nlp.ist.i.kyoto-u.ac.jp/index.php?BERT%E6%97%A5%E6%9C%AC%E8%AA%9EPretrained%E3%83%A2%E3%83%87%E3%83%AB).

paid money or delivered thing for an obligation for an illegal cause may demand the return of the money paid or thing delivered"). After making sentences, a pair of the same sentence is a positive example and a pair of an original sentence and a flipped sentence generated by adding negation or removing negation is a negative example. We suppose these augmentation data are helpful in training the model to handle logical mismatch.

Utilization of these augmented data significantly improves the performance of the entailment system. However, based on the evaluation of different years' test data provided by COLIEE organizers, this BERT model has inconsistent performance for the different datasets (the best performance system for year X does not mean good performance for another year). Therefore, [6] proposed an ensemble approach to use outputs of multiple BERT models trained by different training datasets.

This method utilizes three types of data: overall training data, validation data for ensemble, and test data. Overall training data are randomly split into training and validation data for the BERT model training. For this year's task, we generated 20 models randomly by splitting overall data into training data (90%) and validation data (10%).

Validation data for the ensemble are used for selecting an appropriate ensemble model set as a combination of trained BERT models. Our ensemble models use the output of the entailment system that corresponds to a probability value for the "Yes" case. The original BERT system returns "Yes" if the value is larger than 0.5. We used the average of this probability value for making ensemble results instead of majority voting because we would like to emphasize the output with a larger higher confidence value for "Yes" or a smaller value for "No".

Ensembled models are selected by using the entailment performance of the validation data for the ensemble.

This year we have proposed the following three methods to extend the previous one.

1. Construction of new augmentation data
   Because of the characteristics of the rewriting method used in the previous COLIEE, the system does not have many examples that contain "ただし～この限りでない" ("provided"), because rewritten examples do not contain "ただし～この限りでない" ("provided") for understanding the meaning of this phrase. Therefore, to provide the examples for the phrase "ただし～この限りでない" ("provided"), we propose a new method to make pairs of questions and articles. This method uses original article texts for the article parts. For example, "不法な原因のために給付をした者は、その給付したものの返還を請求することができる。" ("If the illegal cause existed solely in relation to the Beneficiary, A person that has paid money or delivered thing for an obligation for an illegal cause may demand the return of the money paid or thing delivered") and original article text "不法な原因のために給付をした者は、その給付したものの返還を請求することができない。ただし、不法な原因が受益者についてのみ存したときは、この限りでない。" ("A person that has

paid money or delivered thing for an obligation for an illegal cause may not demand the return of the money paid or thing delivered; provided, however, that this does not apply if the illegal cause existed solely in relation to the Beneficiary.") is a positive example.

2. Selection of useful sentences from articles for entailment
There are cases where the system uses (an) article(s) with multiple judicial decisions. In such cases, the length of the article text becomes longer, and BERT cannot handle all text. Therefore, we propose a method to select a useful similar sentence calculated by the similarity score between the question and the sentences. This method also works well to include rewritten articles introduced in the last item. In such a case, it is not necessary to interpret the meaning of " ただし〜この限りでない " ("provided"). The similarity with the sentence of the target article is calculated by using Elasticsearch with a basic BM25 setting. The system selects one sentence with the highest similarity score for each article.

3. Selection of the best ensemble model set using the loss function
The previous system selects the best performance sets by using the accuracy of the validation data for the ensemble. Because this value is a discrete value, there are many tied sets, and it is difficult to select the best one. To solve this problem, we use the loss function to select the best one from the tied sets. The loss function is a simple function defined by Eq. 2, where g_i is a value for representing the correct label for question i ($g_i = 1, 0$ for "Yes" and "No" cases, respectively), and $prob_i$ is a probability value calculated by the system for question i. We select the result with the smallest $loss$ as the best one.

$$loss = \sum_{i=0}^{n} |g_i - prob_i| \tag{2}$$

3   Submitted Runs and Evaluation Results

3.1   Task 3

We submit three runs that combine the output of three different IR systems: keyword-based IR system that uses reconstructed article database (New), keyword-based IR system with original article text (Original), and BERT-based IR system (BERT). The ensemble method of the different models is very simple and just merges all candidates of the models.

We submit the following three results.

HUKB1 Merge results of New, Original, and BERT
HUKB2 Merge results of New and Original
HUKB3 Use New results only

Table 1 shows the evaluation results of our submitted runs and the best runs for each team. HUKB2 achieves the best performance in terms of F2 measure. There are 110 questions and 131 relevant articles.

Table 1. Evaluation results of the submitted runs (Task 3)

ID	F2	Precision	Recall	Returns	Correct
HUKB2	**0.8204**	**0.8180**	0.8405	136	101
HUKB1	0.7908	0.6532	**0.8901**	**223**	**109**
OVGU_run3	0.7790	0.7781	0.8054	161	96
JNLP.longformer	0.7699	0.6865	0.8378	177	101
UA_TFIDF2	0.7638	0.8073	0.7641	115	90
HUKB3	0.7512	0.7890	0.7534	118	90
LLNTU0066cc	0.6416	0.6743	0.6391	113	74

The evaluation results of HUKB3 are not good because this system returns multiple articles only for the combined article cases. This system finds the appropriate results for R03-12-U that have *"mutatis mutandis"* articles. In contrast, there are cases where part of the combined article is relevant, but the other part is not relevant. It may be better to have a mechanism to check whether such a combination is necessary or not.

Comparing the evaluation results of HUKB2 and HUKB3 can be used for discussing the similarity and differences between the new and original databases. Most of the retrieved case results are the same, and only 18 (136–118) articles are newly added as unique findings of the original database. For this test set, 11 (101–90) articles out of 18 are correct. This system significantly improves the performance for two reasons.

One is the case for the side effect of emphasis on judicial decisions. There are cases where the judicial decision does not match the one in the query (mostly for the not entail case). For example, the decision part of R03-05-O is similar to article 152, but the relevant article is article 149. However, the original database can find this article by removing the side effect of the emphasis.

The other is finding complementary articles by using different methods. For example, R03-20-E has two relevant articles: article 470 and article 442. A new database finds article 442, which shares keywords for judicial decisions. The original database found article 470 because it shares many keywords for explaining the situation.

For HUKB1, the system achieves better recall, but the precision is not so good. The BERT IR model can find the relevant article for the case with an anonymized symbol (R03-25-A). However, because of the inconsistent output of the different IR models, the number of returned documents is significantly increased (89 (223–136)). Even though the system found 8 (109–101) unique findings, it degraded the value of precision and caused the lower F2 values.

Based on this evaluation of the results, we found that there are three types of articles from the viewpoint of similarity between the queries and articles.

Simple case: Target question requires only one article that shares many terms. This type of question is easy to retrieve by any system.

Multiple case: Target question requires multiple articles. In such a case, the criteria for selecting these articles may be different. For example, one is the article that explains *"mutatis mutandis"*, and the other is a referred article. For the other case, one is the articles for judicial decision and the other is for analyzing the condition. Therefore, a simple selection of multiple articles based on one similarity measure (e.g., BM25 score for the article database) may not be good enough to find these documents.

Example case: It is necessary to understand the correspondence between the terms used for explaining the case with legal terminologies used in the article.

Our method shows good performance for the *simple* and *multiple cases* (HUKB2). We also found out the BERT-based system may be effective for the *example case* (better recall by HUKB1), but because of the insufficient quality of our system, the overall performance of HUKB1 is not good. For the next step, it is necessary to improve the performance of the BERT-based system for the *example case*.

3.2 Task 4

We submit three runs with different settings.

We submit the following three results. Our baseline system is HUKB3 where BERT models are constructed using the method proposed in [5], and the best ensemble set is selected by using the loss proposed in this paper. HUKB1 uses new augmented data, and HUKB2 uses a method to select useful sentences for each article.

HUKB1 BERT model is trained with the new augmented data.
HUKB2 Select useful sentences by elastic search and use the BERT model for HUKB3.
HUKB3 Baseline method

To make these training data, we split the data by considering the year. When the test data are questions for Year X (e.g., R03), questions for Year X-1 (e.g., R02) are used as an ensemble validation dataset. Documents before Year X-2 (e.g., H18-R01) are randomly split to make the training (90%) and validation (10%) data used for BERT fine-tuning.

Table 2 shows the evaluation results of our submitted runs and the best runs for each team. Our system performance is almost equivalent to the performance of the best team (KIS2). Among three different settings, HUKB1 achieves the best performance.

However, when we check the perforates of other year datasets (Table 3), KIS approach works better for H30, but the HUKB approach works well for the R01 and R02 datasets. This means it is difficult to discuss the superiority of the method from these results.

For the comparison of HUKB1, HUKB2, and HUKB3, it is also difficult to say which method is best. The most critical part of getting better performance

Table 2. Evaluation results of the submitted runs (Task 4)

ID	Correct	Accuracy
KIS2	**74**	**0.6789**
HUKB1	73	0.6697
HUKB2	69	0.6330
HUKB3	69	0.6330
LLNTUdeNgram	66	0.6055
OVGU3	63	0.5780
UA_e	59	0.5413
JNLP1	58	0.5321

is selecting the best ensemble sets. The selection method using loss seems to be good (our system performs 2nd best consistently), but there is no guarantee, as the selected set works best for the test data. Based on the comparison of the performance of the three methods for the better loss (including best), it is difficult to determine which method is the best.

Table 3. Evaluation results of the submitted runs for other years (Task 4)

ID	Accuracy (H30)	Accuracy (R01)	Accuracy (R02)	Macro Average (H30-R02)
KIS2	**0.7000**	**0.6789**	0.5432	0.6407
HUKB1	0.600	0.6577	0.6173	0.625
HUKB2	0.600	0.6667	0.5926	0.6198
HUKB3	0.6286	0.6486	**0.7160**	**0.6644**
LLNTUdeNgram	0.4714	0.5405	0.5802	0.5307
UA_e	0.4571	0.6216	0.5432	0.5406
JNLP1	0.5714	0.5315	0.6173	0.5734

4   Additional Experiments

Based on the evaluation of the submitted runs, utilization of the similarity of descriptions about judicial decisions between questions and articles is effective for Task 3 IR tasks. However, there is no clear discussion about how we merge the score of two IR scores.

So, we modify the Eq. 1 with a new equation that introduces parameter α, which controls the balance between the scores of $DocumentScore_{article}$ and $DecisionScore_{article}$.

$$MergeScore_{article} = DocumentScore_{article} + \alpha DecisionScore_{article} \qquad (3)$$

We experimented by changing the parameter α from 0.1 to 2.0.

Table 4 shows the result of the new IR system with different α sorted by the F2 score of the training data (HUKB3) for $\alpha = 1.0$. From these results, too much emphasis ($\alpha = 2.0$) or too little emphasis ($\alpha = 0.1$) did not work well for training data. However, the performance of $\alpha = 0.1$ is good for the test data. It is difficult to discuss the characteristics of this parameter for the new IR setting only.

Table 5 shows the result of the merged results (original and new) as the same as the setting of HUKB2($\alpha = 1.0$). In this case, the performance of the lower alpha was worse than the others for the training data because of the lower recall. Little emphasis on the judicial decision tends to select the same article that is selected by the original IR system. On the contrary, higher emphasis may select the one that is not selected by the original IR systems. It may improve the recall, but it may cause the precision to deteriorate.

We confirm that merged results (original and new) improve the retrieval performance. It seems that modest α around 1.0 is good for better performance. However, the best parameter may change because of the different characteristics of a query set.

Table 4. Results of using different α values of the new IR system

α or original	Training			Test		
	F2	Precision	Recall	F2	Precision	Recall
1.3	**0.5437**	**0.5755**	**0.5444**	0.7421	0.7798	0.7442
1.0	0.5428	0.5750	0.5429	0.7512	0.7890	0.7534
1.2	0.5426	**0.5755**	0.5427	0.7421	0.7798	0.7442
1.1	0.5411	0.5727	0.5413	0.7421	0.7798	0.7442
0.9	0.5406	0.5722	0.5407	0.7512	0.7890	0.7534
0.5	0.5398	0.5727	0.5390	0.7839	0.8257	0.7855
0.8	0.5391	0.5699	0.5390	0.7512	0.7890	0.7534
0.6	0.5385	0.5710	0.5378	0.7839	0.8257	0.7855
1.4	0.5384	0.5699	0.5389	0.7421	0.7798	0.7442
0.7	0.5375	0.5688	0.5373	0.7747	0.8165	0.7763
0.4	0.5364	0.5693	0.5356	0.7839	0.8257	0.7855
1.5	0.5355	0.5665	0.5361	0.7421	0.7798	0.7442
0.3	0.5353	0.5682	0.5345	0.7839	0.8257	0.7855
1.6	0.5319	0.5626	0.5324	0.7421	0.7798	0.7442
1.8	0.5312	0.5626	0.5312	0.7421	0.7798	0.7442
1.7	0.5300	0.5614	0.5301	0.7421	0.7798	0.7442
0.2	0.5290	0.5620	0.5279	0.7981	0.8440	0.7992
0.1	0.5268	0.5586	0.5259	**0.8058**	**0.8486**	**0.8084**
1.9	0.5246	0.5552	0.5247	0.7399	0.7706	0.7424
2.0	0.5227	0.5524	0.5231	0.7399	0.7706	0.7424
original	0.5439	0.5953	0.5379	0.7974	0.8532	0.7916

Table 5. Results of using different α values for merged results (original +new)

α	Training			Test		
	F2	Precision	Recall	F2	Precision	Recall
1.3	**0.5846**	0.5770	0.6021	0.8127	0.8135	0.8313
1.8	0.5845	0.5710	**0.6038**	0.8116	0.8119	0.8313
1.4	0.5840	0.5744	0.6021	0.8127	0.8135	0.8313
1.6	0.5833	0.5705	0.6027	0.8116	0.8119	0.8313
1.5	0.5831	0.5722	0.6015	0.8116	0.8119	0.8313
1.7	0.5831	0.5705	0.6021	0.8116	0.8119	0.8313
1.2	0.5830	0.5776	0.5993	0.8127	0.8135	0.8313
1.9	0.5821	0.5673	0.6018	0.8156	0.8073	0.8359
2.0	0.5819	0.5660	0.6024	0.8156	0.8073	0.8359
1.1	0.5809	0.5767	0.5968	0.8127	0.8135	0.8313
1.0	0.5806	0.5780	0.5959	0.8204	0.8180	**0.8405**
0.9	0.5775	0.5769	0.5920	0.8163	0.8180	0.8359
0.8	0.5749	0.5759	0.5886	0.8163	0.8180	0.8359
0.7	0.5722	0.5753	0.5852	0.8199	0.8318	0.8359
0.6	0.5707	0.5769	0.5824	0.8214	0.8364	0.8359
0.5	0.5697	**0.5782**	0.5801	0.8214	0.8364	0.8359
0.4	0.5679	0.5770	0.5779	0.8214	0.8364	0.8359
0.3	0.5662	0.5765	0.5756	0.8214	0.8364	0.8359
0.2	0.5635	0.5737	0.5730	**0.8286**	**0.8471**	**0.8405**
0.1	0.5634	0.5716	0.5735	0.8225	**0.8471**	0.8313

5   Summary

In this paper, we introduced our system for participating in Tasks 3 and 4 of
COLIEE 2020. For Task 3, we propose to use a new IR system that utilizes the
similarity of descriptions of judicial decisions between questions and articles. This
IR system can find relevant articles focusing on the similarity of the decision.
Merging the results of the IR system with an ordinal keyword-based IR system
achieves good recall without losing much precision. Merging the results of the
BERT-based IR is good for improving recall but greatly diminishes precision.
Our system using a new IR system with an ordinal keyword-based IR system
achieves the best performance for Task 3. For Task 4, we proposed different
data augmentation methods and preprocess methods to select relevant parts of
articles. Our system generally works well, but it is difficult to say which setting
is the best. Further analysis is necessary to understand the characteristics of the
proposed system.

Acknowledgment. This work was partially supported by JSPS KAKENHI Grant Number 18H0333808.

References

1. Devlin, J., Chang, M.W., Lee, K., Toutanova, K.: BERT: pre-training of deep bidirectional transformers for language understanding. In: Proceedings of the 2019 Conference of the North American Chapter of the Association for Computational Linguistics: Human Language Technologies, Volume 1 (Long and Short Papers), pp. 4171–4186. Association for Computational Linguistics, Minneapolis (2019). https://doi.org/10.18653/v1/N19-1423, https://www.aclweb.org/anthology/N19-1423

2. Kano, Y., Kim, M.Y., Goebel, R., Satoh, K.: Overview of COLIEE 2017. In: Satoh, K., Kim, M.Y., Kano, Y., Goebel, R., Oliveira, T. (eds.) COLIEE 2017. 4th Competition on Legal Information Extraction and Entailment. EPiC Series in Computing, vol. 47, pp. 1–8. EasyChair (2017)

3. Kim, M.Y., Goebel, R., Kano, Y., Satoh, K.: COLIEE-2016: evaluation of the competition on legal information extraction and entailment. In: The Proceedings of the 10th International Workshop on Juris-Informatics (JURISIN2016) (2016). paper 11

4. Kudo, T., Matsumoto, Y.: Japanese dependency analysis using cascaded chunking. In: CoNLL 2002: Proceedings of the 6th Conference on Natural Language Learning 2002 (COLING 2002 Post-Conference Workshops), pp. 63–69 (2002)

5. Rabelo, J., Goebel, R., Kim, M.Y., Kano, Y., Yoshioka, M., Satoh, K.: Overview and discussion of the competition on legal information extraction/entailment (coliee) 2021. Rev. Socionetwork Strategies, 111–133 (2022). https://doi.org/10.1007/s12626-022-00105-z

6. Aoki, Y., Yoshioka, M., Suzuki, Y.: Data-augmentation method for bert-based legal textual entailment systems in coliee statute law task. Rev. Socionetwork Strategies, 175–196 (2022). https://doi.org/10.1007/s12626-022-00104-0

7. Rabelo, J., Kim, M.-Y., Goebel, R., Yoshioka, M., Kano, Y., Satoh, K.: A summary of the COLIEE 2019 competition. In: Sakamoto, M., Okazaki, N., Mineshima, K., Satoh, K. (eds.) JSAI-isAI 2019. LNCS (LNAI), vol. 12331, pp. 34–49. Springer, Cham (2020). https://doi.org/10.1007/978-3-030-58790-1_3

8. Rabelo, J., Kim, M.-Y., Goebel, R., Yoshioka, M., Kano, Y., Satoh, K.: COLIEE 2020: methods for legal document retrieval and entailment. In: Okazaki, N., Yada, K., Satoh, K., Mineshima, K. (eds.) JSAI-isAI 2020. LNCS (LNAI), vol. 12758, pp. 196–210. Springer, Cham (2021). https://doi.org/10.1007/978-3-030-79942-7_13

9. Robertson, S.E., Walker, S.: Okapi/Keenbow at TREC-8. In: Proceedings of TREC-8, pp. 151–162 (2000)

10. Sakata, W., Shibata, T., Tanaka, R., Kurohashi, S.: FAQ retrieval using query-question similarity and BERT-based query-answer relevance. In: Proceedings of the 42nd International ACM SIGIR Conference on Research and Development in Information Retrieval, SIGIR 2019, pp. 1113–1116. Association for Computing Machinery, New York (2019). https://doi.org/10.1145/3331184.3331326

11. Yoshioka, M., Kano, Y., Kiyota, N., Satoh, K.: Overview of Japanese statute law retrieval and entailment task at COLIEE-2018. In: The Proceedings of the 12th International Workshop on Juris-Informatics (JURISIN2018), pp. 117–128. The Japanese Society of Artificial Intelligence (2018)
12. Yoshioka, M., Onodera, D.: A civil code article information retrieval system based on phrase alignment with article structure analysis and ensemble approach. In: Satoh, K., Kim, M.Y., Kano, Y., Goebel, R., Oliveira, T. (eds.) COLIEE 2017. 4th Competition on Legal Information Extraction and Entailment. EPiC Series in Computing, vol. 47, pp. 9–22. EasyChair (2017)
13. Yoshioka, M., Suzuki, Y.: HUKB at COLIEE 2020 information retrieval task. In: The Proceedings of the 14th International Workshop on Juris-Informatics (JURISIN2020), pp. 195–208. The Japanese Society of Artificial Intelligence (2020)

Using Textbook Knowledge for Statute Retrieval and Entailment Classification

Sabine Wehnert[1,2(✉)] , Libin Kutty[1], and Ernesto William De Luca[1,2]

[1] Otto von Guericke University Magdeburg, Magdeburg, Germany
`sabine.wehnert@gei.de`
[2] Leibniz Institute for Educational Media | Georg Eckert Institute,
Braunschweig, Germany

Abstract. In this work, we imitate the process of a legal expert studying the situational application of statutes, in order to infer relevance and entailment relationships between a query statement and a statute. While using transformer-based architectures, we extract additional statute information from textbooks and incorporate this knowledge into the original pipeline. Results indicate that there is a benefit of using the textbook knowledge in Statute Retrieval and Entailment Classification tasks.

Keywords: information extraction · document enrichment · semantic similarity · sentence transformer · statute retrieval · entailment classification

1 Introduction

Developing Artificial Intelligence for the legal domain is challenging. From an outside view, legal jargon seems well-regulated and therefore predisposed to be formalized. However, imitating the reasoning of a human has been done so far only in a very limited scope and does not appear to be generalizable soon. How can we support lawyers though, given the ever-increasing amount of norms and jurisdictions they need to consider? Efforts in legal information retrieval shall help a lawyer to find relevant laws, whereas in the future classifiers for entailment may offer insights into scenarios contradicting a given set of laws.

Why are we not there yet? With the advent of transformer-based architectures in recent times, many Information Retrieval and Entailment Classification tasks have been practically solved. The amount of statistical information that those models encode in their high-dimensional embeddings has been shown to generalize well in many areas. Transformer models may perform well in situations, where semantic similarity is sufficiently captured because the involved terms are common enough. Nevertheless, daily tasks in the legal domain require more problem-solving capabilities than large open-domain models currently have. The knowledge that is required to understand statute relevance and entailment relationships can be highly specialized to a given jurisdiction and may not be present in the statutes themselves. Further domain knowledge can help to

Y. Takama et al. (Eds.): JSAI-isAI 2022 Workshop, LNAI 13859, pp. 125–137, 2023.
https://doi.org/10.1007/978-3-031-29168-5_9

alleviate this problem. Thus, we focus on obtaining knowledge from textbooks and web resources about the situational use of statutes, similar to the knowledge a legal expert may have acquired through years of study and practice. We study how this knowledge can be incorporated into transformer-based approaches and whether it offers a benefit in the Statute Retrieval and Entailment Classification tasks of the Competition on Legal Information Extraction and Entailment (COLIEE) 2022. Our contributions are:

- We use a rule-based approach to extract textbook knowledge about statutes.
- We employ this knowledge in our combined 2-stage Term Frequency - Inverse Document Frequency (TF-IDF) and sentence embedding approach for statute retrieval.
- We test different methods for encoding the external knowledge in a Graph Neural Network for entailment classification.

The remainder of this paper is organized as follows: In Sect. 2, we collect the related research to our approach of obtaining external knowledge about statutes from textbooks and similar documents. Section 3 contains more details about the employed rule-based knowledge extraction process. Our conceptual designs for the downstream tasks of statute retrieval and entailment classification with extracted knowledge are described in Sects. 4 and 5, respectively. In Sect. 6, we present preliminary experimental results, as well as the competition results of our approaches, along with a discussion. The work is concluded in Sect. 7.

2   Related Work

Regarding related work, this section focuses on legal information extraction about statutes, since using textbook knowledge is the main contribution of this work.

In general, extracting information from textbooks is uncommon in the legal field. We often find researchers work on the statutes themselves to create citation networks [11] or on legal cases to detect references to statutes [16]. The work by Winkels et al. [16] is one of the approaches working on case law. They define so-called *reasons for citing* and extract keywords around a reference to a statute. This basic notion has been adopted in this research, as well. We regard the sentence containing a reference to an article as a possible source of useful information about the situational application of that article. In previous work, we developed a pipeline for extracting statute knowledge from textbooks with GATE[1] [12], and more recently using Apache UIMA Ruta[2] [13]. This work is based on a finite set of patterns that are specified to detect article mentions in the text and then to retrieve the surrounding sentence as potentially useful context information. In the following section, we explain how we made use of that approach for the COLIEE tasks.

---

[1] https://gate.ac.uk/.

[2] https://uima.apache.org/ruta.html.

3   Extracting Knowledge About Statutes from Textbooks

Statutes are written in an abstract manner in order to apply to several cases. Knowing in which case a statute is applicable requires domain knowledge, normally from legal domain experts. However, those experts also obtain their knowledge from sources, which may be partially available in digital format. In that regard, we propose an approach to extract auxiliary information for the civil code articles from textbooks to enrich the articles in subsequent processing steps. To this end, we obtained a collection of English textbooks, journal articles and web resources concerning the Japanese Civil Code:

- Journal Articles [1, 10]
- Textbooks [5, 9]
- Web Resources [2–4, 6, 8, 17]

From this collection, we extracted 152 sentences containing references to articles of the Japanese Civil Code. The main motivation behind extracting those sentences is that they may contain some information about the application of a given article. Hence, if we are prompted with a query describing a special scenario, we assume that chances will be higher to detect the similarity between query and article in case we possess auxiliary information from the textbooks describing that situation in the query. Given our extracted knowledge, the gain we expect from adding this information shall be noticeable.

In the following, we first describe the process of extracting the knowledge about Civil Code articles from textbooks, before testing its benefit on the COLIEE tasks in the Sects. 4 and 5. All aforementioned documents are initially obtained in a PDF format. We first perform some preprocessing steps:

1. Convert the PDF to txt format using `pdftotext`[3].
2. Remove hyphens at the end of each line and reconstruct the words that were separated by a hyphen.
3. Remove all line breaks.
4. If there is a table of contents, extract the chapter names. This is either done with `pdfminer`[4] (if there is sufficient metadata) or manually.
5. Parse the fulltext for the chapter titles from the table of contents and use the title strings to section the document hierarchically.
6. Apply the UIMA Ruta rules for detecting references to the Civil Code and extract them along with their surrounding sentence as the context.
7. Map the references and their context to the hierarchical segment they occur in and append the chapter names to the context sentence.
8. Assign the context sentences to the Civil Code articles and encode them according to the subsequent task's pipeline.

Regarding the UIMA Ruta rules, we form patterns based on regular expressions and part-of-speech tagged by the StanfordPosTagger in `DKPro`[5]. We provide

---

[3] https://www.xpdfreader.com/pdftotext-man.html.

[4] https://github.com/pdfminer/pdfminer.six.

[5] https://dkpro.github.io/dkpro-core/.

some examples for the patterns that our rules capture in Table 1. While there is some variability across the documents regarding the way of referring to the Japanese Civil Code, the authors remain mostly consistent with their own citation style. This property limits the complexity of the patterns, such that the most complex references that we account for are itemizations of multiple articles. Although we do not formally evaluate the coverage of the patterns, manual inspections lead us to estimate an effectiveness of our rules in 90% of the references. Given the extra knowledge from textbooks and the web, we can encode it for the downstream tasks, as described in the following.

Table 1. References to Civil Code articles captured by the extraction rules

Pattern Name	Example
Standard	Article 1 (3) of the Civil Code
Abbreviated	Art. 97 CivC
Reversed	Civil Code Art. 120 (1)
Combined	Civil Code Articles 412 and 484
Itemized	Articles 647, 665, 671, 701 et al. of the Civil Code

4   Statute Retrieval Task

The basis for our retrieval approach is our last year's winning contribution in the same task [15]. In short, the approach is a combination of 2 stages of TF-IDF weighting and sentence embeddings, that are combined in a final relevance score R for ranking:

$$R = TFIDF_1 + \text{TFIDF}_2 + S, \tag{1}$$

where TFIDF_1 refers to the cosine similarity between query and article vectors from the first stage of TF-IDF, while TFIDF_2 is the cosine similarity from the second stage. S is the cosine similarity between article and query sentence embeddings. Previous experiments have shown that both TF-IDF stages together yield better performance than separately. TFIDF_1 refers to a TF-IDF weighting of articles which are enriched with metadata from the Japanese Civil Code structure (i.e., section titles). Also, relevant queries for the given article are appended to the original article text, based on the information that can be obtained from the COLIEE 2022 training dataset for Task 4 (Statute Entailment Classification). For this stage, we use sub-linear term frequency scaling and L2-normalization. Between this enriched article and a given query in the test data, we then compute the cosine similarity. For the second stage TFIDF_2, we also enrich the article with metadata, but not with relevant query information, and then also compute the cosine similarity between that enriched article and the query. For the last part of Eq. 1, we enrich the articles with the same structural metadata as in $TFIDF_1$ and additionally crawled article commentary from open source commentary[6]. All this article and query text is then encoded by a sentence transformer and the cosine similarity is determined. Given $TFIDF_1$, $TFIDF_2$ and S, we add up all these similarity scores. For ranking, the score R is normalized by dividing the term by the maximum score for R. The new aspect which we add in this year is the injection of further external knowledge where sentence embeddings S are computed. Instead of simply appending more text to the article text, we divide the original sentence embedding similarity score S in two parts. At this point, the adapted relevance score R' is composed of:

$$R' = TFIDF_1 + \text{TFIDF}_2 + S', \tag{2}$$

with the same two stages $TFIDF_1$ and TFIDF_2, and a new sentence embedding similarity score S'. It consists of the following parts:

$$S' = w \cdot S_{\text{old}} + (1 - w) \cdot S_{\text{book}} \tag{3}$$

This score consists of the previously used sentence embedding similarity score S_{old} and an additional sentence embedding similarity score called S_{book}. The latter score is computed from the cosine similarity between query and extracted information for a given article encoded by the sentence transformer. In case there are multiple sentences extracted for the same article (i.e., this article was referred to multiple times in the textbooks), we separately encode them with the sentence transformer and then average the embeddings. If there is no textbook information available for a given article, we use the original article text with structural metadata for computing S_{book}. Note that even in this case $S' \neq S$ because S_{old} is influenced by additional information from Task 4 (queries that have a positive entailment label for a given article). In contrast, we do not use these relevant queries for computing S_{book}, since we found that precision increased through their omission in preliminary experiments. We balance the two sentence embedding similarity scores S_{old} and S_{book} by introducing a weighting parameter w between 0 and 1. High values of w result in a low influence of the book knowledge on the final relevance score R', and vice versa. To sum up, we incorporate the external knowledge from textbooks as a separate term in the relevance score, which is weighted depending on how much impact the external knowledge shall have on the sentence embedding similarity score S'. We show experimental results in Sect. 6.

5   Statute Entailment Classification Task

Our approach for the Statute Entailment Classification Task of the COLIEE competition is also based on one of the architectures we employed previously, the Graph Neural Networks (GNNs) [14]. Given the below-average results of last time for this architecture and our assumption that more encoded information

---

[6] https://ja.wikibooks.org/.

could lead to better performance, we extend the GNN-based approach towards the textbook knowledge. The main idea of the original setup is to form a graph from the instances, such that we have a query node and one or more article nodes attached to it. We encode the queries and articles with a sentence transformer model. Thereby, we also use the structural metadata to enrich the articles, as in the Statute Retrieval task. Using a unidirectional message passing technique with an average aggregation function [7], we obtain query node embeddings with neighbor information from adjacent article nodes and pass this query node embedding to two linear layers and a final softmax classification layer. Different from the previous COLIEE edition, we now only train one GNN model and do not form an ensemble of models trained on different dataset splits anymore. We implemented three approaches to incorporate external knowledge:

- **GNN_ORIGINAL:** This approach is the basic architecture of the GNN as described above, without the use of any further external textbook knowledge.
- **GNN_CONCAT:** In this approach, we concatenate the article node embeddings with the additional embeddings obtained from the textbooks for a given article. If there is no reference in any textbook to a given article, we use the original article node embedding as a replacement.
- **GNN_AVG:** We average the sentence embeddings for the articles that we obtained in the GNN_ORIGINAL approach with the textbook knowledge for each article, which is also encoded by the sentence transformer model.

6   Evaluation

In this section, we evaluate our approaches for the Statute Retrieval and Entailment Classification tasks of COLIEE 2022. First, we describe the experimental setup, then we share results and finally, we discuss the models' performance. Regarding both tasks, we created internal dataset splits on the English version of the dataset. Our training split contains all provided training data, except for the query-article pairs starting with $R02$-*, which form the validation split. Please note that for the Statute Retrieval task we do not train any machine learning model and only use the splits for parameter selection. However, for the Entailment Classification task, we train models on the training split and select the best performing models based on their performances on the training and validation split, without training any model on the validation data.

6.1   Statute Retrieval Task

Experimental Setup. According to the COLIEE 2022 rules, the model performance on the statute retrieval task is decided by the F2-score. Therefore we performed our preliminary experiments based on this metric. Given the approach which we described in Sect. 4, we aim to select two parameters through experiments: the sentence transformer model and the weight w which controls the influence of the textbook knowledge on the final relevance score R'. The

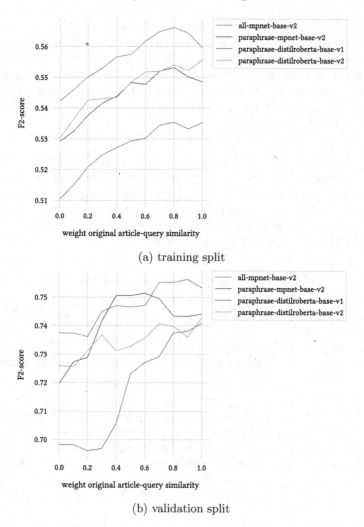

Fig. 1. Performance based on how the original article-query similarity is weighted. Higher weights indicate a lower contribution of the external data to the similarity.

results of the preliminary experiments are shown in Fig. 1. The highest performance on the training and validation split is achieved by the model *"all-mpnet-base-v2"*, with a w value of 0.8 and 0.9, respectively. This indicates that the model benefits from a small influence of the textbook knowledge most, compared to a w value of 1.0, where no external textbook knowledge is used and the performance drops slightly. Although the differences in the F2-scores are not large, the same trend can be observed for the model *"paraphrase-mpnet-base-v2"*, while this model reaches its best performance on the validation split on a w value of 0.6. The model *"paraphrase-distilroberta-base-v2"* performs slightly better than *"paraphrase-mpnet-base-v2"* on the training split, but worse on the validation split. Interestingly, *"paraphrase-distilroberta-base-v2"* does not benefit from external textbook knowledge at all. Its predecessor *"paraphrase-distilroberta-base-v1"* does neither benefit from the textbook knowledge and was outperformed on both splits by the other models. Given the large difference in performance between the training and validation split, we decided to use a w value of 0.7 for all three runs, and we submitted one run for each model, except *"paraphrase-distilroberta-base-v1"*.

Results. The results of the three selected models are shown in Table 2. Our third run with the model *"all-mpnet-base-v2"* achieved the highest performance among our submitted runs with an F2-score of 77.9%. This result is not surprising, given the model's performance on the preliminary experiments. Overall, our best run achieved the third-highest rank in the competition. The best result was attained by the HUKB team with an F2-score of 82.04%.

Table 2. Results on the Statute Retrieval Test Data

Run	Model	F2-score	Precision	Recall
OVGU_run1	paraphrase-distilroberta-base-v2	0.7732	0.7745	0.7962
OVGU_run2	paraphrase-mpnet-base-v2	0.7718	0.7732	0.8008
OVGU_run3	all-mpnet-base-v2	**0.7790**	**0.7781**	**0.8054**

Given that there were only 151 collected article context sentences from textbooks and a much larger corpus of 775 articles in the Japanese Civil Code, we examine the benefit of using the textbook knowledge. In Table 3, we summarize the article coverage. 104 unique articles from the Japanese Civil Code are referenced within our textbook corpus. Thereof the majority is mentioned only once, while two articles are mentioned four times and one article was cited five times.

Table 3. Article Coverage in the Textbook Corpus

Mentions	Articles	Examples
1	71	Art. 97, Art. 667
2	23	Art. 13, Art. 414
3	7	Art. 90, Art. 543
4	2	Art. 1, Art. 487
5	1	Art. 96
Total	**104**	

Figure 2 depicts the sentence length of the extracted passages from the textbooks. Most sentences encompass less than 200 characters.

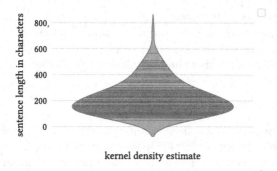

Fig. 2. Distribution of the sentence length for the 151 extracted instances

Upon further inspection, we noticed that there were not many matches between the articles we had textbook knowledge for and those which were considered relevant in the test data. In several cases, the relevant articles were retrieved regardless of the presence or absence of textbook knowledge. Overall, our retrieval system with its composed relevance score shows higher performance when using textbook knowledge, compared to setting the w value to 1.0. Surprisingly, this time the weighting mechanism itself has played an important role in the performance boost. As described before, in case where we have no textbook information, there will be only the original article with structural metadata encoded and compared to the query, resulting in the S_{book} score. Meanwhile, the S_{old} score uses the same articles and structural metadata, but also relevant queries to a given article based on the entailment label from Task 4. As a consequence, the weighting mechanism strengthened the influence of the original article and structural metadata and improved precision in a situation where a large portion of articles was not enhanced by textbooks. In other words, the influence of the relevant queries from Task 4 was diminished and therefore, precision increased.

Despite this observation, there can be article context information from textbooks which is closer to a query than the original article text. One example for an article that got enriched with context information from one of our web resources by Dogauchi [2] is Art. 96 of the Civil Code:

"In a situation in which for example, as a result of a manifestation of intention made as a result of the fraud, the transfer of ownership of land from A to B is registered, there will be a need to protect C, a third party who purchases the land from B. Consequently, article 96 (3) of the Civil Code prescribes "The rescission of the manifestation of intention induced by the fraud pursuant to the provision of the preceding two paragraphs may not be asserted against a third party without knowledge."

In this case, we see that there is a specific situation described with three acting persons (A,B and C). Similar types of queries exist in the COLIEE dataset. Consequently, we assume there could be a performance boost when we have more relevant articles enriched with information from textbooks. We find ourselves in a balancing act between introducing external information which may dilute the original article content and which can reduce precision one one hand, and using no external knowledge while risking that the article texts differ syntactically too much from the queries, making similarity-based approaches less effective.

6.2 Statute Entailment Classification Task

Experimental Setup. The task of Statute Entailment Classification is a binary classification problem with "Y" for positive entailment and "N" otherwise. Accordingly, the evaluation metric is the model's accuracy. Because of the unstable model performance depending on the weight initialization in the training phase, we performed our preliminary experiments on four sentence transformer models with 10 different random seeds. Figure 3 depicts on violin diagrams how the model performs on the different seeds (each observation is a horizontal line within the "violin") and the respective training and validation split. We have three setups: Subfigure 3a shows how the GNN_ORIGINAL performs without any textbook knowledge. We observe that the models *"all-mpnet-base-v2"* and *"paraphrase-distilroberta-base-v2"* yield similar accuracy scores, however the former model exhibits a lower variance in performance on the validation dataset. Therefore, in this setup model *"all-mpnet-base-v2"* becomes run 1. Subfigure 3b shows how GNN_CONCAT performs. In this case, we also choose *"all-mpnet-base-v2"* for run 2 because its performance on the validation split is the best of all models while being mostly on par with the other models on the training split. Finally, we choose the model *"paraphrase-distilroberta-base-v2"* for run 3 from Subfigure 3c in the GNN_AVG setup, because it has many seeds performing well on the training data and also achieves peak performance on the validation data.

Results. The result of our submitted runs is shown in Table 4. Different from what we expected, run 3 performed best among all our runs with the model *"paraphrase-distilroberta-base-v2"* and an accuracy of 57.8%. The best overall performance was achieved by the KIS team with an accuracy of 67.89%. Given this result, it is apparent to us that the external knowledge was helpful to boost performance, since our run 1 without textbook knowledge only achieved 47.71%, despite performing well in many cases on the preliminary experiments. We also attribute the performance of our third run to the model itself, because it was trained on paraphrase data and may be better suited for entailment classification. Compared to the previous year, we achieved our goal to boost the GNN performance, however this performance increase was not sufficient to outperform other approaches. To sum up, adding knowledge from a textbook to a GNN model architecture turns out to be beneficial, and the best performance was achieved when averaging the original article embeddings with the additional textbook embeddings for the respective article.

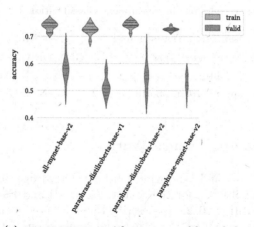

(a) **GNN_ORIGINAL**: without external knowledge

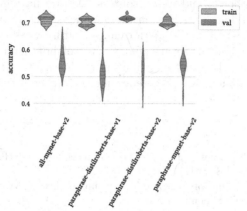

(b) **GNN_CONCAT**: with external knowledge, concatenated with article embeddings

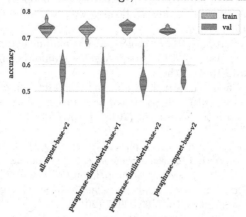

(c) **GNN_AVG**: with external knowledge, averaged with article embeddings

Fig. 3. GNN experiments on the training/validation splits over 10 random seeds.

Table 4. Results on the Entailment Classification Test Data

Run	Sentence Transformer	GNN Model	Accuracy
OVGU_run1	all-mpnet-base-v2	GNN_ORIGINAL	0.4771
OVGU_run2	all-mpnet-base-v2	GNN_CONCAT	0.5321
OVGU_run3	paraphrase-distilroberta-base-v2	GNN_AVG	**0.5780**

7   Conclusion and Future Work

We studied extracting and employing textbook knowledge about the statutes of the Japanese Civil Code for the Statute Retrieval and Entailment Classification tasks of COLIEE 2022. We described how we used a rule-based method to extract information about the situational application of the statutes from a collection of textbooks and web resources. Despite having limited textbook knowledge not covering all articles in the Japanese Civil Code, using our approach boosted the overall model performance. Future work can focus on using textbook knowledge in other setups, and can also elaborate on the content of the textbooks to explain the exact contribution of the involved textbook passages to the models' predictions when there are more enriched articles.

References

1. Danwerth, C.: Principles of Japanese law of succession. Zeitschrift für Japanisches Recht **17**(33), 99–118 (2012)
2. Dogauchi, H.: Outline of contract law in Japan. http://www.law.tohoku.ac.jp/kokusaiB2C/overview/contract.html
3. Hashimoto, Y.: Supreme court judgement on the constitutionality of article 750 of the civil code, which requires a husband and wife to adopt the surname of either spouse at the time of marriage (2017). https://www.waseda.jp/folaw/icl/news-en/2017/03/29/5720/
4. Iimura, T., Takayabashi, R., Rademacher, C.: The binding nature of court decisions in Japan's civil law system (2015). http://cgc.law.stanford.edu/commentaries/14-Iimura-Takabayashi-Rademacher
5. Ishikawa, H.: Codification, decodification, and recodification of the Japanese civil code. In: Rivera, J.C. (ed.) The Scope and Structure of Civil Codes. IGCPLJ, vol. 32, pp. 267–285. Springer, Dordrecht (2013). https://doi.org/10.1007/978-94-007-7942-6_12
6. Kanazawa, T.: The case in which a part of article 733(1) of the civil code, stipulating a prohibition period for remarriage specific to women, was ruled as unconstitutional. (2017). https://www.waseda.jp/folaw/icl/news-en/2017/03/29/5722/
7. Kipf, T.N., Welling, M.: Semi-supervised classification with graph convolutional networks. arXiv preprint arXiv:1609.02907 (2016)
8. Shiraishi, D.: Payment of guarantee obligation, made after a guarantor has inherited principal obligation, can interrupt the extinctive prescription of the principal obligation (2014). https://www.waseda.jp/hiken/en/jalaw_inf/topics2014/precedent/001shiraishi.html

9. Steiner, K.: Postwar changes in the Japanese civil code. Wash. Law Rev. **25**(3), 286 (1950)
10. Taniguchi, Y.: The 1996 code of civil procedure of Japan-a procedure for the coming century? Am. J. Comp. Law **45**(4), 767–791 (1997)
11. Waltl, B., Landthaler, J., Matthes, F.: Differentiation and empirical analysis of reference types in legal documents. In: Legal Knowledge and Information Systems, pp. 211–214. IOS Press (2016)
12. Wehnert, S., Broneske, D., Langer, S., Saake, G.: Concept hierarchy extraction from legal literature. In: Cuzzocrea, A., Bonchi, F., Gunopulos, D. (eds.) Proceedings of the CIKM 2018 Workshops co-located with 27th ACM International Conference on Information and Knowledge Management (CIKM 2018), Torino, Italy, October 22, 2018. CEUR Workshop Proceedings, vol. 2482. CEUR-WS.org (2018). http://ceur-ws.org/Vol-2482/paper33.pdf
13. Wehnert, S., Durand, G.C., Saake, G.: ERST: leveraging topic features for context-aware legal reference linking. In: Araszkiewicz, M., Rodríguez-Doncel, V. (eds.) Legal Knowledge and Information Systems - JURIX 2019: The Thirty-second Annual Conference, Madrid, Spain, December 11–13, 2019. Frontiers in Artificial Intelligence and Applications, vol. 322, pp. 113–122. IOS Press (2019). https://doi.org/10.3233/FAIA190312
14. Wehnert, S., Dureja, S., Kutty, L., Sudhi, V., Luca, E.W.D.: Applying BERT embeddings to predict legal textual entailment. Rev. Socionetw. Strateg. **16**(1), 197–219 (2022). https://doi.org/10.1007/s12626-022-00101-3
15. Wehnert, S., Sudhi, V., Dureja, S., Kutty, L., Shahania, S., De Luca, E.W.: Legal norm retrieval with variations of the BERT model combined with TF-IDF vectorization. In: Proceedings of the Eighteenth International Conference on Artificial Intelligence and Law, pp. 285–294. ICAIL 2021, Association for Computing Machinery, New York, NY, USA (2021). https://doi.org/10.1145/3462757.3466104
16. Winkels, R., Boer, A., Vredebregt, B., van Someren, A.: Towards a legal recommender system. In: JURIX, pp. 169–178 (2014)
17. Yamashiro, K.: The treatment of liability to refund overpayment in case of assignment of operating assets of the moneylender (2012). https://www.waseda.jp/folaw/icl/public/bulletin/back-number31-35/

Legal Textual Entailment Using Ensemble of Rule-Based and BERT-Based Method with Data Augmentation by Related Article Generation

Masaki Fujita, Takaaki Onaga, Ayaka Ueyama, and Yoshinobu Kano[✉]

Shizuoka University, Johoku, 3-5-1, Naka-Ku, Hamamatsu-Shi, Shizuoka 432-8011, Japan
{mfujita,tonaga,aueyama}@kanolab.net, kano@inf.shizuoka.ac.jp

Abstract. We report our system architecture of COLIEE 2022 Task 4, which challenges to solve the textual entailment part of the Japanese legal bar examination problems. We successfully improved the correct answer ratio by an ensemble of a rule-based method and BERT-based method. Our proposed methods mainly consist of two parts: data augmentations of training dataset and an ensemble of the methods. Regarding training data augmentation, the civil law articles are segmented once and reconstructed again with all the combinations. Data expansion is then performed by replacing the data with negative forms and alphabetical symbols. Focusing on the characteristics that the rule-based method is high in its precision but low in its coverage, we employed a modular way in our ensemble. We integrated other proposed methods such as Sentence-BERT to select necessary data, person name inference to replace alphabetical anonymized symbols with the actual role name of the person. We confirmed that our suggested methods are effective by comparing with our baseline models, achieved 0.6789 correct answer ratio in accuracy on the formal run test dataset, which was the best score among the COLIEE 2022 Task 4 submissions.

Keywords: COLIEE · Question Answering · Legal Bar Exam · Legal information Extraction · BERT · Predicate Argument Structure Analysis

1 Introduction

The COLIEE shared task series was held in association with the JURISIN (Jurisinformatics) workshops and ICAIL (International Conference on Artificial Intelligence and Law) workshops [1]. COLIEE 2022 is the ninth shared task, which consists of four tasks. Task 1 and 2 are case law tasks using Canadian law. Task 3 and 4 are statute law tasks which use the Japanese legal bar examination. In Task 3, participants are given a problem text, then search for Japanese civil law articles which are necessary to solve the problem. In Task 4, participants are given a problem text and related article(s), then asked to answer Yes or No whether the content entails the given article(s) or not regarding the given article(s). We describe our participation of COLIEE 2022 Task 4 in this paper.

© The Author(s), under exclusive license to Springer Nature Switzerland AG 2023
Y. Takama et al. (Eds.): JSAI-isAI 2022 Workshop, LNAI 13859, pp. 138–153, 2023.
https://doi.org/10.1007/978-3-031-29168-5_10

In Task 3, participants are given a problem, then search articles which are necessary to solve the problem. In Task 4, participants are given a problem and related article(s), then answer Yes or No whether the content entails the given article(s) or not regarding the given article(s). We challenged Task 4.

Unlike machine learning-based systems, where the reasoning process is a black box, rule-based systems can reason according to human thought, thus are better in terms of explainable output, which is important in practically automating trial process.

In Task 4 of the previous COLIEE 2021 shared task, we built a solver system that uses a rule-based solution method [2]. Other teams mainly used machine learning-based methods, such as teams using BERT [3–5], ensembles based on T5 [6], and graph neural networks [7]. We were the only team who employs a rule-based method.

Our previous rule-based system outputs different correct answers for each module within the rule-base system. Therefore, an ensemble by selecting modules is a straightforward extension of our previous system. While rule-based methods have advantages on their good precision scores for specific problem types, their total performance decreases when increasing their recall scores in general. We implemented a machine learning-based system using BERT, to cover solving other types of problems in higher performance in which our rule-based system shows lower performance.

In addition to the ensemble of the rule-based and BERT-based parts above, we propose three data augmentation methods for the training data of BERT. Firstly, we segment the text once and then reconstruct in various combinations. This process can create texts that are easy for BERT to infer, by containing no excess or deficiency of necessary data, and by reducing string lengths. Secondly, we augment the problem texts by converting into negative forms at the end of sentences. Thirdly, we replace person role names with alphabetical symbols. Fourthly, we replace referring article numbers by their referred actual article texts.

Finally, two new methods were added: data selection, which selects appropriate data from the combinatorial augmented data, and person name inference, which replaces alphabetical person name symbols with actual person role names.

These techniques resulted in a 67.89% correct answer ratio in accuracy on the COLIEE 2022 formal run's test data, which was the best score among the teams that submitted data. We compare results of our proposed methods with our baselines, discusses detailed analysis including effectiveness of the proposed methods in the following sections.

2 Previous Works

Hoshino, et al. [8] suggested a rule-based solver system in COLIEE 2019, which syntactically parses sentences, and then sentences are segmented into clauses by their original definition, based on the parsing results. The parsing results are then used again to extract a clause set (subject, predicate, and object) for each clause. They built a couple of solver modules: for example, their Precise match module compares the relevant civil law clauses with the problem clauses using all elements in the clause sets and answers Yes if they match, while their Loose match module answers Yes if one or more clause elements match. We used one of the modules of Hoshino et al.'s system, but we propose to perform ensemble with machine learning-based systems, while Hoshino et al. employed only the rule-based system.

Yoshioka, et al. [3], the best team in Task 4 of COLIEE 2021, improved its performance mainly by augmenting the training data and by an ensemble of differently trained BERT [9] models. BERT is a frequently used deep learning model, which uses Transformer's encoder part. For their training data expansion, they used a list of civil law articles. They increased the training data size by segmenting the sentences, and by inserting negations that invert the sentence's logic. In the ensemble of BERT models, they selected models which showed better performances among the prepared BERT models. We reused their methods but also added new data augmentation methods to Yoshioka, et al.'s, data extension to the problem texts and data extension by replacing alphabetical symbols and article numbers.

3   System

3.1   System Overview: Rule-Based Part and BERT-Based Part

We only used resources of Japanese languages including the official ones of COLIEE, while organizers provide both English and Japanese versions in Task 4.

Our solver system consists of a rule-based part and a BERT-based part. These parts are integrated by an ensemble, then output the final Yes/No answers.

In the previous work, there were a couple of solver modules. We examined different ways of ensemble of these solver modules, but the modules other than the Precise Match module have not contributed to the scores. Therefore, we only use the Precise Match module in this paper as our rule-based part, which compares all of subjects, objects and predicates of the clause pairs. Based on the syntactic parsing results of the given input text, the Precise Match module divides them into conditional clauses and expansion clauses. Then, each clause is individually parsed again, and a set of {predicate, subject, object} is extracted based on the parsed results for each clause. For example, {"make", "lessor", "contract"} is extracted from a clause of a problem text "the lessor made contract", and {"make", "owner", "contract"} is extracted from a clause of an article text "the owner made contract". The Precise Match module answers *Yes* if the pair of the extracted sets completely match. In the above example, the answer is *No* because the subject does not match. If there are negations, etc. then the module inverts the answer.

The BERT-based part includes multiple BERT models with different fine-tunings, then integrated by an ensemble. This part is similar to the previous work by Yoshioka, et al. [3], but we extended their work as follows.

All of our BERT models use a pre-trained BERT model [10], which was trained by the Japanese Wikipedia articles. Our BERT models are fine-tuned as inputting the given problem text and the given relevant civil law articles, and outputting Yes/No binary answers. We set parameters as follow: the learning rate to 4e−5, the maximum string length to 512, the number of epochs to 6, and the batch size to 32. The difference of our BERT models is that they are fine-tuned by different datasets. We explain our system process flow in the following subsections. Firstly, data augmentation is performed on the training and test data (3.2). Among our three formal run submissions (**KIS1**, **KIS2** and **KIS3**), **KIS2** is our suggested model. **KIS1** and **KIS3** selects which data to use of the augmented data (3.3), in addition to **KIS2**. **KIS3** further performs person name inference (3.4), which replaces anonymous person names with inferred concrete person names to create a new dataset. All these three models finally perform an ensemble of the rule-based and BERT-based parts. Then to output the final solution. Figure 1 illustrates the above process.

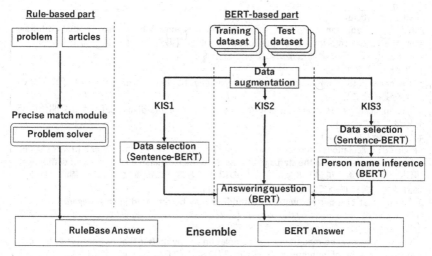

Fig. 1. System Overview

3.2 Data Augmentation

We apply our data augmentation to the BERT-based part only. We apply our data augmentation methods to both the civil law articles and the problem sentences, both training data and test data. Figure 2 shows the flow of our data augmentation with the number of data samples when applied to all past questions.

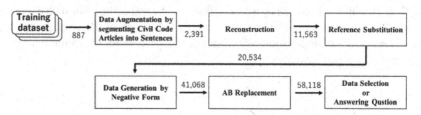

Fig. 2. Flow of our data augmentation with number of samples in past questions

Data Augmentation by Segmenting Civil Code Articles into Sentences. The relevant civil law articles, which are needed to answer a problem by textual entailment, may be segmented into multiple articles (Fig. 3).

[Civil Code Article]

Article 679. In addition to the cases set forth in the preceding Article, a partner shall withdraw from the Partnership for any of the following things. (第六百七十九条　前条の場合のほか、組合員は、次に掲げる事由によって脱退する。)

1, death (一　死亡)

2, The decision to commence bankruptcy proceedings has been made. (二　破産手続開始の決定を受けたこと。)

3, The applicant has received a trial for commencement of guardianship. (三　後見開始の審判を受けたこと。)

4, Expulsion (四　除名)

Article 681 Calculations between a partner who has withdrawn and the other partners shall be made in accordance with the status of the assets of the Partnership at the time of withdrawal. (第六百八十一条　脱退した組合員と他の組合員との間の計算は、脱退の時における組合財産の状況に従ってしなければならない。)

2, The interest of a partner who has withdrawn may be refunded in cash, regardless of the type of contribution made by the partner. (2, 脱退した組合員の持分は、その3 出資の種類を問わず、金銭で払い戻すことができる。)

3, Calculations may be made after the completion of any matter that has not yet been completed at the time of withdrawal. (3, 脱退の時にまだ完了していない事項については、その完了後に計算をすることができる。)

[Problem text]

A partner may receive a refund of his/her interest even if he/she is expelled. (組合員は，除名された場合であっても，持分の払戻しを受けることができる。)

Fig. 3. Examples of multiple article segmentations in Civil Law (H20–27-I)

This segmentation process shortens the input string length and augments the training data. In Fig. 3, the example articles data is segmented into units of *articles* designated as Article 679 and Article 681, and in units of *terms* as well described as *1("一"), 2("二")...*, in the same figure. Article 679 includes the statement *the following things* ("次に掲げる"), which is followed by a description of what it specifies. For such a sentence, we substitute *the following things* ("次に掲げる") by each of the contents specified by the description. Figure 4 shows the result of this process for the example in Fig. 3, segmented into seven sentences.

> 1. In addition to the cases described in the preceding Article, a partner shall withdraw due to death.
> （1，前条の場合のほか、組合員は、死亡によって脱退する。）
> 2. In addition to the cases described in the preceding Article, a partner shall withdraw from the Partnership upon a decision to commence bankruptcy proceedings.
> （2，前条の場合のほか、組合員は、破産手続開始の決定を受けたことによって脱退する。）
> 3, In addition to the cases described in the preceding Article, a partner shall withdraw from the Partnership upon a decision of commencement of guardianship.
> （3，前条の場合のほか、組合員は、後見開始の審判を受けたことによって脱退する。）
> 4, In addition to the cases described in the preceding article, a partner shall withdraw from the Partnership by expulsion.
> （4，前条の場合のほか、組合員は、除名によって脱退する。）
> 5, Calculations between a partner who has withdrawn and the other partners shall be made in accordance with the status of the assets of the Partnership at the time of withdrawal.
> （5，脱退した組合員と他の組合員との間の計算は、脱退の時における組合財産の状況に従ってしなければならない。）
> The interest of a partner who withdraws may be refunded in cash, regardless of the type of investment.
> （6，脱退した組合員の持分は、その出資の種類を問わず、金銭で払い戻すことができる。）
> With respect to matters that have not yet been completed at the time of withdrawal, calculations may be made after the completion of such matters.
> （7，脱退の時にまだ完了していない事項については、その完了後に計算をすることができる。）

Fig. 4. Examples of segmented article texts

Reconstruction. We reconstruct sentences from segmented data, to create dataset that contains necessary data without excesses of deficiencies within all possible combinations, in shorter sentences then the original ones. For example, if a civil law article is segmented into seven sentences, 127 new patterns of sentences are generated. Figure 4 shows an example of such seven sentences (1, 4, 6 only due to the space limitation) (Fig. 5).

In this example, the necessary information to solve the problem is 4 and 6, because 4 indicates that the expulsion is a withdrawal, and 6 indicates that the withdrawn member is entitled to a refund of his/her share. Therefore, in this example, the data constructed with 4 + 6 is an appropriate data set that contains the necessary information without excess or deficiency.

This automatic reconstruction will generate a large dataset, which could include data that are not suitable for the solution. We introduce Data Selection (3.3) as a solution to this issue.

Reference Substitution. Civil law articles sometimes refer to other articles by their article numbers as shown in Fig. 6.

Because the referred "main text of Article 560 paragraph 1" and "Article 565" are not given as relevant articles, we need other information than the relevant articles. Since such reference patterns are complex, e.g., the "main text" excludes the proviso portion, or the section number may be specified after the article number, we manually replaced the references to other articles in all civil law articles. Because the relevant article texts

1, In addition to the cases mentioned in the preceding article, a member shall withdraw from the association upon his/her death. (1,　前条の場合のほか、組合員は、死亡によって脱退する。)
4, In addition to the cases described in the preceding article, a member shall be withdrawn by expulsion from the Partnership. (4,　前条の場合のほか、組合員は、除名によって脱退する。)
6, The interest of a partner who has withdrawn may be refunded in cash, regardless of the type of investment. (6,　脱退した組合員の持分は、その出資の種類を問わず、金銭で払い戻すことができる。)
1+4, In addition to the cases mentioned in the preceding article, a member shall withdraw from the association upon his/her death. In addition to the cases described in the preceding article, a member shall be withdrawn by expulsion from the Partnership. (1+4,　前条の場合のほか、組合員は、死亡によって脱退する。前条の場合のほか、組合員は、除名によって脱退する。)
1+6, In addition to the cases mentioned in the preceding article, a member shall withdraw from the association upon his/her death. The interest of a partner who has withdrawn may be refunded in cash, regardless of the type of investment. (1+6,　前条の場合のほか、組合員は、死亡によって脱退する。脱退した組合員の持分は、その出資の種類を問わず、金銭で払い戻すことができる。)
4+6, In addition to the cases described in the preceding article, a member shall be withdrawn by expulsion from the Partnership. The interest of a partner who has withdrawn may be refunded in cash, regardless of the type of investment. (4+6,　前条の場合のほか、組合員は、除名によって脱退する。脱退した組合員の持分は、その出資の種類を問わず、金銭で払い戻すことができる。)
1+4+6, In addition to the cases mentioned in the preceding article, a member shall withdraw from the association upon his/her death. The interest of a partner who has withdrawn may be refunded in cash, regardless of the type of investment. The interest of a partner who has withdrawn may be refunded in cash, regardless of the type of investment. (1+4+6,　前条の場合のほか、組合員は、死亡によって脱退する。前条の場合のほか、組合員は、除名によって脱退する。脱退した組合員の持分は、その出資の種類を問わず、金銭で払い戻すことができる。)

Fig. 5. Examples of combinations reconstructed from 1, 4, 6

Article 572. Even where the seller has made a covenant not to assume liability for security in the case prescribed in the main text of **Article 560 paragraph 1** or **Article 565**, he/she may not be exempted from liability for facts that he/she knew but did not disclose and for rights that he/she established for a third party or assigned to a third party.
(第五百七十二条　売主は、**第五百六十二条第一項本文又は第五百六十五条**に規定する 場合における担保の責任を負わない旨の特約をしたときであっても、知りながら告げなかった事実及び自ら第三者のために設定し又は第三者に譲り渡した権利については、その責任を免れることができない。)

Fig. 6. Examples of articles referring to other articles by article numbers

are subset of the distributed civil law article, and there is no problem text which specifies article numbers, we do not need to modify the test dataset.

In some cases, the length of replaced sentence could get very long, e.g., when multiple article numbers are specified, or when the specified article refers to other in a nested way. We not only use the replaced data but also the data before the replacement in training and testing, thereby preventing cases in which a problem cannot be answered due to the long sentences.

Data Generation by Negative Form. We apply data expansion by performing a logical inversion at the end of a sentence. For this logical inversion, we manually list pairs of logically opposite character strings in advance, such as "can" and "cannot" or "will" and "will not". When this negative form expansion is applied, we invert the answer labels. This is like the previous work in Sect. 2, but we apply this process to the problem text, in addition to the previous work's civil law text.

For questions which answers are No, the negative form at the end of the sentence does not necessarily result in a Yes. We tried an option that convert Yes to No only.

AB Replacement. Person names are sometimes replaced by alphabetical characters in the problem texts, such as A and B, as a sort of anonymization. In order to deal with such problems, we create an augmentation dataset from the training data, by replacing person names with alphabetic characters.

We applied this expansion when person's names appear more than once, because we aim to fine-tune the model to correctly identify person names when there are two or more choices. As same as the past problem texts, we replace the person's name which firstly appear with A, secondly appear with B, and so on. Since such problem texts are written in the Japanese full-width symbols, we replace them with full-width alphabetic characters (Fig. 7).

```
[Before replacement]
(Civil Code Article)
In the case of possession by an agent, the right of possession shall be extinguished by the
principal's renunciation of the intention to allow the agent to take possession.
(代理人によって占有をする場合には、占有権は、本人が代理人に占有をさせる意
思を放棄したことによって消滅する。)

(Problem text)
When possession is taken by an agent, the right of possession shall be extinguished by the
principal's renunciation of the intention to allow the agent to take possession. (代理人によっ
て占有をする場合には、占有権は、本人が代理人に占有をさせる意思を放棄したこと
によって消滅する。)
```
```
[After replacement]
(Civil Code Article)
same

(Problem text)
When possession is taken by an A, the right of possession shall be extinguished by the B's
renunciation of the intention to allow the A to take possession. (Aによって占有をする場合
には、占有権は、BがAに占有をさせる意思を放棄したことによって消滅する。)
```

Fig. 7. An example applying alphabetical substitution to a problem using Article 204

Variation and Decision of Final Answers. When the above replacements and reconstructions are applied to a single problem, that single problem could be duplicated with different augmentation methods, resulting in potential multiple different answers. For each duplicated problem, we compare BERT's confidence values, then accepts the answer which has largest difference between the confidence scores of Yes and No.

Because different fine-tuning trail could result in different answers even when the same training dataset is used, we tried the fine-tuning five times, then accepted the majority vote results as the final output.

3.3 Data Selection

We calculate the similarity between the problem text and the generated civil law text for this selection, using pretrained Sentence-BERT [11]. We regard top five similar texts among texts after data segmentation, reconstruction, and replacement processes as the appropriate data set.

3.4 Person Name Inference

As described earlier, person names are sometimes replaced by alphabetical characters in the problem texts, such as A and B, as a sort of anonymization. We trained a BERT model to predict which alphabet represents which names, from semi-manually created 49 candidates: the person himself, agent, seller, buyer, etc. **KIS3** uses this prediction result, replacing alphabets with prediction results as preprocessing. Contents of this section are applied to **KIS3** only.

If the problem directly indicates what the alphabet represents as an appositional expression, we apply replacements by the following two rules, before applying the above BERT's predictions. Firstly, we replace all occurrences of "A" with appositions "XX person", when there are indications in the text, such as "the XX person (A)" (XX(人物名)者であるA), "A who is the XX…" (XX者A). Examples include *creditor*, *buyer*, donor, recipient, supporter, protector, appointee, etc. Secondly, we replace expressions such as "between AB" ("AB間") with "between A and B" ("AとBとの間"), to be closer to expressions of the civil code. After these processes applied, our BERT-based system predicts replacements for the rest of the alphabetical characters.

We eliminated problems with alphabetical characters as person names in the training dataset, because such problems are converted into non-alphabetical symbols by applying the above process.

3.5 Ensemble of Rule-Based Part and BERT-Based Part

We built an ensemble of the rule-based part and the BERT-based part. As shown in Fig. 1, the rule-based part (precise match) is applied first, because the rule-based part is better in its precision but lower in its coverage. If the rule-based part can output an answer, then that answer will be used as the system's final output; if the rule-based part cannot output its answer, then output of the BERT-based part will be used as the system's final answer.

4 Result and Experiments

4.1 Formal Run Results

Table 1 shows the COLIEE 2022's Task 4 formal run evaluation results for each team's submission. Table 1 shows the COLIEE 2022's Task 4 formal run evaluation results for each team's submission. **KIS** is our team's name.

Table 1. COLIEE 2022 Task 4's formal run results for each participant's submission. "Correct" column shows the number of correct answers among 109 problems in total; "Accuracy" column shows the accuracy ratio.

Team	Submission ID	Correct	Accuracy	Team	Submission ID	Correct	Accuracy
KIS	**KIS2**	**74**	**0.6789**	UA	UA_e	59	0.5413
HUKB	HUKB1	73	0.6697	UA	UA_r	59	0.5413
KIS	**KIS1**	**72**	**0.6606**	UA	UA_structure	59	0.5413
KIS	**KIS3**	**72**	**0.6606**	JNLP	JNLP1	58	0.5321
HUKB	HUKB2	69	0.633	JNLP	JNLP2	58	0.5321
HUKB	HUKB3	69	0.633	UVGU	OVGU2	58	0.5321
LLNTU	LLNTUdeNgram	66	0.6055	JNLP	JNLP3	56	0.5138
LLNTU	LLNTUdiffSim	63	0.578	OVGU	OVGU1	52	0.4771
OVGU	OVGU3	63	0.578				

4.2   Experiments on Training Dataset

Table 2 shows the evaluation results using the H18-R02 training dataset, which includes 15 years' datasets, 887 problems in total. For each year of the training dataset, we regard that target year's dataset as a test dataset, and the rest of the years' datasets as a training dataset. For H30-R02 datasets, we follow the same setting with the previous formal runs i.e. regard the rest of the past datasets as the training dataset but not use "future" datasets of the target year. Results in Table 2 show total number of answered problems, the total number of correctly answered problems, and correct answer ratios, for each solver.

The first row in Table 2, **Individual**, shows individual solver's results; because we performed the fine-tuning five times as described earlier (3.2), count values in the *BERT-based* columns show summation of these five differently fine-tuned models. The second row, + **Majority Vote**, shows results of the majority vote integration of these five fine-tuned models. The third row, + **Ensemble**, shows results of an ensemble of the **Rule-based** part, which corresponds to the Precise Match module, and the BERT-based part, which corresponds to the majority vote integration.

Baseline column corresponds to our baseline model, which is same as the other BERT-based models but no data expansion is applied. Because the data expansion includes the sentence segmentation, inputs to the *Baseline* model sometimes exceed the maximum length of the BERT model. Our **Baseline** model does not output answers in such cases, thus the total number of the answered problems in Table 2 is different from other models.

KIS1_N is the implementation of the process of making the negative form at the end of the sentence only for the answers with Y.

KIS1_N removes negative form data augmentation from **KIS1** when the original problem's gold standard answer is *No*, because the answer may not be reversed to *Yes* by converting into negative forms when the original problem's gold standard answer is *No*. We did not submit **KIS1_N** as one of our formal runs.

Table 2. Results of training data execution.

	Rule-based	BERT-based			
		KIS1	KIS2	KIS3	Baseline
Individual	545/887	**2688/4435**	2635/4435	2674/4435	2433/4135
	(0.614)	**(0.606)**	(0.594)	(0.603)	(0.588)
+Majority vote		544/887	540/887	**553/887**	494/827
		(0.613)	(0.609)	**(0.623)**	(0.597)
+Ensemble		558/887	557/887	**559/887**	505/827
		(0.629)	(0.628)	**(0.63)**	(0.611)

Table 3 shows the coverage and accuracies of our **Rule-based** system: of the 887 questions in the training data, 142 questions were covered and answered by our **Rule-based** system, which corresponds to the **Rule-coverable Problems** row in Table 3; the rest of the training data is 745 questions, which corresponds to the **Others** row. The cell of **Rule-based/Others** shows the results when we applied our **Rule-based** system to the originally non-applicable problems, which is not used in our formal run systems. In other words, the summation of the cell values of **Rule-based/Rule-coverable Problems** and **KIS3/Others** in Table 3 is equals to the value in the **KIS3/ + Ensemble** cell in Table 2.

Table 3. Coverage of our rule-based systems and accuracy scores for each system (BERT-based KIS1–3 corresponds to the Majority vote version)

	Rule-based	BERT-based		
		KIS1	KIS2	KIS3
Rule-coverable	**114/142**	100/142	97/142	108/142
Problems	**(0.803)**	(0.704)	(0.683)	(0.761)
Others	431/745	444/745	443/745	**445/745**
	(0.579)	(0.596)	(0.595)	**(0.597)**

Our system identified 173 of the 887 questions in the training data as problems that require person name inference (3.4). Table 4 shows the results of the 173 questions, which corresponds to the **Problem Name Inference Problems** row, and the other 714 questions, which corresponds to the **Others** row.

5   Discussion

Our **KIS2** submission achieved the 1st ranked score in Task 4 (Table 1). **KIS1** and **KIS3** were also able to solve the problem with a high percentage of correct answers, indicating that the ensemble of rule-based and BERT-based parts contributed to the improvement of the correct answer rate.

Table 4. Results for questions that require person name inference and others

	Rule-based	BERT-based		
		KIS1	KIS2	KIS3
Person Name	105/173	**107/173**	99/173	101/173
Inference Problems	(0.607)	**(0.618)**	(0.572)	(0.584)
Others	440/714	437/714	441/714	**452/714**
	(0.616)	(0.612)	(0.618)	**(0.633)**

In Table 2, + **Majority Vote** with five fine-tunings shows greatly better scores than **Individual**, suggesting that even when training with the same model, settings, and training data, the answers often differ and unstable. These results imply that fine-tuning results could be unstable, thus an ensemble can be effective in general. More than five times of fine-tuning trials could be a future work.

Such variations of outputs make it difficult to analyze the effectiveness of the individual methods. Adjusting the training settings or further augmenting the training data could solve this issue.

Because the results of **KIS1–3** were always better than **Baseline** in Table 2, we confirmed that our proposed method is effective. + **Ensemble** is always better than corresponding + **Majority Vote**, thus our ensemble with the **Rule-based** part was also confirmed as effective.

Statistically speaking, **KIS3** is slightly better than **KIS1**, suggesting that the person name inference was sometimes effective. Figure 8 shows an example of a person name inference failure. In this case, as inferred from the given civil law text, *agent*("代理人") to be in A and the *principal*("本人") to be in B, but the model inferred inversely. Out-of-vocabulary errors occurred when the answer is not one of the 49 candidates.

However, **KIS3** had higher scores than **KIS1** and **KIS2** in Table 2, suggesting that even replacing alphabetic letters with wrong person names is effective. Further improvement of the person name inference will contribute to the final correct answer.

KIS1_N showed further accuracy improvement over other results. This suggests that negative form generation is more effective when the negative form conversion is limited to the problems which gold standard answers are *Yes*.

In Table 3, the **BERT-based** systems show lower scores than our **Rule-based** system for the questions answered by our **Rule-based** system (**Rule-coverable Problems**), but the **BERT-based** systems show higher scores than our **Rule-based** system for the questions that are *not* answered by our **Rule-based** system (**Others**) These results suggest that the ensemble achieved our goal, which aims to compensate our **Rule-based** system by machine learning methods, regarding the problems which our **Rule-based** system is not good at. In Table 4, **KIS3**, which made the person name inference separately, does not show a very high correct answer rate in **Person Name Inference Problems**. On the other hand, the correct answer rate for **Others** questions was improved, suggesting that exclusion of **Person Name Inference Problems** in the training data may improve the general accuracy regarding the **Others** questions.

[Before replacement]
(Civil Code Article)
代理人が自己の占有物を以後本人のために占有する意思を表示したときは、本人は、これによって占有権を取得する。
When an agent has manifested his/her intention to take possession of his/her own possessions for the principal thereafter, the principal shall thereby acquire the right of possession.

(Problem text)
When A sells movable property X("甲") in his possession to B and expresses his intention to take possession of X("甲") for B thereafter, B shall acquire the right of possession of X("甲").
(Aが、自己が占有する動産甲をBに売却し、甲を以後Bのために占有する旨の意思を表示したときは、Bは、甲の占有権を取得する。)

[After replacement]
(Civil Code Article)
same

(Problem text)
When the principal sells movable property X("甲") that he/she possesses to the agent and indicates his/her intention to possess X("甲") for the agent thereafter, the agent shall acquire the right of possession of X("甲").
(本人が、自己が占有する動産甲を代理人に売却し、甲を以後代理人のために占有する旨の意思を表示したときは、代理人は、甲の占有権を取得する。)

Fig. 8. Example of the inversed substitution of person names (R03–08-E)

The similarity between the Civil Code articles and the problem texts was calculated by our data selection. As a result, the number of training data has decreased from **KIS2** (58,118) to **KIS1** (8,758) by the data selection. Meanwhile, there is not significant clear difference between the accuracies of **KIS1** and **KIS2**. These indicates that our data selection method was able to extract sentences of better quality. The figures below include examples of extracted sentences and selections.

Figure 9 shows the top five similar articles given an example problem text (Fig. 2), where bold parts indicate texts that are considered to be necessary in solving the problem.

These similar articles include the **bold** necessary parts, and in particular, the second ranked article includes information without excesses of deficiencies. This example suggests that Sentence-BERT works well in selecting relevant sentences. On the other hand, the article text without excesses of deficiencies is not always ranked as the highest, thus the current method is considered appropriate which uses the top five results but not only the highest.

> 1: **The interest of a partner who withdraws may be refunded in cash, regardless of the type of investment.**
> (脱退した組合員の持分は、その出資の種類を問わず、金銭で払い戻すことができる。)
>
> 2: **In addition to the cases described in the preceding article, a partner shall withdraw from the Partnership by expulsion. The interest of a partner who withdraws may be refunded in cash, regardless of the type of investment.**
> (前条の場合のほか、組合員は、除名によって脱退する。脱退した組合員の持分は、その出資の種類を問わず、金銭で払い戻すことができる。)
>
> 3: **In addition to the cases described in the preceding article, a partner shall withdraw from the Partnership by expulsion. The interest of a partner who withdraws may be refunded in cash, regardless of the type of investment.** With respect to matters that have not yet been completed at the time of withdrawal, calculations may be made after the completion of such matters.
> (前条の場合のほか、組合員は、除名によって脱退する。脱退した組合員の持分は、その出資の種類を問わず、金銭で払い戻すことができる。脱退の時にまだ完了していない事項については、その完了後に計算をすることができる。)
>
> 4: **The interest of a partner who withdraws may be refunded in cash, regardless of the type of investment.** With respect to matters that have not yet been completed at the time of withdrawal, calculations may be made after the completion of such matters.
> (脱退した組合員の持分は、その出資の種類を問わず、金銭で払い戻すことができる。脱退の時にまだ完了していない事項については、その完了後に計算をすることができる。)
>
> 5: **In addition to the cases described in the preceding article, a partner shall withdraw from the Partnership by expulsion. The interest of a partner who withdraws may be refunded in cash, regardless of the type of investment.** Calculations between a partner who has withdrawn and the other partners shall be made in accordance with the status of the assets of the Partnership at the time of withdrawal.
> (前条の場合のほか、組合員は、除名によって脱退する。脱退した組合員の持分は、その出資の種類を問わず、金銭で払い戻すことができる。脱退した組合員と他の組合員との間の計算は、脱退の時における組合財産の状況に従ってしなければならない。)

Fig. 9. Top five similar articles given an example problem text

Given another problem text (R03–20-O), Fig. 10 shows the replaced article text with the highest similarity score within our data selection results obtained from the original article text.

This problem is difficult to solve in general because this problem does not contain information on the assumption of exculpatory obligations. However, we obtained a higher similarity score by our proposed method. Our reference substitution method, as described in 3.2, substitutes the actual article number by the article text, which augments the information on the assumption of indemnifiable obligations that is not given in the related articles. In this way, our reference substitution method could refer to articles that are not given as related articles, and our data selection method could allow using the substituted sentences. We manually verified and corrected our reference substitution results, so there were no failures in the reference substitution. On the other hand, sentences after substitutions get longer, sometimes exceed the maximum input length of BERT, which are not included in the selection.

[civil code article with the highest degree of similarity]

A creditor may transfer a security interest created as security for an obligation discharged by the debtor under the provisions of the **"The underwriter of an exculpatory debt assumption shall assume an obligation with the same terms and conditions as the obligation owed by the obligor to the obligee, and the obligor shall be discharged from his/her own obligation."** to the obligation incurred by the underwriter. However, if a person other than the underwriter has established such a security interest, the underwriter's consent must be obtained.

(債権者は、「免責的債務引受の引受人は債務者が債権者に対して負担する債務と同一の内容の債務を負担し、債務者は自己の債務を免れる。」の規定により債務者が免れる債務の担保として設定された担保権を引受人が負担する債務に移すことができる。ただし、引受人以外の者がこれを設定した場合には、その承諾を得なければならない。)

[Problem text]

In an exculpatory assumption of debt, a creditor may not transfer a security interest created as security for the debtor's exculpatory obligation to the obligation assumed by the assumer.

(免責的債務引受において債権者は債務者が免れる債務の担保として設定された担保権を引受人が負担する債務に移すことはできない。)

Fig. 10. An example problem (R03–20-O) where our reference substitution method successfully included new article information

6 Conclusion and Future Works

We implemented BERT-based solvers and rule-based solver, integrated them by an ensemble. We improved the correct answer ratio through data expansions and ensembles, achieved 67.89% in accuracy on the COLIEE 2022 test data, placing first among the 18 formal runs of the participating teams.

Our original intention to develop the rule-based method was to make the process white-boxed, but the rule-based method is confirmed as effective through the ensemble. Since the rule-based method can explicitly select which problems to solve, it is possible to create rule-based modules specialized for problems that other types of methods, such as BERT, are not good at, thus further improvement in accuracy can be expected by creating rule-based modules specialized for ensembles.

The results of BERT's fine-tuning varied, making it difficult to determine whether there are consistent improvements, probably due to the randomness of the initial values. On the other hand, because the rule-based method always outputs the same result for the same data input, it was easier to judge whether the improvements are stable. In order to overcome this issue, we integrated five fine-tuning results of the BERT model, confirmed that it stabilizes the results and improves its overall accuracy.

We segmented and reconstructed the texts to contain necessary information without excess or deficiency, where Sentence-BERT was used to determine which data should be included. We also augmented the text data by replacing the article number with the actual article texts, transforming the data into negative forms, and replacing the data with alphabetical characters, resulting in better accuracy scores than our baseline which does not use these data augmentations. We found that our data selection method properly selects appropriate texts by combining our reconstruction method and our reference substitution method.

Our future work includes employments of other machine learning methods than BERT, ensembles of such different machine learning methods or multiple models. Another future work is to improve the performance of our person name inference.

Acknowledgments. This research was partially supported by MEXT Kakenhi 00271635, 22H00804, and 21K18115,Japan.

References

1. Rabelo, J., Goebel, R., Kim, M.-Y., Kano, Y., Yoshioka, M., Satoh, K.: Summary of the competition on legal information extraction/entailment (COLIEE) 2021. In: Proceedings of the Eighth International Competition on Legal Information Extraction/Entailment (COLIEE 2021), pp.1–7 (2021)
2. Fujita, M., Kiyota, N., Kano, Y.: Predicate's argument resolver and entity abstraction for legal question answering: KIS teams at COLIEE 2021 shared task. In: Proceedings of the Eighth International Competition on Legal Information Extraction/Entailment (COLIEE 2021), pp. 15–24 (2021)
3. Yoshioka, M., Aoki, Y., Suzuki, Y.: BERT-based ensemble methods with data augmentation for legal textual entailment in COLIEE statute law task. In: ICAIL 2021 Proceedings of the Eighteenth International Conference on Artificial Intelligence and Law, pp.278–284 (2021)
4. Nguyen, H.-T., et al.: ParaLaw nets - cross-lingual sentence-level pretraining for legal text processing. In: Proceedings of the Eighth International Competition on Legal Information Extraction/Entailment (COLIEE 2021) , pp.54–59 (2021)
5. Kim, M.-Y., Rabelo, J., Goebel, R.: BM25 and transformer-based legal information extraction and entailment. In: Proceedings of the Eighth International Competition on Legal Information Extraction/Entailment (COLIEE 2021) , pp.25–30 (2021)
6. Schilder, F., et al.: A pentapus grapples with legal reasoning. In: Proceedings of the Eighth International Competition on Legal Information Extraction/Entailment (COLIEE 2021) , pp.60–68 (2021)
7. Wehnert, S., Dureja, S., Kutty, L., Sudhi, V.: E.W.D. luca, using contextual word embeddings and graph embeddings for legal textual entailment classification. In: Proceedings of the Eighth International Competition on Legal Information Extraction/Entailment (COLIEE 2021), pp.69–77 (2021)
8. Hoshino, R., Kiyota, N., Kano, Y.: Question answering system for legal bar examination using predicate argument structures focusing on exceptions. In: Proceedings of the Sixth International Competition on Legal Information Extraction/Entailment (COLIEE 2019) (2019)
9. Devlin, J., Chang, M-W., Lee, K., Toutanova, K.: BERT: pre-training of deep bidirectional transformers for language understanding (2019) arXiv:1810.04805v2
10. Pretrained Japanese BERT models. https://github.com/cl-tohoku/bert-japanese
11. "【日本語モデル付き】2020年に自然言語処理をする人にお勧めしたい文ベクトルモデル (Japanese model attached: sentence vector models recommended to developers of natural language processing in 2020)", https://qiita.com/sonoisa/items/1df94d0a98cd4f2 09051. (in Japanese)

Less is Better: Constructing Legal Question Answering System by Weighing Longest Common Subsequence of Disjunctive Union Text

Minae Lin[1], Sieh-chuen Huang[1] (ID), and Hsuan-lei Shao[2]([✉]) (ID)

[1] National Taiwan University, Roosevelt Rd., Taipei City 106, Taiwan
{R09341057,schhuang}@ntu.edu.tw
[2] National Taiwan Normal University, Heping E. Rd., Taipei City 106, Taiwan
hlshao@ntnu.edu.tw

Abstract. This article is prepared for submission to *Competition on Legal Information Extraction/Entailment (COLIEE 2022)*, an international competitive event organized to focus on information processing and retrieval. The proposed method tackles on how to construct an answering system capable of responding Yes/No legal questions, ultimately recognizing entailment between legal queries from past Japanese bar exams and relevant articles of Japan Civil Code (both in Japanese). We first attempted to extract disjunctive union text from each training query and relevant article(s) with corresponding 'Y/N' answers as their labels, eventually forming our reference database (training set). Then the same process was repeated on a sample of different queries and relevant articles yet without a 'Y/N' label as the input (testing set). Finally, when constructing our model, the similarity ratio between the test disjunctive union and the training disjunctive union by longest common subsequence was calculated as its basis. As a result, this model achieved an accuracy of 0.6055 in Task 4 (rank 3rd as a team, and 7th as a trial). This is an extremely simple and efficient model capable of satisfactory performance.

Keywords: Textual Entailment · Disjunctive Union Text · Longest Common Subsequence · Legal Analytics · COLIEE 2022 · Lexical Features

1 Introduction

Competition on Legal Information Extraction/Entailment (COLIEE), widely known as an international event for people to work on the perfection of legal information retrieval techniques and methodologies, had its ninth run in 2022 [1–3]. There are four tasks presented in the 2022 competition: two of them (Task 1 and 2) are part of the case law competition, and the other two (Task 3 and 4) are part of the statute law competition. This paper focuses on Task 4, which requires participants to devise creative ways to confirm whether the entailment of a yes/no answer corresponds with the most relevant Civil Code articles provided [4]. We attempted a simple approach known as the longest

---

M. Lin, S.-C. Huang and H.-L. Shao—All authors contributed equally to this work.
H.-L. Shao—Corresponding author

common subsequence (LCS) [15] to challenge Task 4, and reached a satisfactory score. This can serve as a basis to derive further thoughts when tackling similar tasks or even be potentially applied on ensemble learning as one the building pieces to construct more complex models in the future.

In detail, our team, *Legal Analytics Laboratory of National Taiwan University (LLNTU)*, participated in Task 3 (the Statute Law Retrieval Task) and Task 4 (the Legal Question Answering Task). In Task 4, we collected and structured a dataset of disjunctive union text based on training queries and relevant articles. Next, the same process was applied to other unprocessed legal queries and the respective relevant articles. Finally, we compared the disjunctive union text of the test data to those of the training data, i.e., establishing a longest common subsequence similarity comparison model to find the most similar disjunctive union text in the training data. The 'Y/N' labels of the most resembling queries in the training data will be the recommended answer for the test queries. The accuracy of the model without stop words is 0.5780, while the accuracy of the model with punctuations as stop words is 0.6055 (ranked 3rd as a team).

2   Competition Data and Task Description

The COLIEE organizers provided the *"Statute Law Competition Data Corpus"* which consists of Japanese bar exams' legal questions, and Japanese Civil Code articles in original Japanese as well as translated English. The format of the COLIEE competition corpus is RITEVAL, developed for one of the previous NTCIR projects [4]. The corpus is composed of bar exam 'Yes/No' questions and the corresponding articles along with a label indicating that whether their relationships are confirmed, as illustrated in the following example:

"R02-27-O"

```
<pair id="R02-27-O" label="N">
<t1>
Article 676 (3) A partner may not seek the division of the
partnership property before liquidation.
</t1>
<t2>
A partner may seek the division of the partnership property
before liquidation if the consent of the majority of partners
exists.
</t2>
</pair>
```

The part enclosed by <t2> contains the full text of a legal bar exam question Q, and the part enclosed by <t1> contains the full text of the article of Japan Civil Code relevant to Q. The above example indicates that the query id "R02-27-O" is confirmed to be answerable according to the Article 676 (3) (relevant to Task 3). The pair in this example is labelled "N" according to its attribute, meaning the answer for this query is "No," which says the legal question is not entailed by the relevant article (relevant to Task 4). For both Task 3 and 4, the training data should remain the same. These training data were provided for two sub-tasks as following:

1) Task 3: Legal Information Retrieval Task. A bar exam 'Yes/No' question is provided as input. In correspondence, relevant Civil Code articles should be the respective output.
2) Task 4: Recognizing Entailment between Law Articles and Queries. A bar exam question and its relevant article(s) are provided as input. In correspondence, 'Yes/No' should be the respective answer [4].

For Task 3, the suggested evaluation measures consist of precision, recall and F2-measure. The COLIEE organizers emphasize recall more since the goal of information retrieval in this scenario is selecting articles for further usage in the following entailment process [4]. The formulas for calculating those measures are specified as following:

$$Precision = \frac{average\ of\ (the\ number\ of\ correctly\ retrieved\ articles\ for\ each\ query)}{the\ number\ of\ retrieved\ articles\ for\ each\ query}$$

$$Recall = \frac{average\ of\ (the\ number\ of\ correctly\ retrieved\ articles\ for\ each\ query)}{the\ number\ of\ relevant\ articles\ for\ each\ query}$$

$$F2\ measure = \frac{5 \times Precision \times Recall}{4 \times Precision + Recall}$$

The goal of Task 4 is to construct a 'Yes/No' question answering system for legal queries, interpreting entailment between queries and their relevant articles. How the proposed system performs will be evaluated using its 'Yes' or 'No' answers to previously unprocessed queries, after evaluating input queries and provided Civil Code article(s). Training data include triplets of a query, its relevant article(s), and a label in 'Y' or 'N' representing the correct answer. Test data includes only queries and relevant articles, but no 'Y/N' label [4]. We will focus on Task 4 in the following part of this article.

3 Data Preprocessing

Our research only utilized the original Japanese data corpus provided by the COLIEE organizers but the English translation of data corpus. In the beginning, we had 1,086 bar exam questions functioning as <t2> from H18-R02, and 768 Civil Code articles functioning as <t1>. Our design is to find the disjunctive union text from training questions and relevant articles. Our approach first compares words of <t2> with those of <t1> and then picks up words appearing in either <t2> or <t1> as "disjunctive union text", while discarding words existing in both <t2> and <t1>. Mathematically speaking, it is a process of finding the symmetric difference of <t2> and <t1> sets, as Fig. 1 shows.

For example, as Table 1 indicates, in the training data <pair label = "N", id = "R02-27-O">, the query id "R02-27-O" (<t2>) is believed to be relevant with Article 676 (3) (<t1>). First, in order to reduce noises, the article number of the Civil Code, i.e., "Article 676 (3)" was excluded while constructing disjunctive union text (B). Next, the words appearing in both <t2> and <t1>, "組合員は、清算前に組合財産の分割を求めることができ" in Japanese and "*A partner may seek the division of the partnership property before liquidation.*"

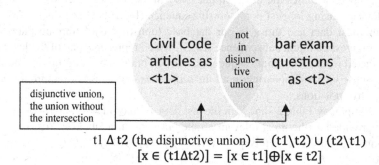

$$t1 \, \Delta \, t2 \text{ (the disjunctive union)} = (t1\backslash t2) \cup (t2\backslash t1)$$
$$[x \in (t1\Delta t2)] = [x \in t1] \oplus [x \in t2]$$

Fig. 1. Venn diagram of $<t1> \, \Delta \, <t2>$

in English, will be abandoned, while words existing in either $<t2>$ or $<t1>$, "組合員の過半数の同意がある場合には，る。ない。" in Japanese and "*if the consent of the majority of partners exists. not.*" in English will be recorded as "disjunctive union text." It should be noticed that only Japanese data is processed so the content's English translation may not be literally equivalent to its Japanese counterpart. Finally, we obtained a new set of data (B) by combining "disjunctive union text" with the provided 'Y/N' labels. In the result dataset, there are a total number of 1,086 (B).

Table 1. Constructing disjunctive union text for $<$pair id="R02-27-O"$>$

Bar exam question for Training "R02-27-O" ($<t2>$)	Japan Civil Code article(s) ($<t1>$)	Disjunctive union text (B)	Label
組合員は，組合員の過半数の同意がある場合には，清算前に組合財産の分割を求めることができる。	~~第六百七十六条　3~~ 組合員は、清算前に組合財産の分割を求めることができない。	組合員の過半数の同意がある場合には，る。ない。	N
A partner may seek the division of the partnership property before liquidation if the consent of the majority of partners exists.	~~Article 676 (3)~~ *A partner may not seek the division of the partnership property before liquidation.*	*if the consent of the majority of partners exists. not.*	N

After performing transformation described above, we obtained a dataset in which 1,086 disjunctive union text and corresponding 'Y/N' labels are included, which will function as our database to work with in the next step.

When handling the test data, we also preprocessed queries and relevant article(s) in the same manner like the approach described above. In other words, disjunctive union text of the test data will also be produced, but without the corresponding 'Y/N' labels.

Next, our model searches the most similar entry in the dataset based on the similarity ratio calculated using longest common subsequence (LCS) between disjunctive union text of this test data and those in our database (constituted of training data) as the weights. Longest common subsequence (LCS), which represents one of the lexical features extracted from two or more sequences, can be obtained by counting the number of common subsequences appearing in all the sequences, but does not require those to be in consecutive positions.

For example, as Table 2 shows, in the test data a <pair id = "R03-28-U">, Article 677 was provided as the most relevant article but without a label of 'Yes/No' answer. The disjunctive union text of this query (A) is "組合員の持分の限度でる。ない。" in Japanese and "*to the extent of the partner's interest. not*" in English.

Table 2. Answering Yes/No Question <pair id="R03-28-U">

Bar exam question for Testing "R03-28-U" (<t2>)	Japan Civil Code article(s) (<t1>)	Disjunctive union text (A)	Most similar datum ("R02-27-O")
組合員の債権者は、組合財産について、その組合員の持分の限度で権利を行使することができる。	第六百七十七条 組合員の債権者は、組合財産についてその権利を行使することができない。	組合員の持分の限度でる。ない。	["組合員の過半数の同意がある場合には，る。ない。", "N"]
A partner's creditor may exercise the rights of that creditor against the partnership property to the extent of the partner's interest.	~~Article 677~~ *A partner's creditor may not exercise the rights of that creditor against the partnership property.*	*to the extent of the partner's interest. not*	["*if the consent of the majority of partners exists. not.*", "N"]

Finally, the model found that the most similar disjunctive union text, which is the entry containing the highest ratio of LCS in our database, "R02-27-O" ["組合員の過半数の同意がある場合には，る。ない。", "N"] in Japanese and ["*if the consent of the majority of partners exists. not.*", "N"] in English. Therefore, our system will output the response to this query as "N," suggested by the most similar data text contained in "R02-27-O" as indicated in Table 1.

The degrees of similarity between the querying disjunctive union text (i.e., (A) in the Table 2) and other text in our database (for example, (B) in the Table 1) are calculated using the Sequence Matcher Similarity ratios (hereinafter referred to as SMS-ratios) of longest common subsequence intersecting both. Figure 2 visualizes the core concept when performing the LCS comparison.

The following formula shows how to calculate SMS ratio of (A) and (B).

$$Sequence\ Matcher\ Similaraty(SMS)ratio = \frac{2 \times amount\ of\ A \cap B}{amount\ of\ A + amount\ of\ B}$$

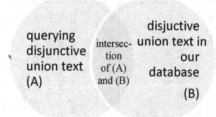

Fig. 2. Intersection of (A) and (B)

4 The Result

To improve the accuracy, we attempted to perform the disjunctive union text detection differently: with and without stop words. In our case, punctuations are chosen to be stop words. We used the training data of H18-H29 to construct the database of disjunctive union text. And the data of H30-R03 are utilized as the test set (self-testing sets). Table 3 shows both scenarios' performances in these four self-testing sets respectively.

Table 3. Accuracy in self-testing sets with two different constructions of the model

model	H30-accuracy	H30-performance	R01-accuracy	R01-performance	R02-accuracy	R02-performance	R03-accuracy	R03-performance
Without stop words (diffSim)	51.4%	36/70	50.5%	56/111	60.5%	49/81	57.8%	63/109
With stop words (deNgram)	47.1%	33/70	54.1%	60/111	58%	47/81	60.1%	66/109

In terms of performance, we achieve 0.5780 accuracy for the model without defining any stop words, and 0.6055 accuracy with the punctuations defined as stop words regarding the official test data (R03). Overall, it is ranked as 7th and 8th among 17 teams/trials. The performance of this non-deep-learning model shows the potential of employing a simple method on the task of answering legal questions.

5 Discussion and Conclusion

Our model is quite simple yet effective when utilized to interpret most of the queries. The symmetric difference of a query and its relevant article(s) may be correlated with similar patterns extracted from the 'Yes/No' question triplets and hence those corresponding answers ('Y/N' label) associated with the specified pattern can be used to answer unseen queries. In concise, what this article proposed is an analogical approach relying on detecting resembling symmetric differences between processed queries and unprocessed ones presented as the input question. This approach can correctly identify responses to not only short queries but also long queries containing a lot of text. Table 4 demonstrates how our model could be applied to a lengthy question. By calculating the ratio of SMS

Table 4. Calculating SMS ratio to solve a 'Yes/No' question with long text <pair id="R03-02-I">

Bar exam question "R03-02-I" (<t2>)	Japan Civil Code article(s) (<t1>)	Disjunctive union text (A)	Most similar datum (similarity=0.654) ("H20-30-I")
表意者の意思表示がその真意ではないことを理由として無効とされた場合において、その無効は、善意であるが過失がある第三者に対抗することができる。	第九十三条 意思表示は、表意者がその真意ではないことを知ってしたときであっても、そのためにその効力を妨げられない。ただし、相手方がその意思表示が表意者の真意ではないことを知り、又は知ることができたときは、その意思表示は、無効とする。2 前頃ただし書による意思表示の無効は、善意ただし書による意思表示の無効は、善意の第三者に対抗することができない。	の理由としてとされた場合において、そであるが過失があるある。は、知ってしたときであっても、そのためにその効力を妨げられない。ただし、相手方がその意思表示が表意者の真意ではないことを知り、又は知ることができたとき、その意思表示は、する。2 前頃ただし書の規定によるのない。	["心裡留保の場合、相手方が知らなかったとし、知らないことについて重大な過失がなければ、有であ意思表示は、がそではないことをってしたときであっ、そのためにその効力を妨げられない。ただし、相手方が表意者の真意を知り、又は知ることができたときは、無とす", "N"]
If the manifestation of intention of a person is held void on the ground that it does not reflect that person's true intention, such nullity may be duly asserted against a third party in good faith acting with negligence.	*Article 93* (1) *The manifestation of intention of a person is not impaired even if the person making it does so while knowing that it does not reflect that person's true intention;* (2) *The nullity of a manifestation of intention under the proviso to the preceding paragraph may not be duly asserted against a third party in good faith.*	*If the of a person is held void on the ground, such nullity may be duly asserted against The validity of a is not impaired even if the person making it does so while knowing....The nullity of a manifestation of intention under the provisions of the proviso to the preceding paragraph may not be*	["*In the case of concealment of, assuming was unaware of party making the manifestation, and there was no gross negligence...knew or that lack of knowledge...knew or could have known that the manifestation was not person who made it, that is void.*", "N"]

(continued)

Table 4. (*continued*)

Bar exam question "R03-02-I" (<t2>)	Japan Civil Code article(s) (<t1>)	Disjunctive union text (A)	Second similar datum (similarity=0.562) ("H26-2-A")
表意者の意思表示が、その真意ではないことを理由として無効とされた場合において、善意であるが過失がある第三者に対抗することができる。	第九十三条 意思表示は、表意者がその真意ではないことを知ってしたときであっても、そのためにその効力を妨げられない。ただし、相手方がその意思表示が表意者の真意ではないことを知り、又は知ることができたときは、その意思表示は、無効とする。 2 前項ただし書の意思表示の無効は、善意の第三者に対抗することができない。	の理由としてとされた場合において、そであるが過失がある。は、知ってしたときであっても、そのためにその効力を妨げられない。ただし、相手方がその意思表示が表意者の真意ではないことを知り、又は、その意思表示は、その意思表示は、2 前項ただし書による第三者に意思表示の無効は、対抗することができない。	［「前二項規定よよし善が過失抗るな。相手方すにいてが行った場合て相手方を事実を知ってってきたはその意思表示をりとると第三者が強迫を行った場合において相手方その意思表示の事実を知らなかったときも方がその意思表示を取り消こととができ。", "Y"］
If the manifestation of intention of a person is held void on the ground that it does not reflect that person's true intention, such nullity may be duly asserted against a third party in good faith acting with negligence.	~~Article 93~~ (1) The validity of a manifestation of intention is not impaired even if the person making it does so while knowing that it does not reflect that person's true intention; … (2) The nullity of a manifestation of intention under the proviso to the preceding paragraph may not be duly asserted against a third party in good faith.	If the of a person is held void on the ground, such nullity may be duly asserted against The validity of a is not impaired even if the person making it does so while knowing… The nullity of a manifestation of intention under the provisions of the proviso to the preceding paragraph may not be	["A manifestation of intention based on fraud or duress is voidable. If a first party In cases any person a second that is voidable only second or could have known that The rescission of induced by fraud under provisions preceding two paragraphs may be duly asserted against a third party in good faith acting without negligence.. the other such may be rescinded other such On the other hand, in cases any third party commits any duress inducing any person to make to other party, such manifestation other party did know such fact.", "Y"]

(LCS) and identifying the nearest triplet, an answer ("N" in this cases) of acceptable accuracy should be obtained.

Table 5 shows how to generate disjunctive union text of "H20-30-I" (B).

As Table 4 shows, the SMS similarity ratio of the most similar pair, (A) "R03-02-I" and (B) "H20-30-I," was 0.654, which was determined by LCS. Compared to that, the ratio of the second most similar pair, (A) "R03-02-I" and (B) "H26-2-A," was merely 0.562. The rest 1,084 entries of (B) in our database had lower ratios when compared with the above two. Therefore, (B) of "H20-30-I" was determined to be the most similar datum.

The disjunctive union text of the unseen query (A) may contain words similar to the instances of (B) in the database including but not limited to "意思表示 (manifestation of intention)", "表意者(person who made it)", and "真意 (true intention)." This approach naturally leads the model to pair the data with the same topic, "心裡留保 (concealment of intention)." However, the number of the Civil Code article, for example, "Article 93" in Table 4, was not included in the database while constructing disjunctive union text (B).

Table 7 shows how to generate disjunctive union text of "H24-10-5" (B).

As Table 6 and 7 indicate, when the model is too focused on camouflage examples, it misses some obvious questions. In the case that a relevant article of the unprocessed query shares several words with a disjunctive union text in the database, our model was misled. This happens in the "R03-08-E" (which is relevant to Article 183), in which our model incorrectly pairs it with the disjunctive union text of "H24-10-5" (which is more relevant to Article 184 and the label is "N"). We could determine the reason that our algorithm generates an erroneous response to "R03-08-E" because Article 184 is the proviso postscript of Article 183 and therefore worded in a very similar fashion to it. However, our model fails to distinguish them due to the lack of successfully answered bar exam questions relevant to Article 184. This should improve in the future, as more applicable data should be accumulated each year and will be utilized to update training data.

Employing disjunctive text in semantic analysis is not a brand new idea [7, 8], yet it can quickly reach its potential limit as semantics can get really complex. Also, the calculation of disjunctive union text can incur intensive computation costs when processing lengthy and complicated text [9]. On the other hand, longest common subsequence (LCS) had been used by past participants [10, 11] as an approach to performing lexical matching in the previous COLIEE for Task 1 (legal case retrieval task). LCS method is also a traditional method and faces its limit [12, 13].

The idea of combining disjunctive union text and LCS stems from one co-author's experience of preparing for the bar exam. The disjunctive union text, which is the non-overlapping part of a query and its relevant article, demonstrates a pattern of the question maker's attempts to "camouflage" examinees. That is, it entails a designated set of rules to incorporate statutes with the exam questions. Hence, it is not the intersection of a query and its relevant article that is important, but the symmetric difference between those two matters the most. Our model compares the patterns of bfuscate detected in previous exams with similar patterns found in unseen questions by measuring their longest common subsequence (LSC). This model deals merely with lexical features and

Table 5. Constructing disjunctive union text of <pair label="N" id="H20-30-I">

Bar exam questions for training "H20-30-I" (<t2>)	Japan Civil Code article(s) (<t1>)	Disjunctive union text (B)	Label
心裡留保の場合、相手方が表意者の真意を知らなかったとしても、知らないことについて重大な過失があれば、その意思表示は有効である。	第九十三条　意思表示は、表意者がその真意ではないことを知ってしたときであっても、そのためにその効力を妨げられない。ただし、相手方が表意者の真意を知り、又は知ることができたときは、その意思表示は、無効とする。	心裡留保の場合、相手方が表意者の真意を知らなかったとし、知らないことについて重大な過失があなければ、有である意思表示は、がではないことをもってしたときであって、そのためにその効力を妨げられない。ただし、相手方が表意者の真意を知り、又は知ることができたときは、無とす	N
In the case of concealment of true intention, assuming the other party was unaware of the true intention of the party making the manifestation, and there was no gross negligence regarding that lack of knowledge, that manifestation of intention shall be valid.	_Article 93_ _The validity of a manifestation of intention is not impaired even if the person making it does not reflect that person's true intention; provided, however, that if the other party knew or could have known that the manifestation was not the true intention of the person who made it, that manifestation of intention is void._	_In the case of concealment of, assuming was unaware of party making the manifestation, and there was no gross negligence regarding that lack of knowledge, that...knew or could have known that the manifestation was not person who made it, that is void._	N

Table 6. Calculating SMS ratio to pair a 'Yes/No' question with incorrect short text <pair id="R03-08-E">

Bar exam questions "R03-08-E" (<t2>)	Japan Civil Code Articles (<t1>)	Disjunctive union text	Most similar datum (similarity=0.576)("H24-10-5")
Aが・自己が占有する動産甲をBに売却し、甲を以後Bのために占有する旨の意思を表示したときは・Bは、甲の占有権を取得する。	第百八十三条 代理人が自己の占有物を以後本人のために占有する意思を表示したときは・本人は、これによって占有権を取得する。	Aがする動産甲をBに売却し、甲B代理人の物本人Bの本人これによって	["Aは、B動産甲代理人によって占有をする場合において、本人とその代理人に対して以後その物、受寄、その第三、A、動産甲の、その第三者","N"]
When A sells movable X in his possession to B, and manifests the intention to thenceforward possess X on behalf of B, B acquires the possessory rights of X.	*Article 183 If an agent manifests the intention to thenceforward possess a thing under the agent's own possession on behalf of the principal, the principal thereby acquires the possessory rights.*	When A sells movable X in his possession to B, and X B, B rights of X. If an agent a thing under the agent's own possession the principal, the principal thereby rights.	["In cases where (A) bought movable A which (B) had owned and deposited to ...third party, that third party the third party acquires rights.", "N"]

Table 7. Constructing disjunctive union text of <pair label="N" id="H24-10-5">

examed bar query "H24-10-5" (<t2>)	Japan Civil Code Articles (<t1>)	Disjunctive union text	Label
Ａは，Ｂが第三者に寄託している動産甲をＢから買い受け，自ら受寄者に対し，以後Ａのために動産甲を占有することを命じ，受寄者がこれを承諾したときは，Ａは，動産甲の占有権を取得する。 *In cases where (A) bought the movable A which (B) had owned and deposited to the depositary, if A orders the depositary to thenceforward possess it on behalf of A, and such depositary consents thereto, A shall acquire the possessory right.*	第百八十四条　代理人によって占有をする場合において，本人がその代理人に対し以後その第三者のためにその物を占有することを命じ，その第三者がこれを承諾したときは，その第三者は，占有権を取得する。 *Article 184 If a thing is possessed through an agent, the principal orders that agent to thenceforward possess that thing on behalf of a third party, and that third party consents thereto, the third party acquires the possessory rights.*	Ａは，Ｂ動産甲代理人によって占有をする場合において，本人その代理人に対して以後その物，受寄，その第三，Ａ，動産甲の，その第三者 In cases where (A) bought movable A which (B) had owned and deposited to the depositary, if A the depositary it A, such depositary A shall acquire right. If a thing is possessed through an agent, principal that agent that thing a third party, that third party the third party acquires rights.	N

takes no account of semantics. Therefore, we cannot determine that our model correctly answers the question. Perhaps it produces closely estimated answers by exploiting the question makers' biases. For example, in the case of human observation, when the word, "不動産 (real property)" in the statutes was replaced by "動産 (movables)" in the query, the label (answer) is usually "No" since they cannot be used interchangeably. On the contrary, when the word, "物 (thing)" in the statutes was replaced by "動産 (movables)" in the query, the label (answer) is usually "Yes" because the former is a broader concept that can be narrowed down to the latter.

Our experiment showed that a purely rule-based approach may still prove to be an effective solution, although limited to a very specific kind of corpuses. Overall, when compared to other models applying complicated algorithms such as deep learning technique (which has been used by our LLNTU team in previous year, mainly based on the BERT [5, 6]), the model we proposed this time is simple enough to run without computational burden, which takes less than 1 s to preprocess the training data and 8.14 s for processing the test data and doing the LCS comparison. Compared to this, the BERT-based model we introduced previously took several days to produce the outcome [14]. This is because the time complexity of preprocessing is $O(m^2)$ per pair with m as lengths of queries, and the time complexity of LCS detection is $O(n \cdot m^2)$ per query which n accounts for the number of entries in the training data. Of course, it shall be noticed that the described scenario is based on our own experience. The cost of computation time for the LCS approach is shorter than the BERT approach. So, it might be valuable to apply this approach in practice for the reason of explainability. We recognize this simple model has its limits. To increase the model's performance, it may be necessary to perform a more precise failure analysis and add additional rules when constructing the model. That will be our main goal next year.

Acknowledgment. Hsuan-lei Shao, "Knowledge Graph of China Studies: Knowledge Extraction, Graph Database, Knowledge Generation" (110-2628-H-003-002-MY4, *Ministry of Science and Technology, the MOST*), Taiwan.

Sieh-chuen Huang, "A Study on Property Management Regimes in Family and Succession Law in Taiwan" (110-2410-H-002-026-MY3, *Ministry of Science and Technology, the MOST*), Taiwan.

References

1. Rabelo, J., Kim, M.-Y., Goebel, R., Yoshioka, M., Kano, Y., Satoh, K.: A summary of the COLIEE 2019 competition. In: Sakamoto, M., Okazaki, N., Mineshima, K., Satoh, K. (eds.) JSAI-isAI 2019. LNCS (LNAI), vol. 12331, pp. 34–49. Springer, Cham (2020). https://doi.org/10.1007/978-3-030-58790-1_3

2. Rabelo, J., Kim, M.Y., Goebel, R., Yoshioka, M., Kano, Y., Satoh, K.: COLIEE 2020: methods for legal document retrieval and entailment (2020). https://sites.ualberta.ca/~rabelo/COLIEE 2021/COLIEE_2020_summary.pdf

3. Rabelo, J., Goebel, R., Kim, M.Y., Kano, Y., Yoshioka, M., Satoh, K.: Overview and discussion of the competition on legal information extraction/entailment (COLIEE) 2021. Rev. Socionetwork Strat. **16**, 111–133 (2022). https://doi.org/10.1007/s12626-022-00105-z

4. COLIEE organizer. COLIEE-2022 main webpage, Online (2022). https://sites.ualberta.ca/~rabelo/COLIEE2022/

5. Tohoku NLP Group. Pretrained Japanese BERT models (BERT-base_mecab-ipadic-char-4k_whole-word-mask) (2022). https://github.com/cl-tohoku/bert-japanese

6. Alinear-corp, albert-japanese. https://github.com/alinear-corp/albert-japanese

7. Kasper, R.T.: A logical semantics for feature structures. In: 24th Annual Meeting of the Association for Computational Linguistics, pp. 257–266 (1986)

8. Eiter, T., Gottlob, G., Mannila, H.: Disjunctive datalog. ACM Trans. Database Syst. (TODS) **22**(3), 364–418 (1997)

9. Eiter, T., Gottlob, G.: On the computational cost of disjunctive logic programming: propositional case. Ann. Math. Artif. Intell. **15**(3), 289–323 (1995)

10. Tran, V., Le Nguyen, M., Tojo, S., Satoh, K.: Encoded summarization: summarizing documents into continuous vector space for legal case retrieval. Artif. Intell. Law **28**(4), 441–467 (2020). https://doi.org/10.1007/s10506-020-09262-4

11. Tran, V., Nguyen, M., Satoh, K.: Building legal case retrieval systems with lexical matching and summarization using a pre-trained phrase scoring model. In: ICAIL 2019: Proceedings of the Seventeenth International Conference on Artificial Intelligence and Law June 2019 (2020). https://doi.org/10.1145/3322640.3326740

12. Anan, Y., Hatano, K., Bannai, H., Takeda, M., Satoh, K.: Polyphonic music classification on symbolic data using dissimilarity functions. In: ISMIR, pp. 229–234 (2012)

13. Deken, J.G.: Some limit results for longest common subsequences. Discret. Math. **26**(1), 17–31 (1979)

14. Shao, H.-L., Chen, Y.-C., Huang, S.-C.: BERT-based ensemble model for statute law retrieval and legal information entailment. In: Okazaki, N., Yada, K., Satoh, K., Mineshima, K. (eds.) JSAI-isAI 2020. LNCS (LNAI), vol. 12758, pp. 226–239. Springer, Cham (2021). https://doi.org/10.1007/978-3-030-79942-7_15

15. Bergroth, L., Hakonen, H., Raita, T.: A survey of longest common subsequence algorithms. In: Proceedings Seventh International Symposium on String Processing and Information Retrieval. SPIRE 2000, pp. 39–48. IEEE (2000)

JSAI 2022 International Session

JSAI 2022 International Sessions

Yasufumi Takama[1], Sachiyo Arai[2], Daisuke Katagami[3], Takahiro Uchiya[4],
Akinori Abe[2], Katsutoshi Yada[5], Rafał Rzepka[6], Toshihiro Hiraoka[7],
and Hisashi Kashima[8]

[1] Tokyo Metropolitan University, Japan
[2] Chiba University, Japan
[3] Tokyo Polytechnic University, Japan
[4] Nagoya Institute of Technology, Japan
[5] Kansai University, Japan
[6] Hokkaido University, Japan
[7] University of Tokyo, Japan
[8] Kyoto University, Japan

The JSAI annual conferences are considered key events for the Japanese Society for Artificial Intelligence (JSAI), and the international sessions held at these conferences play a key role for the society in its efforts to share Japan's research on artificial intelligence with other countries. With the increased impact of AI on the world, the JSAI annual conferences have recently attracted many participants not only from academia but also from industries. The international sessions of JSAI 2022 were held online, and various research ideas were shared through active discussion with many participants. We are extremely pleased to publish this collection of papers as the research results of our international sessions.

The topics of the international sessions cover five categories: knowledge engineering, machine learning, agents, robots and real worlds, and human interface and education aid, which have been important topics for the JSAI community. The international sessions have 41 oral presentations, among which 32 papers submitted to a regular category were handled as the candidate papers for this post-proceedings. Each of the candidate papers was reviewed by at least two experts from the viewpoint of originality (the novelty of the paper), significance (impact on sciences and business), and quality of presentation. As a result of this review process, 17 papers were selected and invited to submit their extended version from papers presented at JSAI 2022. After checking the quality of submitted extended versions of papers by JSAI 2022 International Program Committee members, 7 papers were included in this book. All of the papers are original and high quality, representing key contributions to AI research.

We would like to extend our deepest appreciation to President Itsuki Noda, Vice President Chie Morita (General Chair of JSAI 2022), and Executive Committee Chair Hiroyuki Toda, as well as to the JSAI administrative staff and Springer publishing staff for their tremendous assistance on this project. We would also like to thank the authors of the papers contained in this book and all international session contributors.

Proposal for Turning Point Detection Method Using Financial Text and Transformer

Rei Taguchi[1][✉], Hikaru Watanabe[1], Hiroki Sakaji[1], Kiyoshi Izumi[1], and Kenji Hiramatsu[2]

[1] School of Engineering, The University of Tokyo, Tokyo, Japan
s5abadiee@g.ecc.u-tokyo.ac.jp
[2] IFIS Japan Limited, Tokyo, Japan

Abstract. In this study, we demonstrate whether analysts' sentiment toward individual stocks is useful for stock market analysis. This can be achieved by creating a polarity index in analyst reports using natural language processing. In this study, we calculated anomaly scores for the created polarity index using anomaly detection algorithms. The results show that the proposed method is effective in detecting the turning point of the polarity index.

Keywords: Stock market · Financial time series analysis · Natural language processing · Machine learning · Anomaly detection

1 Introduction

In recent years, with the explosive development of artificial intelligence, the use of alternative data has been attracting worldwide attention. The use of alternative data is particularly prominent in the financial and economic fields, where it is beginning to be widely used for economic forecasting and investment strategies, in addition to traditional financial data. In Japan, the Japan Alternative Data Accelerator Association (JADAA)[1], and other cross-industry organizations have been established to actively promote the use of alternative data. Among them, text data is particularly versatile, and it has been found that it is possible to extract predictions and classifications from the author's writing style and content bias [1,2]. In addition, analyst reports are considered to have a very high information value among text data [5]. It has been found that the polarity index generated from analyst reports has a leading edge over macroeconomic index such as exchange rates and issuance of government bonds. In this study, we use analyst reports to demonstrate that the future sentiment of individual stocks is useful for market analysis. The expected outcome is to show that the method proposed in this study is effective in detecting turning points of the polarity index. The contribution of this research is the development of fundamental techniques in a new market analysis framework using a polarity index generated from analyst reports.

[1] https://alternativedata.or.jp.

Y. Takama et al. (Eds.): JSAI-isAI 2022 Workshop, LNAI 13859, pp. 171–181, 2023.
https://doi.org/10.1007/978-3-031-29168-5_12

2   Related Works

The following studies have been conducted on the creation of a polarity index by machine learning. In Yono et al. [3], the monthly financial and economic reports are trained using Long Short Term Memory (LSTM), and Latent Dirichlet Allocation (LDA) is used to create an index for each topic such as consumer spending, capital investment, and inventory. We also analyze which macroeconomic factors are more influential by determining how much each topic's sentiment contributes to the overall sentiment. Jin et al. [4] created a polarity index to predict the closing price of a stock from Stocktwits' data, a social networking site for investors in the financial sector. The model used LSTM.

While the above studies use similar texts such as the Monthly Financial and Economic Report and the Economic Watcher Survey, our study differs in that we use analyst reports as an index by summing up the sentiment of individual stocks. As an example of research on text mining using analyst reports, the following studies have been conducted. In Hiramatsu et al. [5], not only do stock prices respond strongly to the sentiment of the report, but also drift in stock prices is observed after the report is issued, suggesting that the textual information in analyst reports is useful in asset management practice. Further, Asquith et al. [6] investigates the association between market returns and the content of analyst reports using regression analysis. In Suzuki et al. [7], opinion and non-opinion text are extracted from analyst reports using LSTM and other methods, and forecasts of net income and stock prices are made.

On the other hand, we also differ from other studies in that we use BERT to train analyst reports. An example of a study using BERT is Hiew et al. [8]. Hiew et al. [8] uses Weibo, a Chinese social networking service, as text data, assigns polarity using BERT, and performs stock price prediction using LSTM.

In addition, we use Transformer and anomaly detection algorithms as part of the framework, which is different from other research. An example of research using the Transformer in the financial field is Ding et al. [9]. Ding et al. [9] introduced the Transformer and a multiscale Gaussian prior distribution to predict stock prices. Another example of the use of anomaly detection algorithms in the financial sector is Ahmed et al. [10]. Ahmed et al. [10] used algorithms such as Local Outlier Factor to perform turning point detection on stocks listed on the Australian Stock Exchange.

3   Method

In this study, we perform empirical analysis in the following three steps.
Step1: BERT is used to learn the text of analyst reports and classify them into three polarity categories: "positive", "negative", and "neutral".
Step2: Learn the created polarity indices (all industries and industry-specific) using Time2Vec+Transformer.
Step3 : For the output of **Step2**, we create anomaly scores using Hotelling's T^2 method. In addition, we aggregate the results.

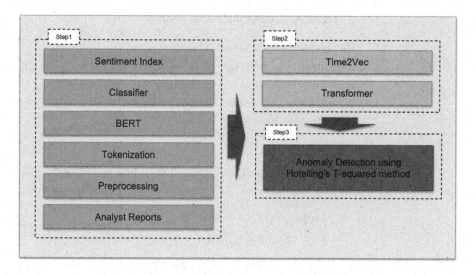

Fig. 1. Architecture of This Study

In addition, the architecture in this study can be described as shown in Fig. 1.

3.1 Polarity Classification Method Using Bidirectional Encoder Representations from Transformers (BERT)

The contents of this section correspond to **Step1** in Sect. 3. BERT is a Transformer-based language model proposed by Devlin et al. [11]. BERT allows for successful bidirectional learning by masking some tokens in the input and predicting the masked words. In this study, we use the model[2] published by Inui and Suzuki Laboratory at Tohoku University as a trained model for Japanese BERT. In this study, we use the method of Taguchi et al. [12] to create two types of models (UP Model and DOWN Model) using BERT. In the Taguchi et al. [12] method, a report in which the rating changes to "buy" is set to 1, a report in which the rating does not change to 0, and a report in which the rating changes to "sell" is set to −1. See Table 1 for the method of the final judgment. For details of this method, please refer to Taguchi et al. [12]. This architecture replaces the model in Sakaji et al. [13] with BERT. For the calculation results, see Sect. 5.

3.2 Transformer+Time2Vec

The contents of this section correspond to **Step2** in Sect. 3. In this section, we describe a learning method using Transformer+Time2Vec. In this method, the polarity index created in Sect. 3.1 is vectorized by Time2Vec, and its output is used as input for the Transformer.

---

[2] https://github.com/cl-tohoku/bert-japanese.

Table 1. Polarity Judgment Method

UP Model	DOWN Model	Final Judgment
0: Neutral	−1: Negative	−1: Negative
1: Positive	0: Neutral	1: Positive
1: Positive	−1: Negative	high likelihood
0: Neutral	0: Neutral	0: Neutral

First, we use Time2Vec to encode the concept of time into the Transformer. Time2Vec was proposed by Kazemi et al. [14]. Time2Vec is formulated as follows.

$$\begin{cases} \mathbf{t2v}(\tau)[i] = \omega_i \tau + \varphi_i, \ \text{if} \ i = 0 \\ \mathcal{F}(\omega_i \tau + \varphi_i), \ \text{if} \ 1 \leq i \leq k \end{cases} \tag{1}$$

Time2Vec for the time scalar τ is defined as $\mathbf{t2v}$. $\mathbf{t2v}[i]$ is an element of $\mathbf{t2v}$ at i. $\mathcal{F}$ is an active function with periodicity. The ω_i and φ_i are the parameters that can be learned.

Next, we use the Transformer for the training part. The Transformer is based on the Encoder-Decoder Model and incorporates Self-Attention and Feed Forward Neural Networks. The Transformer was proposed by Vaswani et al. [15]. And, the application of the Transformer to series data was proposed by Wu et al. [16].

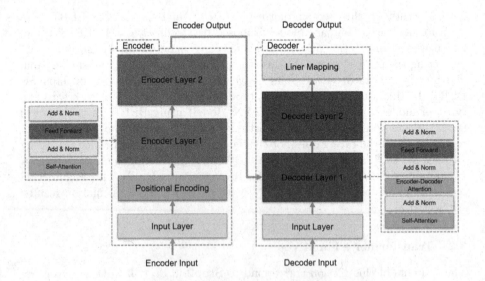

Fig. 2. Architecture of Transformer

The architecture of the transformer for time series can be represented in Fig. 2. MAE (Mean Absolute Error), MSE (Mean Squared Error), RMSE (Root Mean Squared Error), and MSLE (Mean Squared Logarithmic Error) are used to evaluate the transformer and comparison methods. See Sect. 5 for the reason for choosing the Transformer for the proposed method. See Appendix A for the definition of each evaluation metric.

3.3 Hotelling's T^2 Method

The contents of this section correspond to **Step3** in Sect. 3. To calculate the anomaly score for anomaly detection, we use Hotelling's T^2 method. The anomaly score is calculated by applying Hotelling's T^2 method to the Output of Sect. 3.2. The reason for using Hotelling's theory for the turning point detection part is that it uses the basic distribution information of the data such as mean and variance, and thus avoids to some extent the problem of empirical determination of parameters that occurs in change point detection algorithms such as ChangeFinder [17]. The T^2 method is an anomaly detection algorithm proposed by Hotelling [18]. Data are given by $\mathcal{D} = \{x_1, ..., x_n\}$. Assume that data $\mathcal{D}$ follows a normal distribution. From this, we can estimate the sample mean $\hat{\mu}$ and variance-covariance matrix $\hat{\Sigma}$ of the data $\mathcal{D}$. In this case, the anomaly score $a(\boldsymbol{x}')$ for the observed value x' is defined as follows.

$$a(\boldsymbol{x}') = (\boldsymbol{x}' - \hat{\boldsymbol{\mu}})^\mathsf{T} \hat{\boldsymbol{\Sigma}}^{-1} (\boldsymbol{x}' - \hat{\boldsymbol{\mu}}) \tag{2}$$

The threshold in this study is set based on the maximum value of the verification data. In addition, the ROC (Receiver Operating Characteristic) Curve is used to evaluate the performance of anomaly detection. AUC (Area Under the Curve) under ROC Curve ranges from 0 to 1, and it is said that the performance of the model is high if the AUC is 0.7 or higher. The author manually assigned the correct labels[3] necessary for the evaluation using the ROC Curve.

4 Experiments

Analyst report data (373,050) is used to create the BERT polarity index. Data cleansing is done using IFIS technology. The period of the data is from 2010/1 to 2020/12. In the experiment, we create polarity indices for all industries and each industry, respectively. For details on how to create a polarity index see Sect. 3.1. The all-industry polarity index is the sum of all the outputs (1, 0, −1) of the industry-specific polarity index. Five-time series deep learning models were used for the selection. The first one is Transformer+Time2Vec. The second is Bidirectional LSTM (BiLSTM). The third is LSTM. The fourth is GRU. The fifth is Bi-directional GRU (BiGRU). As a preprocessing of the data, we take three-month moving averages for all industries and industry-specific polarity index. The ratio of train:valid:test in each model is 3:1:1. The number of epochs in

---

[3] We labeled the correct answers as 1 and the incorrect answers as 0.

each model is 200. For the comparison experiments with stock prices, we used the monthly data of the Nikkei Stock Average and the monthly stock price data of Yahoo! Finance[4].

5   Results

First, as shown in Sect. 4, we create the all-industry polarity index and the industry-specific polarity index, respectively.

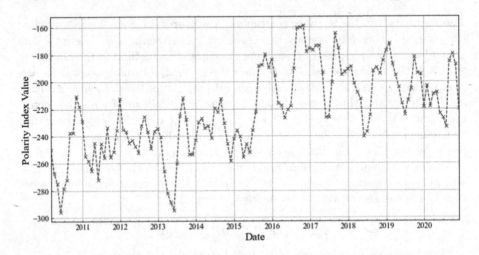

Fig. 3. All Industry Polarity Index with 3-Month Moving Average

The results of the three-month moving averages of the polarity indices for all industries, sorted by time series, are shown in Fig. 3. Next, we show the results of the experiments with Transformer+Time2Vec and the comparison model.

Table 2. Model Comparison

Model	MAE	MSE	RMSE	MSLE
Transformer+Time2Vec	**0.1186**	**0.0221**	**0.1485**	**0.0071**
BiLSTM	0.2355	0.0684	0.2616	0.0299
LSTM	0.2243	0.0663	0.2574	0.0296
BiGRU	0.2302	0.0688	0.2622	0.0301
GRU	0.2278	0.0684	0.2616	0.0304

The results of the comparison experiments are shown in Table 2. In this study, we chose Transformer+Time2Vec, which has the smallest MAE, MSE, RMSE, and MSLE among the five.

---

[4] https://finance.yahoo.co.jp/.

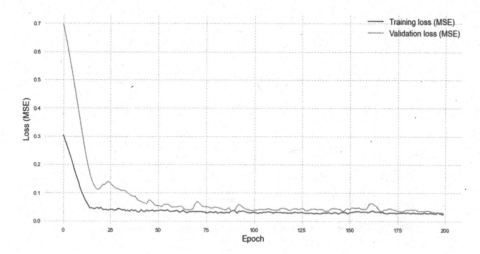

Fig. 4. Learning Curve of Transformer+Time2Vec

The learning curve of the all-industry polarity index Transformer+Time2Vec is shown in Fig. 4. Figure 4 shows that there is no over-learning and the loss does not change drastically from 100 epochs. The same trend was observed for the industry-specific polarity indices.

Figure 5 shows the anomaly scores for all industry polarity index. See Appendix B for industry-specific polarity index results.

Figure 6 shows the ROC Curve of the proposed method in Sect. 3. The value of AUC is 0.82.

6   Discussion

In this study, we created a new fundamental technology for market analysis by creating a polarity index created using BERT and implementing turning point detection using Transformer+Time2Vec and Hotelling's T^2 theory. First, for Table 2, Transformer+Time2Vec gave the highest result among the five. In this study, the feature value of input was set to 1 (only for stocks and the corresponding industry polarity index), but the accuracy of each evaluation index can be improved when the feature value is increased to 2 or more. In the future, we would like to examine the case where the number of input features is increased. Second, from Fig. 6, the value of AUC is 0.82, which indicates that the turning point detection method proposed in this study is effective to some extent for the polarity index. In the future, we would like to verify the effectiveness of the proposed method for market analysis by using actual stock price data. Third, we would like to compare and verify the threshold value setting methods using quantile and chi-squared distributions in addition to the method using validation data.

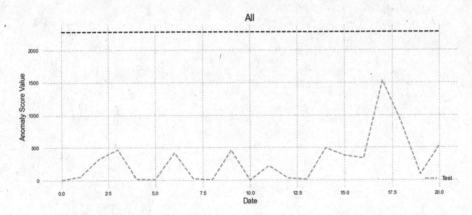

Fig. 5. Turning Point Detection for All-Industry Polarity Index

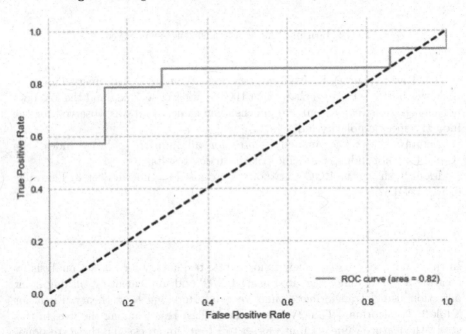

Fig. 6. ROC Curve for All-Industry Polarity Index

7   Summary

In this study, we created polarity indexes using BERT, trained the polarity indices with Transformer+Time2Vec, and performed turning point detection on the outputs using Hotelling's T^2 theory. The results show that the proposed method is effective to some extent in detecting the turning point of the polarity index. In the future, we would like to extend our method to develop a framework for market analysis using multivariate analysis.

Acknowledgment. This work was partially supported by JST-Mirai Program Grant Number JPMJMI20B1, Japan. This work was also supported by IFIS Japan Limited.

Appendix A   Evaluation Metrics for Time Series Deep Learning Models

In this section, we define the comparison metrics used in the comparison experiments.

$$MAE = \frac{1}{N} \sum_{i=1}^{N} |y_i - \hat{y}_i| \tag{3}$$

$$MSE = \frac{1}{N} \sum_{i=1}^{N} (y_i - \hat{y}_i)^2 \tag{4}$$

$$RMSE = \sqrt{\frac{1}{N} \sum_{i=1}^{N} (y_i - \hat{y}_i)^2} \tag{5}$$

$$MSLE = \frac{1}{N} \sum_{i=1}^{N} (log(y_i + 1) - log(\hat{y}_i + 1))^2 \tag{6}$$

where $\hat{y}_i$ is the predicted value at i and $\hat{y}_i$ is the measured value at i. The closer to zero each evaluation index is, the better it is.

Appendix B   Empirical Results for Industry-Specific Polarity Index

This appendix shows the anomaly scores of the polarity index by industry. The selection of industries was done randomly among 33 industries (Figs. 7, 8 and 9).

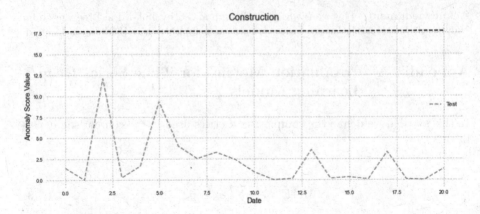

Fig. 7. Turning Point Detection for Construction Polarity Index

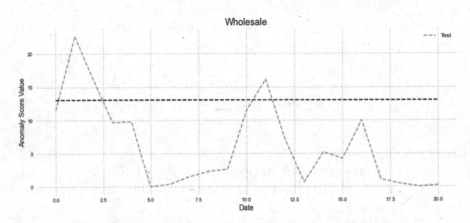

Fig. 8. Turning Point Detection for Wholesale Polarity Index

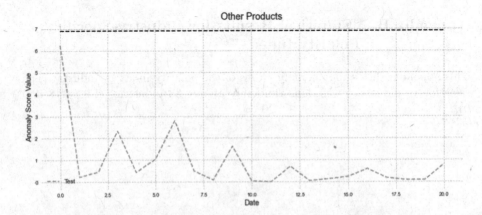

Fig. 9. Turning Point Detection for Other Products Polarity Index

References

1. Ito, T., Tsubouchi, K., Sakaji, H., Yamashita, T., Izumi, K.: Contextual sentiment neural network for document sentiment analysis. Data Sci. Eng. **5**(2), 180–192 (2020)
2. Sakaji, H., Kuramoto, R., Matsushima, H., Izumi, K., Shimada, T., Sunakawa, K.: Financial text data analytics framework for business confidence indices and inter-industry relations. In: Proceedings of the First Workshop on Financial Technology and Natural Language Processing, pp. 40–46 (2019)
3. Yono, K., Sakaji, H., Matsushima, H., Shimada, T., Izumi, K.: Construction of macroeconomic uncertainty indices for financial market analysis using a supervised topic model. J. Risk Finan. Manag. **13**(4), 79 (2020)
4. Jin, Z., Yang, Y., Liu, Y.: Stock closing price prediction based on sentiment analysis and LSTM. Neural Comput. Appl. **32**(13), 9713–9729 (2020)
5. Hiramatsu, K., Miwa, K., Sakai, H., Sakaji, H.: [Analyst Report Tone Information Value] Anarisutorepōto no tōn no jōhō kachi (in Japanese), Shōken anarisutojānaru **59**(2), Securities Anal. J. **59**(2), 86–97 (2021)
6. Asquith, P., Mikhail, M.B., Au, A.S.: Information content of equity analyst reports. J. Financ. Econ. **75**(2), 245–282 (2005)
7. Suzuki, M., Sakaji, H., Izumi, K., Matsushima, H., Ishikawa, Y.: Forecasting net income estimate and stock price using text mining from economic reports. Information **11**(6), 292 (2020)
8. Hiew, J.Z.G., Huang, X., Mou, H., Li, D., Wu, Q., Xu, Y.: BERT-based financial sentiment index and LSTM-based stock return predictability. arXiv preprint arXiv:1906.09024 (2019)
9. Ding, Q., Wu, S., Sun, H., Guo, J., Guo, J.: Hierarchical multi-scale gaussian transformer for stock movement prediction. In: IJCAI, pp. 4640–4646 (2020)
10. Ahmed, M., Choudhury, N., Uddin, S.: Anomaly detection on big data in financial markets. In: 2017 IEEE/ACM International Conference on Advances in Social Networks Analysis and Mining (ASONAM), pp. 998–1001. IEEE (2017)
11. Devlin, J., Chang, M.W., Lee, K., Toutanova, K.: Bert: pre-training of deep bidirectional transformers for language understanding. arXiv preprint arXiv:1810.04805 (2018)
12. Taguchi, R., et al.: Market trend analysis using polarity index generated from analyst reports. In: 2021 IEEE International Conference on Big Data (Big Data), pp. 3486–3494. IEEE (2021)
13. Sakaji, H., Sakai, H., Masuyama, S.: Automatic extraction of basis expressions that indicate economic trends. In: Washio, T., Suzuki, E., Ting, K.M., Inokuchi, A. (eds.) PAKDD 2008. LNCS (LNAI), vol. 5012, pp. 977–984. Springer, Heidelberg (2008). https://doi.org/10.1007/978-3-540-68125-0_102
14. Kazemi, S.M., et al.: Time2vec: learning a vector representation of time. arXiv preprint arXiv:1907.05321 (2019)
15. Vaswani, A., et al.: Attention is all you need. In: Advances in Neural Information Processing Systems, vol. 30 (2017)
16. Wu, N., Green, B., Ben, X., O'Banion, S.: Deep transformer models for time series forecasting: the influenza prevalence case. arXiv preprint arXiv:2001.08317 (2020)
17. Yamanishi, K., Takeuchi, J.I.: A unifying framework for detecting outliers and change points from non-stationary time series data. In: Proceedings of the Eighth ACM SIGKDD International Conference on Knowledge Discovery and Data Mining, pp. 676–681 (2002)
18. Hotelling, H.: Multivariate quality control. Techniques of statistical analysis (1947)

Product Portfolio Optimization for LTV Maximization

Kazuhiro Koike[1]([⊠])(iD), Masumi Kawamura[1], Kenichi Machida[1],
Kazuaki Takenaka[1], Daishi Sagawa[2], and Kenji Tanaka[2]

[1] ASKUL Corporation, 3-2-3 Toyosu Koto-ku, Tokyo 135-0061, Japan
kazuhiro.koike@askul.com
[2] The University of Tokyo, 7-3-1 Hongo Bunkyo-ku, Tokyo 113-8656, Japan
https://www.askul.co.jp/kaisya/english/
https://www.u-tokyo.ac.jp/en/index.html

Abstract. To maximize customer lifetime value (LTV), we conduct
sales promotions periodically for internet shopping, such as coupons and
points, or recommend attractive products to stimulate purchase motivation. For recommendation, it is essential to narrow the target to effective
customers and choose appropriate recommended products to maximize
the effect with little cost. We formulated this problem as a product portfolio optimization problem to maximize LTV using Markowitz's mean-
variance model, which we generally use for deciding the portfolio of diver-
sified investment stocks. This study proposes a method to increase sales
and improve LTV by adding optimal products to the customer's portfolio. First, we build an LTV mean-variance model for each customer based
on their purchase history and select a group of customers with good performance as the sales promotion target. We then estimate which product recommendations from the product groups not purchased by those
customers improve the performance on the product sales mean-variance
model. Thus, we can obtain the expected LTV while reducing the fluctuation risk. As a result of verification with actual data, we confirmed
the effectiveness of the proposed method.

Keywords: Portfolio optimization · Mean-Variance model · Lifetime
value · Recommender system

1 Introduction

LTV is an abbreviation for Life Time Value, and although CLV, i.e., customer
lifetime value, is sometimes used in general, LTV is used synonymously in this
paper. According to Dwyer [1], LTV represents the present value of the expected
benefits (e.g., gross margin) less the burdens (e.g., direct costs of servicing and
communicating) from customers.

In the EC business, it is a management issue to build and maintain a good
relationship with customers in the long term, and customer lifetime value has
been attracting attention as an essential indicator. For the interest in CLV,
Berger & Nasr [2] cite the following two points.

© The Author(s), under exclusive license to Springer Nature Switzerland AG 2023
Y. Takama et al. (Eds.): JSAI-isAI 2022 Workshop, LNAI 13859, pp. 182–195, 2023.
https://doi.org/10.1007/978-3-031-29168-5_13

The first is that since the early 1980s, the marketing field has been evolving toward relationship marketing. The second is that technological changes have made it possible to understand and track customer behavior. They argue that CLV calculates the present value of the cash flows a company expects to receive from its customers over the long term and proposed a general systematic approach for CLV calculation. Moreover, they use as inputs to the CLV calculation the costs of acquiring and retaining customers, the probability of purchase, which changes over time, and how that probability varies with promotional costs.

In this study, we focused on the fact that CLV is an index that changes with time and promotion. We used modern portfolio theory to examine a method for quantitatively evaluating the effects of promotion on which customer groups are under such changes.

Specifically, we used Markowitz's mean-variance model, which was the origin of modern portfolio theory [3]. The mean-variance model is straightforward. Moreover, we need only the expected return value and variance [4]. Therefore we expect it to be applied to sales and multiple indicators in EC logistics if we have daily changing quantitative data.

We have two research questions as follows.

1. Can we use the LTV mean-variance model to choose the target customers to promote to maximize LTV?
2. Suppose we recommend a product to a selected target customer it has not yet purchased. The customer's portfolio contains a new product if the customer purchases it. That can be considered a rebalancing of the product portfolio. Is it possible to evaluate the portfolio's performance before and after the rebalancing?

These research questions aim to find a top-down strategy method in which we determine the expected LTV increment first. In the conventional bottom-up strategy, we conduct individual measures to increase sales by each division and evaluate the overall increase in LTV last.

In this study, we propose a method to determine target customers using Markowitz's Mean-Variance Model and then to increase sales by the mean-variance model of product sales for each customer.

2 Methods

2.1 How to Calculate LTV

LTV is an essential concept in marketing, but its definition varies from one literature to another and has not been settled. According to Bendle [5], the reason for the different definitions is that they include wrong formulas and false claims.

As an example, Fader [6] gives three LTV formulas that are often used in marketing courses, and states that which formula is "correct" depends on two factors:

1. Whether the first payment from the customer is included in the calculation.
2. Whether the net cash flow associated with each period is "booked" at the beginning or end of the period.

Although this study does not aim to explore the correct LTV, we would like to start by clarifying the definition of LTV used in this study in light of Fader's point.

We refer to the definition by Berger & Nasr [2] given in Eq. (1).

$$CLV = GC * \Sigma_{i=0}^{n} \frac{r^i}{(1+d)^i}$$
$$- M * \Sigma_{i=0}^{n} \frac{r^{i-1}}{(1+d)^{i-0.5}} \tag{1}$$

GC is the expected yearly gross contribution margin per customer. It is equal to revenues minus the cost of sales.

M is the relevant promotion costs per customer per year. n is the length of time (in years) over which projected cash flows. r is the yearly retention rate, i.e., the proportion of customers expected to continue buying the company's goods or services in the subsequent year. d is the yearly discount rate which is appropriate for marketing investments.

Starting from Eq. (1), we define the LTV used in this study. We made the following three changes to this equation:

1. We did not consider the promotion cost M and the discount rate d, and $M = 0, d = 0$.
2. We use an infinite time horizon instead of n because we do not know when the customer will stop buying.
3. We adopt monthly sales S instead of GC.

As a result, Eq. (1) becomes Eq. (2).

$$LTV = S * \Sigma_{i=0}^{\infty} r^i \tag{2}$$

Promotion cost M and discount rate d are essential variables in calculating CLV. However, the main reason for omitting these two critical variables is that no appropriate numerical data exists. The effects of missing M and d are that the costs used for continuity are not taken into account and that the future value is not discounted to the present value, resulting in an overestimation.

Therefore, the value of LTV itself is larger than the original CLV. Since this study does not discuss the validity of the absolute value of LTV but only focuses on the expected value of LTV, its change over time, and its correlation with other customers, the omission of the two variables is acceptable for this study. However, we should note the omitted critical factors.

The term of Σ in Eq. (2) is $r^0 + r^1 + r^2 + ...$ This is a geometric series. The formula for the sum of an infinite geometric series is given by Eq. (3). Because of the retention rate is $0 < r < 1$, Eq. (2) can be transformed to Eq. (4) by Eq. (3).

$$\Sigma_{i=0}^{\infty} r^i = \frac{1}{1-r}, 0 < r < 1 \tag{3}$$

$$LTV = S * \frac{1}{1-r} \tag{4}$$

Here, $(1-r)$ can be considered the Churn Rate c, which can be further transformed into Eq. (5).

$$LTV = S * \frac{1}{c} \tag{5}$$

It should be noted that the monthly sales are a value for each customer, while the Churn Rate is a shared value for all customers since it is calculated based on the number of customers who left the service in a unit period.

Suppose the case of customer A with monthly sales of 100 yen and B with 200 yen. We can calculate the average usage months and LTV when the Churn Rate varies from 0.1 to 1.0, as shown in Table 1.

Note that the Churn Rate of 0 means that usage months are infinite, while 1.0 means months are 1.0; the user will leave the service in the next month.

Table 1. Churn Rate and LTV

Churn Rate	Usage months	LTV of A	LTV of B
0.1	10.00	1000.00	2000.00
0.2	5.00	500.00	1000.00
0.3	3.33	333.33	666.66
0.4	2.50	250.00	500.00
0.5	2.00	200.00	400.00
0.6	1.67	166.67	334.00
0.7	1.43	142.86	286.00
0.8	1.25	125.00	250.00
0.9	1.11	111.11	222.22
1.0	1.00	100.00	200.00

Figure 1 shows the change in the number of customers when the retention rate is 0.9, i.e., the Churn Rate is 0.1. Here, the number of customers at $t = 0$ is 100; not considered new customers, the number will be reduced to 50 in half a year. The red dotted line is 50. After 48 months, it is almost zero.

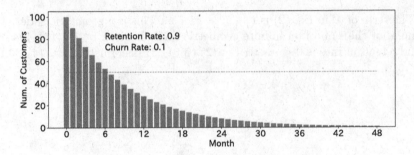

Fig. 1. Change in number of customers when Churn Rate is 0.1

2.2   Markowitz's Mean-Variance Model

Based on Markowitz's mean-variance model, the portfolio candidates are obtained by solving the quadratic programming problem formulated by Eq. (6). Where μ is a vector of expected returns of products, w is a vector of ratios of products, ρ is a given target return, Σ is a variance-covariance matrix of each products, 1 is a vector whose components are all 1, and w_i is the ith component of w. w_i is the ith component of w.

$$
\begin{aligned}
\text{minimize} \quad & w^T \Sigma w \\
\text{subject to} \quad & w^T \mu \geq \rho \\
& w^T 1 = 1 \\
& w_i \geq 0
\end{aligned}
\tag{6}
$$

The portfolio candidates lie on the curve of a quadratic function called the efficient frontier, and the portfolio with the maximum Sharpe ratio is selected from among them. The Sharpe ratio SR is the rate of return of the portfolio over the risk-free rate per unit risk or volatility, and is calculated by Eq. (7). The risk-free rate is assumed to be zero in this study because there is no corresponding concept in EC logistics.

$$
SR = \frac{R_p - R_f}{\sigma}
$$
R_p Portfolio Return
R_f Risk-free rate
σ Portfolio excess return standard deviation
$$
\tag{7}
$$

2.3   Dataset

We used the sales data of ASKUL Corporation for a period from February 2017 to January 2022. It includes whole categories of products and customers in the period. The sampling method for the experimental data is to select a population of 10,000 customers in order of frequency of use from the sales data. Then 200 customers were randomly sampled from it. As for the products, 50 were randomly selected from the products purchased by the target customer group in the period.

The Churn Rate c was calculated every month using Eq. (8), where the "churn" is defined as customers who did not purchase any products within six months after the base month. Variable n_0 is the base month number of the customer, and n_1 is the number of the customer six months later. That means if num. of customers is 100 in January 2021 as the base month and 90 in July 2021, the Churn Rate of January 2021 is one minus 90 divided by 100 equals 0.1.

$$c = 1 - \frac{n_1}{n_0} \tag{8}$$

The LTV was calculated monthly for each customer using Eq. (9). S is a 6-month moving average of sales per customer.

$$LTV = \frac{S}{c} \tag{9}$$

2.4   Algorithm

Extraction of Target Customer Groups. The following procedure is used to extract target customer groups for sales promotion to maximize LTV. For a sample group of 200 people, the LTV mean-variance model is used to extract the target group with the maximum Sharpe ratio.

At this time, the vertical axis of the mean-variance plane is the expected return value of LTV. In this study, we use the average value of past data. The horizontal axis is the risk or volatility, the standard deviation of LTV. We use an exponentially weighted covariance matrix to give greater weight to more recent data.

We then solve the quadratic programming problem of Eq. (6) to obtain the optimal solution. This portfolio maximizes the Sharpe ratio among the efficient frontier curve and the solution sets on the curve.

The meaning of the obtained portfolio is that it is a group of clients that can be expected to be effective in maximizing LTV. However, it is a group that maximizes the excess return per unit risk rather than merely maximizing the expected return.

Performance Evaluation of Rebalancing. We aim to lift sales by providing some sales promotion to the extracted sales promotion target. In this study, we simulate that one product is recommended for each customer, and the customer purchases the product. The recommended product is determined by the covariance with the products that have been purchased. Moreover, the change in the Sharpe ratio evaluates the performance of the product portfolio before and after the rebalancing. Precisely, we follow the next procedure.

We create a sales mean-variance model for the 50 products we sampled and obtain the efficient frontier and the Sharpe ratio maximizing portfolio. Plot the actual product portfolio for each customer on the sales mean-variance model. For each customer, we add a product that improves the Sharpe ratio.

Then select the product that minimizes the sum of the covariance between the products that have been purchased and the products that have not been purchased (See Algorithm 1). For example, in Table 2, columns are products that have been purchased, rows are products that have not been purchased, and numbers are covariance. In order to increase the portfolio effect, we should select the product's row with the smallest sum of covariance, so we select the product '1' in the first row.

Add randomly selected products for each customer for comparison (replace lines 21–23 of Algorithm 1 with random choice). Compare the actual, proposed method, and random solutions, using the performance of the product portfolio for each customer as the Sharpe ratio.

Table 2. Minimum sum of covariance example

Product	6	7	8	9	10	11	12	13	14	15	16	Sum
1	−5.16e−01	−1.46e−01	−0.07	0.27	0.18	−0.37	0.37	−8.07e−01	−0.06	−0.18	1.10	−0.22
2	6.86e−02	−2.08e−01	−0.14	−0.03	−0.13	−0.02	0.32	3.67e−03	0.21	−0.04	0.90	0.93
3	1.64e−01	5.04e−06	0.47	0.11	0.24	0.06	−0.27	1.72e−01	0.17	0.07	−0.12	1.07
4	3.28e−03	2.10e−01	0.29	0.16	0.26	0.16	0.17	1.29e−01	0.15	0.17	0.19	1.90
5	−3.25e−01	4.02e−01	−0.65	0.47	0.73	0.19	0.39	1.81e−01	−0.04	0.29	0.71	2.34

3   Results

3.1   Extraction of Target Customer Groups

Figure 2 shows the LTV mean and variance model for 200 customers sampled by the method shown in Sect. 2.3. In the left chart, the vertical axis is the expected LTV return, the horizontal axis is the risk or volatility, the blue curve is the efficient frontier, the red × (optimal) is the customer portfolio with the maximum Sharpe ratio, and the black dots represent the customers. The bar chart on the right shows the ratio of customers in the optimal customer portfolio, i.e., the result of extracting the target customer group for sales promotion to maximize the LTV.

Algorithm 1. Optimal additional product select

Input: $COVARIANCE\_MATRIX, ACTUAL\_RATIO$
Output: $OPTIMAL\_RATIO$
1: $rx \leftarrow 0.1$
2: $i \leftarrow 0$
3: **while** $i \neq len(ACTUAL\_RATIO)$ **do**
4:    $u, W \leftarrow ACTUAL\_RATIO[i]$
5:    $j \leftarrow 0$
6:    $zero \leftarrow dict()$
7:    **while** $j \neq len(W)$ **do**
8:      **if** $W[j].v = 0$ **then**
9:        $zero \leftarrow zero.append(W[j])$
10:      **end if**
11:      $j \leftarrow j + 1$
12:    **end while**
13:    $j \leftarrow 0$
14:    $nonzero \leftarrow dict()$
15:    **while** $j \neq len(W)$ **do**
16:      **if** $W[j].v > 0$ **then**
17:        $nonzero \leftarrow nonzero.append(W[j])$
18:      **end if**
19:      $j \leftarrow j + 1$
20:    **end while**
21:    $s \leftarrow COVARIANCE\_MATRIX[list(nonzero.keys())]$
22:    $ix \leftarrow s.sum(axis = 1).argmin()$
23:    $one \leftarrow s.iloc[ix].name$
24:    $d \leftarrow copy.deepcopy(W)$
25:    $d[one] \leftarrow rx$
26:    $j \leftarrow 0$
27:    **while** $j \neq len(nonzero)$ **do**
28:      $k, r \leftarrow nonzero[j]$
29:      $d[k] \leftarrow r(1 - rx)$
30:      $j \leftarrow j + 1$
31:    **end while**
32:    $OPTIMAL\_RATIO[u] \leftarrow d$
33: **end while**

Figure 3 shows the monthly LTV of each customer in the optimal customer portfolio. The vertical axis is the monthly LTV, and the horizontal axis is the month. The vertical axis of LTV is logarithmic because the fluctuation range varies significantly for each customer. We can see that the trends are different for each customer.

3.2 Performance Evaluation of Rebalancing

Figure 4 shows the monthly sales of 50 randomly sampled products among the products purchased by the customers of the optimal customer portfolio. The vertical axis is the logarithmic monthly sales amount, and the horizontal axis is the month. We can see that the trends differ, as in the case of customer LTV.

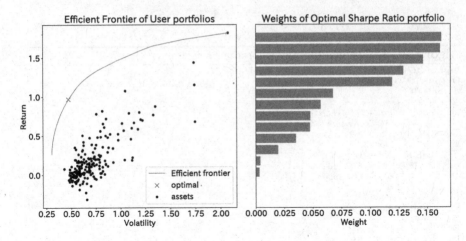

Fig. 2. LTV Mean-Variance model

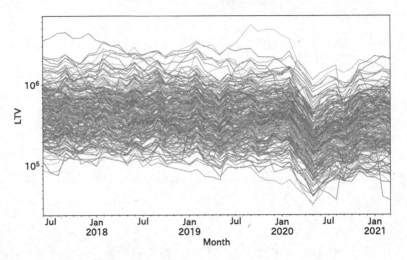

Fig. 3. Change in LTV per customer

Figure 5 shows the sales mean and variance model for 50 randomly sampled products. In the above chart, the vertical axis is the expected return on sales; the horizontal axis is the risk or volatility; the blue curve is the efficient frontier; the red × (optimal) is the product portfolio with the maximum Sharpe Ratio, and the black dots represent products. The right bar chart shows the ratio of actual client inclusion of the optimal product portfolio.

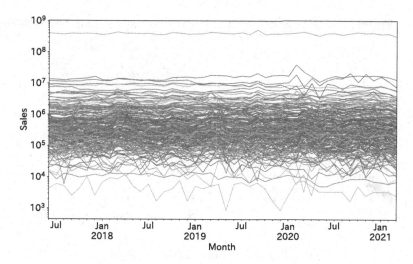

Fig. 4. Change in Sales per product

Figure 6 shows each customer's product portfolio performance (left) and the rebalanced product portfolio performance after adding randomly selected products (right).

Figure 7 shows the change between actual and random rebalanced portfolios for each customer. The left chart magnifies at the bottom left of the Volatility Return plane, and the right side is upper right.

In the same way, Fig. 8 shows the actual product portfolio (left) and the rebalanced product portfolio (right) after adding selected products by the proposed method.

Figure 9 shows the change between the actual and optimal rebalanced portfolios. The left chart is bottom left, and the right side is upper right.

Table 3 shows the performance evaluation by the sharpe ratio for each customer of the proposed method and random. As for the random results, the average of 10 random solutions was taken.

Figure 10 shows the evaluation results in a bar chart. From this result, we can see that the performance increase of the proposed method is larger than that of the random rebalancing.

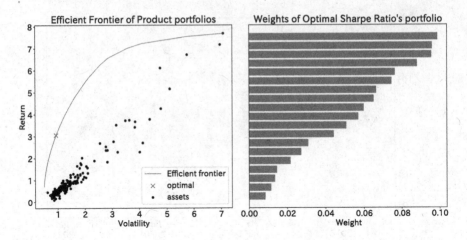

Fig. 5. Product Sales Efficient Frontier

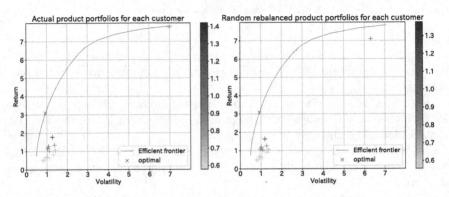

Fig. 6. Actual vs. Random rebalanced portfolio for each customer

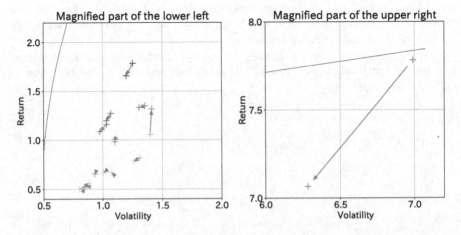

Fig. 7. Change between Actual and Random rebalanced portfolio for each customer

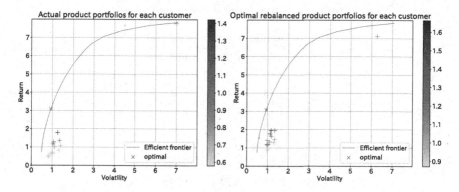

Fig. 8. Actual vs. Optimal rebalanced portfolio for each customer

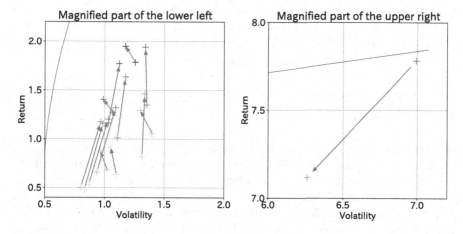

Fig. 9. Change between Actual and Optimal rebalanced portfolio for each customer

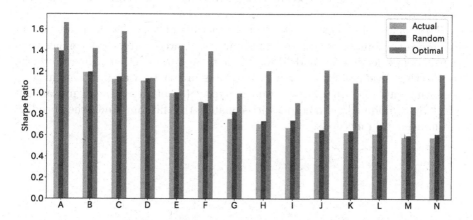

Fig. 10. Sharpe Ratio Result Comparison

Table 3. Sharpe Ratio Result Comparison

User	Actual	Random	Optimal
A	1.42	1.39	1.66
B	1.19	1.20	1.42
C	1.13	1.15	1.58
D	1.11	1.13	1.14
E	1.00	1.00	1.44
F	0.91	0.90	1.39
G	0.76	0.82	0.99
H	0.71	0.73	1.21
I	0.67	0.74	0.91
J	0.62	0.65	1.21
K	0.62	0.64	1.09
L	0.61	0.70	1.17
M	0.58	0.60	0.87
N	0.58	0.61	1.18

4   Discussion

Since the definition of LTV in this paper is a simplified version of the general definition of CLV, and the ratio of customer retention cost and future value to present value is set to zero, the absolute value of LTV is likely to be overestimated. As mentioned above, we believe this will not affect the results of our proposed method, which focuses on the correlation between LTV fluctuation and customers, not the absolute value of LTV. However, suppose the appropriateness of customer retention costs is to be evaluated based on the results of this study. In that case, LTV will need to be redefined to include the variables omitted in this study.

As a rebalancing method, we used the method of selecting the product that minimizes the sum of covariance. This method showed better performance than the random selection method. However, it tended to select the same products, so selecting products from several candidates in practical applications may be necessary randomly. In addition, we can expect to obtain a more significant lift effect by combining the method with collaborative filtering and other product recommendation methods.

5   Conclusions

In this study, we proposed a method to select the most suitable customer group as the sales promotion target using the LTV mean-variance model. We evaluated the sales promotion results using the mean-variance model of product sales purchased by each customer and conducted numerical experiments using actual EC data.

The novelty of the proposed method lies in the fact that the mean-variance model is applied to marketing domains other than stock diversification investment and that the LTV mean-variance model and the product sales mean-variance model are linked on a customer-by-customer basis. The LTV mean-variance model treats the customer as a single asset. While in the product sales model, customers are treated as a portfolio of products, like an ETF.

The mean-variance model can evaluate the performance of a portfolio by expected return, risk, and Sharpe ratio, as long as there is quantitative data on the frequency over a certain period, and it can be linked to multiple models. For example, it can be used for overall optimization, such as balancing EC sales and logistics costs in the EC logistics business. In this study, we have confirmed the effectiveness of the proposed method, and the next step is to expand its application to the EC logistics domain.

Acknowledgements. This research was conducted in collaboration with Kenji Tanaka Laboratory, Department of Technology Management and Strategy, Graduate School of Engineering, the University of Tokyo, and ASKUL Corporation, and we would like to express our sincere gratitude to all the people involved for their useful advice and warm guidance. We would like to express our sincere gratitude to them.

References

1. Dwyer, F.R.: Customer lifetime valuation to support marketing decision making. J. Direct Mark. **3**(4), 8–15 (1989)
2. Berger, P.D., Nasr, N.I.: Customer lifetime value: marketing models and applications. J. Interact. Mark. **12**(1), 17–30 (1998)
3. Markowitz, H.: Portfolio selection*. J. Financ. **7**(1), 77–91 (1952)
4. Cardozo, R.N., Smith, D.K.: Applying financial portfolio theory to product portfolio decisions: an empirical study. J. Mark. **47**(2), 110–119 (1983)
5. Bendle, N.T., Bagga, C.K.: The confusion about clv in case-based teaching materials. Mark. Educ. Rev. **27**(1), 27–38 (2017)
6. Fader, P.S., Hardie, B.G.S.: Reconciling and clarifying clv formulas (2016)

An Examination of Eating Experiences in Relation to Psychological States, Loneliness, and Depression Using BERT

Kentaro Nakai[1], Ritsuko Iwai[2], and Takatsune Kumada[1(✉)]

[1] Graduate School of Informatics, Kyoto University, Kyoto, Japan
kumada.takatsune.7w@kyoto-u.ac.jp
[2] Guardian Robot Project, RIKEN, Tokyo, Japan

Abstract. For humans, meals are significant, not only to intake nutrients or feel satisfaction but also to feel connected with family and society through interpersonal communication. This study aimed to estimate and examine the psychological states and traits of texts describing eating experiences using BERT. Texts about positive, negative, and neutral eating experiences were collected from 877 crowd workers along with their psychological traits (loneliness and depression). The accuracy of the 6-label classification of the three psychological states × two eating situations (co-eating or eating alone) was 72%. Although the accuracies of the binary classification of loneliness and depression are approximately 55%, they are comparable with those of crowd workers. These results suggest that estimating psychological traits is more difficult than estimating psychological states from a single text per crowd worker. Further analyses revealed that the fine-tuned BERT classifiers of psychological traits use language features different from those of human raters.

Keywords: BERT · Psychological states · Psychological traits

1 Introduction

For humans, meals are significant, not only to intake nutrients or feel satisfaction but also to feel connected with family and friends through interpersonal communication. The amount of food [1] and sensitivity to taste [2] are improved when meals are consumed with others (i.e., co-eating). Eating alone is also a risk factor for mental health problems (e.g., depression) among older people, especially among older males [3]. Thus, eating alone is closely related to the mental health and psychological state. Therefore, we expect that mental health risks can be predicted by monitoring the eating habits of individuals.

In this study, as the first step in developing a mental health monitoring system for eating situations, we investigated whether eating experiences are related to psychological states or traits. In psychological studies, "states" and "traits" are distinguished. Psychological states refer to the functioning of the mind to unconsciously feel emotions in response to perceived changes in the surrounding situations or the individuality of how one feels about an event at one moment. However, psychological traits are relatively

Y. Takama et al. (Eds.): JSAI-isAI 2022 Workshop, LNAI 13859, pp. 196–214, 2023.
https://doi.org/10.1007/978-3-031-29168-5_14

persistent tendencies in thoughts, feelings, and actions that characterize an individual across different situations. A critical difference between psychological states and traits is that psychological states change depending on events and environments at a certain time, whereas psychological traits are persistent. In this study, we used the psychological evaluation (positive, neutral, or negative) of eating as a psychological state evoked by eating. Regarding psychological traits, we were interested in loneliness and depression because eating alone can be a critical factor for mental health, as mentioned above. Loneliness is defined as "feeling subjectively unpleasant and painful caused by dissatisfaction with his/her social relationships". Depression is defined as "a serious mental illness like feeling down and not being able to do anything, and various mental activities".

In this study, we investigated whether individual psychological states or traits were estimated based on written texts about each eating experience. We used bidirectional encoder representations from transformers (BERT) [4] as a natural language processing model for text-based analysis to examine the degree to which psychological states and traits can be estimated. In the past, natural language models used separate models for specific learning tasks, such as sentence classification, translation, and sentiment analysis. However, BERT is based on two frameworks: pre-training and fine-tuning. Because BERT has high accuracy in natural language processing tasks owing to pre-training and fine-tuning, we consider it to be suitable for estimating psychological states and traits from the eating experience texts in this study.

The purpose of this study was to estimate and examine psychological states and traits from texts describing eating experiences, such as daily diaries, using BERT. We fine-tuned a pre-trained BERT model to automatically classify eating situations (eating alone or eating), psychological states (positive, neutral, negative), and traits (loneliness and depression) from the texts. Psychological traits do not change easily in a short time; therefore, it is expected to be difficult in principle to estimate them from a single text relative to psychological states.

2 Related Work

In psychological studies, traits are measured using questionnaires. Regarding loneliness, which is featured in this study, Masuda et al. tested the reliability and validity of the Japanese version of the UCLA' Loneliness Scale (3rd edition) [5] and proved it to be a useful scale for measuring loneliness in the elderly. In that paper, loneliness is defined to "be due to the individual's lack of social relationships; be a subjective state; be an unpleasant and painful experience". The Japanese version of the UCLA Loneliness Scale has 20 items, with four options (1–4 points) for each item: "Always," "Sometimes," "Almost never," and "Never. The overall score on the scale ranges from 20 to 80, with higher scores indicating greater loneliness.

Regarding depression, Shima et al. translated a self-rating scale (the Center for Epidemiologic Studies Depression Scale, CES-D Scale) developed for epidemiological studies of depression at the National Institute of Mental Health in the United States into Japanese, examined its clinical usefulness, and proved its usefulness in Japan [6]. The CES-D has a 20-item self-rating scale of depression, with four options for each item: "rarely or never (less than 1 day)," "some or a little (1–2 days)," "sometimes or a lot

(3–4 days)," and "usually or always (5–7 days)" in the past week. The lowest score was 0 and the highest was 60. The higher the score, the higher the tendency toward depression. A total of 15 or 16 points was used as the division score of depression. In this study, the scores of these psychologically validated questionnaires were used as the correct answer values for fine-tuning BERT.

To date, some previous studies have estimated psychographic characteristics using NLP techniques such as BERT. For example, Munikar et al. compared BERT with word embeddings, recursive networks [7], and recurrent networks [8] for sentiment analysis of movie review sites in the United States [9]. They reported that BERT shows higher accuracy than the other models in a five-label classification of emotions: very positive, positive, neutral, negative, and very negative, whereas conventional sentiment analysis is limited to a binary classification of positive and negative emotions. However, to the best of our knowledge, no study has estimated or classified the psychological states and traits of daily eating experiences using BERT.

3   Data Collection

3.1   Purpose

We collected textual data on eating experiences, satisfaction with meals, and psychological traits to estimate eating situations, psychological states, and psychological traits from the texts.

3.2   Method

Through a crowdsourcing service (CrowdWorks, Inc.), 877 crowd workers participated in the survey: 100 men and 100 women in their 20s to 50s and 51 men and 26 women in their 60s or older. It includes questions about gender, age, living status (living alone or living with family/cohabitants), depression (Japanese version of the CES-D) measures, and loneliness (Japanese version of the UCLA Loneliness Scale). We also collected texts (between 30 and 500 characters) of the most enjoyable (satisfying), most boring (unsatisfying), and most ordinary (usual) eating experiences within the last week. For each of the three meals, we also collected the time of the meal (breakfast, lunch, dinner, or other), number of people at the meal, and satisfaction with the meal. The most enjoyable (satisfying) text of the eating experience was defined as positive, the most ordinary (usual) as neutral, and the most boring (unsatisfying) as negative. Since the purpose of this study was to estimate psychological states and traits from diary-like texts, we asked the respondents to respond to the questions in an open-ended format. The instructions (positive examples) were as follows:

(1)   Please select one meal during the week that you enjoyed (or were satisfied with) the most and describe that meal experience in as much detail as possible, including the food you ate, in 500 words or fewer. When and with whom did you eat (or eat alone)? What was your state of mind at that time? Please describe the situation, feelings, and emotions at the time in as much detail as possible.

We also used juman++ [10] and knp [11] to analyze the text length and the number of words that appeared in the texts of positive, neutral, and negative eating experiences, respectively.

3.3 Result and Discussion

Table 1 shows the number and percentage of respondents by gender and residence type, in the collected data. The mean age of the respondents was 41.5 years, and the standard deviation was 12.6. Descriptive statistics for the UCLA Loneliness Scale, CES-D, and Cronbach's alpha are shown in Table 2. Table 3 shows the length (characters) and words in the texts regarding eating experiences. The targets of this analysis were nouns, verbs, and adjectives. Positive texts were the longest, and neutral texts were the shortest. It is reasonable to consider that there were no special events to write about during neutral meals.

Table 1. Number and percentage of respondents by gender and type of residence

Gender	Male	450 (51.3%)
	Female	426 (48.6%)
Living status	Living alone	162 (18.5%)
	Living with family/cohabitants	715 (81.5%)

Table 2. Means, standard deviations (SDs), and Cronbach's alphas of UCLA Loneliness Scale and CES-D alphas

	Mean	SD	Cronbach's alpha
UCLA Loneliness Scale	48.0	11.8	0.94
CES-D	16.3	10.0	0.90

Examples of texts on eating experiences are shown in (2)–(4): positive eating experience (2), neutral eating experience (3), and negative eating experience (4). In the positive texts, words such as "美味しい (delicious)" and "楽しい (enjoyable)" are often used, and the overall impression is positive. In the neutral texts, words such as "いつも (always)" and "普段 (usually)" are often used, and the texts as a whole give an impression of the contents of ordinary meals. In the negative texts, words with negative meanings such as "退屈 (boring)" are often used, and the overall text has a gloomy impression.

Table 3. Length and words of texts about eating experiences

	Positive	Neutral	Negative
Texts length (characters)			
Mean per text	124.2	91.9	101.5
Maximum	500	440	475
Minimum	31	30	30
Number of words			
Mean per text	29.0	21.9	23.4
Whole texts	25,448	19,250	20,554
Analyzes word	22,792	17,281	18,133

(2)　昨日の夕飯で主人がお好み焼きを作ってくれて家族3人で食べました。味はとても美味しいです、大阪風と広島風を作ってくれました。昨日の夜は料理を作ることを私自身が休めて楽でした。また週末というとこでいつもより高い酎ハイも飲んで満足です。

(2)　My husband made an okonomiyaki for dinner last night, and we ate it together with three family members. The taste was very good; he created both the Osaka and Hiroshima styles. I felt it was easy because I was free from cooking that night. Also, because it was the weekend, I drank more expensive "chuhai" than usual and was satisfied.

(3)　金曜日の朝食です。至っていつもと変わらないルーティンです。朝食メニューは大人はピザトースト、スープ、ヨーグルト、コーヒーです。娘はバナナパン、バナナ、お茶です。

(3)　Breakfast on Friday. This routine was the same as usual. The breakfast menus for grown-ups were pizza toast, soup, yogurt, and coffee. My daughter had banana bread, bananas, and tea.

(4)　今週の木曜日の昼ご飯です。午前中に嫌なことがあったのを引きずっての昼ごはんでしたのであまりいい思い出ではありません。食事をしたのは自宅で娘と2人です。食べたご飯の内容は家にあるものを食したぐらいです。

(4)　Lunch on Thursday this week. I had a bad feeling in the morning, and I still had a bad feeling at lunch, so it was not a good memory. I ate at home with my daughter. We only ate what we had at home.

Regarding the psychological traits of loneliness, since no cut-off point was set, a median split was used to define those who scored 47 or less on the scale as the low loneliness group and those who scored 48 or more as the high loneliness group. The high loneliness group comprised 445 participants, and the low loneliness group comprised 432 participants. Table 4 shows the length and words of the texts about eating experiences for each loneliness group. Table 4 shows that the average length of texts is shorter, and the words are fewer for those with high loneliness in all texts, whether positive, neutral, or negative.

Regarding depression, following the criteria of a previous study [6], those who scored 15 or less on the CES-D were defined as the low depression group and those who scored 16 or more as the high depression group. As a result, the high depression group comprised 492 participants, and the low depression group comprised 385 participants. Table 5 shows the length and words of the texts on eating experiences for each depression group. Table 5 shows that similar to loneliness, the average length of texts is shorter, and the words are fewer for those with high depression in all texts, whether positive, neutral, or negative. In general, it is known that people with high depression show less motivation and spontaneity, and such tendencies may be reflected in eating experience texts.

Table 4. Length and words of texts about eating experiences in loneliness

	Positive		Neutral		Negative	
	L	H	L	H	L	H
Texts length (characters)						
Mean per text	128.6	120.0	94.0	89.9	104.9	98.2
Maximum	450	500	292	440	380	475
Minimum	32	31	30	31	30	31
Number of words						
Mean per text	30.1	27.9	22.5	21.4	24.2	22.6
Whole texts	13,010	12,438	9,706	9,544	10,479	10,075
Analyzed words	11,632	11,160	8,692	8,589	9,242	8,891

Note: L = lower loneliness (<48); H = higher loneliness (≥48)

Table 5. Length and words of texts about eating experiences with depression

	Positive		Neutral		Negative	
	L	H	L	H	L	H
Texts length (characters)						
Mean per text	126.7	121.1	93.7	89.6	102.6	100.1
Maximum	443	500	300	440	380	475
Minimum	32	31	31	30	31	30
Number of words						
Mean per text	29.6	28.3	22.4	21.4	23.7	23.1
Whole texts	14,560	10,888	11,011	8,239	11,662	8,892
Analyzed words	13,084	97,08	9,870	7,411	10,297	7,836

Note: L = lower depression (<16); H = higher loneliness (≧16)

4   Experiments

Three experiments were conducted using the collected data. In Experiment 1, we examined how well BERT can classify psychological states (positive, neutral, or negative) and eating situations using texts of eating experiences. In Experiment 2, we classified psychological traits (loneliness and depression) using texts. In Experiment 3, we compared and discussed the results of the BERT classification with those of human assessments that estimated the writer's psychological traits (loneliness and depression) from texts that reflect the psychological states of eating experiences.

In this study, we used the Japanese pre-trained BERT model developed by the Inui Laboratory, Tohoku University [12]. Table 6 lists the experimental conditions. We inserted an affine layer into the final layer of the pre-trained BERT model for classification. We fine-tuned the last four layers of the pre-trained BERT model and the affine layer.

Table 6. Experimental environment

	Model
Optimizer	Adaptive Moment Estimation (Adam)
Loss function	Negative log-likelihood loss
Learning rate of hidden layer	5×10^{-5}
Batch size	16
Learning rate of the final layer	1×10^{-4}

4.1   Experiment 1

4.1.1   Purpose

To determine the extent to which fine-tuned BERT can predict psychological states and eating situations in texts of eating experiences, a six-label classification was used by combining psychological states and eating situations: positive and eating alone, positive and co-eating, neutral and eating alone, neutral and co-eating, negative and eating alone, and negative and co-eating. Since writers are aware of their psychological states during writing experiences and their psychological states are consistent with what they write, we expect that the classification results of psychological states are highly accurate.

4.1.2   Method

Because the number of texts in a class of positive and eating alone data is 161,180, texts are randomly selected in each of the other five classes to match the number of texts. The total number of datasets used in the experiment was 1061. The training and test datasets were divided in an 8:2 ratio with 849 and 212 datasets, respectively.

4.1.3   Results and Discussion

Figure 1 shows the losses for each epoch. The loss decreases as learning progresses. The number of epochs was set as 15. The accuracy of the six-label classification on the test dataset was 72%. The precision, recall, and f1-score are shown in Table 7. The f1-scores for all psychological states were higher for co-eating than for eating alone. In addition, the classifications of positive psychological states are more accurate than those of the other two psychological states. The confusion matrix is presented in Table 8. The true class rows show that for all psychological states, there are more misclassification errors in the same eating-alone text and the same co-eating text. This suggests that it is more difficult to classify psychological states than to classify eating situations.

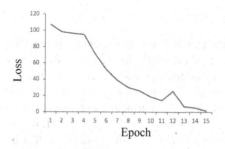

Fig. 1. Trend of the loss for each epoch

Table 7. Precision, recall, and f1-score

		Precision	Recall	F1-score
Positive	EA	0.85	0.81	0.83
	CE	1.00	0.76	0.86
Neutral	EA	0.52	0.59	0.55
	CE	0.56	0.79	0.66
Negative	EA	0.68	0.64	0.66
	CE	0.78	0.77	0.77

Note. EA = eating alone, CE = co-eating

Table 8. Confusion matrix of the six-label classification

True class		Predictive class					
		Positive		Neutral		Negative	
		EA	CE	EA	CE	EA	CE
Positive	EA	0.81	0.00	0.08	0.03	0.08	0.00
	CE	0.03	0.76	0.03	0.15	0.00	0.03
Neutral	EA	0.10	0.00	0.59	0.14	0.17	0.00
	CE	0.00	0.00	0.13	0.79	0.00	0.08
Negative	EA	0.00	0.00	0.20	0.00	0.64	0.16
	CE	0.02	0.00	0.00	0.11	0.11	0.77

Note. EA = eating alone, CE = co-eating

4.2 Experiment 2

4.2.1 Purpose

To investigate the extent to which psychological traits are estimated from texts about eating experiences, we used the BERT to classify positive, neutral, and negative texts as high or low in loneliness and depression, respectively, based on the scores on the UCLA Loneliness Scale and CES-D. As psychological traits do not change in a short time, it is expected to be difficult in principle to estimate the eating experience from a single text. However, given the learning ability of BERT, it is also expected that it will be possible to estimate psychological traits from contextual information that humans cannot discriminate.

4.2.2 Method

Using BERT, positive, neutral, and negative texts of eating experiences were dichotomized separately for high and low loneliness (cut-off:48 or higher) and depression (cut-off:16 or higher) based on scores on the UCLA Loneliness Scale and CES-D.

For loneliness and depression, positive, neutral, and negative texts of eating experiences were divided in an 8:2 ratio into training and test datasets with 701 and 176 texts, respectively. Table 9 presents the means and standard deviations for the training and testing datasets for loneliness and depression. The training and test datasets were split into neutral and negative texts of the UCLA Loneliness Scale and positive, neutral, and negative texts of the CES-D, with the number of individuals fixed based on the mean and variance of the UCLA Loneliness Scale scores in positive texts.

Table 9. Means and standard deviations for the training and testing data sets for loneliness and depression

	Mean	Standard deviation
Loneliness		
Training data	47.8	11.8
Test data	49.0	11.8
Depression		
Training data	16.5	10.1
Test data	15.2	9.4

4.2.3   Result and Discussion

Table 10 shows the accuracy of the binary classification of high or low loneliness and depression for positive, neutral, and negative texts. The accuracy ranged from 53% to 60%, which was less than the accuracy for the classification of psychological states in Experiment 1. The reason for this is that psychological states represent feelings at the time and can be expressed in the text because we explicitly asked participants to report them, so high accuracy was obtained. However, persistent traits may not easily be expressed in the text of a single experience. Table 11 shows the precision, recall, and f1-score of loneliness and depression for positive, neutral, and negative texts. The accuracy of both low loneliness and depression was higher than that of high loneliness and depression in all texts except for the positive text on depression. This suggests that it is more difficult to classify higher scores for loneliness and depression than lower scores. Figure 2a shows the distribution of correct answers, which represents the distribution of the number of texts in which the classification of loneliness was correct among the three positive, neutral, and negative texts for an individual. Figure 2b shows the distribution of correct answers, which represents the distribution of the number of texts in which the classification of depression was correct among the three positive, neutral, and negative texts for an individual. In Figs. 2a and 2b, the three-digit numbers on the horizontal axis represent, from left to right, positive, neutral, and negative texts. Table 12 shows the percentage of correct answers among individuals for loneliness and depression classifications by BERT. In the text classification of each psychological state within an individual, most crowd workers correctly answered all psychological state texts for both loneliness and depression, and the percentage of correct texts for two or more psychological state texts was approximately 58%. The percentage of correct texts is approximately 58%, but we consider that BERT is trying to determine psychological traits by some criterion because the largest number of texts are all correct.

Table 10. Accuracy for the binary classification by BERT

	Positive	Neutral	Negative
Loneliness	0.60	0.55	0.55
Depression	0.53	0.55	0.56

Table 11. Precision, recall, and f1-score

		Precision	Recall	F1-score
Loneliness				
Positive	Low	0.77	0.53	0.62
	High	0.46	0.72	0.56
Neutral	Low	0.69	0.49	0.57
	High	0.44	0.65	0.53
Negative	Low	0.65	0.49	0.56
	High	0.47	0.64	0.54
Depression				
Positive	Low	0.46	0.64	0.53
	High	0.63	0.45	0.53
Neutral	Low	0.59	0.62	0.61
	High	0.49	0.46	0.48
Negative	Low	0.53	0.65	0.59
	High	0.60	0.48	0.53

4.3 Experiment 3

4.3.1 Purpose

To test the extent to which BERT's classification of discriminators differs from human judgments about loneliness and depression from texts of eating experiences, we asked crowd workers to rate the degree of their psychological traits of loneliness and depression from texts of their eating experiences.

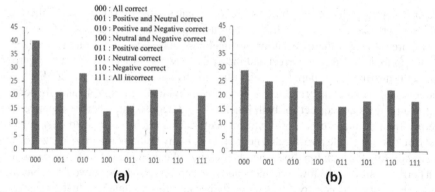

Fig. 2. Distribution of loneliness (left) and depression (right) classification by BERT according to the pattern of correct and incorrect answers within individuals

Table 12. Percentage of correct texts within individuals for the loneliness and depression classification by BERT.

	Loneliness	Depression
2 or more texts correct	0.59	0.58
Only 1 text correct	0.30	0.32
All incorrect	0.11	0.10

4.3.2 Method

Using a crowdsourcing service (Yahoo! Crowdsourcing), we asked crowd workers, who were expected to have no special expertise related to this task, to rate the degree of the writer's loneliness and depression based on each text of the eating experience used in Experiment 2. A total of 528 positive, neutral, and negative texts from the test dataset used in Experiment 2 are randomly selected and asked crowd workers to rate through "high," "middle high," "middle low," and "low" for loneliness and depression, respectively. Twenty-four questions, including two check questions, were asked per crowd worker, and 10 participants responded to each text.

4.3.3 Result and Discussion

We classified the positive, neutral, and negative texts into two classes: high when six or more respondents answered high or middle-high for loneliness and depression, respectively, and low when six or more respondents answered low or middle-low. Other texts were not used for further analyses.

Figures 3a and 3b show the distribution of responses (N = 1760) for four levels of loneliness and depression, respectively, for positive, neutral, and negative texts. Many human evaluators indicate that loneliness and depression are low in positive texts, and loneliness and depression are high in negative texts. We consider that it is difficult for human evaluators to judge psychological traits, which are a constant trait of the writer because they are influenced by the psychological states expressed at the time in the single eating experience text, which reflects the writer's psychological states.

Figure 4a shows the distribution of loneliness classification by human evaluation according to the pattern of correct and incorrect answers among individuals. Figure 4b shows the distribution of depression classification by human evaluation, according to the pattern of correct and incorrect answers among individuals. In Figs. 4a and 4b, positive and neutral texts are correct for both loneliness and depression, whereas negative texts are incorrect. In many cases, positive and neutral texts are incorrect, and only negative texts are correct. In the positive and neutral texts, many human evaluators answered low or slightly low for both loneliness and depression. We assume that this is because they can correctly answer the low loneliness and low depression for these two texts, but were unable to answer the negative texts correctly because many human evaluators answered high or slightly high for the negative.

Table 13 shows the percentage of correct answers for the loneliness and depression categories within individuals by human evaluation. We consider that the low values for all incorrect texts (6% for loneliness and 3% for depression) are because evaluators tend to judge loneliness and depression to be low for positive and neutral texts, respectively, and loneliness and depression are high for negative texts.

Table 14 shows the accuracy of the binary classification of the degree of loneliness and depression for positive, negative, and neutral texts. In loneliness classification, the accuracy for positive texts was the lowest at 44%, and in depression classification, the accuracy for positive texts was the highest at 59%. The accuracy of loneliness or depression classification is not high in any of the positive, neutral, or negative texts, so it is difficult for crowd workers to estimate psychological traits from the text of a single eating experience written by a stranger.

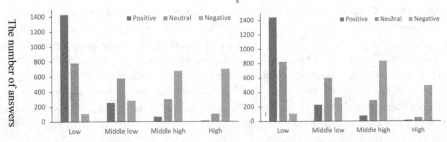

Fig. 3. Distribution of responses of loneliness (left) and depression (right), for each of the positive, neutral and negative texts, respectively

4.3.4 Comparison of Classification by BERT and Human Evaluation

Tables 15, 16, 17 and 18 show the percentages of the class in which the text is classified by BERT and human for the true class. The results showed that the majority of positive and neutral texts were classified as low in both loneliness and depression, while the majority of negative texts were classified as high in both loneliness and depression. It is thought that crowd workers are influenced by the psychological states of the text

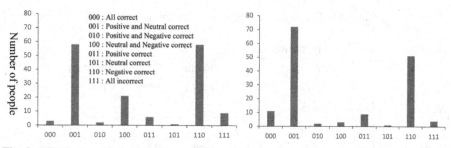

Fig. 4. Distribution of the loneliness (left) and depression (right) classification by human evaluation according to the pattern of correct and incorrect answers within individuals

Table 13. Percentages of correct answers for the loneliness and depression categories within individuals by human evaluation

	Loneliness	Depression
2 or more texts correct	0.53	0.57
Only 1 text correct	0.41	0.40
All incorrect	0.06	0.03

Table 14. Accuracy for the binary classification by crowd workers

	Positive	Neutral	Negative
Loneliness	0.44	0.53	0.53
Depression	0.59	0.56	0.48

when estimating their psychological traits. Conversely, the results of BERT's binary classification of loneliness and depression from positive, neutral, and negative texts were not biased by the psychological states of the text. This suggests that BERT has different criteria for classifying psychological traits from texts that reflect the writer's psychological states than it does for classifying psychological states.

Table 15. Loneliness classification for the true class by BERT

True class		Predictive class					
		Positive		Neutral		Negative	
		Low	High	Low	High	Low	High
Positive	Low	0.78	0.24	-	-	-	-
	High	0.54	0.46	-	-	-	-
Neutral	Low	-	-	0.69	0.31	-	-
	High	-	-	0.56	0.44	-	-
Negative	Low	-	-	-	-	0.65	0.35
	High	-	-	-	-	0.53	0.47

Table 16. Loneliness classification for the true class by crowd workers

True class		Predictive class					
		Positive		Neutral		Negative	
		Low	High	Low	High	Low	High
Positive	Low	1.00	0.00	-	-	-	-
	High	1.00	0.00	-	-	-	-
Neutral	Low	-	-	0.88	0.12	-	-
	High	-	-	0.93	0.07	-	-
Negative	Low	-	-	-	-	0.13	0.87
	High	-	-	-	-	0.09	0.91

Table 17. Depression classification for the true class by BERT

True class		Predictive class					
		Positive		Neutral		Negative	
		Low	High	Low	High	Low	High
Positive	Low	0.46	0.54	-	-	-	-
	High	0.37	0.63	-	-	-	-
Neutral	Low	-	-	0.59	0.41	-	-
	High	-	-	0.51	0.49	-	-
Negative	Low	-	-	-	-	0.53	0.47
	High	-	-	-	-	0.40	0.60

Table 18. Depression classification for the true class by crowd workers

True class		Predictive class					
		Positive		Neutral		Negative	
		Low	High	Low	High	Low	High
Positive	Low	1.00	0.00	-	-	-	-
	High	1.00	0.00	-	-	-	-
Neutral	Low	-	-	0.89	0.11	-	-
	High	-	-	0.76	0.24	-	-
Negative	Low	-	-	-	-	0.07	0.93
	High	-	-	-	-	0.12	0.88

We further examined whether the attention patterns of the loneliness classifier were different from those of the depression classifier. Texts (5) and (6) show examples of attention. In texts (5) and (6), red indicates that attention is strongly directed toward loneliness and blue indicates that attention is strongly directed toward depression. The example in (5) is a positive text written by a person with high loneliness and depression, for which BERT is correct. The attention of the discriminator for loneliness is strongly oriented to words that describe a person, such as "義理の母 (mother-in-law)" and "夫 (husband)," or "一人 (alone)". The example in (6) is the negative text of a person with low loneliness and low depression. BERT classifies loneliness as low, and depression as high. The attention of the discriminator for loneliness is directed toward "家族 (family)" and "人数 (number of people)," suggesting that person judged loneliness to be low. In the latter part of the text, the writer said that he/she lost interest in eating because he/she had to eat alone, and the attention of the discriminator for depression is strongly directed toward words after "結局 (after all)," suggesting that BERT judged depression as high.

(5)   Positive
             Loneliness : True Class : High, Predicted class : High
             Depression : True Class : High, Predicted class : High

[CLS] 義理 の 母 の 家 に 遊び に 行き まし た 。 以前 から 美味 ##し
い と 聞い て い た カルボ ##ナー ##ラ を 作っ て いただ ##き 、 ご ##
馳 ##走 に なり まし た 。 普段 一 人 で 食べる 事 が 多い の
で 、 夫 と 並ん で 食べ た の が 楽し ##く 、 カルボ ##ナー ##ラ も す
ご ##く 美味 ##しかっ た です 。

(5)   We visited my mother-in-law's house. She cooked spaghetti carbonara,
             which I heard was delicious, and served us. I usually eat alone, so it was fun
             to eat side-by-side with my husband, and it was really delicious.

(6)   Negative
             Loneliness : True Class : Low, Predicted class : Low
             Depression : True Class : Low, Predicted class : High

[CLS] 朝 は 他 の 家族 も 、 夕 ##飯 を 食べる と 言っ て い た の
で 、 い つも 通り 人数 分 作っ た のに 、 ひとり また 一 人 と 、 やっ ##
ぱ ##り いら な く な っ た と 連絡 が 来 て 、 結局 、 一 人 で 夕 ##
飯 に なっ て しまっ た の が は 不満 ##足 な 食事 でし た 。 結局 、 作
っ た もの を 食べる 気 に も なれ ず 、 納 ##豆 ご飯 で サ ##ッ ##
と す ##ま ##せ て しまい まし た 。

(6)   In the morning, the rest of the family said they were going to have dinner at
             home, so I cooked dinner enough for everyone as usual, but one by one, they
             came to tell me they would not need it after all, and I ended up having dinner
             by myself, which was an unsatisfying meal. In the end, I did not feel like
             eating what I had made, so I just had a quick meal with natto (fermented soy
             beans) and rice.

5   General Discussion

This study aimed to estimate and examine psychological states and psychological traits
from texts describing eating experiences using BERT.

The results of this study indicate that it is possible for BERT to estimate the psychological states and eating situations of a person from a single text on the eating experience.
Analyzing the attention that is correctly classified, the texts show that eating alone and
co-eating focus on words such as "1人(alone)" and "家族 (family)" that can be used to
infer the person. The results also show that attention focused on positive words such as
"delicious" when the psychological state is positive, and on words with negative impres-
sions such as "not delicious" when the psychological state was negative. The attention is
focused on reasonable words as the basis for classifying psychological states and eating
situations. Thus, we consider BERT to estimate the psychological states and eating situations of a person from a single text of the eating experience. Since writers are instructed
to write about eating experiences with awareness of the state, psychological states are

more apparent in the text. However, it is difficult to estimate a writer's psychological traits from the same text. It is also difficult for humans to estimate the psychological traits of a writer from texts of eating experiences that reflect the psychological states of the writer. However, the reason why it is difficult to estimate psychological traits for BERT and crowd workers may be different because humans may use implicit social knowledge about psychological traits learned through their daily life, but BERT does not have enough information. However, such knowledge biases human evaluation. The writer's psychological state influences the evaluation of psychological traits. Conversely, BERT extracts its own criteria for the classification of psychological traits from a single text that reflects the writer's psychological state while taking into account the context. We consider that the criteria for the loneliness classification are words that can recognize the presence of others, such as "一人 (alone)" and "家族 (family)", as shown in (5) while the criteria for the depression classification are context and words that express the psychological state and mood at the time, such as "食べる気にもなれず (I don't even feel like eating)" as shown in (6).

The relatively low accuracy of the psychological traits may be due to the use of only a single text. To improve the classification accuracy of psychological traits in BERT, we should consider using a time series of texts instead of a single text because psychological traits are difficult to express in a single text due to their persistent characteristics. To implement time-series text classification, we can prepare multiple BERT models, train each model with a single text, and then create a model that learns the output of each model together, as in ensemble learning.

6 Conclusion

BERT is more effective in classifying psychological states and eating situations from a single text than psychological traits. Although the classification of psychological traits by human raters is biased by state-related descriptions in texts, BERT classifies psychological traits using learned context. This shows the possibility that BERT predicts psychological traits more accurately than human raters do, which contributes to supporting persons with risk factors for mental health.

References

1. Higgs, S., Thomas, J.: Social influences on eating. Curr. Opin. Behav. Sci. **9**, 1–6 (2016)
2. Boothby, E.J., Clark, M.S., Bargh, J.A.: Shared experiences are amplified. Psychol. Sci. **25**(12), 2209–2216 (2014)
3. Yukako, T., et al.: Combined effect of eating alone and living alone on unhealthy dietary behaviors, obesity and underweight in older Japanese adults: results of the JAGES. Appetite **95**, 1–8 (2015)
4. Devlin, J., Chang, M., Lee, K., Toutanova, K.: BERT: pre-training of deep bidirectional transformers for language understanding. In: Proceedings of the 2019 Conference of the North American Chapter of the Association for Computational Linguistics: Human Language Technologies, Minneapolis, Minnesota, pp. 4171–4186. Association for Computational Linguistics (2019)

5. Russell, D.W.: The UCLA loneliness scale (version3): reliability, validity, and factor structure. J. Pers. Assess. **66**(1), 20–40 (1996)
6. Satoru, S., Tatsuo, S., Toshinori, K., Masahiro, A.: New self-rating scale for depression. Clin. Psychiatry **27**, 717–723 (1985)
7. Socher, R., et al.: Recursive deep models for semantic compositionality over a sentiment treebank. In: Proceedings of the 2013 Conference on Empirical Methods in Natural Language Processing, Seattle, Washington, USA, pp. 1631–1642. Association for Computational Linguistics (2013)
8. Tai, K.S., Socher, R., Manning, C.D.: Improved semantic representations from tree-structured long short-term memory networks. In: Proceedings of the 53rd Annual Meeting of the Association for Computational Linguistics and the 7th International Joint Conference on Natural Language Processing, Beijing, China, pp. 1556–1566. Association for Computational Linguistics (2015)
9. Munikar, M., Shakya, S., Shrestha, A.: Fine-grained sentiment classification using BERT. In: 2019 Artificial Intelligence for Transforming Business and Society (AITB), pp. 1–5 (2019)
10. https://nlp.ist.i.kyoto-u.ac.jp/?JUMAN%2B%2B. Accessed 22 Oct 2022
11. https://nlp.ist.i.kyoto-u.ac.jp/?KNP. Accessed 22 Oct 2022
12. https://huggingface.co/cl-tohoku/bert-base-japanese-whole-word-masking. Accessed 22 Oct 2022

Objective Detection of High-Risk Tackle in Rugby by Combination of Pose Estimation and Machine Learning

Monami Nishio[1], Naoki Nonaka[1], Ryo Fujihira[1], Hidetaka Murakami[2], Takuya Tajima[3], Mutsuo Yamada[4], Akira Maeda[5,6], and Jun Seita[1(✉)]

[1] Advanced Data Science Project, RIKEN Information R&D and Strategy Headquarters, Tokyo, Japan
jun.seita@riken.jp
[2] Murakami Surgical Hospital, Tagawa, Japan
[3] Division of Orthopaedic Surgery, Department of Sensory and Motor Organs, Faculty of Medicine, University of Miyazaki, Miyazaki, Japan
[4] Faculty of Health and Sport Sciences, Ryutsu Keizai University, Ryugasaki, Japan
[5] Hakata Knee & Sports Clinic, Fukuoka, Japan
[6] Department of Sports Medicine and Science, Faculty of Human Health, Kurume University, Kurume, Japan

Abstract. To provide suitable care for concussion, objective and timely detection of high-risk event is crucial. Currently it depends on monitoring by medical doctors, and there is a certain risk of missing high-risk events. A few attempts introducing video analysis have been reported, but those approaches require labeling by experts, which is skill-dependent, and time and cost consuming. To achieve objective detection of high-risk tackle without human intervention, we developed a method combining pose estimation by deep learning and pose evaluation by machine learning. From match videos of Japan Rugby Top League in 2016–2018 seasons, 238 low-risk tackles and 155 high-risk tackles were extracted. Poses of tackler and ball carrier were estimated by deep learning, then were evaluated by machine learning. The proposed method resulted AUC 0.85, and outperformed the previously reported rule-based method. Also, the features extracted by the machine learning model, such as upright positions of tackler/ball carrier, tackler's arm dropped in extended position, were consistent with the known risk factors of concussion. This result indicates that our approach combining deep learning and machine learning opens the way for objective and timely detection of high-risk events in rugby and other contact sports.

Keywords: Pose estimation · Machine learning · Rugby

1 Introduction

Injury prevention is in high priority especially for contact sports, such as rugby, which has high-risk of serious injuries due to frequent collisions between

Y. Takama et al. (Eds.): JSAI-isAI 2022 Workshop, LNAI 13859, pp. 215–228, 2023.
https://doi.org/10.1007/978-3-031-29168-5_15

players. Overall incidence of match-play concussion in Men's Rugby Union[1] is 4.73 per 1,000 player match hours, with tackle being the most common cause [Gardner 14]. Repeated concussions are known to cause long-term damage to the brain, leading to serious sequalae such as dementia and parkinsonism [Williams 13, Morissette 20]. In fact, the study using brain imaging suggest that about half of professional rugby players have brain atrophy [Zimmerman 21]. Therefore, it is crucial to detect concussions at the first time.

To reduce the number of missed concussions, the World Rugby has introduced a match day concussion management protocol, referred to as Head Injury Assessment (HIA) from August 2015 [Fuller 17]. HIA protocol is a three-stage process for the identification, diagnosis, and management of head impact events with the potential for a concussion and it allows doctors to temporarily remove a player from the game to make clear diagnosis by an off-field assessment. However, since the rugby league playing field is quite huge and players are intricately intertwined during the match, it is difficult for doctors to detect all HIA candidates by human monitoring alone. Also, not all teams are affordable for professional team doctors, although sub-elite level, such as students, have higher risk of concussions compared to elite [Vincent 21]. Therefore, automated high-risk events detection system which can be utilized as a support of doctors or as a stand alone system is desired.

There are several attempts to detect head impact events utilizing video analysis. For example, *Tucker et al.,* [Tucker 17] have identified the risk factor of tackles resulting in HIA based on categorical features such as tackle types, tackle direction and body positions of tackler and ball carrier, which is manually extracted from videos by a professional rugby video analyst. However, labeling by experts is time and cost consuming, thus are not suitable for real-time detection. In addition, the objectivity of those methods is questionable as input features are designed by humans.

To overcome these issues, we developed a method to automatically detect high-risk tackle combining pose estimation by deep learning and pose evaluation by machine learning. Our method achieved AUC of 0.85 which outperformed the subjective evaluation by doctors, or the rule-based method using manually extracted features as input. Also, the features highlighted by the proposed model, such as upright positions of tackler/ball carrier, tackler's elbows dropped in extended position, were consistent with the known risk factors of concussion. This result indicates that our approach, combining deep learning and machine learning, opens the way for objective and real-time detection of high-risk event in rugby and other contact sports.

This paper is organized as follows. First, Sect. 2 describes the related studies and Sect. 3 describes details of data used for this study. Then, in Sect. 4, we explain the details of model and experiments and the results are presented in Sect. 5. We discuss about the result in Sect. 6, show our limitation in Sect. 7, and describes the future direction of our study in Sect. 8.

---

[1] Among several variants of Rugby, here we focus on Rugby Union, played between two teams of 15 players each.

2   Related Works

Recent advance in deep learning enables the quantitative assessment of player performance, which is highly useful for athletes and their coaches in several ways. First is to improve their training efficiency. Domain specific pose estimation models for the sports with complex poses such as athletics [Nekoui 20, Einfalt 20] or swimming [Einfalt 20, Zecha 18, Zecha 19] are useful to analyze the form of players and make appropriate feedback for the performance improvement. Furthermore, pose information can be utilized for automatic detection or classification of events during match [Kulkarni 21, Ogata 19, Cai 19], which enable record automation and improve efficiency of reflection. Second application is to mitigate the risk of injury and improve the safety of players. *Piergiovanni and Ryoo* proposed the method to detect and predict injuries of baseball pitchers using convolutional neural networks [Piergiovanni 19]. Also, *Murthy and Goecke* proposed an injury mechanism classification method during soccer match with a Bag-of-Words framework [Ramana Murthy 15].

In the field of rugby, there are several attempts to utilize the video analysis to prevent concussion. For example, *Tucker et al.*, [Tucker 17] have identified the risk factor of tackles resulting in HIA based on features manually extracted from videos by a professional rugby video analyst. One of the findings of this research, that upright or face-to-face tackle are 4.5 times more dangerous than bent at the waist tackle, led to the introduction of High Tackle Sanction Framework since the Rugby World Cup 2019, which has reduced the number of tackle-related concussions by 37%. In addition, this finding led World Rugby to launch Tackle Ready, an educational program for coaches to promote safe tackle.

However, those approaches require labeling by experts, which is skill-dependent, time and cost consuming. To achieve real-time detection and widely applicable approach, we propose a method to combine pose estimation by deep learning with pose evaluation by machine learning. This approach enables more objective classification in near real-time manner.

3   Dataset

Broadcasted videos of 360 matches in 3 seasons (2016–2018) of Japan Rugby Top League were used in this study. The videos were recorded by multiple cameras at 24 or 25 frame per second, and the frame size was 1920×1080 or 1280×720. The videos were edited for broadcasting including review of highlight from different angles. The videos began before the game start and stopped after the game end.

To make the dataset for binary classification of high-risk and low-risk tackles, video frames of high-risk and low-risk tackles were extracted manually and poses of tackler and ball carrier within the frames were estimated by pretrained deep learning model. Figure 1 shows overview of the dataset preparation process described in Sect. 3.

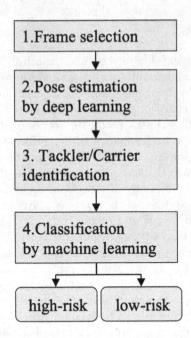

Fig. 1. Strategy for high-risk tackle identification. We define a high-risk tackle as a tackle that has led to a Head Injury Assessment. The frame just before the contact of tackler and ball carrier were manually extracted for all obtained tackles and pose estimation model was applied to the frame. Then, tackler and ball carrier were manually identified and pose information of those 2 players are used as the input for the tackle classification model.

3.1   High Risk Tackle Identification

In this work, we defined high-risk tackle as a tackle that has led to HIA. Among 360 matches, HIA was conducted for 226 times in total. Time points of causative events for 172 HIAs were identified based on the official match records. Causative events of the other 54 HIAs were difficult to identify because HIAs were conducted after a certain time had passed from the events. Out of 172 causative events, 149 (86%) were tackles, of which 34 (23%) were HIA to the ball carrier and the else were to the tacklers (Fig. 2). *Tucker et al.,* [Tucker 17] reported similar demographics by analysis of six major professional competitions in the world (Six Nations Rugby Championship, Rugby World Cup, England Premiership, Super Rugby, Top 14, Pro 12 and European Champions Cup), which indicates sampling bias of our dataset is quite small. Since some tackles were broadcasted several times from different angles and magnifications, 230 video clips of high-risk tackle were obtained in total.

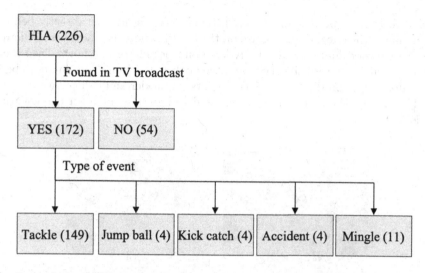

Fig. 2. Analysis of HIA causing events. Time points of causative events for HIA were identified in TV broadcast based on the official records. 172 events were successfully identified and 86%(149) of those events were tackles.

3.2 Low Risk Tackle Identification

In each rugby match, tackle occurs hundreds of times. From 87 videos in which at least one video clip of high-risk tackle was successfully obtained, tackles not causing HIA were randomly selected as low-risk tackles. The number of low-risk tackles selected per video were 1–3 times of high-risk tackles and 400 video clips of low-risk tackle were obtained in total.

3.3 Frame Selection and Pose Estimation

The frame just before the contact of tackler and ball carrier was selected manually for all obtained tackles. This frame is called 'event frame' from now on. Subsequently, pose estimation model called CenterTrack, proposed by *Xingyi et al.,* [Xingyi 20] was applied to the event frames. In this study, we used the model which was pretrained on COCO dataset [Lin 14]. Since the videos used in this study were a combination of videos taken by multiple cameras, there was a variation in the size of players depending on the scene.

3.4 Tackler and Ball Carrier Identification

Tackler and ball carrier in the event frames were manually identified. In 155 out of 230 high-risk tackles and 238 out of 400 low-risk tackles, at least 5 body key-points for both tackler and ball carrier were successfully identified (Fig. 3). For those samples, missing key-points were padded with zero. Pose estimation tended to fail when tackler or carrier was in extreme posture (ex. bend down), occluded by other players, or captured from directly in front or directly behind. To eliminate the effect of player size on the classification accuracy, we calculated the relative coordinates of each body key-point per player and normalized them for the distance between the origin and the farthest key-point coordinate to be 1. Normalized x, y coordinates of 17 key-points for tackler and ball carrier, in total $2 \times 17 \times 2 = 68$ features, were concatenated and used as input for classification model.

(a) High risk tackles   (b) Low risk tackles

Fig. 3. Example of event frames for high risk and low risk tackle.

4   Training and Experiments

4.1   Train/Test Split

Eighty-seven videos containing at least one high-risk tackle were randomly divided into train set and test set in the ratio of 9:1. The train set contained 143 high-risk tackles and 217 low-risk tackles, and the test set contained 12 high-risk tackles and 21 low-risk tackles.

4.2   Initial Selection of Machine Learning Models with Parameter Tuning

In this study, we evaluated the classification performance of 10 different machine learning models based on the area under the curve in test set (test AUC). For parameter tuning of each model, train set was split into train: valid at a ratio of 9:1 for 10 times, and the parameter with the best weight-F1 in valid set in average was selected. Top 3 models were selected for the next step.

4.3   Final Selection of the Model with Data Augmentation

Three models selected in the previous stage were further optimized with 2 data augmentation methods. First one is Omit, which is to randomly select x keypoints and pad with zero, add to the original data for y times. 2 parameters, x and y were determined through grid search. This augmentation might be useful to mitigate the effect of missing coordinates in the original data. Second is Flip, for which x-coordinates of all key-points were multiplied with -1. This might contribute to the performance improvement by mitigating the effect of left-right positional relationship between tackle and ball carrier.

4.4   Comparison with Human Labeled Methods

We compare performance of our proposed model with 2 alternative methods based on human labeling. First is a subjective risk evaluation by official match day doctors. Four official match day doctors of Japan Rugby Football Union watched 4 s video clips (2 s before and after the event frame) of tackles in test set and individually made 5 grade evaluation of head injury risk. Scores of 4 doctors were averaged and used to calculate test AUC.

Second is a rule-based method using tackle features manually labeled by official match day doctors as input. *Tucker et al.,* analyzed relevance between tackles resulting in HIA and 33 tackle features in 7 categories[2], and reported tackles with 12 out of 33 features had tendency to result in HIA. Based on this study, we built a rule-based method which use normalized sum of those 12 features as predict probability of HIA. For each sample in the test set, 12 features were manually labeled as 0 or 1 by 4 official match day doctors, and the final features were decided by taking the average of 4 doctors. Among 7 categories, only tackle type was multiple choice and others were single choice.

5   Results

5.1   Initial Selection of Machine Learning Models

Ten machine learning models were evaluated based on test AUC. Parameters for each model were selected with grid search. Naïve Bayes achieved the best AUC of 0.76, followed by Decision Tree of 0.75 and Ada Boost of 0.72 (Table 1). We compared those top 3 models in the following sections.

---

[2] Tackle type: {Active shoulder tackle, Passive shoulder tackle, Smother tackle, Tap tackle, Lift tackle, No arm tackle, High tackle}, Tackle direction: {Front-on, On angle, Side-on, Back}, Accelerating player: {Tackler, Ball carrier, Both, Neither}, Tackler and BC speed: {High, Low, Stationary}, Tackler and BC body positions: {Upright, Bent at the waist, Falling/diving}.

Table 1. Initial Selection of machine learning models. Ten machine learning models were evaluated based on the area under the curve in test set (test AUC). Parameters for each model were selected with grid search at the range in [brackets].

Model	Test AUC	Parameters
Naive Bayes	0.76	Var-smoothing [1e-1 - 1e-9]
Decision Tree	0.75	Criterion [gini, entropy] Max-depth [1-10]
Ada Boost	0.72	N-estimators [1-10] Learning-rate [0.01,0.1,1,1.5]
Nearest Neighbors	0.71	N-neighbors [10-60] Weights [uniform, distance] Metric [euclidean, manhattan]
Polynomial SVM	0.69	C [1e-3 - 1e+1] Gamma [1e-5 - 1e-1]
RBF SVM	0.69	C [1e-3 - 1e+1] Gamma [1e-5 - 1e-1]
Logistic Regression	0.63	C [1e-3 - 1e+1] Penalty [none, L1, L2, elasticnet] Solver [newton-cg,lhfgs,liblinear]
Random Forest	0.59	N-estimators [1-50] Max-depth [none, 2, 10]
Sigmoid SVM	0.41	C [1e-3 - 1e+1] Gamma [1e-5 - 1e-1]
Linear SVM	0.38	C [1e-3 - 1e+1] Gamma [1e-5 - 1e-1]

5.2   Final Selection of the Model with Data Augmentation

First data augmentation method, Omit, was applied for the top 3 models. Number of omitted key points (x) and Number of repeat (y) were greedily searched and the parameters which achieved the maximum improvement from baseline ($x = 0$, $y = 0$) was selected. The best AUC was achieved with $x = 4$, $y = 1$ for Naïve Bayes, $x = 7$, $y = 2$ for Decision Tree, and $x = 6$, $y = 1$ for Ada Boost (Fig. 4).

Second data augmentation method is Flip. Flip is a method to multiply -1 to x-coordinates of all body key points. Flip significantly improved the performance of Naïve Bayes and Ada Boost. In contrast, performance of Decision Tree was degraded.

Figure 5 shows the comparison of test AUC in the condition of no augmentation, Omit only, Flip only and combination of Omit and Flip. For Omit, optimized x and y for each model shown in Fig. 4 were applied. Naïve Bayes improved the performance with both Omit and Flip and achieved the best AUC of 0.85 when both were applied.

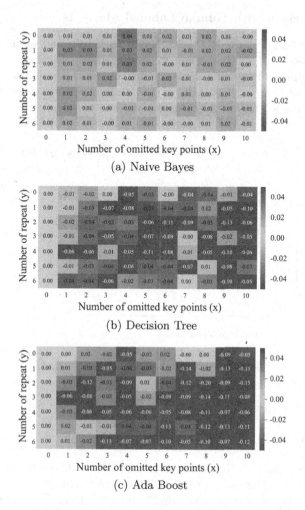

Fig. 4. Parameter search for Omit.

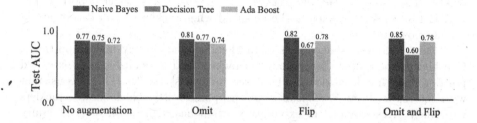

Fig. 5. Comparison of augmentation methods. Naïve Bayes with Omit and Flip achieved the best score test AUC of 0.85.

5.3   Comparison with Human Labeled Methods

We compared our best model, Naïve Bayes with Flip and Omit ($x = 4$, $y = 1$), with a rule-based method using manually labeled features as input and a subjective evaluation by official match day doctors. As shown in Fig. 6, our proposed model achieved test AUC of 0.85 and outperformed manually labeled method of 0.70 and subjective evaluation method of 0.68.

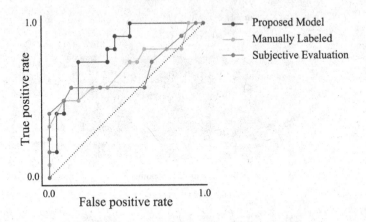

Fig. 6. ROC-curve evaluated on the test set.

6   Discussion and Conclusion

To deepen our understanding about what kind of pose features are important for classification, permutation feature importance [Altmann 10] of each body key-point of our model were calculated (Fig. 7). It shows head and hip of both tackler and carrier have high importance. Considering the average pose of samples classified as high/low-risk tackles (Fig. 8), it is cleared that in samples classified as high-risk, tackler and ball carrier tend to be in upright position than in low-risk tackles. This is consistent with *Tucker et al.,* [Tucker 17], which reported that HIA is 1.5 times more likely to be occurred when tackler or ball carrier are in upright position.

It is also notable that elbows of tackler have moderately high importance. Considering the average pose, elbows of tackler tend to be dropped in extended position in high-risk tackles and be flexed in low-risk tackles. This is consistent with the report from *Hopkinson et al.,* [Hopkinson 21], which showed tacklers with their arms dropped in extended position has higher risk of head injury than those with their elbows flexed. Those result suggest that our proposed model learned the feasible features.

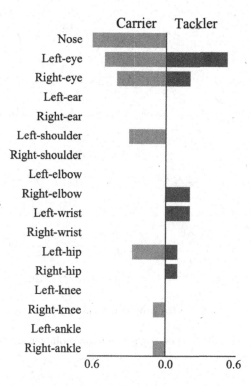

Fig. 7. Feature importance of each body key-points used as input for our proposed model. It shows head and hip of both tackler and ball carrier, and elbow of tackler have high importance.

7   Limitation

There are two major limitations in this study. First is the limitation in data selection process. In this study, HIAs conducted after a certain time had passed from the causative event were excluded because of identification difficulty, which possibly results in the selection of relatively severe cases. Also, samples failed with pose estimation are removed in this study. In contact sports such as rugby, performance of pose estimation model is relatively low because of frequent occlusion, thus more robust pose estimation model with against occlusion is needed to overcome this limitation.

The second limitation is the variation of shooting direction. The direction from which the tackle event is captured differs from sample to sample, and this may have a certain effect on the classification accuracy. For example, feature importance of carrier's shoulder is relatively high in this study, although there is no evidence about the relationship between shoulder position and head injury risk. This may result from accidental tendency of carriers to face directly toward the camera in high-risk tackles. One technical solution for this limitation is to reconstruct the 3D coordinates of players and align the shooting direction. Sev-

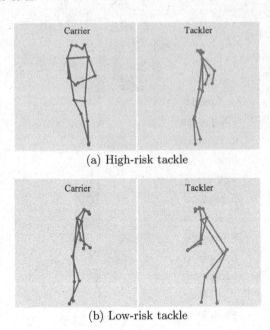

(a) High-risk tackle

(b) Low-risk tackle

Fig. 8. Average x,y-coordinates of each body key-points for samples classified as high/low-risk tackles.

eral deep learning models are proposed for 3D reconstruction from multiple 2D images [Takahashi 18, Bridgeman 19] and those might be useful for this purpose.

8   Future Directions

Results of this study indicate that our approach combining deep learning and machine learning opens the way for objective and real-time detection of high-risk event in rugby and other contact sports. Although our model is not yet ready for real time use since extraction of event frame and identification of tackler/ball carrier still require manual selection, we are planning to automate those process with deep learning as well. This enables us to build a model which can identify high-risk events completely automatically using only videos as input. This model will make significant contribution for detection of high-risk event as a support tool of medical doctors in professional matches, or the stand-alone system in sub-elite matches without professional medical teams.

Acknowledgement. The authors would like to thank Japan Rugby Football Union for their support. We also thank J Sports Corporation for providing video data. This work was supported by MEXT "Innovation Platform for Society 5.0" Program Grant Number JP-MXP0518071489.

References

[Altmann 10] Altmann, A.: Permutation importance: a corrected feature importance measure. Bioinformatics **26**, 1340–1347 (2010)

[Bridgeman 19] Bridgeman, L.: Multi-person 3D pose estimation and tracking in sports. In: CVPRW (2019)

[Cai 19] Cai, Z.: Temporal hockey action recognition via pose and optical flows. In: CVPRW (2019)

[Einfalt 20] Einfalt, M.: Decoupling video and human motion: towards practical event detection in athlete recordings. In: CVPRW (2020)

[Fuller 17] Fuller, C.W.: Evaluation of World Rugby's concussion management process: results from Rugby World Cup 2015. Br. J. Sports Med. **51**, 64–69 (2017)

[Gardner 14] Gardner, A.J.: A systematic review and meta-analysis of concussion in rugby union. Sports Med. **44**, 1717–1731 (2014)

[Hopkinson 21] Hopkinson, M.: Rugby league ball carrier injuries: the relative importance of tackle characteristics during the European Super League. Eur. J. Sport Sci. **22**, 269–278 (2021)

[Kulkarni 21] Kulkarni, K.M.: Table tennis stroke recognition using two-dimensional human pose estimation. In: CVPRW (2021)

[Lin 14] Lin, T.-Y., et al.: Microsoft COCO: common objects in context. In: Fleet, D., Pajdla, T., Schiele, B., Tuytelaars, T. (eds.) ECCV 2014. LNCS, vol. 8693, pp. 740–755. Springer, Cham (2014). https://doi.org/10.1007/978-3-319-10602-1_48

[Morissette 20] Morissette, M.P.: Associations between concussion and risk of diagnosis of psychological and neurological disorders: a retrospective population-based cohort study. Family Med. Commun. Health (2020)

[Nekoui 20] Nekoui, M.: FALCONS: FAst learner-grader for CONtorted poses in sports. In: CVPRW (2020)

[Ogata 19] Ogata, R.: Temporal distance matrices for squat classification. In: CVPRW (2019)

[Piergiovanni 19] Piergiovanni, A.J.: Early detection of injuries in MLB pitchers from video. In: CVPRW (2019)

[Ramana Murthy 15] Ramana Murthy, O.V.: Injury mechanism classification in soccer videos. In: ICCVW (2015)

[Takahashi 18] Takahashi, K.: Human pose as calibration pattern: 3D human pose estimation with multiple unsynchronized and uncalibrated cameras. In: CVPRW (2018)

[Tucker 17] Tucker, R.: Risk factors for head injury events in professional rugby union: a video analysis of 464 head injury events to inform proposed injury prevention strategies. Br. J. Sports Med. (2017)

[Vincent 21] Vincent, M.: Tackler and ball-carrier technique during moderate and severe injuries ($\geq$8 days lost) compared with player-matched and team-matched injury-free controls in Elite Rugby Union. Br. J. Sports Med. (2021)

[Williams 13] Williams, S.: A meta-analysis of injuries in senior men's professional rugby union. Sports Med. (2013)

[Xingyi 20] Xingyi, Z.: Tracking objects as points. arXiv (2020)

[Zecha 18] Zecha, D.: Kinematic pose rectification for performance analysis and retrieval in sports. In: CVPRW (2018)

[Zecha 19] Zecga, D.: Refining joint locations for human pose tracking in sports videos. In: CVPRW (2019)

[Zimmerman 21] Zimmerman, K.A.: White matter abnormalities in active elite adult rugby players. Brain Commun. (2021)

Incremental Informational Value of Floorplans for Rent Price Prediction

Applications of Modern Computer Vision Techniques in Real-Estate

Jiyan Jonas Schneider[1,2(✉)] and Takahiro Hoshino[1,2]

[1] Graduate School of Economics, Keio University, Minato City, Japan
jiyan.schneider@keio.jp, hoshino@econ.keio.ac.jp
[2] AIP Center, RIKEN, Chuo City, Japan

Abstract. This study strives to examine whether consideration of floor-plan images of real-estate apartments could be effective for improving rental price predictions. We use a well-established computer vision technique to predict the rental price of apartments exclusively using their floorplan. Afterward, we use these predictions in a traditional hedonic pricing method to see whether its predictions improved. We found that by including floorplans, we were able to increase the accuracy of the out-of-sample predictions from an R^2 of 0.914 to an R^2 of 0.923. This suggests that floorplans contain considerable information about rent prices, not captured in the other explanatory variables used. Further investigation, including more explanatory variables about the apartment itself, could be used in future research to further examine the price structure of real estate and better understand consumer behavior.

1 Introduction

The problem of real estate value estimation comes up in multiple forms throughout economics and society, with many kinds of agents being interested in predicting housing and real estate prices. Real-estate appraisers conduct property valuations, investors conduct fundamental value analyses, and it is reasonable to assume that other agents, such as banks, have methods of assessing the price of a property as well, for example, for their mortgage lending operations. [10] The real estate appraisal done by appraisers and tax assessors is often done individually. This kind of appraisal is usually done on a by-house basis, with nationally certified appraisers estimating the value of a property.

On the other hand, in other larger-scale contexts, real-estate prices have to be estimated with quantitative methods. For example, the potential rent an estate would receive on the market at a given time has to be imputed to determine certain economic variables such as the GDP. In economics, real estate prices are often considered hedonic prices, meaning that the total price of a good is determined by the parts that make it up, and hedonic methods are often the de facto methods for real estate price estimation. These methods, however, do not

Y. Takama et al. (Eds.): JSAI-isAI 2022 Workshop, LNAI 13859, pp. 229–250, 2023.
https://doi.org/10.1007/978-3-031-29168-5_16

readily incorporate information about the real estate properties at the apartment level, as this kind of information is hard to obtain and formulate into distinct features. Most previous research uses tabular data for price estimation, and detailed information on, for example, apartment level is not available. Such features might include the size of the kitchen or the bathtub. However, such information would be expected to affect real-estate prices as well.

The underlying hypothesis of this research paper is that floorplans contain information about characteristics that are valuable to consumers, neglected with traditional methods, and can be leveraged with Deep Learning. In the long run, we hope to advance insight into the price structure of real estate and consumer behavior surrounding real estate.

To test this hypothesis, we first collected tabular data and floorplans of over 140,000 rental apartments in the Tokyo Metropolitan area from a publicly available website. Then we devised some minor adjustments to a widely used neural network architecture and trained a Residual Neural Network (NN hereafter) to predict the rent of an apartment given only its floorplan. Finally, we combined the NN's prediction with a linear regression model and analyzed the effects of including the NN's predictions. Doing this, we find that the NN can explain a sizable proportion of the rent price of many real-estate properties and considerably improve the explanatory power of the hedonic regression model. Including the NN does not overly remove explanatory power from variables considered important in a more traditional model or affect the other variables in unexpected ways, showing that the NN captures at least partly some previously unconsidered factors.

The structure of the remaining paper is as follows: First, we will introduce the reader to some background about the topic of real estate prices. After that, in Sect. 3, we describe the dataset used, explain the architecture and training process of the NN, and the linear regression base model we used. Finally, we will present our results, discussing the implications and limitations of this study and our methods.

2   Background

2.1   Price Structure of Real Estate

First, some past research on the price structure of real estate will be lined out, and afterward, we will discuss the machine learning methods with this research in mind. When considering the price structure of real estate, it is important to note that while the value of a house and its rent are certainly related, they are not the same. This was noted in Krainer and Wei [10], where the authors identify the change in the price-rent ratio between the years from 1982 to 2002. In this research, we are strictly considering rent and not the property's actual value.

Furthermore, in general, determining the price structure of real estate is more complicated than doing a regular regression, as noted in Rosen [17] and Nelson [14]. Most studies in the literature, starting from Nelson [14], assume that factors for real-estate prices can primarily be divided into two categories, the physical and environmental characteristics of the property. This paper will refer to what Nelson [14] called "physical" characteristics as "structural" characteristics. Examples of structural characteristics might be an apartment's size, the number of rooms, or layout type. On the other hand, the environmental factors are not directly a part of the apartment but are related to its environment. Examples could be the name of the closest train station, the distance to it, or the distance to the city center. Structural and environmental factors might change depending on the market, as different markets tend to have their peculiarities. For example, in big Japanese cities, people spend a higher proportion of their income on rent and tend to put a higher relative value on property location than in other places [20].

The importance of markets is a topic that often comes up in the discussion about real-estate price estimation and is dealt with in different ways. An example of a paper dealing with this problem of different markets is Akiyama [1]. They want to conduct their analysis using all available data but want to differentiate between the markets. Thus they rely on the K-Means++ algorithm to create clusters and use the Gap statistic to determine the optimal amount of clusters to use. Afterward, they can then use these clusters in their research to analyze their data on a by-market basis.

The price structure of real estate is expected to be largely influenced by consumer preferences. Choi and Asami [2], is a study about the causes of residential satisfaction. This study's unique quality relevant to our research is that it considers real estate prices not only econometrically but also tries to understand the survey participants' consumer preferences. This is relevant for our paper because, as such, it provides insight into the price structure of real estate.

Their survey asks participants to list their satisfaction levels about several items in their current apartment. These items are subdivided into the aforementioned categories: "Structural" and "Environmental". While conducting their analysis, they obtain results of how much each item influences overall residential satisfaction. In Table 1, we show the items that the survey participants were asked about. One of the findings of their study is that overall structural factors have a greater impact than environmental factors. A similar conclusion is shared by Akiyama [1], mentioned earlier, who find that structural characteristics are generally more impactful than environmental features, even in Tokyo, where environmental features are regularly valued more highly than in other parts of Japan.

While structural features seem to be more impactful, they are also harder to obtain. Although apartment size is a standard characteristic available in most datasets, more specific features like storage space or kitchen size are harder to acquire. Having said that, many of the structural features shown in Table 1 are available in floorplan images, and humans should be able to identify them from the images alone. Furthermore, many floorplans even contain more detailed information, for example, about balconies, the position of windows, and the cardinal direction of the apartment. Some floorplans even include the placement of air conditioning machines or other regularly used household appliances. All

Table 1. Table showing items Choi and Asami [2] asked participants to judge their satisfaction by, and their rough classifications into Fundamental and Structural.

Fundamental	Structural
Traffic	Overall Size
Shops	Floorplan
Medical facilities	number of rooms
Educational institutions	Interior design and Finish
Nature/Parks	Storage space
Exposure to sun	Kitchen space
Airflow	Kitchen facilities
Security (Natural disasters)	Washing room space
Crime and crime prevention	Washing room facilities
	Bathtub size
	Ventilation
	Heat Insulation
	Outward appearance
	Sound insulation
	Privacy
	View
	Lighting

of this information seems like it should be relevant for predicting rent. Lastly, floorplans also expose information about more complicated notions not posed in the survey of Choi and Asami [2], possibly because they are complicated and thus too difficult to ask survey participants. However, consumers might still have preferences about such criteria. Some examples of this could be the proportions of rooms relative to each other, whether the shower and toilet are in the same room, or how much cooking space is available in the kitchen.

2.2   Machine Learning Methods

The earliest example of the use of NNs for rent price prediction the authors could find was Gan, and Lee [11], in which the authors already argue for the use of NNs in real-estate price predictions over hedonic methods in spite of the hardships of interpreting NNs, simply due to their increased predictive powers. However, in this early paper, the authors were not yet using floorplans or computer vision techniques.

Moving onto research utilizing computer vision techniques in real estate. Matera, and Belongie [16] uses pictures of the exteriors and interiors of properties to improve price predictions. They succeeded with their approach and improved on the base model used in their study. Their research differs from ours in that they are not using the actual floorplans of the estates. Their approach certainly seems valuable, especially for agents who have access to pictures of the interiors of the apartments. However, floorplans contain characteristics that are intrinsic to their real estate property, while pictures of interiors entail much subjectivity. When analyzing photographs, lighting, angles, and interior furniture would all be expected to affect the evaluation of a property. Floorplans, however, especially when prepared professionally, include information inherent to a specific estate, for example, the sizes of the different rooms and their relative location to each other. Even when different parties prepare the floorplans, the results would be expected to look similar.

Lastly, previous research on using Machine learning methods for real estate data using floorplans has been conducted as well, and has yielded some contradictory results. For example, Solovev and Pröllochs [19] successfully used a ResNet50 architecture to improve rent appraisal in a European real-estate market. However, research conducted slightly earlier in the Japanese markets showed less success. Hattori, Okamoto, and Shibata [5] use PCA and a CNN to create a feature vector for use in a linear model in the Tokyo markets. They find that while PCA does improve predictions in the Tokyo market, the CNN-based method does not. Furthermore, in the same year Hattori, Okamoto, and Shibata [6] find that using PCA for apartments throughout all of Japan does not seem to improve predictions noticeably. While Solovev and Pröllochs [19] were successful using the CNN and Hattori, Okamoto, and Shibata [5] were not, the sample size that Hattori, Okamoto, and Shibata [5] used was an order of magnitude greater. Solovev and Pröllochs [19] used 9174 samples, and Hattori, Okamoto, and Shibata [5] used over 90,000 samples. There are multiple plausible causes for these contradictory findings. Examples of some of these could be a difference in European and Japanese markets, the difference in the size of the sample, or a difference in the Computer vision techniques used. We found that by using a residual network and employing some slight adjustments to the architecture and data input, we were able to train a network to noticeably improve predictions in the Tokyo real estate market, with a sample size similar to Hattori, Okamoto, and Shibata [5].

3   Methodology

3.1   Data

The dataset used is a mix of tabular and image data of around 140,000 rental real estate properties listed on a public website from the Tokyo Metropolitan area. The data was collected to write this paper.

We focused on rental apartments in Tokyo in particular because, as outlined in Moriizumi [13] and Fujisawa, Inui, and Hiromatsu [4] and Akiyama [1], estimating real estate prices throughout different markets is more challenging and causes complications. An intuitive way to see this is that the same property would have different prices based on whether it is based in Tokyo or a more rural place. This paper is primarily an exploratory study, so we decided that by focusing on "roughly" a single market, we can sidestep the problem of considering multiple markets and focus on establishing the viability of these computer vision methods first. Furthermore, Hattori, Okamoto, and Shibata [5] were not able to utilize a CNN on this scale, so our results will not be trivial.

For each listing, we have the monthly rent of the apartment, the image of the floorplan of the apartment, 6 continuous and 3 categorical variables. The details for the tabular variables are described in Table 2. The data collected is observational only and not representative of the Tokyo real estate market as a whole. In Fig. 1 we can see the distribution of values our variables take on and summary statistics in the appendix (Tables 7 and 6).

Table 2. Explanation of the variables collected and used in this study.

Variable	Explanation
Apt. Floor	The floor the property is on property
Size in m^2	Size of property in m^2
Time to station	No. minutes of taking "method" to the next station
Age bldg	No. of years ago, the property was built
No Floors bldg	No of floors of the building
Admin fee 10, 000¥	Amount of monthly administration fee
Station	Name of the closest public transport station
Method	How "Time to station" is measured (foot, bus, or car)
Style	Description of the layout type of the apartment (1K, 1LDK,...)
apt_rent	Rent per month of the listing. In units of 10000 Yen

3.2   Neural Network Architecture

This subsection will explain the architecture of the NN we used, the preprocessing and augmentation steps we performed and the changes devised to the original architecture.

For the construction of the NN, we relied on the software libraries `fastai` [8], `pytorch` and `torchvision`. (Pytorch and torchvision both by the PyTorch team [15]). We built on the `resnet50` implementation by Paszke et al. [15] of the model outlined in He et al. [7]. We initialized the model's weights to the pre-trained weights available in `torchvision`. These weights are trained using the "ImageNet" [3] dataset.

Initially, we used the pre-trained weights for all layers except the final fully connected one, which was randomly initialized. However, we found that when doing this, sometimes the model would make unreasonably high predictions, which complicated model training by abnormally increasing the loss, resulting in "exploding gradients". Thus, we decided to add another layer after the fully connected one to scale the outputs to a predetermined range. In particular, we scaled the last layer's outputs with a sigmoid function. This layer scales the output vector elementwise according to the following formula. $s(x) = \sigma(x)(h-l)+l$, where $\sigma(x) = \frac{1}{1+e^{-x}}$, l is the lower bound, and h is the upper bound.

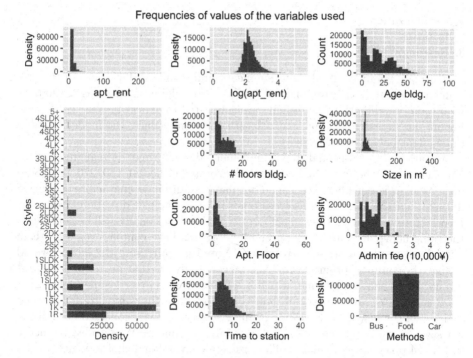

Fig. 1. This figure depicts the value frequencies of the variables used in our paper. Note that for the "Styles" variable, the x and y axes have been flipped for the readability of the labels.

The outputs of this function are then used to calculate the loss, ensuring that initial predictions of the network are never unreasonably high, ultimately resulting in smoother training and convergence.

By forcibly scaling the outputs of the NN, we prevented the above problem at the expense of introducing one hyperparameter, the y-range. Before introducing this change, the ResNet would not converge reliably due to the abovementioned problem. However, after its introduction, the convergence of the network went smoothly. To decide on the y-range for the NN, we used the log-transformed target variable's greatest lower and least upper integer bounds. Since the extreme values were 0.095, and 5.521, we chose 0 and 6 as our bounds.

We used the mean squared error as a loss function, and before training the whole model, we "froze" the base model and trained the head only. After initial rounds of training the head only, we "unfroze" the pre-trained weights and trained the whole NN. The ResNet model was optimized with Adam [9], and the learning rate schedule and initial learning rate were chosen as suggested in Smith [18].

The resolution of the images we used was generally larger than the ones Hattori, Okamoto, and Shibata [5] were using; however, their size was not uniform, and in order to efficiently train with these images, we had to preprocess them to make them a uniform size. We performed three steps of preprocessing for all of the floorplan images.

1. Normalization
2. Rotation
3. Resizing

Normalization: We used the same means and standard deviations of the pre-trained model to normalize all input images. The original model was normalized with those weights; thus, all weights are calibrated to expect normalized inputs. Should our inputs not be normalized with the same values, the model's predictions might behave unexpectedly.

Rotation: The rotational step is implemented as a form of data augmentation. For each image, there is a 25% chance to be rotated either 90, 180, 270, or 0 (360) degrees. This is done because some floorplans usually have characters or writing in them, but the images themselves do not have an intrinsic direction. With only its orientation changed, the same floorplan should functionally still be considered the same floorplan. Furthermore, many floorplans have compass roses on them to find out the orientation of the rooms. Note that mirroring the images would change the compass' orientation. Thus we can easily see that mirrored floorplans are not functionally the same, which is why we avoid mirroring the images.

Resizing: As said earlier, all images have to have the same size for efficient training of the network. However, the images in the dataset collected have different sizes, so we had to choose how to prepare the images. We decided to choose 224×224 pixels for our images. This size is a conventional choice, which we did not find any problems with. Most images in the dataset are between 200 and 400 pixels in height and length, and we did not see a reason to adjust the conventional size. Images were cropped lazily before feeding them into our model, so we were able to try different approaches to resizing the image. Each approach has advantages and disadvantages, and some are outlined below. We tried the following three approaches.

Distorting the image by "squashing and squeezing" it to fit into the 224×224 pixels. This approach makes it possible to retain information from all image regions. However, when resizing this way, the degree of distortion for each image varies based on the original size, and the model has to process different degrees of distortions and the distorted proportions these entail. A consequence of distorted proportions could be that important markers, such as the width of doors or tatami mats, lose their meaning. For example, the size of a Tatami mat is standardized, so if a floorplan is not distorted, it is possible to get hints about the size of an apartment based on the relative size of a Tatami mat. However, if floorplans are distorted and we do not provide any additional information about the distortion, it is impossible to use such markers reliably.

Cropping out the center part of the image and padding with black if the image's height or size is smaller than 224 pixels. One drawback of this method is that if we excluded an essential part of the image, there would be no information for the model to refer to. Furthermore, since the padded values are all 0's, they result in wasted computation and inefficient training.

Randomly cropping out a part of the image with the desired size. This method has the same problem as the second approach, however by cropping out a random part, rather than just the center, we can use a wider variety of images, since even if we use the same image twice, there is a high probability that the images are cropped differently. Furthermore, we can perform test time augmentation. Meaning that at evaluation time, we can crop the image multiple times, predict for the different crops and then aggregate the predictions to obtain a prediction that considers more area of each floorplan.

Figure 2 (Fig. 9 in the appendix shows a larger version) shows how different techniques influence the different cropping methods and lets us observe some of the problems outlined. The first row shows the distorted images. The second shows the center-cropped images, and the third shows some random crops of the leftmost apartment in the other two rows. All images with the label 7.7 look highly alike and are actually from the same building. However, while the first and eighth picture images look the same, the ninth does not because the original image contains more white on either side. Even though all three images depict rooms with almost the same layout, one room looks quite different from the other two after the distortion. In the second row, we can see that the compass rose of the pictures labeled 8.0 and 8.57 is cropped out, while it is included in their squished versions. The last row depicts some images obtained using the random crop method for the floorplan in the first column of the above two rows. While we get most of the details, with the correct proportions, due to the random nature of our cropping, we do not have any image containing the apartment's balcony. The third approach yielded the best results in some preliminary experiments. Thus all results in this paper are reported using a model trained on predictions by using the "Random Crop" strategy.

3.3   Multiple Linear Regression

The price estimation was performed via a multiple linear regression model using all collected variables outlined in Table 2. We log-transform the target variable of apartment rent. While preliminary tests of the multiple regression model only showed a slight improvement in R^2 by using the log-transformed rent, the NN's predictions improved significantly. Furthermore, many of the research papers cited in this paper use log-transformed rents as well, so we will side with convention. We created dummy matrices for each categorical variable, ending up with 724 columns, including the intercept and continuous columns. The "station" variable's cardinality of 684 and the "style" variable's cardinality of 31 caused this significant increase. Furthermore, we added a squared term for the "Time to station." variable to the design matrix. We estimated three different models,

- Model 1: using all variables, without NN's floorplan predictions
- Model 2: using all variables, with NN's floorplan predictions
- Model 3: using only NN's prediction and an intercept

4   Results

In this section, we will first present the results of our analysis. Table 3 shows the results for three models described in Sect. 3.3. Note that we included all

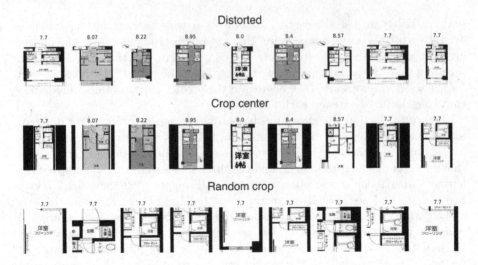

Fig. 2. This figure showcases the properties of each resizing method. The first and second rows compare nine floorplans. The third shows different crops of the leftmost floorplan.

categorical variables in Models 1 and 2, but did not include their coefficients in the table due to their high cardinality. We observe a considerable increase in the model's predictive power using the NN's predictions over the one that does not include the NN's predictions. The R^2 value moves from 0.915, to 0.945, and the Residual Std. Error is reduced from 0.127 to 0.101, a reduction of $\approx 20\%$. The signs of the coefficients in the models are as one would expect them to be and do not change with the inclusion of the NN prediction. However, the magnitude of the coefficients moved toward 0 in every case. A similar pattern holds for the categorical variables not included in this table. Most of these coefficients moved toward 0 without changing the sign.

Table 4 shows the differences in model performance for the three models on the train and test datasets. While we can see that the NN's performance is much better on the train than on the test dataset, there is an increase in R^2 nonetheless. Table 5 shows the total error in prediction for models 1 and 2 on the test dataset rounded to (10,000 Yen units). We can see that including floorplans with the ResNet decreases total error and mean absolute error substantially, by 26%.

Table 3. Estimated coefficients (Standard Errors) for the variables in Table 2. These coefficients were estimated with the hedonic price model explained. However, because of the high cardinality of the categorical variables of Apartment style and closest station, we excluded them here.

	Dependent variable: $log(apt\_rent)$		
	1) Without NN	2) With NN	3) Only NN
Intercept	1.962***	1.050***	0.032***
	(0.011)	(0.009)	(0.002)
Apartment Size(m^2)	0.015***	0.007***	
	(0.000)	(0.000)	
Building age	-0.008***	-0.005***	
	(0.000)	(0.000)	
No. Floors(Building)	0.006***	0.003***	
	(0.000)	(0.000)	
Apartment Floor	0.006***	0.004***	
	(0.000)	(0.000)	
Administration Price	-0.000	-0.000***	
	(0.000)	(0.000)	
Time to station	-0.003***	-0.002***	
	(0.000)	(0.000)	
Time to station^2	-0.000***	-0.000***	
	(0.000)	(0.000)	
NN Factor		0.485***	0.986***
		(0.002)	(0.001)
Degrees of Freedom	722.0	723.0	1.0
Observations	141,394	141,394	141,394
R^2	0.915	0.946	0.897
Adjusted R^2	0.915	0.945	0.897
Residual Std. Error	0.127	0.101	0.139
F Statistic	2098.527***	3383.452***	1237891.037***

Note: *p<0.1; **p<0.05; ***p<0.01

Table 4. R^2 and sample size for the three models obtained on different parts of the dataset.

	total	train	test
Model 1: R^2 MLR Without NN	0.915	0.915	0.914
Model 2: R^2 MLR With NN	0.945	0.951	0.923
Model 3: R^2 LR NN only	0.897	0.917	0.817
N	141,394	113,116	28,278

Table 5. Reduction of error in predictions on the test set. ($N = 28,278$)

Model	Total Error (10,000 Yen)	MAE (10,000 Yen)
Model 1 (Baseline)	43813	1.5493
Model 2 (w/ NN)	32131	1.1362

5   Discussion

Our discussion section consists of two parts. The first part discusses the models' predictions, the models' shortcomings, and some potential remedies. The second part discusses the overall results of our papers in a general sense.

5.1   Discussion and Critique of the Neural Network

In this section, we will look at our models' predictions qualitatively. All predictions and images in this section are taken from the test dataset. In Fig. 3 we plotted the predictions against their actual values to try and see whether there are any patterns of mispredictions in our models. The dotted line is drawn at $x = log(100) \approx 4.6$. We can see that all models seem to overpredict rents greatly when the rents get too high. While the linear models have few but very high over-predictions, the NN's residuals are smaller but seem to have shifted systematically above the identity line. One of the reasons for the somewhat low residuals of the NN is probably that we forcibly scaled its predictions with the sigmoid layer discussed in Sect. 3. The NN also seems to make greater errors with low rent properties. A possible reason for this could be a relatively high contribution of environmental factors, which can not be observed from the floorplans alone. Overall, we can see that the second model's predictions are wound more tightly around the identity and that its predictions seem to have been improved.

Next, we will look at some predictions of the NN and their floorplans, first looking at some randomly chosen predictions to see what a standard floorplan and its predictions might look like. Afterward, we will look at the highest and lowest predictions that the model made. A sample of randomly extracted images is shown in Fig. 4. The neural network is not radically off with any prediction in

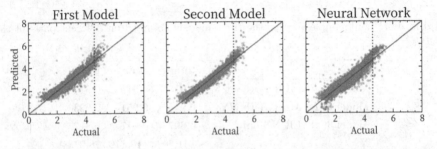

Fig. 3. Image of residuals of predictions of the three models. The dotted blue line is drawn at $x = log(100) \approx 4.6$. (Color figure online)

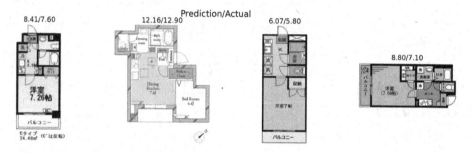

Fig. 4. Randomly extracted sample with ground truths and NN's prediction (in 10,000¥). (Taken from test dataset)

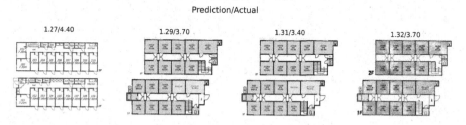

Fig. 5. Four of the lowest predictions of the NN (in 10,000¥). (Taken from test dataset)

this example, with the highest difference in prediction and price being 17,000¥. Seen in relative terms, the model overpredicts the apartment's value by about 25%. However, it is hard to tell exactly why the NN made the predictions it did, and some of the more extreme predictions show more easily discernible patterns. While some of these extreme predictions come about simply due to problems with the dataset. They also provide insight into how the NN is making its predictions. (Larger images are provided in the appendix)

Figures 5 and 6 exhibit images that the NN's predictions were the lowest and highest for. The floorplans for Fig. 5, the models' lowest predictions are solely for dormitory or boarding house-like apartments. The model seems to have noticed the repetitive pattern in the floorplan often present in these apartments. Although the overall size of the floors is quite spacious, and the floorplan spans multiple floors, the model's predictions, having been exposed to many of these kinds of plans, seem to predict the price for only a single room. However, as we see later in Fig. 8, the model cannot always correctly tell these kinds of shared-living spaces apart from big apartments intended for a single household. Note that the predictions for the middle two floorplans were different even though the floorplans are the same. This is due to the preprocessing step, where we randomly crop our images. When making the two predictions for the middle floorplans, the model thus had slightly different inputs and outputs. This image appears twice in the dataset because two different rooms in this building were open for rent, which explains the difference in actual prices. If the prices for each room

Prediction/Actual

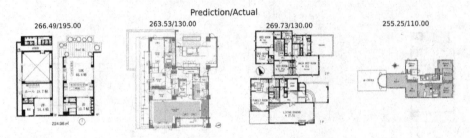

Fig. 6. Four of the highest predictions of the NN (in 10,000¥). (Taken from test dataset)

Model1/Model2/NN/Actual

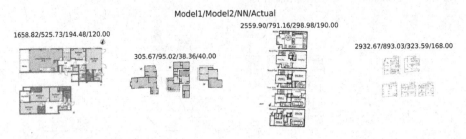

Fig. 7. Image showing floorplans of apartments with the biggest decreases in prediction after considering NN (in 10,000¥). (Taken from test dataset)

Model1/Model2/NN/Actual

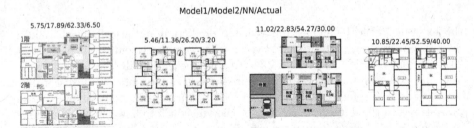

Fig. 8. The floorplans of the apartments with the biggest increases in predicted rent due to the NN's prediction (in 10,000¥). (Taken from test dataset)

are close, like in this case, the model not having any information about which room to predict the rent for is not overly detrimental. A potential failure point is a situation where several apartments that differ significantly in rent prices are depicted in the same floor plan.

Figure 6 shows the floorplans with the highest predictions, and the residuals are much higher relatively as well as absolutely. The model appears to choose spacious apartments with multiple floors, prominent balconies, and a non-repetitive layout for its highest predictions. Overall, however, it is harder to find a definitive pattern in the highest predictions of the model. To see some more edge cases, we will present the predictions that changed the most due to the input of the NN factor.

We will look at the largest downward changes first and at the largest upward changes afterward. The floorplans for these can be seen in Figs. 7 and 8 and have a slight format change. In these figures, we compare the differences in the predictions of models 1 and 2 for a given apartment. Furthermore, we also depict the NN's prediction and the actual rent value. Figure 7 shows downward shifts due to consideration of the NN. We can see that most of the depicted downward shifts are caused by the linear model's large over-predictions being somewhat corrected by the NN. However, in 3 out of the 4 examples, the NN is still overpredicting by a large amount. Finally, we will look at the greatest upward movements after considering the predictions of the NN. In Fig. 8, the first and second postings seem to be for share-houses or shared flats. The NN, however, having no information other than the floorplan, did not successfully predict a very low rent price as it did in Fig. 5, causing Model 2's prediction to stray away from the actual rent rather than improving it.

In the third and fourth posting, the NN's prediction does improve Model 2's prediction. The linear model seems to assign a very low rent to these properties, possibly based on environmental factors, which the NN did not have information about. While these properties were located in the Tokyo Metropolitan area, they were located quite remotely. The NN did not have any information about this location, but seeing only data from Tokyo, it was conditioned on Tokyo prices and thus gave these apartments a comparably high prediction.

5.2 General Discussion

In this paper, we found that utilizing the floorplans of rental apartments can improve the predictive power of linear regression models when not many variables are available, and they can do so, even if we use a large sample size.

We suppose that the reason for the effectiveness of the NN reported in this paper is twofold:

1. By using the floorplans, the NN had access to information that influences rent and residential satisfaction of a particular real estate. Thus it can find features that influence rent that are not available in the tabular dataset, and leverage these for its prediction.
2. The increase in explanatory power seems extraordinarily high because of our relatively simple dataset. While we had a sizable amount of apartments and floorplans, we had much fewer explanatory variables than other studies on hedonic pricing. Furthermore, we only had apartments from the Tokyo Metropolitan area.

To further expand on the second point, many studies about the price structure of real estate make use of more explanatory variables, especially about structural features of the apartments. We presume that by using those, the regression models' predictive power would increase, and that of the NN would decrease when used in combination with the new features. However, under circumstances where it might be easier to obtain floorplans of apartments rather than the tabular data of the categorical features, an approach utilizing computer vision might be worth considering. Moreover, our method could be used by entities who do not have the resources to gather a dataset of tabular features but could obtain the necessary floorplans.

This study was exploratory only, and further investigation might include how this method fares with floorplans in different markets. The current dataset only includes a limited area of rental apartments in and around Tokyo. This, however, means that the rents we encountered did not deviate as much as they would when considering more markets. We can easily imagine that bigger discrepancies in rent, coming from location exclusively, could disturb our model. The same problem, less pronounced, is present in the current dataset already because apartments with mostly the same layout in different locations will have different prices.

Another problem with NNs, in general, is that they are hard to interpret. This also applies to the current study. We have trouble explaining why the model is making some of its predictions. Lundberg and Lee [12], for example, provide an approach for general model interpretation, which can be applied to computer vision. Analyzing the current model using the outlined technique might give us more insight into its internals and allow us to observe its focus when making predictions. This, in turn, might lead to insights into consumer behavior.

6   Conclusion

We used real estate data collected from a publicly available website to train a residual-based convolutional NN to predict rents based solely on that property's floor plan. We proposed some tweaks to enhance the original model to allow for smoother convergence in the case of real-estate prediction. We showed that it is possible to effectively leverage floorplan image information to improve the prediction of rents and that these predictions can enhance other, more traditional models' predictive power. We only had limited access to detailed information at the apartment level and thus could not test the effectiveness of floorplan image analysis against models using a wider variety of tabular data. We suspect that using floorplan data could be an option for entities trying to estimate rents without the need for interviewing participants or employing other costly means of gaining apartment-level information. Furthermore, we believe that this paper shows initial evidence that using computer vision for rent prediction in low data-availability situations can be practical.

A   Appendix

Table 6. Summary statistics for the categorical variables

Name	Unique	Most Frequent	No. Occurrences
Style	31	1K	63573
Station	684	Tokyo Metro Kasai st.	1839
Method	3	Walking	140329

Table 7. Summary statistics for the continuous variables

Name	mean	std	min	25%	50%	75%	max
Bldg. Age	17.70	15.08	0.00	4.00	15.0	30.0	99.00
Bldg. No Floors	7.30	5.73	1.00	3.00	6.0	10.0	60.00
Size m^2	30.50	17.25	1.94	21.16	25.6	35.0	491.88
Admin Fee	6554.48	5220.71	0.00	3000.00	6000.0	10000.0	220600.00
Floor	4.10	3.61	1.00	2.00	3.0	5.0	57.00
Time to station	6.03	3.29	1.00	4.00	5.0	8.0	40.00
Rent 10,000¥	11.12	8.23	1.10	7.50	9.1	12.1	250.00

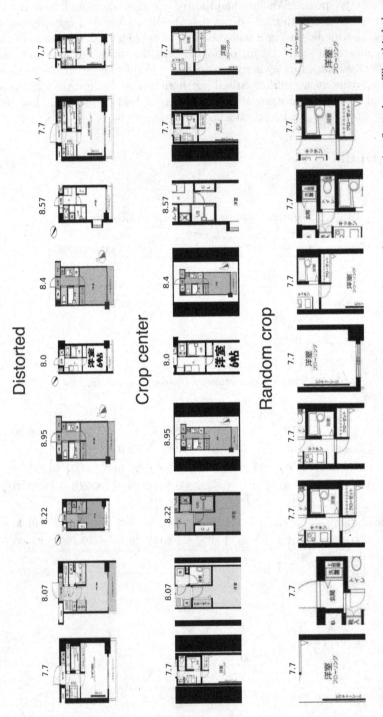

Fig. 9. This figure showcases the properties of each resizing method. The first and second rows compare nine floorplans. The third shows different crops of the leftmost floorplan.

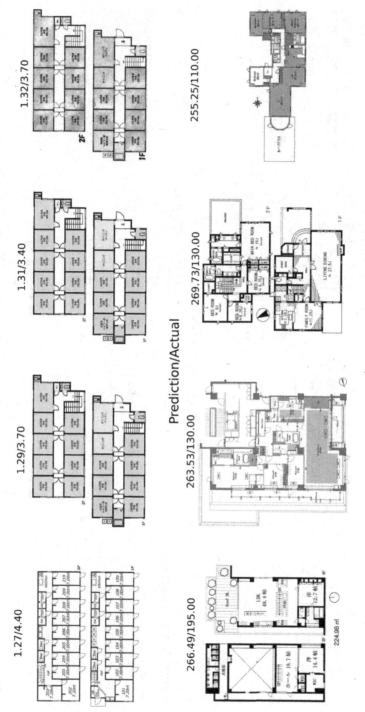

Fig. 10. This figure shows some of the NN's minimal and maximal predictions (in 10,000¥). (Taken from test dataset)

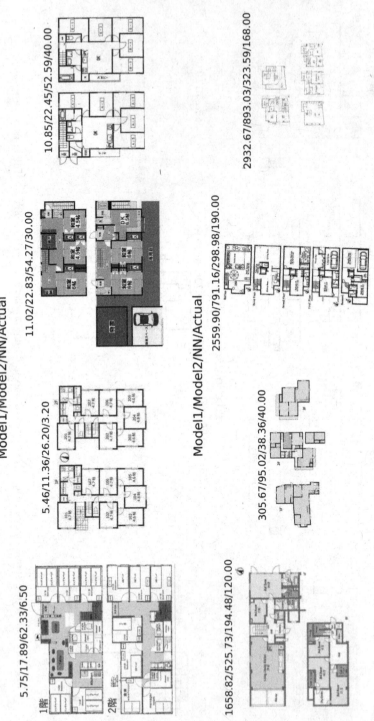

Fig. 11. This figure shows floorplans of the predictions where an inclusion of the NN's predictions introduced the largest changes (in 10,000¥). (Taken from test dataset)

References

1. Akiyama, Y.: A study for the mechanism of house rent formation using micro geo-data. Unexpected relationship between living environment and market value of housing. Soc. Environ. Sci. Jpn. **32**(2), 53–64 (2019). https://doi.org/10.11353/sesj.32.53

2. Choi, J.M., Asami, Y.: A study on the hidden structure of residents' segmentation and evaluation structure on residential satisfaction; the case of UDC rental housing residents in Japan. Urban Housing Sci. **42**, 86–97 (2003). https://doi.org/10.11531/uhs1993.2003.42_86. https://cir.nii.ac.jp/crid/1390001205257564032. ISSN 1341-8157

3. Deng, J., et al.: ImageNet: a large-scale hierarchical image database. In: 2009 IEEE Conference on Computer Vision and Pattern Recognition, pp. 248–255 (2009). https://doi.org/10.1109/CVPR.2009.5206848

4. Fujisawa, M., Inui, T., Hiromatsu, T.: Examination of imputed rent estimation method for considering the quality of housing in subregions: a case study using data from the housing and land survey. Hitotsubashi Univ. Discussion Pap. **20**(013), 1–11 (2021)

5. Hattori, R., Okamoto, K., Shibata, A.: Evaluation of rent prediction models using floor plan images. In: Proceedings of the Annual Conference of JSAI JSAI2019 (2019). https://doi.org/10.11517/pjsai.JSAI2019.0_1D2OS10a05

6. Hattori, R., Okamoto, K., Shibata, A.: Rent prediction models with floor plan images. In: 2019 IEEE 8th Global Conference on Consumer Electronics (GCCE), pp. 451–452 (2019). https://doi.org/10.1109/GCCE46687.2019.9015208

7. He, K., et al.: Deep residual learning for image recognition (2015). arXiv:1512.03385v1

8. Howard, J., Gugger, S.: FastAI: a layered API for deep learning. CoRR (2020). arXiv:2002.04688 [cs.LG]

9. Kingma, D.P., Ba, J.: Adam: a method for stochastic optimization (2017). arXiv:1412.6980 [cs.LG]

10. Krainer, J., Wei, C.: House prices and fundamental value. In: FRBSF Economic Letter (2004)

11. Limsombunchai, V., Gan, C., Lee, M.: House price prediction: hedonic price model vs. artificial neural network. Am. J. Appl. Sci. **1** (2004). https://doi.org/10.3844/ajassp.2004.193.201

12. Lundberg, S.M., Lee, S.-I.: A unified approach to interpreting model predictions. In: Guyon, I., et al. (eds.) Advances in Neural Information Processing Systems, vol. 30, pp. 4765–4774. Curran Associates Inc. (2017)

13. Moriizumi, Y.: Estimation of housing price index and demand price elasticity for urban housing in Japan. J. Jpn. Stat. Soc. **16**(1), 81–100 (1986)

14. Nelson, J.P.: Residential choice, hedonic prices, and the demand for urban air quality. J. Urban Econ. **5**(3), 357–369 (1978). https://doi.org/10.1016/0094-1190(78)90016-5. https://www.sciencedirect.com/science/article/pii/0094119078900165. ISSN 0094-1190

15. Paszke, A., et al.: PyTorch: an imperative style, high-performance deep learning library. In: Wallach, H., et al. (eds.) Advances in Neural Information Processing Systems, vol. 32, pp. 8024–8035. Curran Associates Inc. (2019)

16. Poursaeed, O., Matera, T., Belongie, S.: Vision-based real estate price estimation. Mach. Vis. Appl. **29**(4), 667–676 (2018). https://doi.org/10.1007/s00138-018-0922-2

17. Rosen, S.: Hedonic prices and implicit markets: product differentiation in pure competition. J. Polit. Econ. **82**(1), 34–55 (1974). http://www.jstor.org/stable/1830899. ISSN 00223808, 1537534X
18. Smith, L.N.: Cyclical learning rates for training neural networks (2017). arXiv:1506.01186 [cs.CV]
19. Solovev, K., Prollochs, N.: Integrating floor plans into hedonic models for rent price appraisal. In: Proceedings of the Web Conference 2021, WWW 2021, Ljubljana, Slovenia, pp. 2838–2847. Association for Computing Machinery (2021). https://doi.org/10.1145/3442381.3449967. ISBN 9781450383127
20. Urban Developers' Association of Japan. Divergence between the price of medium-high rise buildings and the household income of office workers: Survey result announcement of the three big cities for the year Heisei 10. Urban Developers' Association of Japan (1999)

Transaction Prediction by Using Graph Neural Network and Textual Industry Information

Naoto Minakawa$^{(\boxtimes)}$, Kiyoshi Izumi, Hiroki Sakaji, and Hitomi Sano

The University of Tokyo, School of Engineering, Tokyo, Japan
`naoto-minakawa@g.ecc.u-tokyo.ac.jp`

Abstract. Transaction data owned by financial institutions can be alternative source of information to comprehend real-time corporate activities. Such transaction data can be applied to predict macroeconomic indicators as well as to sophisticate credit management, customer relationship management, and etc. However, it needs attention when a financial institution uses transaction data for aforementioned applications since occurrence of transactions depends on miscellaneous factors including customer loyalty, implying missing potential transactions. To solve this issue, we can predict occurrence of transactions by formulating the problem as a link prediction task in a transaction network with bank accounts as nodes and transaction volume as edges. With the recent advances in deep learning on graphs, we can expect better link prediction. We introduce an approach to predict transaction occurrence by using graph neural network with a special attention mechanism and textual industry information, analyzing the effectiveness of the proposed method, attention mechanism and node feature design as well as demonstrating its usage as an industry importance explainer.

Keywords: Graph Neural Network · Natural Language Processing · Financial Transaction Network

1 Introduction

Transaction data owned by financial institutions can tell us real-time corporate activities. Large financial institutions possess huge amount of transactions, covering most companies from listed companies to start-ups in almost all industries. Indeed, the previous work to nowcast GDP using Turkish bank transactions reports that individual-to-firm transactions in Garanti BBVA database account for 6% of Turkish GDP as well as firm-to-firm transactions in the same database account for 36% of Turkish GDP, verifying the usefulness of banking transaction data [1]. We can leverage such data to predict miscellaneous macroeconomic indicators and sophisticate credit and customer relationship management. Extracting information from banking transactions is beneficial for financial institutions in many ways.

Y. Takama et al. (Eds.): JSAI-isAI 2022 Workshop, LNAI 13859, pp. 251–266, 2023.
https://doi.org/10.1007/978-3-031-29168-5_17

However, it needs attention when a financial institution uses transaction data for aforementioned applications since occurrence of transactions depends on miscellaneous factors including customer loyalty, implying missing potential transactions. For example, a bank can comprehend almost all activities of a company which uses the bank as its main bank. On the other hand, the bank has limited information about the activities of a customer which main bank is different from the bank. In this case, if a bank can predict occurrence of transactions for a particular customer, the bank can estimate whether it is missing potential transactions from a customer by the prediction.

If we are to predict occurrence of transactions, orthodox statistical or machine learning methods such as regression and gradient boosting [8,18] can be used. For instance, a bank can predict occurrence of money transfer between two companies by using features such as industry information, number of counterparties, and respective transaction amount. However, in these approaches, we cannot sufficiently take into account inter-company relationships.

To solve this issue, we can formulate a transaction network with bank accounts as nodes, transaction occurrence as edges, and transaction amount as edge weights. Whereas complex network analysis can be an effective approach to analyze such network [4], there have been recent advances in the area of deep learning on graphs to capture more complex information [13,22,27]. We can obtain embedding of nodes that represents information about each account considering the aforementioned inter-company relationship, applying such embedding to predict transaction occurrence.

In this paper, we propose a novel approach to capture such information using graph neural networks (GNNs) with a special attention mechanism and textual industry information. Specifically, we adopt textual description of bank accounts as node features when representing banking transaction data as a network. Then, we introduce an efficient attention mechanism for a financial transaction network to consider nodes and edges equally in case the dimension of edge features is significantly smaller than that of node features, which can be a common issue when we construct financial networks. Compared to our previous work [16], we conducted additional experiments from different perspectives to verify the effectiveness of our proposed method. We also analyze the novel attention mechanism, node feature design and demonstrate its usage as an industry importance explainer.

2   Related Work

Recently, applications of GNNs have been investigated in a wide range of domains, such as physical systems modeling, protein interface prediction, side effects prediction, knowledge graph completion, traffic state prediction, user-item interaction prediction, social recommendation, question answering, and image classification [27]. In the financial domain, GNNs have been applied in the following categories: stock movement prediction, loan default risk prediction, recommendation system of e-commerce, fraud detection, and event prediction [13,22,27].

The most similar previous works to this paper are which applied various graph embedding methods to banking transactions. For instance, Fujitsuka et al. [5] applied node2vec [6] and network analysis, such as Jaccard coefficient [14], to banking transactions and then predicted transaction occurrence between companies. A different approach is to consider sequences of financial transactions as a graph, where a customer engaging in a transaction at two merchants within a specified time window constitutes an edge between those two merchants [9]. They formulate bipartite graphs of credit card transactions and learn embeddings of account and merchant entities inspired by metapath2vec [3]. In those two previous works, neither GNNs nor textual information was used. Only topological information of the network is considered.

Shumovskaia et al. [20] proposed a GNN based approach, which uses not only the topological information but rich time-series data available for nodes and edges, evaluating the developed method by link prediction task using the data provided by a large European bank and applying to credit scoring. They leverage concepts from graph convolutional network (GCN) [11], graph attention network (GAT) [21], and SEAL [26], focusing on the temporal characteristics appearing in banking transaction data. Although its focus is different from transaction prediction, Mori et al. [17] applied GCN [11] and GAT [21] to predict credit rating of companies. Their method can be applied to prediction of transaction occurrence.

Our approach is different from previous works in the sense that we enrich node features, efficiently capture edge information to compute neighbor nodes importance, and explore different design of GNNs from their work.

3   Proposed Methods

In this section, we present the architecture to efficiently extract information from a banking transaction network for prediction of transaction occurrence. Its idea is to use embedded textual description of banking accounts as node features, encode transaction network by modified GAT [21] to consider transaction amount effectively as well as graph isomorphism network (GIN) [25] to obtain graph embedding in an injective manner and then to decode using graph embedding to predict transaction occurrence.

3.1   Node Features

First, textual data describing the industry of each account are extracted. Table 1 presents an example of textual data. As shown in Table 1, such texts include information about the industry of the corresponding account. In this example, textual data possess information that Company X, the account holder, deals with petroleum or coal products and is considered to be in the oil industry. Then, extracted textual data are cleaned since it includes irregular characters, such as spaces and newline characters. Once the data are cleaned, we apply stemming and lemmatization, remove stopwords (e.g., "a," "the," "of," ...) and finally feed into Doc2Vec [12] model to obtain embedding for accounts.

Doc2Vec [12] is a model used to obtain sentence embedding, which is similar to Word2Vec [15]. Doc2Vec [12] has two variations: PV-DM takes an additional paragraph vector on top of context words to predict a current word. The paragraph vector is shared across all contexts generated from the same paragraph but not across paragraphs. After being trained to predict a current word, the paragraph vectors can be used as features for the paragraph. PV-DBOW forces the model to predict words randomly sampled from the paragraph in the output. After being trained to predict words randomly sampled from the paragraph, the paragraph vectors can be used as features for the paragraph.

Table 1. Illustrative example of industry textual data.

Account	Description
Company X	company involved in the process of petroleum refining, producing petroleum and coal products such as lubricating oil and grease

3.2 Edge Features

The transaction amount is the most important information for an edge from the practical viewpoint[1] regarding banking transactions since it indicates how much money are transferred between two companies. Hence, we adopt the transaction amount between two companies as an edge feature. Please be advised that the dimension of edge features is much smaller than that of node features in this setting where dimension of embedded textual data can be large. We discuss this problem in succeeding subsections.

3.3 Graph Attention Network

Let us denote a network as $G(V, E)$, node as $u \in V$, edge as $(u, v) \in E$, neighbor nodes of node $u \in V$ as $\mathcal{N}(u)$, $\mathbf{A}$ as the adjacency matrix. We denote $\mathbf{h}_u^{(k)}$ as an embedding of node u in k-th layer in the neural network. $\mathbf{h}_u^{(0)}$ is equivalent to the feature vector of node u, which is a look up of node feature matrix $\mathbf{H} \in \mathbb{R}^{|V| \times d}$. $\mathbf{W}^{(k)} \in \mathbb{R}^{|\text{Hidden dim.}| \times |\text{Input dim.}|}$ is a shared trainable parameter in k-th layer in the network, where |Hidden dim.| and |Input dim.| represents the dimensions of the hidden and input layers, respectively. $\alpha_{u,v}$ is an attention score from node u to node v, indicating importance of neighbor nodes. σ represents an activation function. We adopted the most widely used **ReLU** as an activation function.

With those notations, GAT [21] is formulated as follows. The message aggregating function $\mathbf{m}_{\mathcal{N}(u)}^{(k)}$ from neighbor nodes $\mathcal{N}(u)$ in the k-th layer is given by the equation below. Then, the embedding for node u is updated accordingly.

---

[1] Transaction frequency and descriptive statistics can be other candidates to be concatenated with transaction amount to increase the dimension of edge features. However, importance of features other than transaction amount is limited even when we adopt multi-dimensional edge features since how much money transferred between two parties is critical.

$$\mathbf{m}_{\mathcal{N}(u)}^{(k)} = \sum_{v \in \mathcal{N}(u)} \alpha_{u,v} \mathbf{h}_v^{(k)}, \quad \mathbf{h}_u^{(k+1)} = \sigma \left(\mathbf{W}^{(k)} \mathbf{m}_{\mathcal{N}(u)}^{(k)} \right). \tag{1}$$

Here, the attention score is computed by denoting $\|$ as the concatenation operation and $\mathbf{a}^\top \in \mathbb{R}^{2|\text{Hidden dim.}|}$ as a weight vector.

$$\alpha_{u,v} = \frac{exp \left(\mathbf{LeakyReLU}(\mathbf{a}^\top [\mathbf{W}^{(k)} \mathbf{h}_u^{(k)} \| \mathbf{W}^{(k)} \mathbf{h}_v^{(k)}]) \right)}{\sum_{v' \in \mathcal{N}(u)} exp \left(\mathbf{LeakyReLU}(\mathbf{a}^\top [\mathbf{W}^{(k)} \mathbf{h}_u^{(k)} \| \mathbf{W}^{(k)} \mathbf{h}_{v'}^{(k)}]) \right)}. \tag{2}$$

3.4 Edge Weight-Enhanced Attention Mechanism for Banking Transactions

Arguably, one of the most standard formulations[2] to consider edge features when computing attention scores is to concatenate edge feature vector $\mathbf{e}$, where $\mathbf{e}_{u,v}$ represents transaction amount from node u to node v in this case, to node features $\mathbf{h}_u^{(k)}$ and $\mathbf{h}_v^{(k)}$ when computing attention from node u to node v [2].

$$\alpha_{u,v} = \frac{exp \left(\mathbf{LeakyReLU}(\mathbf{a}'^\top [\mathbf{W}^{(k)} \mathbf{h}_u^{(k)} \| \mathbf{W}^{(k)} \mathbf{h}_v^{(k)} \| \mathbf{W}_e^{(k)} \mathbf{e}_{u,v}]) \right)}{\sum_{v' \in \mathcal{N}(u)} exp \left(\mathbf{LeakyReLU}(\mathbf{a}'^\top [\mathbf{W}^{(k)} \mathbf{h}_u^{(k)} \| \mathbf{W}^{(k)} \mathbf{h}_{v'}^{(k)} \| \mathbf{W}_e^{(k)} \mathbf{e}_{u,v'}]) \right)}. \tag{3}$$

Here, $\mathbf{W}_e^{(k)} \in \mathbb{R}^{|E| \times d_e}$ is a shared weight parameter in k-th layer for edge features; d_e denotes the dimension of edge features and $\mathbf{a}'^\top \in \mathbb{R}^{2|\text{Hidden dim.}|+d_e}$ is a weight vector. The message aggregating function $\mathbf{m}_{\mathcal{N}(u)}^{(k)}$ and the update function for node u are the same as the above original GAT.

However, the effect of edge feature in the above attention mechanism is considered limited in our case since the dimension of edge features is much smaller than that of node features in this setting as mentioned in Subsect. 3.2. Although a node feature vector obtained by Doc2Vec has d dimensions, and $|\text{Hidden dim.}|$ appeared in the weight vector $\mathbf{W}^{(k)}$ is in the order of ten or hundred, an edge feature vector, a transaction amount, is a scalar value. That is to say, $\mathbf{W}_e^{(k)} \mathbf{e}_{u,v}$ accounts for only 1 dimension out of $2|\text{Hidden dim.}| + 1$ dimensions, which is the dimension of the concatenated feature $\mathbf{W}^{(k)} \mathbf{h}_u^{(k)} \| \mathbf{W}^{(k)} \mathbf{h}_v^{(k)} \| \mathbf{W}_e^{(k)} \mathbf{e}_{u,v}$, indicating that edge information contributes little in determining the importance of neighbor nodes.

This issue can appear when we represent financial transactions like banking transactions as a network. More specifically, the dimension of node features can

---

[2] This type of edge feature enhanced attention mechanism is implemented in PyTorch Geometric (https://pytorch-geometric.readthedocs.io/en/latest/modules/nn.html) which is a popular GNN library built upon PyTorch (https://pytorch.org/).

easily be scaled up to a higher dimension by taking different kinds of information about the nodes, such as textual data about nodes like our formulation. As another example, one can concatenate miscellaneous information about the account, such as the number of employers, revenue, profit, asset, and liabilities. However, there are few candidates for edge features as important as the transaction amount as mentioned in Subsect. 3.2.

To alleviate this issue, we propose an alternative modification to the aforementioned attention mechanism [2] to consider node features and edge weights in a well-balanced fashion as follows:

$$\alpha_{u,v} = \frac{exp\left(\textbf{LeakyReLU}\left(\mathbf{a}^\top[\mathbf{W}^{(k)}\mathbf{h}_u^{(k)}||\mathbf{W}^{(k)}\mathbf{h}_v^{(k)}] + \frac{log(e_{u,v})}{\gamma}\right)\right)}{\sum_{v'\in\mathcal{N}(u)} exp\left(\textbf{LeakyReLU}\left(\mathbf{a}^\top[\mathbf{W}^{(k)}\mathbf{h}_u^{(k)}||\mathbf{W}^{(k)}\mathbf{h}_{v'}^{(k)}] + \frac{log(e_{u,v'})}{\gamma}\right)\right)}.$$

(4)

Here, $\mathbf{a}^\top[\mathbf{W}^{(k)}\mathbf{h}_u^{(k)}||\mathbf{W}^{(k)}\mathbf{h}_v^{(k)}]$ is 1-dimensional since it is a dot product of $1\times 2|$Hidden dim.$|$- vector $\mathbf{a}^\top$ and $2|$Hidden dim.$|\times 1$- vector $[\mathbf{W}^{(k)}\mathbf{h}_u^{(k)}||\mathbf{W}^{(k)}\mathbf{h}_v^{(k)}]$. Inside **LeakyReLU**(), we sum 1-dimensional node information and 1-dimensional edge weight. The influence of an edge weight is the same as that of a node feature in terms of dimension.

The reason for taking $log()$ for an edge weight is that the transaction amount varies from the order of 10 (USD) to the order of 100,000,000 (USD). Only a handful of accounts possess such huge transactions; thus, we intend to mitigate the skewness of large values. Additionally, we do not place parameter in front of $log(e_{u,v})$ because we consider transaction amount $log(e_{u,v})$ itself to be a sort of weight parameter, which is the importance of an account to another account.

Furthermore, γ is the parameter used to adjust the influence of the edge weight $log(e_{u,v})$. We can adjust the value range of $log(e_{u,v})$ similar to that of $\mathbf{a}^\top[\mathbf{W}^{(k)}\mathbf{h}_u^{(k)}||\mathbf{W}^{(k)}\mathbf{h}_v^{(k)}]$, by observing them and controlling the edge influence more flexibly. We adopted $\gamma = 10000$ by observing the value range of $\mathbf{a}^\top[\mathbf{W}^{(k)}\mathbf{h}_u^{(k)}||\mathbf{W}^{(k)}\mathbf{h}_v^{(k)}]$ and $log(e_{u,v})$. While we adopted a fixed scaler as γ for simplicity, γ can be a learnable parameter.

Here, for simplicity, we assume that we are only interested in transaction amount as an 1-dimensional edge feature because it is the most important edge information when formulating a banking transaction network[3].

3.5   Graph Isomorphism Network

Typical GNNs are based on message aggregation from neighbor nodes and update on the aggregated features. Such message passing GNNs are proven to be

---

[3] If we want to consider multi-dimensional features, we can set $e_{u,v} = \sum_i \beta_i \mathbf{e}_{u,v}^{(i)}$, for instance. Note that $\mathbf{e}_{u,v}^{(i)}$ represents i-th component of an edge feature vector $\mathbf{e}_{u,v}$ and β_i represents a weight parameter.

as powerful as the Weisfeiler-Lehman graph isomorphism test[4] in distinguishing different graphs [25].

Among message passing GNNs, it is proven that the network is as powerful as the Weisfeiler-Lehman test when the neighbor aggregation functions are injective. GIN [25] is a network that satisfies the injectivity of neighbor aggregation function. By denoting $\epsilon^{(k)}$ as a learnable parameter or a fixed scaler in the k-th layer. GIN [25] is described as follows:

$$\mathbf{m}_{\mathcal{N}(u)}^{(k)} = \sum_{v \in \mathcal{N}(u)} \mathbf{h}_v^{(k)}, \quad \mathbf{h}_u^{(k+1)} = \mathbf{MLP}^{(k+1)}\left((1 + \epsilon^{(k+1)})\mathbf{h}_u^{(k)} + \mathbf{m}_{\mathcal{N}(u)}^{(k)}\right). \quad (5)$$

In previous studies, the authors used one-hot encodings as input node features. Thus, they do not need multilayer perceptrons (MLPs) before summation since the summation of one-hot encodings alone satisfies injectivity. In our case, node features are not necessarily unique since account description is about an industry of a particular account, which can be common for some accounts. To increase the chance of obtaining injectivity, we applied MLP for node features followingly:

$$\mathbf{m}_{\mathcal{N}(u)}^{(k)} = \sum_{v \in \mathcal{N}(u)} \mathbf{MLP}^{(k)}(\mathbf{h}_v^{(k)}), \quad (6)$$

$$\mathbf{h}_u^{(k+1)} = \mathbf{MLP}^{(k+1)}\left((1 + \epsilon^{(k+1)})\mathbf{MLP}^{(k)}(\mathbf{h}_u^{(k)}) + \mathbf{m}_{\mathcal{N}(u)}^{(k)}\right). \quad (7)$$

3.6   Injectivity and Motivation to Use Textual Information

The use of industry description is indeed less effective than one-hot encodings in terms of injectivity because the number of industry is less than the number of accounts. However, adding more textual descriptions on industry information easily defines a unique description of a particular account. Moreover, we can introduce the similarity of different nodes by using textual information, which is not achieved by one-hot encodings. For example, suppose Company X is a petroleum refining company, Company Y is a petroleum products company, and Company Z is a fast-fashion clothing retailer. Companies X, Y, and Z are represented as $(1, 0, 0)$, $(0, 1, 0)$, and $(0, 0, 1)$ with one-hot encodings, respectively, and there is no more information than they are distinguishable. However, they are represented as dense vectors with Doc2Vec, which can capture similarity among companies: Companies X and Y should be embedded close, and Company Z should be embedded far from Companies X and Y. This is because Companies X and Y are in the oil industry, and Company Z is in the fashion industry. Additionally, Doc2Vec can learn the nuance of a slight difference between Companies

---

[4] Weisfeiler-Lehman graph isomorphism test is to distinguish different graphs. First, an initial label is assigned to each node. Then, a new label is iteratively assigned by hashing the multiset of the current labels, which are assigned to neighbor nodes of each node. The iteration halts when relabeling of each node converges [7,23].

X and Y that they are in the same industry but located in the different part of the oil supply chain.

3.7 Non-probabilistic Graph Autoencoder

Once node features are passed through the GAT layer and succeeding GIN layer, we obtain embedded node features. The obtained embedding is decoded using a non-probabilistic graph autoencoder (GAE) [10].

Let us denote the obtained embedding through the GAT layer and succeeding GIN layer as $\mathbf{Z}$. Then, the adjacency matrix $\mathbf{A}$ of the original network, which can be interpreted as occurrence of transactions, can be reconstructed as follows[5]:

$$\mathbf{A} \approx \mathbf{sigmoid}(\mathbf{Z}\mathbf{Z}^T). \tag{8}$$

4   Evaluation

4.1   Dataset

The dataset is provided by one of large Asian banks with all data in the depersonalized format. The data consist of monthly aggregated transactions that companies send or receive money to its counterparties, as shown in Table 2.

Textual data shown in Table 1, which describe industry in English for each account, are originally obtained from Asian central bank. The central bank defines descriptions of different industries. The above Asian bank mapped the defined industry to each account on their side. Thereafter, the monthly aggregated transactions and textual data were given to us in the depersonalized format.

Table 2. Illustrative example of aggregated transactions.

Sender	Receiver	Amount
Company X	Company Y	20,000,000
Company X	Company Z	800,000,000
Company X	Company W	100,000,000
Company U	Company X	50,000,000
Company V	Company X	700,000,000

Based on the transaction data, we construct a directed network with embedded description of accounts as node features, transaction occurrence for pairs of nodes as edges, and monthly aggregated transaction amount from an account to its counterparties as edge weights. The constructed network consists of 170,094 nodes and 1,244,639 edges, as presented in Table 3. Max degree, which is the

---

[5] For a particular edge, its linkage is reconstructed as $\mathbf{A}_{u,v} \approx \mathbf{sigmoid}(\mathbf{Z}_u \mathbf{Z}_v^T)$. In this case, $\mathbf{Z}_u$ represents a node embedding for node u.

number of counterparties an account has, is 15,431. The average degree is 7.2863; median degree is 3; min degree is 1. The average clustering coefficient is 0.0573. As mentioned in the previous section, the edge weights vary from the order of 10 (USD) to 100,000,000 (USD).

Table 3. Basic information of banking transaction network.

Information	Value
Number of Nodes	170,094
Number of Edges	1,244,639
Max Degree	15,431
Average Degree	7.2863
Median Degree	3
Min Degree	1
Average Clustering Coefficient	0.0573

4.2 Task

We adopted the link prediction task to learn embeddings since the link prediction problem is interpreted as the prediction of transaction occurrence. Additionally, prediction of transaction occurrence is beneficial from the practical viewpoint. For instance, if we can accurately predict the transaction occurrence of a client, a bank can estimate if they are missing potential transactions from a client, implying useful for customer relationship management.

We adopted ROC-AUC (Receiver Operating Characteristic - Area Under the Curve) score [18] as evaluation metrics. ROC Curve is a probability curve that plots the true positive rate $(= \frac{TP}{TP+FN})$ against false positive rate $(= \frac{FP}{TN+FP})$ by denoting using true positive as TP, true negative as TN, false positive as FP and false negative as FN. ROC-AUC stands for the area under the ROC curve. It is a standard practice to evaluate link prediction tasks by ROC-AUC scores as seen in previous works [5,17,20]. We also used accuracy $(= \frac{TP+TN}{TP+FP+FN+TN})$, precision $(= \frac{TP}{TP+FP})$ and recall $(= \frac{TP}{TP+FN})$ as well.

4.3 Baseline Methods

As baselines, we adopted several popular methods: node2vec [6], GCN [11], GAT [21] and GIN [25]. Complex network analysis methods, such as Jaccard coefficient [14], are also widely used for link prediction; however, they have been tested in previous work and did not outperform node2vec [5]. Therefore, we did not use them in our experiment. GAT [21] and GIN [25] are explained in detail in the previous section, the rest of models are explained in this section.

node2vec [6] is one of the most popular graph embedding approaches. It runs a second-order random walk for each node in a graph to generate random sequences of nodes, generating node embeddings by training a skip-gram of Word2Vec [15]. The random walk has two parameters to control focuses if it explores the close area or far area from the current node. It basically captures network topology only.

GCN [11] is one of the most popular models among GNNs. The model structure of GCN is relatively simple and often shows good performance. Therefore, it is commonly used as a benchmark for comparison. It is categorized as a spectral-based method since it has a solid mathematical foundation in graph signal processing [24]. GCN [11] is formulated as follows:

$$\mathbf{H}^{(k+1)} = \sigma\left(\tilde{\mathbf{D}}^{-1/2}\tilde{\mathbf{A}}\tilde{\mathbf{D}}^{-1/2}\mathbf{H}^{(k)}\mathbf{W}^{(k)}\right). \tag{9}$$

Here, $\mathbf{H} \in \mathbb{R}^{|V| \times d}$ is a node feature matrix; $\tilde{\mathbf{D}}$ is a degree matrix[6]; k is the number of layers; $\mathbf{H}^{(k)} \in \mathbb{R}^{|\text{Hidden dim.}| \times |\text{Input dim.}|}$ as a node embedding in k-th layer in the network; $\tilde{\mathbf{A}}$ is the adjacency matrix with added self-connections; $\mathbf{W}^{(k)} \in \mathbb{R}^{|\text{Hidden dim.}| \times |\text{Input dim.}|}$ is a shared trainable parameter in k-th layer in the network; σ is an activation function. We used **ReLU** as an activation function and k as the number of layers. Note that $\mathbf{H}^{(0)} = \mathbf{H}$.

4.4   Experiment

We conducted experiments to evaluate the performance of the proposed method and aforementioned baseline models. For the implementation, we used nltk[7] for preprocessing text data, gensim[8] for Doc2Vec, PyTorch geometric[9] for different baseline methods as well as our proposed method, and scikit-learn[10] for evaluation metrics.

For node2vec [6], the bias parameter of the random walk is $p = q = 1$; the walk length of the random walk is 15; the context size is 10. The dimension of embedding is 128, and the window size is 10. For GNN baseline models and our proposed method, we adopted the following settings. The dimension of node features d obtained from Doc2Vec is 300. We adopted 128 as the dimension of the output of the GAT layer and 64 as the output of the GIN layer. More specifically, for node $u \in V$, the dimension of $\mathbf{h}_u^{(0)}$ is 300; the dimension of $\mathbf{h}_u^{(1)}$ is 128; the dimension of $\mathbf{h}_u^{(2)}$ is 64.

We adopted cross entropy as loss function, 0.001 as learning rate, 100 as the number of epochs, Adam as an optimizer. We limit the layer as shallow as two layers to simply avoid the over-smoothing problems, in which adding more layers into the network results in that the node representations converge to indistinguishable features [19]. We use 80% of the entire edges as train edges, 10% of the entire edges as validation edges, and 10% of the entire edges as test edges to compare with baseline methods. We record ROC-AUC score for test

---

[6] Degree matrix is represented as $\tilde{\mathbf{D}}_{i,i} = \sum_j \tilde{\mathbf{A}}_{i,j}$.
[7] https://www.nltk.org/.
[8] https://pypi.org/project/gensim/.
[9] https://pytorch-geometric.readthedocs.io/en/latest/index.html.
[10] https://scikit-learn.org/stable/.

edges when the validation score is the best through running epochs. The results of the experiment is shown in Fig. 1.

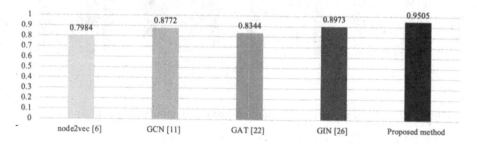

Fig. 1. ROC-AUC comparison with baseline methods.

Compared to our previous work [16], we conducted additional experiments from different perspectives to verify the effectiveness of our proposed method. First, similar to previous works, we change ratio of training edges to study model behaviors [5,17]. On top of the aforementioned train-test split, additional two patterns are tested for node2vec [6], GCN [11] and proposed method; (1) 50% of the entire edges as train edges, 10% of the entire edges as validation edges, and 40% of the entire edges as test edges; (2) 20% of the entire edges as train edges, 10% of the entire edges as validation edges, and 70% of the entire edges as test edges. We record ROC-AUC score for test edges when the validation score is the best through running epochs. Those results are presented in Fig 2.

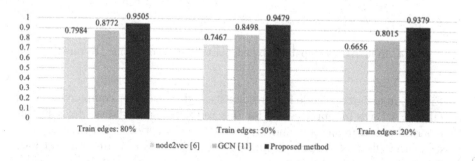

Fig. 2. ROC-AUC comparison by training edges ratios.

We also studied the behavior of the proposed method by the node degrees (i.e. the number of counterparties), as studied in previous works [5,17]. We record ROC-AUC score for test edges when the validation score is the best through running epochs. Those results are presented in Fig. 3.

Moreover, we compared the proposed edge enhanced mechanism presented in Subsect. 3.4 with the existing edge enhanced attention mechanism [2] to see

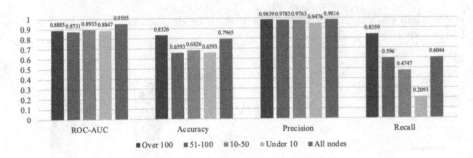

Fig. 3. Evaluation metrics by the node degrees (i.e. number of counterparties).

the expected improvements to consider node information and edge information in well-balanced fashion. We record ROC-AUC score for test edges when the validation score is the best through running the same experiments 10 times for each method. Then, we compare average, max, and min of ROC-AUC scores for each method. Those results are presented in Fig. 4.

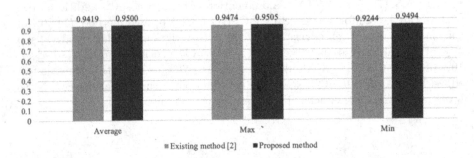

Fig. 4. ROC-AUC comparison by edge attention mechanisms (10 runs).

Finally, injectivity of node features are studied. Since inter-company network in Subsect. 4.1 was inappropriate[11] for this study, the same dataset for different time period was aggregated by industry level to construct inter-industry network to study the effect of assigning unique information. Here, high-level and low-level industry classification are used as node features respectively to consider the effect of uniqueness and similarity. Low-level classification is unique to each node while it is not the case with high-level classification. We record ROC-AUC score for test edges when the validation score is the best through running the same experiments 5 times for each pattern. Then, average, max, and min of ROC-AUC scores are compared. Those results are presented in Fig. 5.

---

[11] There was data limitation that unique textual description was not available on each account. Also, individual firm information such as the firm's transaction amount cannot be disclosed due to data privacy.

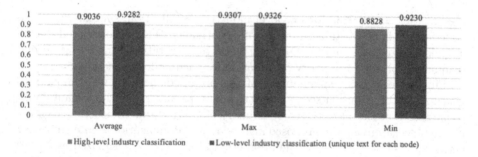

Fig. 5. Study of injectivity of node features (5 runs).

5 Discussion

As presented in Fig. 1, ROC-AUC score of the proposed method is the highest as 0.9505. We analyze this is due to the expected effect of considering textual information, edge weight-enhanced attention mechanism, and choice of GNNs to capture importance of neighbor nodes in the first GAT layer and to increase representation power in the succeeding GIN layer. When we compare node2vec with GNNs, such as GCN, GAT, and GIN, one of the key differences is whether we leverage node features, which is account description in this case, on top of network topology. As explained in the previous section, GIN has a higher score than GCN and GAT because of its representation power.

As shown in Fig. 2, deterioration of ROC-AUC scores is milder in proposed method and GCN than node2vec, indicating the effectiveness of GNN based methods by considering node features on top of network topology.

Regarding evaluation by the node degrees, whereas there cannot be seen significant changes in ROC-AUC scores, recall gets worse when node degrees are smaller as shown in Fig. 3. This is considered due to the network property: the accounts with small number of counterparties are not likely to have links and vice versa. Similar results are seen in previous work [17].

Also, the effectiveness of edge enhanced attention mechanisms are studied. As presented in Fig. 4, our proposed attention mechanism outperform the existing method [2] in average, max and min of ROC-AUC scores when running the experiments 10 times. Whereas differences of average and max ROC-AUC scores are small, min ROC-AUC scores is 0.9494 for propose method and 0.9244 for the existing method [2], suggesting the proposed method is more stable in terms of performance. This is considered due to that the novel attention mechanism works as intended to consider node and edge information with equal importance, implying transaction amount is important whereas we lose some information from node features with the proposed attention mechanism.

Moreover, injectivity of node features are studied. As presented in Fig. 5, average, max and min of ROC-AUC scores for low-level node features are higher when running the experiments 5 times. Whereas differences of average and max ROC-AUC scores are close, min ROC-AUC score is 0.8828 for high-level industry classification and 0.9230 for low-level industry classification, suggesting unique node feature is more stable in terms of performance. This is considered due to intended uniqueness and similarity of node representation, suggesting adding unique text on top of industry information for each node is effective.

Finally, regarding explainability of the proposed method, we demonstrate visualization of attention scores is instrumental to understand important counterparties from the perspective of industry similarity and transaction volume. For instance, applying the proposed method to the aforementioned inter-industry network, attention scores for the apparel retail industry is visualized as Fig. 6. The results are consistent with transaction volume and practical knowledge (i.e. similarity in some sense); There are lot of internal transactions within the same apparel industry; amount spent by consumers via online shopping is transferred to apparel retailers from credit card company; amount spent by consumers at on-site stores is transferred to apparel retailers from department stores.

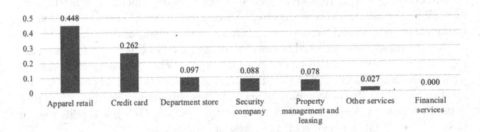

Fig. 6. Visualization of attention scores.

In future studies, we can consider applications of the proposed method for downstream tasks, such as macroeconomic indicator predictions, credit scoring and customer relationship management.

6   Conclusion

In this paper, we propose an approach to predict transaction occurrence by using GNNs with special attention mechanism and textual industry information. To capture information of each banking account, we use Doc2Vec [12] to obtain an embedded vector of the textual industry description for each account, enabling consideration of similarity among different nodes and scalable node representation to a more detailed unique description of accounts. Additionally, we use embedded descriptions of accounts as node features, transaction occurrence as edges, and monthly aggregated transaction amount from an account to its counterparties as edge weight to model banking transaction networks. Consequently, we achieved a better ROC-AUC score for predicting transaction occurrence using the novel edge weight-enhanced attention mechanism in GAT [21] and GIN [11]. We also discussed the effectiveness of the proposed method, the novel attention mechanism and node feature design while demonstrating its usage as an industry importance explainer. The proposed method can be applied to macroeconomic indicator predictions as well as credit and customer relationship management.

Acknowledgement. This work was supported by JST-Mirai Program Grant Number JPMJMI20B1, Japan.

References

1. Barlas, A.B., et al.: Big data information and nowcasting: Consumption and investment from bank transactions in turkey (2021). https://arxiv.org/abs/2107.03299
2. Chen, J., Chen, H.: Edge-featured graph attention network (2021). https://arxiv.org/abs/2101.07671
3. Dong, Y., Chawla, N.V., Swami, A.: Metapath2vec: scalable representation learning for heterogeneous networks. In: Proceedings of the 23rd ACM SIGKDD International Conference on Knowledge Discovery and Data Mining, pp. 135–144. KDD 2017, Association for Computing Machinery, New York (2017). https://doi.org/10.1145/3097983.3098036
4. Engel, J., Nardo, M., Rancan, M.: Network analysis for economics and finance: an application to firm ownership. In: Consoli, S., Reforgiato Recupero, D., Saisana, M. (eds.) Data Science for Economics and Finance, pp. 331–355. Springer, Cham (2021). https://doi.org/10.1007/978-3-030-66891-4_14
5. Fujitsuka, M., Kudo, T.: Latent transaction prediction using graph embedding. In: The Japanese Society for Artificial Intelligence - 23th Workshop on Special Interest Group on Financial Informatics. SIG-FIN 2019 (2019)
6. Grover, A., Leskovec, J.: Node2vec: scalable feature learning for networks. In: Proceedings of the 22nd ACM SIGKDD International Conference on Knowledge Discovery and Data Mining, pp. 855–864. KDD 2016, Association for Computing Machinery (2016). https://doi.org/10.1145/2939672.2939754
7. Hamilton, W.L.: Graph representation learning. Synth. Lect. Artif. Intell. Mach. Learn. **14**(3), 1–159 (2020)
8. Hastie, T., Tibshirani, R., Friedman, J.: The Elements of Statistical Learning. SSS, Springer, New York (2009). https://doi.org/10.1007/978-0-387-84858-7
9. Khazane, A., et al.: DeepTrax: embedding graphs of financial transactions. In: 2019 18th IEEE International Conference On Machine Learning And Applications (ICMLA), pp. 126–133 (2019). https://doi.org/10.1109/ICMLA.2019.00028
10. Kipf, T.N., Welling, M.: Variational graph auto-encoders. In: NIPS 2016 Workshop on Bayesian Deep Learning. BDL 2016 (2016)
11. Kipf, T.N., Welling, M.: Semi-supervised classification with graph convolutional networks. In: Proceedings of the 5th International Conference on Learning Representations. ICLR 2017 (2017)
12. Le, Q., Mikolov, T.: Distributed representations of sentences and documents. In: Proceedings of the 31st International Conference on International Conference on Machine Learning - Volume 32, pp. II-1188-II-1196. ICML2014, JMLR.org (2014)
13. Li, X., Saude, J., Reddy, P., Veloso, M., Morgan, J., Research, A.: Classifying and understanding financial data using graph neural network. In: The AAAI-20 Workshop on Knowledge Discovery from Unstructured Data in Financial Services. AAAI-KDF 2020 (2020)

14. Lu, L., Zhou, T.: Link prediction in complex networks: a survey. Phys. A **390**(6), 1150–1170 (2011)
15. Mikolov, T., Chen, K., Corrado, G., Dean, J.: Efficient estimation of word representations in vector space. In: Proceedings of the 1st International Conference on Learning Representations. ICLR 2013 (2013)
16. Minakawa, N., Izumi, K., Sakaji, H., Sano, H.: Graph representation learning of banking transaction network with edge weight-enhanced attention and textual information. In: Companion Proceedings of the Web Conference 2022, pp. 630–637. WWW 2022, Association for Computing Machinery, New York (2022). https://doi.org/10.1145/3487553.3524643
17. Mori, M., Yogosawa, M., Kudo, T.: Feature extraction of companies from business relationship graphs by GCN. In: The Japanese Society for Artificial Intelligence - 24th Workshop on Special Interest Group on Financial Informatics. SIG-FIN-024 (2019)
18. Murphy, K.P.: Machine Learning: A Probabilistic Perspective. MIT press, Cambridge (2012). Adaptive computation and machine learning series
19. Oono, K., Suzuki, T.: Graph neural networks exponentially lose expressive power for node classification. In: Proceedings of the 8th International Conference on Learning Representations. ICLR 2020 (2020)
20. Shumovskaia, V., Fedyanin, K., Sukharev, I., Berestnev, D., Panov, M.: Linking bank clients using graph neural networks powered by rich transactional data: Extended abstract. In: 2020 IEEE 7th International Conference on Data Science and Advanced Analytics (DSAA), pp. 787–788 (2020). https://doi.org/10.1109/DSAA49011.2020.00117
21. Velickovic, P., Cucurull, G., Casanova, A., Romero, A., Lio, P., Bengio, Y.: Graph attention networks. In: Proceedings of the 6th International Conference on Learning Representations. ICLR 2018 (2018)
22. Wang, J., Zhang, S., Xiao, Y., Song, R.: A review on graph neural network methods in financial applications (2021). https://arxiv.org/abs/2111.15367
23. Weisfeiler, B., Lehman, A.A.: A reduction of a graph to a canonical form and an algebra arising during this reduction. Nauchno-Technicheskaya Informatsia Ser. **2**(N9), 12–16 (1968)
24. Wu, Z., Pan, S., Chen, F., Long, G., Zhang, C., Yu, P.S.: A comprehensive survey on graph neural networks. IEEE Trans. Neural Netw. Learn. Syst. **32**(1), 4–24 (2021). https://doi.org/10.1109/TNNLS.2020.2978386
25. Xu, K., Hu, W., Leskovec, J., Jegelka, S.: How powerful are graph neural networks? In: Proceedings of the 7th International Conference on Learning Representations, pp. 1–17. ICLR 2019 (2019)
26. Zhang, M., Chen, Y.: Link prediction based on graph neural networks. In: Advances in Neural Information Processing Systems 31. NeurIPS 2018, vol. 31, pp. 5165–5175. Curran Associates, Inc. (2018)
27. Zhou, J., et al.: Graph neural networks: a review of methods and applications. AI Open **1**, 57–81 (2020)

Overfitting Problem in the Approximate Bayesian Computation Method Based on Maxima Weighted Isolation Kernel

Iurii S. Nagornov[✉]

National Institute of Advanced Industrial Science and Technology, Tokyo Waterfront,
2-4-7 Aomi, Koto-ku, Tokyo 135-0064, Japan
iurii.nagornov@aist.go.jp
https://www.airc.aist.go.jp/en/project/overview.html

Abstract. A branching processes model yields an unevenly stochastically distributed dataset that consists of highly sparse and highly dense regions. This work addresses the problem of precisely evaluating parameters for such a model. An approximate Bayesian computation method is developed that is based on Isolation Kernel mapping with additional parameter generation and selection processes, i.e. meta-sampling. The method involves the transformation of row data to a Hilbert space and the measurement of the similarity between generated parameters and maxima weighted Isolation Kernel mapping related to the observation point. Meta-sampling algorithm requires no gradient calculation and is dimension independent. This work is devoted to the problem of the fitting and overfitting of the hyperparameters for the method such as a number of Voronoi sites and a number of trees of isolation forest. Here, we discuss the reasons for overfitting and how to fit parameters properly. The advantages of the proposed meta-sampling method are illustrated using multidimensional test data as well as a specific example focused on cancer cell evolution.

Keywords: Isolation Kernel · Overfitting Problem · Approximate Bayesian Computation · Maxima Weighted Isolation Kernel Mapping · Branching Processes

1 Introduction

This paper addresses the problem of precisely estimating the parameters of a stochastic model corresponding to branching processes. A branching process is a stochastic process consisting of collections of random variables indexed by the natural numbers. Branching processes are often used to describe population models [18] and [1]; for example, models in population genetics showing genetic drift [6]. However, particularly in the case of cancer cell evolution, as well as in branching processes in general, the ultimate extinction of a population often occurs [10]. It is for this reason that branching processes models straight up tend to yield strong unevenly distributed data consisting of very sparse and very dense regions.

Y. Takama et al. (Eds.): JSAI-isAI 2022 Workshop, LNAI 13859, pp. 267–282, 2023.
https://doi.org/10.1007/978-3-031-29168-5_18

Well-known method to estimating model parameters under a given observation is Approximate Bayesian Computation (ABC) that has many different approaches [9]. Unfortunately, it has been found even kernel ABC produces inaccurate estimates in the case of unevenly distributed data in a multidimensional space of parameters [27] and [34]. In light of this limitation, we propose the use of a machine learning method, combined with kernel ABC, to improve estimation accuracy. Because of its unique properties, Isolation Kernel (iKernel) would appear to be the most appropriate method for this class of problem [34].

Our method is based on the ABC kernel method and an additional process of generating parameters and selecting them based on similarity to a maxima weighted kernel mean mapping of an observation point. For this purpose, the method first computes the kernel mean mapping of an observation point using Isolation kernel based on Voronoi diagrams. Only those Voronoi sites that have maxima weighted similarity to an observation point are extracted from it, that is, only part of the kernel mean embedding is used. Then, the parameters are heuristically generated, translated into Hilbert space, and the similarity matrix with the observation point is calculated. As a result, the parameters most similar to the observation are selected. No simulation is performed using the generated parameters and only already known data are used. Thus, the proposed method adds an additional algorithmic step between kernel ABC and sampling (meta-sampling), due to which the method achieves significant accuracy in the sparse data domain in stochastic modeling under condition of correct fitting of hyper-parameters. This study is devoted to the overfitting problem, reasons for that and the related task of choosing internal parameters.

2   Related Work

Kernel ABC is evolving toward a kernel search based on the principles of incorporating as much useful information as possible from the available data. The most interesting works in this direction are K2-ABC [28] that used maximum mean discrepancy (MMD) [5] and kernel-based distribution regression (DR-ABC) [23]. However, these methods provide an advantage for high-dimensional data, provided that there is some dense enough distribution to carry out MMD estimation. In the formulation of our problem, this condition is not initially satisfied. Adjusted methods are used in various situations, such as ABC based on linear regression, regression using deep learning, kernel ridge regression. These are the approaches that will be used to compare with the proposed method because they involve changing the weights in the data sample depending on the learning process.

Our approach is a continuation of the Isolation kernel development work and uses algorithms from the recent works [34] and [35]. The Isolation Kernel was specifically chosen as a kernel that depends on data density, requires low computational cost, and is the least of all the others dependent on the dimensionality of the problem [33]. A significant difference with previous works straight is the use of kernel mean embedding in the explicit form of Voronoi cells and an additional search algorithm in the parameter space based on the similarity with kernel mapping related to an observation point. This approach makes it possible to generate points in the parameter space and select the most suitable ones, i.e. meta-sampling, which was not implemented in previous works.

3   Background

3.1   Kernel Mean Embedding

In short the general idea of the kernel method is to transform real data $x \in \mathcal{X}$ to Hilbert space $\mathcal{H}$ where a similarity measure is used instead of the distance. $\mathcal{H}$ is a vector space with an inner product in it $\langle \cdot, \cdot \rangle$ and feature transformation from real data $\phi(x) : \mathcal{X} \to \mathcal{H}$ also called mapping [24]. The inner product plays role the similarity measure function in $\mathcal{H}$ and it is represented by kernel function such that $k(x, y) = \langle \phi(x), \phi(y) \rangle$ for any points $x, y \in R^d$ and $\phi(x), \phi(y) \in \mathcal{H}$ with dimension $d_{\mathcal{H}}$ [30]. The kernel is chosen as the positive definite function and symmetric, i.e. $k(x, y) = k(y, x)$ that is a necessary condition [14]. The feature mapping includes the data transformation with increasing dimensionality $d_{\mathcal{H}} \gg d$ and, in principle, dimension of Hilbert space can be infinity $d_{\mathcal{H}} = \infty$, Thus, the most attractive in the usage of kernel methods is that they avoid the explicit calculation of $\phi(x)$ and use only kernel function instead. This procedure is called a kernel trick that is a very convenient, efficient and accurate algorithm [15]. So, one can calculate the similarity between all data points in the form of a Gram matrix that is also positive definite.

For ML they use a reproducing kernel Hilbert space (RKHS) with reproducing kernel which has the reproducing property:

$$f(x) = \langle f, k(\cdot, x) \rangle \tag{1}$$

for any function $f(x) \in \mathcal{H}$ and any point $x \in R^d$ where dot in $k(\cdot, x)$ means all possible points in a Hilbert space. There is a one-to-one correspondence between the reproducing kernel k and the RKHS $\mathcal{H}$ (Theorem 2.5 in review [24]). For RKHS the feature function can be derived as follow:

$$\phi(x) = k(\cdot, x), \tag{2}$$

and it's called as a canonical feature map.

The kernel mean embedding based on a random variable that is described as a measurable function defined on a probability space [37]. Let $X \subset R^d$ and $Y \subset R^d$ are two random variables. The probabilities defined on X, Y may be marginal ($P(X)$ and $P(Y)$), joint ($P(X, Y)$), or conditional ($P(Y|X)$) [13]. To make a distribution mapping the **kernel mean embedding** is used with P probability measure in the form [3]:

$$\mu_P := \mathbf{E}_P[\phi(X)]_{\mathcal{H}} = \int_{\mathcal{X}} \phi(x) dP(x) = \int_{\mathcal{X}} k(\cdot, x) dP(x), \tag{3}$$

where $k(\cdot, x)$ is a kernel on $\mathcal{X}$, $\mathbf{E}$ is expectation in feature space. The important condition for kernel $k(\cdot, x)$ is that they should be Bochner integrable [14].

3.2 Kernel ABC

In the rejection ABC, to get the posterior distribution it iteratively generates a lot of simulations, gets summary statistics for each simulation to reduce a dimension of a problem and finally decides on rejection or acceptance of the simulation [19] and [9]. Accepted simulations give us a posterior distribution of parameters. where maximum a posterior is usually used as parameters' estimation for the given observation. The target of kernel ABC is to get kernel mean embedding of posterior distribution using the formulation of Eq. (3). Let us assume a stochastic model which has a measurable variable $\Theta \in \mathcal{Q}$ as an input d-dimension parameter and, the results of the model's simulation are represented by another measurable variable $S \in \mathcal{S}$ of d_s dimension. The $\mathcal{Q}$ and $\mathcal{S}$ are corresponding domains. Let consider an observation point $s^* \in \mathcal{S}$ and given sample of n simulations $S = \{s_1, s_2, \ldots, s_n\} \in \mathcal{S}$ based on related input parameters $\Theta = \{\theta_1, ..., \theta_n\} \in \mathcal{Q}$. The corresponding prior distributions of parameters $\pi(\theta)$ and simulations $P(s)$ are given by:

$$s \sim P(s) \qquad \text{and} \qquad \theta \sim \pi(\theta). \tag{4}$$

Therefore, the posterior distribution $P(\theta|s^*)$ of the parameters θ on given observation s^* can be obtained in the form:

$$P(\theta|S = s^*) \propto P(s^*|\theta) \cdot \pi(\theta), \tag{5}$$

where $P(s, \theta)$ is a joint distribution of s and θ, $P(s|\theta)$ is a conditional distribution. In the kernel ABC, the kernel mean embedding of the posterior distribution $P(\theta|S = s^*)$ is defined as follow [28] and [19]:

$$\mu_{P(\theta|S=s^*)} = \int_{\mathcal{Q}} l(\cdot, \theta) dP(\theta|s^*) \in \mathcal{G}, \tag{6}$$

where $l(\cdot, \theta) \in \mathcal{G}$ denotes the kernel in reproducing kernel Hilbert space $\mathcal{G}$. In order to exploit the Eq. (6) one must define two kernels: $l(\cdot, \theta)$ for domain of parameters $\mathcal{Q}$ and $k(\cdot, s)$ for domain of simulations $\mathcal{S}$:

$$
\begin{aligned}
k : \mathcal{S} \times \mathcal{S} \to R \qquad &\text{and} \qquad l : \mathcal{Q} \times \mathcal{Q} \to R \\
k(\cdot, s) = \phi(s) \in \mathcal{H} \qquad &\text{and} \qquad l(\cdot, \theta) = \psi(\theta) \in \mathcal{G},
\end{aligned} \tag{7}
$$

where $\mathcal{H}$ is reproducing kernel Hilbert space for $k(\cdot, s)$, $\phi(s)$ and $\psi(\theta)$ are mapping function for $\mathcal{H}$ and $\mathcal{G}$ respectively. Kernel mean embedding Eq. (6) can be written as [24]:

$$
\begin{aligned}
\mu_{P(\theta|S=s^*)} &\approx \Psi(\mathbf{G} + n\lambda \mathbb{I}_n)^{-1} \Phi^\mathsf{T} k(\cdot, s^*), \\
\Psi^\mathsf{T} &:= [\psi(\theta_1), \psi(\theta_2), ..., \psi(\theta_n)]^\mathsf{T} \\
\Phi^\mathsf{T} &:= [\phi(s_1), \phi(s_2), ..., \phi(s_n)]^\mathsf{T},
\end{aligned} \tag{8}
$$

where $\mathbf{G} = \Phi^\mathsf{T} \Phi$ is Gram matrix. Under conditions of $n \to \infty$ and $\lambda \to 0$, the estimation will converge to true-value consistently [14].

3.3   Isolation Kernel Based on Voronoi Diagram

Isolation Kernel (iKernel) was proposed in the paper [35] and it is based on Isolation Forest (iForest) algorithm [21] and [34]. In the simplest two dimensional case, a Voronoi diagram is a partition of a plane into regions close to each of a given set of points (called Voronoi sites or seeds) [12] and [36]. For each site, there is a corresponding region, called Voronoi cell, consisting of all points of the plane closer to that site than to any other [2] and [16]. The advantage of Voronoi diagram is in a very simple method of dividing all points into cells by just calculating distances and choosing the minimal one.

The algorithm of Voronoi diagram is based on the calculation of feature mapping $\Phi(x)$ for each point x in dataset $D = \{x_1, x_2, ..., x_n\} \in R^d$, where d is dimension, t is a number of partitionings. For each partitioning $\mathcal{H}_i$ the number of partitions is fixed and equals ξ and the value of feature mapping for each point x equals $\Phi_i(x)$ which is binary vector with just one 1 and all zeros in other positions that represents fact that x falls into either only one partition in each partitioning H_i. The feature mapping is achieved by concatenation of all $\Phi_i(x)$. This mechanism has been shown to produce large partitions in a sparse region and small partitions in a dense region [34]. Voronoi diagram requires a subset of ξ points for t Trees at the Training stage, so, the computational cost is $O(\xi \times t)$.

To produce the posterior distribution for parameters $P(\theta | S = s^*)$ under given observation s^*, it is necessary to generate sampling of θ from $\mathcal{Q}$ Eqs. (5 and 6). A number of appropriate methods to generate such sampling are available, including Kernel Herding [8], Markov Chain Monte Carlo (MCMC) [11], Sequential Monte Carlo (SMC) [22], Sequential Kernel Herding [20].

Note that the dimensions d_ϕ and d_ψ of Hilbert spaces $\mathcal{H}$ and $\mathcal{G}$ can be infinite in principle, which is the reason that the kernel trick is used in computations to avoid the direct calculation of kernel mean embedding. A common approach to checking convergence is to use the maximum mean discrepancy **MMD**, which also employs the kernel trick [5] and [28]. To produce the initial and generated sampling, weights such as $\Phi^\mathsf{T} k(\cdot, s^*)$ are used. These, too, are based on the kernel trick.

4   Overfitting Problem in Maxima Weighted iKernel ABC

4.1   Maxima Weighted iKernel Mapping

As an alternative to the kernel trick method, we straight up suggest the calculation of the maxima weighted state of the kernel mean embedding $\mu_{P(\theta|S=s*)}$ in RKHS $\mathcal{G}$ explicitly using Eq. 8 with a transformation based on properties of Isolation Kernel. The most important and interesting idea is that we produce $\mu_{P(\theta|S=s*)}$ in RKHS $\mathcal{G}$ related to the space of parameters, which means that iKernel will give us information about the parameters related to the observation directly. Maintaining the notation of Eq. (4) and in order to prepare iKernel, we can define Voronoi diagrams using a sample of parameters Θ with size n for each tree in accordance with paper [35]:

$$z_{jk} \subset \Theta \qquad j \in [1,t] \qquad k \in [1,\xi] \text{ and } \xi \ll n$$
$$V_{jk}(z_{jk}) = \{\theta \in \mathcal{Q} | d(\theta, z_{jk}) \leq d(\theta, z_{pk}), p \neq j\}, \qquad (9)$$

where z_{jk} is the k-th site of the j-th tree or Voronoi diagram and element of a sample of parameters Θ, ξ is a number of sites in each Voronoi diagram/tree, t is the number of trees/Voronoi diagrams, $V_{jk}(z_{jk})$ is the Voronoi cell related to site z_{jk}, and $d(\cdot, \cdot)$ is a distance metric. Next, we can define Isolation Kernel and feature mapping $l(\cdot, \theta) = \psi(\theta)$ related to [34] as follows:

$$V_{jk}(z_{jk}) \rightarrow \psi(\theta)$$
$$\psi(\theta_i) \Longleftrightarrow \{\zeta_{i1}, ..., \zeta_{it}\} = \{\zeta_{ij}\} \qquad (10)$$
$$\zeta_{ij} = \arg\min_{k \in [1,\xi]} \quad d(\theta_i, z_{jk}),$$

where ζ_{ij} is the Voronoi site with minimal distance to the θ_i parameter from the set of sites $\{z_{jk}\}$ of the jth Voronoi diagram/tree.

Equation (8) gives information regarding the contribution of each sample point to the kernel mean embedding of the observation point in RKHS $\mathcal{G}$. The weights $\Phi^T k(\cdot, s^*)$ are similarity coefficients between sample points and the observation point. Thus, the series of the sum in Eq. (8) gives information about the Voronoi diagrams in the parameters space through the similarity between the sample points and the observation point in the space of S from results of simulations. Incorporating Eqs. (8, 9 and 10) together enables us to describe iKernel mean embedding $\mu_{P(\theta|S=s*)}$ as a weighted distribution of Voronoi sites for each jth tree:

$$P_{jk}(z_{jk}) \Longleftrightarrow \mu_{P(\theta|S=s*)} = \sum_{i=1}^{n} w_i \psi(\theta_i)$$

$$P_{jk}(z_{jk}) \propto \frac{1}{n} \sum_{i=1}^{n} w_i \times \mathbf{1}(\zeta_{ij} = z_{jk}), \qquad (11)$$

where $P_{jk}(z_{jk})$ is the probability of finding a parameter related to observation s^* close to the kth Voronoi site z_{jk} of the jth tree/diagram.

We now turn to an algorithm for seeking the parameter related to observation s^* using the maxima weighted state of $\mu_{P(\theta|S=s*)}$. This procedure reduces the information from iKernel mean $\mu_{P(\theta|S=s*)}$ but allows for the possibility of finding a position in multi-dimensional space of parameters with high probability related to s^*. In this way, our strategy is based on the obvious hypothesis that the true value is near a point related to the maxima weighted iKernel mapping. For this purpose let us determine the maxima weighted probabilities $P_{jk}(z_{jk})$ across the trees:

$$z_j^* = \arg\max_{k \in [1,\xi]} \quad P_{jk}(z_{jk})$$
$$v_j^* = v_j(z_j^*) \qquad (12)$$
$$\mu_{v^*} \Longleftrightarrow \{z_1^*, ..., z_t^*\},$$

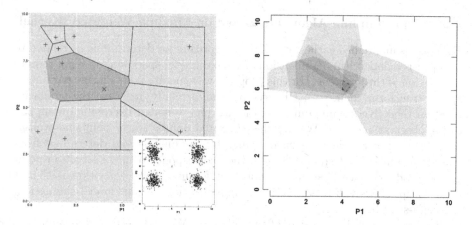

Fig. 1. (left) Voronoi diagram in the parameter space with dimensions $P1$ and $P2$: straight crosses (+) are Voronoi sites, the partitions are related to Voronoi cells, the oblique cross (×) is the truth observation parameter and the shaded area is the Voronoi cell to which the observation belongs. Insert: Points in the sample dataset; the straight crosses (+) are a subset of Voronoi sites and the oblique cross (×) is the truth observation parameter. (right) Intersection of the Voronoi cells from different Voronoi diagrams. Voronoi cells are shown as semi-transparent areas; the intersection is enclosed by a dashed line.

where $\{v_1^*, ...v_t^*\}$ and $\{z_1^*, ..., z_t^*\}$ are Voronoi cells and sites related to the maxima weighted state of $\mu_{P(\theta|S=s*)}$ (denoted as μ_{v^*}) of the observation point s^* in the parameter space $\mathcal{Q}$. After producing the maxima weighted iKernel mapping μ_{v^*} in the explicit form of the list of Voronoi cells of trees as well as an element of Hilbert space $\mathcal{G}$, it is possible to detect with high probability the position or tiny area v^* in the parameter space related to the observation as an intersection of all the Voronoi cells:

$$v^* = \bigcap_{j=1}^{t} v_j^*. \tag{13}$$

We should note that v^* can, in principle, be the empty set which is why we do not use the intersection area for calculation; we use it here simply to demonstrate the algorithmic features of our method and to show an example of a two-dimensional case. To explain the use of Eqs. (11, 12 and 13) of Isolation Kernel, let us consider an example with unevenly distributed sample data (insert in Fig. 1) of two-dimensional parameters ($P1$ and $P2$) and only twelve sites $\xi = 12$ with only five trees $t = 5$. A similar unevenness of the sample data appears under stochastic simulation with frequent null-output in a certain area of the parameters space. We insert the truth observation point into the plots to show the closeness that enables the algorithm to make a decision (oblique cross in Fig. 1).

4.2   Meta-sampling Algorithm Based on Maxima Weighted iKernel

For reasons mentioned earlier, we seek an algorithm for determining θ^* related to μ_{v^*} that is independent of dimension of the parameter space and does not require calculation of the gradient. For this propose, we generate points in the parameter space, transform them to a Hilbert space and, finally, measure the similarity between their iKernel mapping and the maxima weighted iKernel mapping μ_{v^*} of the observation point. We call the generated points 'tracer points' as well as algorithm 'Tracers'. The algorithm generates parameters and determines from their image in Hilbert space how well they correspond to the observation point in the product space. The most important feature of the algorithm is that it straight up allows you to search in parameter space without model simulation, i.e. meta-sampling.

The meta-sampling consists of several steps. We first need to determine the Voronoi sites $z_j^*(j \in [1,t]$, Eq. 11). Then for each site, we need to find the most distant site z_m^* and generate points between those sites, i.e., tracer points:

$$\{\theta_i^{tr}\} = \{\alpha_i \times z_j^* + (1-\alpha_i) \times z_m^*\} \qquad \alpha_i \in [0,1] \forall i. \tag{14}$$

Algorithmic steps include the acquisition of the iKernel mapping $\psi(\theta_i^{tr})$ and calculating the similarity between the tracer points and the maxima weighted iKernel mapping μ_{v^*}:

$$l(\theta_i^{tr}, v^*) = \psi(\theta_i^{tr})\mu_{v^*}. \tag{15}$$

Finally, we heuristically generate new points around the 'top' tracer points with $\Theta_{select} = \{\theta_i^{tr}|l(\theta_i^{tr}, v^*) > 0.5\}$. All steps are repeated until similarity (Eq. 15) ceases to change with criterion ϵ. Algorithm 'Tracers' gives the approximate position in the parameter space with the highest value of similarity $l(\theta_\tau, v^*) = \psi(\theta_\tau)\mu_{v^*}$.

Figure 1 shows us an example of the Voronoi diagram and the Voronoi cell to which the observation point belongs. Iteratively, the applied algorithm finds all Voronoi cells, and, ultimately, it is possible to find the intersection v^* (Eq. 13) of all Voronoi cells from all Voronoi diagrams (Fig. 1). As shown, the intersection v^* of the Voronoi cells is a very small area, even with five cells or trees. In many calculations, we usually used 10–70 sites and 20–400 trees which are much more than in the example. In the supplementary video, the iterative process is shown for the selection of sites, construction of the Voronoi diagram, and determination of the intersection. The machine learning algorithm of ABC based on maxima weighted iKernel mapping μ_{v^*} consists of the following steps:

– Define the kernel and feature mapping $k(\cdot, s) = \phi(s) \in \mathcal{H}$ in the space of the results of simulation S Eqs. (4, 7). Note that any type of kernel with the reproducing property is acceptable (i.e., it does not need to be iKernel).
– Use Eq. (8) to determine the Gram matrix $\mathbf{G}$ and weights $\Phi^T k(\cdot, s^*)$ of similarity between the simulation and the observation points.

- **Training step:** Execute algorithm of Voronoi diagram with iKernel $l(\cdot, \theta) = \psi(\theta) \in \mathcal{G}$ (Eq. 7) to produce Voronoi sites (z_{jk}) and cells $V_{jk}(z_{jk})$ (Eqs. 9, 10) as well as Voronoi cells $v_i(\theta)$ (where $i \in [1, t]$) related to all the simulation points in parameter space $\Theta = \{\theta_1, \theta_2, ..., \theta_n\} \in \mathcal{Q}$.
- Use Eq. (8) to calculate $\mu_{P(\theta|S=s*)}$ related to observation point s^*.
- Use Eqs. (11 and 12) to determine the maxima weighted iKernel mapping μ_{v^*}.
- Execute **meta-sampling algorithm** Tracers to find a point or points corresponding to the intersection of the Voronoi cells v^* (Eq. 13) in the parameter space $\mathcal{Q}$.

Note that, in principle, the intersection can be empty, i.e., $v^* = \varnothing$; thus, to find the corresponding point θ^*, we use maxima weighted-iKernel mapping μ_{v^*} in an additional algorithm for calculating similarity measure $l(\theta, v^*) = \psi(\theta)\mu_{v^*}$, where θ is any parameter.

It should be noted that the meta-sampling algorithm Tracers is independent of the dimension of parameter space $\mathcal{Q}$ and that, rather than calculating the gradient, we generate tracer points, with calculation of $l(\theta_i^{tr}, v^*)$ for each tracer θ_i^{tr}. It is for this reason that the algorithm is suitable for multidimensional data as well as for stochastic simulation based on branching processes.

4.3   Weaknesses of the Algorithm and the Overfitting Problem

To study the overfitting problem, we used a simple two-dimensional case. The maxima weighted iKernel mappings μ_{v^*} were obtained for different internal parameters t and ξ of Eq. 12. To see how μ_{v^*} reflect the distance in the parameter space between truth value and all the other points, we calculated the similarity based on μ_{v^*} and kernel mapping of all the points: $l(\theta, v^*) = \mu_{v^*} \times \psi(\theta)$. Figure 2 shows the successful fitting of the number of Voronoi cells $\xi = 5$ and the number of trees $t = 7$ where $l(\theta, v^*)$ riches maximum equal 1 in a small region of parameters. In this case, the position of the maximum of $l(\theta, v^*)$ corresponds to the truth parameter.

To improve the accuracy and to reduce the region of the parameter estimation, one may increase the number of trees and/or the number of Voronoi sites like in the second example, where $\xi = 35$ and $t = 70$ (Fig. 2). The maximum of similarity equals just 0.17 and the position of it is far from the truth value.

There are several possible reasons. The first one is that the intersection of all Voronoi cells v^* is empty. At the second, the region in the Hilbert space corresponding to the observation point is "blurred" for a large number of Voronoi cells and too long a tree length. As a result, kernel mean embedding does not have a clear maximum and fluctuations in numerical calculations play a significant role, which leads to an increase in the error value.

Let consider kernel mean embedding $\mu_{P(\theta|s^*)}$ (Eq. 8) to analyze the source of the overfitting problem. Explicitly $\mu_{P(\theta|s^*)}$ can be represented as a matrix $\xi \times t$ where each element is a weight related to similarity between observation and Voronoi cell from a sample of sites. Equation 12 allows to get maxima weighted

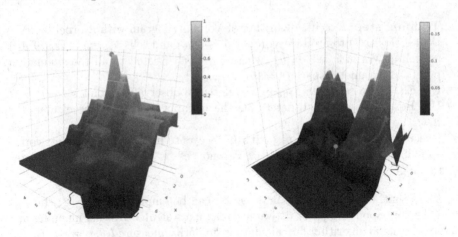

Fig. 2. Similarity measure for two-dimensional example with next internal parameters: (left) number of Voronoi cells $\xi = 5$ and number of trees $t = 7$; (right) $\xi = 35$ and $t = 70$. The ball demonstrate truth value for θ. The similarity $l(\theta, v^*) \in [0; 1]$ for the left plot and $l(\theta, v^*) \in [0; 0.17]$ for the right.

iKernel mapping μ_{v^*} which is based on a set of Voronoi cells z_i^* ($i \in [1, t]$) related to observation point s^*. Practically, each Voronoi cell z_i^* is derived from an independent sample of sites in a tree building algorithm with maximum weight in $\mu_{P(\theta|s^*)}$ matrix.

Two main parameters are used to construct the μ_{v^*}: the number of trees t and the number of Voronoi cells ξ. If ξ is too large then the size of each Voronoi cell v_j^* (Eq. 13) will be too small to obtain a non-zero intersection v^* corresponding to μ_{v^*}. As a result, several areas will appear as the intersections of parts of set v_j^*, $j \in [1; t]$ with several local maxima of the similarity (Fig. 2). As the number of trees t grows, the intersection area v^* first decreases, but then disappears and several areas with partial overlaps appear instead, which also gives false extrema. In both cases, the values of similarity decrease due to a partial coverage of Voronoi cells. So, to keep a balance between the accuracy and overfitting effect, one should check the similarity values as well as area of intersection.

Thus, the meta-sampling algorithm Tracers in combination with maxima weighted iKernel mapping based on the Voronoi diagram, gives approximate parameters for unevenly distributed sample data produced by a stochastic model. To evaluate the efficiency of the proposed algorithms, we used Gauss processes and stochastic linear model with low probability to find a point near region of interest. To determine the degree to which the accuracy of an estimated parameter depends on the stochasticity of the model, we increased the noise in the simulations.

5   Experiments

5.1   Synthetic Data

To check the efficiency of the proposed algorithm we used multidimensional data from two models: the first is Gaussian processes with unevenly distributed points and lack of data points near the region of interest; the second is a linear model with stochastic term η_{stoch}. In this research, we eschew the generation of new points and compare methods based on a given sample of points using the mean squared error (MSE). This is simply to avoid the effect of the sampling method and to compare ABC methods based solely on a given sample, using only four methods in the comparison: rejection ABC [29] (Rejection in Fig. 3), and ABC using the regression-based correction methods that employ either local linear regression [3] (Linear regression in Fig. 3) or neural networks (NN) [4] (Neural Network in Fig. 3). For our calculations, we used the 'abc' package in R that includes all of the above methods. The proposed method and kernel ABC based on Isolation Kernel are shown denoted in Fig. 3 as Maxima weighted and iKernel, respectively.

For the Gaussian processes for each dimension iKernel ABC, and ABC based on Maxima weighted iKernel mapping gave the best results for all simulations with different dimensions (Maxima weighted iKernel mapping typically had 3.5–20 times the accuracy of iKernel ABC. Results for the linear model depended on the stochastic term: for $\eta_{stoch} = 0$ linear regression gave the exact values with MSE $< 10^{-20}$; for $\eta_{stoch} = 0.3$ and range of output $Y \in [0, 10]$ ABC based on linear regression, NN and Maxima weighted iKernel mapping yielded results with similar MSE, while iKernel and rejection ABC produced MSEs that were several times larger; for $\eta_{stoch} \geq 0.6$ (and the same output range) MSE for Maxima weighted iKernel mapping was best in all cases (Fig. 3).

5.2   Cancer Cell Evolution

The cancer cell evolution model serves as an interesting example of branching processes with a high probability of cell population extinction. In this research the tugHall simulator from [25] was used, together with the simulation dataset from [26]. The model has 27 parameters, seven of which were fixed based on expert estimation [25]. The remaining 20 parameters represent the hallmark–gene relationship that is an analogue to gene–phenotype relations. The dataset includes the results of 9,600,000 simulations using different models, initial conditions, and input parameters. Here, the model with threshold metastatic transformation was used with the initial mutated cell in the pull of 1000 normal cells. This sample has the largest number of successful simulations (34,602) and among them the largest number non-zero outputs (34,059) from 400,000 simulations.

Based on the given sample of the dataset and the VAF of a patient from the Cancer Genome Atlas (TCGA) database [17] as an observation (ID record TCGA-AF-5654-01A-01D-1657-10), parameter estimation was performed using the various methods. For rejection ABC, NN ABC and linear regression ABC,

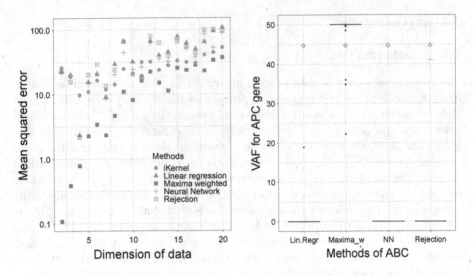

Fig. 3. (left) Mean squared error vs dimension of data with stochastic term $\eta_{stoch} = 0.6$ from ABC estimations using different methods: linear regression, maxima weighted iKernel mapping, Isolation Kernel ABC, neural network and rejection ABC. (right) Box plot of VAF of APC gene obtained by various methods. The observation point is shown as a diamond.

the mean, median and mode values were used in 100 repetitions of the simulation for each parameter set. Unfortunately, only one measure of the central tendency produced a non-zero output for each method (denoted in parentheses in Table 1) while the others led to extinction for all repetitions. It is for this reason that Table 1 shows the results of simulations for only one successful attempt at determining the parameter set, excluding iKernel ABC which led to extinction in all 100 simulations. The observation data are represented as a vector with four VAF values for each gene (APC, KRAS, TP53, and PIK3CA) related to colorectal cancer. Table 1 shows the statistical characteristics of the results of the simulations for each method. In addition to MSE, the portion of successful simulations with survival cells is represented ($\eta_{succeed}$). Standard deviation σ shows the degree to which the simulation data are concentrated around their center (for NN ABC $\sigma = 0$ because of the low probability of successful simulation). The energy distance, E-dist, which is the statistical distance between observation and simulation, is also included in Table 1 and was calculated using the 'energy' R package [31, 32].

According to Table 1, the ABC method based on Maxima weighted iKernel mapping shows the best accuracy under correct hyperparameter selection. Rejection ABC and ABC based on correction with NN have a large mean squared error and a high energy distance, as they are in good agreement only with the VAF of the PIK3CA gene. ABC based on correction with linear regression diverges from the observation for the VAF of the APC gene (Fig. 3), which is the most frequent

Table 1. Simulation statistics based on parameter estimation using the different methods: $\eta_{succeed}$ is the portion of successful simulations with non-zero output, σ is the standard deviation, and E-dist is the energy distance.

Method	MSE	$\eta_{succeed}$, %	σ	E-dist
Rejection (Median)	6956	38%	212	1.616
Neural Network (Mean)	6999	7%	0	1.464
Linear Regression (Mode)	1975	43%	206	0.847
iKernel	×	×	×	×
Maxima weighted iKernel	68	52%	97	0.086

driver gene in colorectal cancer evolution [7]. Only the proposed method gives good agreement for the VAF of all four genes.

6   Conclusion

We have proposed a heuristic ABC based on the part of Isolation Kernel mean embedding with maximal weights μ_{v*} (Eqs. 9, 10, 11, and 12). Isolation Kernel is implemented with a Voronoi diagram algorithm, which makes possible the explicit transformation of simulation row data to a Hilbert space corresponding to the model's parameters. In the simplest case, the interpretation of μ_{v*} is the intersection of all the Voronoi cells of μ_{v*} corresponding to an observation point (Eq. 13).

The study of the overfitting problem was performed for the approximate Bayesian computation method based on maxima weighted isolation kernel mapping using two-dimensional example. Two main hyperparameters are important for the learning process: the number of trees in the isolation forest algorithm and the number of Voronoi cells in a generation of partitionings. In both cases, when numbers t and ξ became too large, the intersection of Voronoi cells corresponding to the observation point disappears, and, therefore, the several overlapping areas give false extrema in the similarity function. The similarity value at maximum can be an indicator of successful fitting: the value is closed to 1 is better and vice versa.

The proposed method allows parameter estimation with good accuracy even when the observation point lies in the sparse region of a given data sample. Maxima weighted iKernel mapping is also effective in dealing with the stochasticity of the simulation data, as well as high dimensionality. Application of the method to synthetic 2–20 dimension data with a stochastic term and the simulator of cancer cell evolution showed much better results in comparison to well-known ABC methods.

Acknowledgements. The author wishes to thank Prof. Takashi Washio for his detailed discussion of the theoretical part of this research, as well as for all the valuable critical comments.

References

1. Athreya, K., Ney, P.: Branching Processes. Grundlehren der mathematischen Wissenschaften. Springer, Berlin (2012). https://books.google.co.jp/books?id=CE3uCAAAQBAJ

2. Aurenhammer, F., Edelsbrunner, H.: An optimal algorithm for constructing the weighted Voronoi diagram in the plane. Pattern Recogn. **17**(2), 251–257 (1984). https://doi.org/10.1016/0031-3203(84)90064-5

3. Beaumont, M.A., Zhang, W., Balding, D.J.: Approximate Bayesian computation in population genetics. Genetics **162**(4), 2025–2035 (2002). https://doi.org/10.1093/genetics/162.4.2025. https://pubmed.ncbi.nlm.nih.gov/12524368

4. Blum, M.G.B., François, O.: Non-linear regression models for approximate Bayesian computation. Stat. Comput. **20**(1), 63–73 (2010)

5. Borgwardt, K.M., Gretton, A., Rasch, M.J., Kriegel, H.P., Schölkopf, B., Smola, A.J.: Integrating structured biological data by kernel maximum mean discrepancy. Bioinformatics **22**(14), e49–e57 (2006). https://doi.org/10.1093/bioinformatics/btl242

6. Burden, C.J., Simon, H.: Genetic drift in populations governed by a Galton-Watson branching process. Theoret. Popul. Biol. **109**, 63–74 (2016)

7. Campbell, P.J., et al.: Pan-cancer analysis of whole genomes. Nature **578**(7793), 82–93 (2020). https://doi.org/10.1038/s41586-020-1969-6

8. Chen, Y., Welling, M.: Parametric herding. In: Teh, Y.W., Titterington, M. (eds.) Proceedings of the Thirteenth International Conference on Artificial Intelligence and Statistics. Proceedings of Machine Learning Research, vol. 9, pp. 97–104. PMLR, Chia Laguna Resort, Sardinia, Italy (13–15 May 2010). https://proceedings.mlr.press/v9/chen10a.html

9. Csillery, K., Blum, M.G., Gaggiotti, O.E., François, O.: Approximate Bayesian computation (ABC) in practice. Trends Ecol. Evol. **25**(7), 410–418 (2010)

10. Devroye, L.: Branching processes and their applications in the analysis of tree structures and tree algorithms. In: Habib, M., McDiarmid, C., Ramirez-Alfonsin, J., Reed, B. (eds.) Probabilistic Methods for Algorithmic Discrete Mathematics. Algorithms and Combinatorics, vol. 16, pp. 249–314. Springer, Berlin (1998). https://doi.org/10.1007/978-3-662-12788-9_7

11. Dyer, M., Frieze, A., Kannan, R.: A random polynomial-time algorithm for approximating the volume of convex bodies. J. ACM **38**(1), 1–17 (1991)

12. Fortune, S.: A sweepline algorithm for Voronoi diagrams. Algorithmica **2**(1), 153 (1987)

13. Fukumizu, K., Gretton, A., Sun, X., Schölkopf, B.: Kernel measures of conditional dependence. In: Platt, J., Koller, D., Singer, Y., Roweis, S. (eds.) Advances in Neural Information Processing Systems, vol. 20. Curran Associates, Inc. (2008). https://proceedings.neurips.cc/paper/2007/file/3a0772443a0739141292a5429b952fe6-Paper.pdf

14. Fukumizu, K., Song, L., Gretton, A.: Kernel Bayes' rule: Bayesian inference with positive definite kernels. J. Mach. Learn. Res. **14**(1), 3753–3783 (2013)

15. Gretton, A., Borgwardt, K.M., Rasch, M.J., Schölkopf, B., Smola, A.: A kernel two-sample test. J. Mach. Learn. Res. **13**(null), 723–773 (2012)

16. Huang, L., Huang, S., Lai, Z.: On the optimization of site investigation programs using centroidal Voronoi tessellation and random field theory. Comput. Geotech. **118**, 103331 (2020)

17. Hudson, T.J., et al.: International network of cancer genome projects. Nature **464**(7291), 993–998 (2010)
18. Jagers, P.: General branching processes as Markov fields. Stochast. Process. Appl. **32**(2), 183–212 (1989)
19. Kajihara, T., Kanagawa, M., Yamazaki, K., Fukumizu, K.: Kernel recursive ABC: point estimation with intractable likelihood. In: Dy, J., Krause, A. (eds.) Proceedings of the 35th International Conference on Machine Learning. Proceedings of Machine Learning Research, vol. 80, pp. 2400–2409. PMLR (2018). https:// proceedings.mlr.press/v80/kajihara18a.html
20. Lacoste-Julien, S., Lindsten, F., Bach, F.R.: Sequential kernel herding: Frank-Wolfe optimization for particle filtering. ArXiv abs/1501.02056 (2015)
21. Liu, F.T., Ting, K.M., Zhou, Z.H.: Isolation forest. In: 2008 Eighth IEEE International Conference on Data Mining, pp. 413–422 (2008). https://doi.org/10.1109/ ICDM.2008.17
22. Liu, J.S., Chen, R.: Sequential monte carlo methods for dynamic systems. J. Am. Stat. Assoc. **93**(443), 1032–1044 (1998)
23. Mitrovic, J., Sejdinovic, D., Teh, Y.W.: DR-ABC: approximate Bayesian computation with kernel-based distribution regression. In: Balcan, M.F., Weinberger, K.Q. (eds.) Proceedings of the 33rd International Conference on Machine Learning. Proceedings of Machine Learning Research, vol. 48, pp. 1482–1491. PMLR New York (2016). https://proceedings.mlr.press/v48/mitrovic16.html
24. Muandet, K., Fukumizu, K., Sriperumbudur, B., Schölkopf, B.: Kernel mean embedding of distributions: a review and beyond. Found. Trends® Mach. Learn. **10**(1–2), 1–141 (2017). https://doi.org/10.1561/2200000060
25. Nagornov, I.S., Kato, M.: tugHall: a simulator of cancer-cell evolution based on the hallmarks of cancer and tumor-related genes. Bioinformatics **36**(11), 3597– 3599 (2020). https://doi.org/10.1093/bioinformatics/btaa182
26. Nagornov, I.S., Nishino, J., Kato, M.: Dataset of tughall simulations of cell evolution for colorectal cancer. Data Brief **34**, 106719 (2021)
27. Nakagome, S., Fukumizu, K., Mano, S.: Kernel approximate bayesian computation in population genetic inferences. Statistical Applications in Genetics and Molecular Biology **12**(6), 667–678 (2013). https://doi.org/10.1515/sagmb-2012-0050
28. Park, M., Jitkrittum, W., Sejdinovic, D.: K2-ABC: approximate Bayesian computation with kernel embeddings. In: Gretton, A., Robert, C.C. (eds.) Proceedings of the 19th International Conference on Artificial Intelligence and Statistics. Proceedings of Machine Learning Research, vol. 51, pp. 398–407. PMLR, Cadiz, Spain (2016). https://proceedings.mlr.press/v51/park16.html
29. Pritchard, J.K., Seielstad, M.T., Perez-Lezaun, A., Feldman, M.W.: Population growth of human Y chromosomes: a study of Y chromosome microsatellites. Mol. Biol. Evol. **16**(12), 1791–1798 (1999). https://doi.org/10.1093/oxfordjournals. molbev.a026091
30. Scholkopf, B., Smola., A.J.: Learning with Kernels: Support Vector Machines, Regularization, Optimization, and Beyond. MIT Press, Cambridge (2002)
31. Székely, G.J., Rizzo, M.L.: Energy statistics: a class of statistics based on distances. J. Stat. Plann. Infer. **143**(8), 1249–1272 (2013)
32. Székely, G.J., Rizzo, M.L.: The energy of data. Annu. Rev. Stat. Appl. **4**(1), 447– 479 (2017)
33. Ting, K.M., Washio, T., Zhu, Y., Xu, Y.: Breaking the curse of dimensionality with isolation kernel (2021)

34. Ting, K.M., Xu, B.C., Washio, T., Zhou, Z.H.: Isolation distributional kernel: a new tool for kernel based anomaly detection. In: Proceedings of the 26th ACM SIGKDD International Conference on Knowledge Discovery and Data Mining, pp. 198–206. KDD 2020, Association for Computing Machinery, New York, NY, USA (2020). https://doi.org/10.1145/3394486.3403062

35. Ting, K.M., Zhu, Y., Zhou, Z.H.: Isolation kernel and its effect on SVM. In: Proceedings of the 24th ACM SIGKDD International Conference on Knowledge Discovery and Data Mining, pp. 2329–2337. KDD 2018, Association for Computing Machinery, New York, NY, USA (2018). https://doi.org/10.1145/3219819.3219990

36. Wan, S., Zhao, Y., Wang, T., Gu, Z., Abbasi, Q.H., Choo, K.K.R.: Multi-dimensional data indexing and range query processing via Voronoi diagram for internet of things. Future Gener. Comput. Syst. **91**, 382–391 (2019)

37. Wasserman, L.: All of Statistics: A Concise Course in Statistical Inference. Springer, Cham (2010)

Author Index

Y. Takama et al. (Eds.): JSAI-isAI 2022 Workshop, LNAI 13859, pp. 283–284, 2023.
https://doi.org/10.1007/978-3-031-29168-5

Printed in the United States
by Baker & Taylor Publisher Services